GLOBETROTTER™

Travel Atlas

AUSTRALIA

NEW HOLLAND

This edition published in 2000 by
New Holland Publishers (UK) Ltd

London • Sydney • Cape Town • Auckland

First Published in 1995

10 9 8 7 6 5 4 3 2 1

24 Nutford Place
London W1H 6DQ, United Kingdom

80 McKenzie Street
Cape Town 8001, South Africa

14 Aquatic Drive
Frenchs Forest, NSW 2086, Australia

218 Lake Road, Northcote
Auckland, New Zealand

ISBN: 1 85368 781 2

Text: Bruce Elder
Manager Globetrotter Maps: John Loubser
Editors: Claudia Dos Santos, Catherine Mallinick, Mary Duncan, Thea Grobbelaar
Design and DTP: Éloïse Moss, Catherine Mallinick, John Loubser
Cartographers: William Smuts, Elaine Fick, Carl Germishuys
Cartographic researcher: Elaine Fick
Indexer: Tania Micheals

Reproduction by Disk Express Cape (Pty) Ltd.
Printed by Kyodo Printing Company (Singapore) (Pte) Ltd.

Cover: *The Great Ocean Road, Victoria.*
Half title page: *The Kennedy Developmental Road near Boulia.*

Distance and Climate Charts

APPROXIMATE DISTANCES IN KILOMETRES	ADELAIDE	ALICE SPRINGS	BRISBANE	BROKEN HILL	BROOME	CAIRNS	CANBERRA	COOBER PEDY	DARWIN	MELBOURNE	MT GAMBIER	MT ISA	PERTH	PORT AUGUSTA	SYDNEY
ADELAIDE		1530	2068	517	4280	2900	1209	846	3050	944	462	2700	2680	318	1427
ALBANY	2630	3515	4350	2710	2658	5426	3820	2903	4459	3370	3141	4753	409	2296	3877
ALICE SPRINGS	1530		3009	1649	2741	2325	2751	687	1492	2268	1993	1160	3628	1226	2680
BRISBANE	2068	3009		1550	4660	1720	1262	2516	3412	1690	2153	1817	4350	1961	1021
BROKEN HILL	517	1649	1550		4101	2557	1132	964	3165	855	960	2300	2820	413	1148
BROOME	4280	2741	4660	4101		3962	5218	3605	1863	5020	4739	2850	2229	3970	5234
CAIRNS	2900	2325	1720	2557	3962		2610	3011	2750	3052	3350	1124	5540	2712	2544
CANBERRA	1209	2751	1262	1132	5218	2610		2009	3967	651	801	2369	3910	1516	286
CARNARVON	3468	4133	5560	3665	1456	5039	4710	3762	3275	4312	4020	3903	900	3294	4730
CEDUNA	783	1687	2428	890	3518	3331	1910	1000	3192	1520	1245	2892	1863	475	2051
CHARLEVILLE	1603	2336	750	1149	3990	1392	1185	2051	2751	1832	1987	1143	3922	1560	1235
COOBER PEDY	846	687	2516	964	3605	3011	2009		2200	1583	1310	1880	2884	541	1975
DARWIN	3050	1492	3412	3165	1863	2750	3967	2200		3760	3502	1607	4043	2726	3997
DUBBO	1182	2376	860	740	4816	2221	400	1693	3571	849	1266	1947	3489	1166	408
EUCLA	1205	2111	2854	1310	3107	3759	2341	1428	3612	1940	1659	3309	1432	889	2472
GRAFTON	1832	3022	352	1396	5049	2074	901	2342	3796	1505	1929	2188	4132	1812	669
KALGOORLIE	2129	3026	3801	2232	2178	4689	3260	2445	4004	2863	2576	4223	600	1811	3392
KATHERINE	2701	1178	3116	2819	1570	2448	3654	1871	314	3451	3168	1309	3732	2405	3718
MEEKATHARRA	2839	3750	4492	2938	1469	5410	3976	3061	3282	3578	3293	4273	738	2542	4112
MELBOURNE	944	2268	1690	855	5020	3052	651	1583	3760		482	2803	3432	1042	879
MILDURA	386	1850	1675	302	4602	3019	819	1172	3351	559	585	2357	2964	627	1022
MT GAMBIER	462	1993	2153	960	4739	3350	801	1310	3502	482		2902	3160	772	1292
MT ISA	2700	1160	1817	2300	2850	1124	2369	1880	1607	2803	2902		4780	2418	2378
ORBOST	1112	2641	1642	1232	5390	3086	470	1955	4129	375	806	2879	3752	1422	673
PERTH	2680	3628	4350	2820	2229	5540	3910	2884	4043	3432	3160	4780		2407	3985
PORT AUGUSTA	318	1226	1961	413	3970	2712	1516	541	2726	1042	772	2418	2407		1585
PORT HEDLAND	4182	3200	5150	4198	570	4500	5018	4020	2418	4381	4380	3850	1762	3656	5020
PORT LINCOLN	672	1570	2325	777	4118	3030	1820	885	3078	1386	1116	2770	2336	354	1943
ROCKHAMPTON	2381	2509	649	1879	4145	1084	1597	2849	2912	2037	2488	1315	4715	2305	1624
SYDNEY	1427	2680	1021	1148	5234	2544	286	1975	3997	879	1292	2378	395	1585	
TENNANT CREEK	2073	507	2486	2182	2221	1818	3058	1211	985	2801	2523	677	4131	1753	3040
TOWNSVILLE	3127	2090	1384	2305	3723	351	2322	3028	2491	2763	3221	883	5444	2860	2339
WAGGA-WAGGA	929	2410	1285	862	5159	2642	245	1736	3850	436	866	2301	3630	1203	470
WYNDHAM	3333	1802	3730	3435	1063	3054	4271	2490	929	4055	3792	1923	3231	3010	4343

Photographic credits:
All photographs (including cover) by **Shaen Adey, New Holland Image Library [NHIL]** with the exception of those on pages 8, 10 (bottom left), 14 (bottom), 20, 22, 34 (bottom), 78 (top and bottom), 84 (top and bottom), 117 by **Anthony Johnson [NHIL]**; pages 10 (bottom right), 56, 60 (top), 63, 65, 68, 76 (top and bottom), 80 (top and bottom), 92, 100, 112 (top) from **Australian Picture Library [NHIL]**; page 12 (bottom) by **Denise Greig [NHIL]**; title page, pages 36 (bottom), 40 by **Nick Rains [NHIL]**; page 94 (bottom) from **Wildside**.

Distance Charts

In order to find the distance between two of Australia's major centres, locate the name of the town or city in the vertical or horizontal column, then locate the name of the other town or city in the other column. The number where the vertical and horizontal lines intersect is the approximate distance between the two places.

Climate Charts

Below is an example of a climate chart. These charts occur throughout the atlas, and give you the average temperatures and rainfall for the relevant city.

SYDNEY	J	F	M	A	M	J	J	A	S	O	N	D
AV. TEMP. °F	73	73	72	66	63	57	54	57	61	64	68	72
AV. TEMP. °C	23	23	22	19	17	14	12	14	16	18	20	22
DAILY SUN hrs	8	7	7	6	6	6	7	8	8	8	8	8
RAINFALL in	4	4.5	5	5	5	5	4	3	3	3	3	3
RAINFALL mm	102	117	135	129	121	131	100	81	69	79	82	78
RAINFALL days	12	12	13	12	12	12	10	10	10	11	11	12

Contents

The design for the Australian flag was chosen from entries for a competition run at the time of Australia's Federation in 1901. The flag's status and dimensions were officially established by an Act of Parliament in November 1953.

National Grid Planner

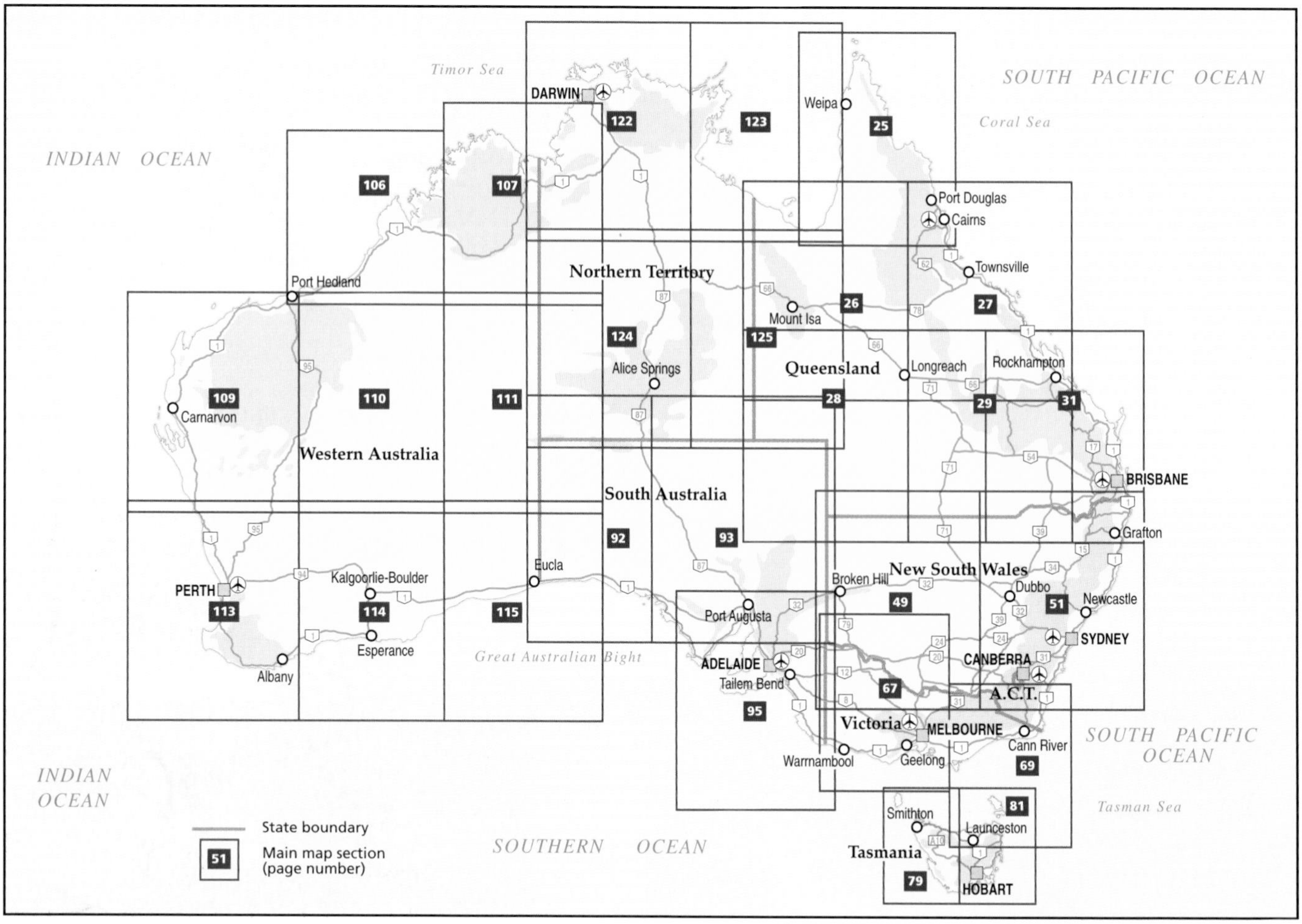

Main & Regional Areas Legend

Directional to Main Map

Directional to Regional Map

National road Nationalstraße Route nationale	Tarred / Untarred	City Großstadt Grande ville		Place of interest Sehenswürdigkeit Endroit à voir	Uluru
Motorway Autobahn Autoroute		Town Stadt Ville secondaire		Picnic site Picknickplatz Lieu de pique-nique	
Highway Fernstraße Grande route	Tarred / Untarred FLINDERS HWY	Small town Kleinstadt Petite ville		Lookout Ausschau Point de vue	
Main road Hauptstraße Route principale	Tarred / Untarred	Large village Größere Ortschaft Village		Airport Flughafen Aéroport	INT. / Other
Minor road Nebenstraße Route secondaire	Tarred / Untarred	Village / Locality Dorf Petit village	Village Locality	Aboriginal land Land der Aborigines Terre Aborigène	ARNHEM
Track Sandweg Piste		Homestead Anwesen Propriété		Peak in metres Höhe in Metern Sommet en mètres	Mt Bailey 1140m
Route number Routennummer Numéro de route	1 4 97 A10	Major petrol stop Große Tankstelle Station-service		Water features Gewässer Hydrographie	River Dam Non-perennial
Distance in kilometres Entfernung in Kilometern Distance en kilomètres	19 15	Camp Ferienlager Camping		Mountain range Gebirgskette Chaîne de montagnes	JAMES
Railway Eisenbahn Chemin de fer		Caravan park Wohnwagenpark Camping-caravaning		Ferry Fähre Ferry/bac	F
State boundary Provinzgrenze Frontière d'état		Golf course Golfplatz Terrains de golf		National park Wild- und Naturschutzgebiet Réserve naturelle	Kakadu N.P.
Scenic route Malerische Landschaft Route panoramique		Station (selected) Bahnhof Gare		State name Bundesstaat/Provinz Nom d'état	Victoria

Key Regional Maps Planner

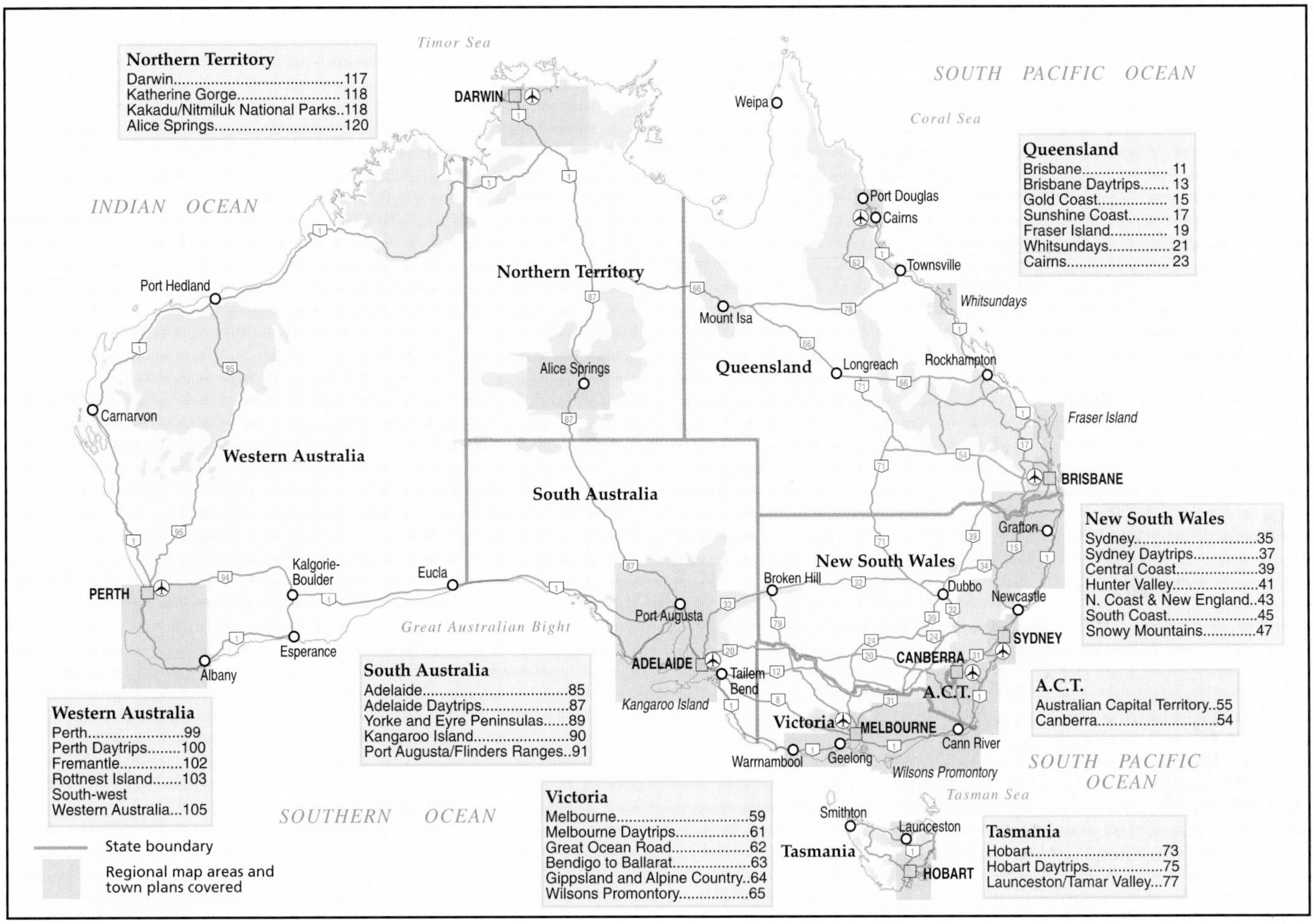

Town Plan Legend

Motorway & slip road
Autobahn/ Autobahnausfahrt
Autoroute et jonction

Main road & mall
Hauptstraße und Fußgängerzone
Route principale et Mall

Road
Straße
Route

Railway
Eisenbahn
Chemin de fer

Tramway
Straßenbahn
Tramway

Park & sports field
Park und Sportplatz
Parc et terrain de sports

Route number
Routennummer
Numéro de route

Building of interest
Sehenswertes Bauwerk
Monument à voir

Place of worship
Religiöse Stätte
Lieu du culte

Police station
Polizeirevier
Poste de police

Parking area
Parkplatz
Parking

Hotel
Hotel
Hôtel

Bus terminus
Busbahnhof
Terminus d'autobus

Hospital
Krankenhaus
Hôpital

Place of interest
Sehenswürdigkeit
Endroit à voir

Post office
Postamt
Bureau de poste

Library
Bibliothek
Bibliothèque

Ferry
Fähre
Ferry/bac

Information
Information
Centre d'information

Built-up area
Wohngebiet
Agglomération

One-way street
Einbahnstraße
Rue à sens-unique

Golf course
Golfplatz
Terrain de Golf

Strip Route Legend

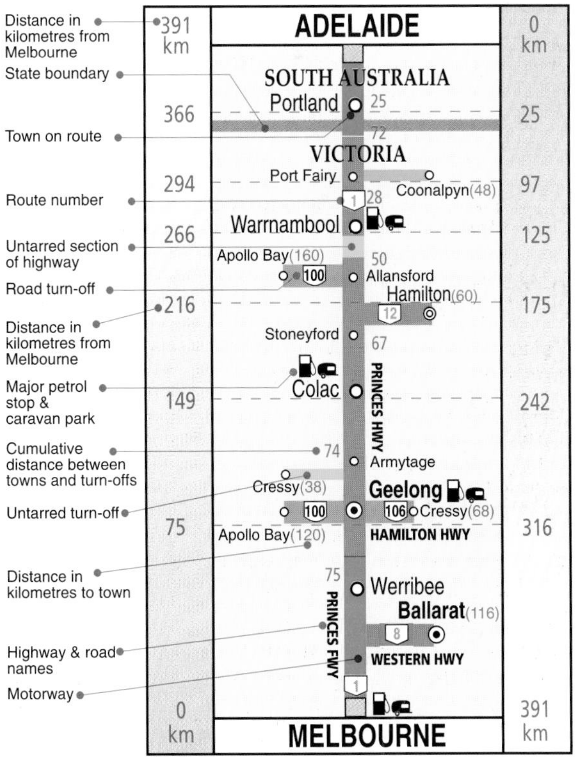

TOURING AUSTRALIA

Australia is a continent of remarkable diversity. It comprises 7 682 300km² (2 965 368 sq miles) and stretches across more than 30 degrees of latitude. The great appeal of the country, with the exception of cool, moist Tasmania which defies every generalisation, is the vastness of the landscape, the extent of the desert areas (it has the second-largest dry desert region in the world, the Sahara being the largest) and the incredibly blue skies. Because most of the continent enjoys long periods of sunny dry weather, the population is essentially an outdoor society characterised by informality, egalitarianism, friendliness and a genuine dislike of protocol and pretentiousness. Nearly 85 per cent of the people have settled in the major urban areas dotted along the coastline. The long distances between these centres create vast areas that are still sparsely populated despite over 40 000 years of human migration. While it has been popular to view Australians as 18.5 million exiled Europeans on the other side of the planet, it is an inaccurate image of a society which, in the 1990s, is proudly and happily multicultural.

The visitor who comes to Australia, or any Australians heading out to explore their own country, will be confronted by a continent of bewildering variation. They will experience the tropical magic of the Great Barrier Reef with its fantastic coral formations, and the vastness of the Great Artesian Basin, which runs down the centre of the country, subjecting the residents to foul-smelling showers and baths from steaming bores that bring valuable water to the parched land from hundreds of metres below the earth's surface. They will marvel at the beauty and elegance of the modern cities and wonder at how they can travel for hundreds of kilometres in Western Australia, the Northern Territory and in the south without ever seeing another human being. They will be seduced by the wild beaches of Tasmania, where waves, uninterrupted by land since leaving South America, crash onto lonely shores, and they will marvel at the dramatic glaciation of that state's cold and forbidding Cradle Mountain area, standing in sharp contrast to the red deserts of the mainland.

Beyond these features there is the beauty of the Snowy Mountains, covered by snow in wintertime and wildflowers in spring; the gently undulating cattle country between the Great Dividing Range and the Pacific Ocean, virtually all the way up the eastern coast; the vast plains where sheep and wheat sustain small rural communities; the dramatic red soils and awesome beaches of the Kimberley; and the huge jarrah and karri trees on the south-western tip of Western Australia. But no journey around Australia, and certainly no one wanting to understand this strange and deeply spiritual continent, can avoid the 'dead heart': Alice Springs with its dry Todd River; the MacDonnell Ranges stretching to the east and west of the Alice; Uluru (previously known as Ayers Rock), 'the greatest stone on Earth', always marvellous at dusk and dawn; the huge mounds that are Kata Tjuta (previously called the Olgas); and the jagged canyons – Standley Chasm, Simpsons Gap and Kings Canyon. These are all places that seem to have been designed by nature to take the visitor's breath away.

It is common for Australians to declare that 'Australia is the oldest continent on earth' without fully understanding what such a statement actually means. Geologists have dated parts of the Western Australian shield and believe it to be 3000 million years old, but it would, perhaps, be more accurate and more descriptive to say, 'Australia seems to be the most stable and the most eroded continent on earth' as it is the lowest and flattest. Only some 6 per cent of the country has an elevation above 700m (2300ft) and the highest mountain, Mount Kosciuszko, is only 2228m (7310ft) above sea level. By European standards it is scarcely more than a substantial hill that can be conquered in an easy day's hike.

It is hard to imagine that hundreds of millions of years ago there was once a mountain range in central Australia, higher than Mount Everest. Yet, when the traveller arrives at Ellery Creek Big Hole, one of the many gorges and chasms that split the MacDonnell Ranges, they will see a notice board near the car park which explains: 'All around you there is evidence of a great mountain building episode in the formation of Central Australia. You can see tortured folds of rock which formed deep in the earth and which great heat and pressure pushed up to 10 000-metre mountains, but 350 million years of erosion have almost worn them away exposing the deeper folded rock. These rocks were formed from mud and sand which were deposited as flat layers on the bed of an inland sea'.

To understand the physical shape of Australia it is best to think in terms of four distinct regions. Along the east coast (where most of the country's population lives) there is the region known as the Eastern Uplands or Great Dividing Range. This is a series of plateaux, high plains and, in some places, spectacular gorges, which run from Cape York in northern Queensland all the way down to Tasmania's southern tip. This is the country's most productive land, enjoying good rainfall and moderate temperatures.

Beyond the Great Dividing Range are the Murray, Eyre and Carpentaria basins, which stretch from the Gulf of Carpentaria in northern Queensland down through western Queensland and New South Wales into western Victoria and parts of South Australia. This is the region that early European explorers thought contained a huge inland sea because the major river systems, instead of running to the east, run in a south-westerly direction, either reaching Lake Eyre (Australia's largest lake) or joining the Murray–Darling basin and reaching the sea at Lake Alexandrina in South Australia. Lake Eyre, incidentally, may be Australia's largest lake but it only fills about twice a century.

Over half of Australia is taken up by the vast Western Craton, a series of low-lying plateaux and desert areas which extend from the Barkly Tableland of the Northern Territory across to the Kimberley and Pilbara region through the vast arid stretches of the Great Victoria, Gibson and Great Sandy deserts. This is an area characterised by the seemingly endless ridges of sand dunes (from the air much of the region looks like an uninhabited piece of corrugated iron) and the almost blood-red soils of this land, whose colour derives from its rich iron ore content. This is where nature, over millions of years, eroded all the major formations – with the notable exceptions of Uluru, the MacDonnell Ranges and the strange formations of the Kimberley – to such a point that all that is left are a series of low-lying hills.

Australia is justifiably famous for its coastline. Although it is almost exactly the same size as the USA, most of the population lives near the coast. More than half of the towns in the country are located in New South Wales and Victoria, and over 80 per cent of the population lives in the narrow coastal strip from Cairns in north Queensland to Adelaide in the south.

From Bundaberg through to the northern coast of Victoria the coastline is characterised by many excellent swimming and surfing beaches (some have an international reputation because of the shape and form of their waves) set between low-lying headlands which are popular haunts for fishermen. These formations continue into South Australia and around much of the coast of Tasmania.

At particular points, notably along the Great Ocean Road in Victoria and along the west coast of Tasmania, the beaches give way to rugged cliffs and spectacular scenery. Most of the coast offers good mooring facilities for fishing boats and pleasure craft and the local communities have constructed breakwaters and wharves where the circumstances are difficult.

Beyond the Eyre Peninsula in South Australia, dramatic cliffs which fall sheer to the sea form the edge of the Nullarbor Plain. It is not until Western Australia that the cliffs give way to beaches and harbours again. One of the country's best-kept secrets is the coastline from Esperance to Albany and around to Busselton and Perth. Characterised by breathtaking white sands and beautiful granite headlands, this coastline is arguably the most beautiful in the country. Only its isolation and the cold winds of the Southern Ocean have protected it from tourist development.

The coastline of Western Australia has many beautiful beaches and is noted for its excellent fishing. Of particular note is Shark Bay with its famous friendly dolphins at Monkey Mia and the glorious beaches around Broome. Beyond Broome, around the northern coastline to Cairns and the magnificent Barrier Reef, the waters are characterised by dense mangrove swamps, broad estuaries from the rivers that are swollen by the rains sweeping across the coast every summer during the wet season, and the ever-present dangers of crocodiles, sharks and deadly jellyfish and stingrays.

Below: *Uluru (Ayers Rock) is an icon in Australia, and millions of people have visited this giant red monolith.*

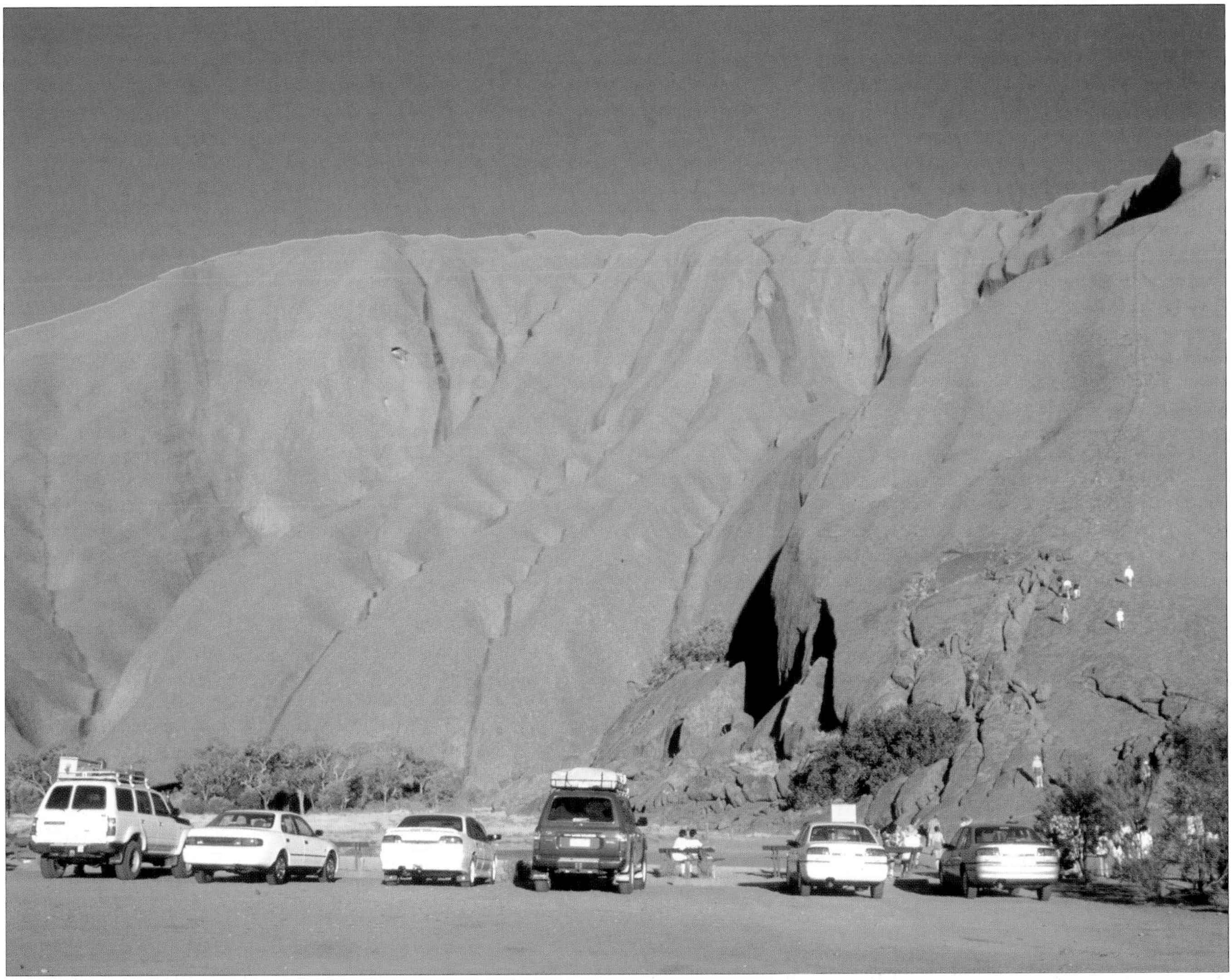

QUEENSLAND

Queensland is Australia's tropical paradise. The state boasts the warmest, most perfect weather but, like so many tropical areas, is prone to the wild winds and drenching rains of cyclones. Queensland is Australia's second-largest state. It covers an area of 1 727 200km² (666 700 sq miles), which is 22.4 per cent of the continent. The majority of the state's three million residents live either in Brisbane or along the coast in large areas like the Gold Coast, the Sunshine Coast, and the cities of Townsville, Bundaberg, Cairns and Rockhampton. The waters off the coast are rich with fish and crustaceans. The slopes of the Great Dividing Range were an important source of timber, and the coastal plains provide an ideal agricultural environment for a variety of crops. The state boasts many international hotels and holiday resorts, more than a dozen huge marinas, and a network of ancillary facilities such as casinos, charter cruises, sporting complexes and hundreds of motels and restaurants. Little wonder then, that over 60 per cent of all tourists arriving in Australia nominate Queensland as their primary destination.

Queensland likes to think of itself as 'The Sunshine State'. Tourist advertising declares that it is the state where it's 'beautiful one day – perfect the next'. This perception is based on the state's magnificent coastal scenery, which from Coolangatta on the New South Wales border to Cairns in far northern Queensland has an almost non-stop stretch of beautiful beaches, coral cays, tropical islands and waterways that are impossibly clear and blue. It is also based on the amount of sunshine the state experiences, with both coastal and inland areas enjoying long periods – particularly during the winter – when the sun shines day after day.

Queensland comprises over 7400km (4600 miles) of coastline stretching north from the headlands and beaches of Coolangatta and the Gold Coast to Cape York, and south and west around the Gulf of Carpentaria. The great attraction of this coastline is the remarkable Great Barrier Reef which was declared a World Heritage site in 1981. This spectacular marine wonderland extends from Cape York to Rockhampton, but actually forms part of a 2000-km (1243-mile) chain of over 2100 individual reefs stretching from Papua New Guinea in the north, down to Lady Elliot Island along Queensland's central coast. It has been estimated that the reef is home to more than 350 species of coral, 4000 species of mollusc and over 1200 varieties of fish.

Because the state is so large, its landscape is more complex and varied than the tropical tourist image it presents to the world. In winter the far south can experience snow with sub-zero temperatures, while the weather in the Gulf Savanna around the Gulf of Carpentaria and the area north of Townsville is so mild that these areas have become popular destinations during winter. In summer, while the Gold Coast and Sunshine Coast are recognised as desirable holiday destinations, the rains and the presence of box jellyfish make the far north far from attractive. Beyond the fertile narrow coastal plain and the Great Dividing Range the state slowly dries out until in the far west it becomes, at best, marginal land moving towards desert.

Further north, beyond Cairns and around the coast to the border with the Northern Territory, the land is characterised by impenetrable rainforest, low-grade tropical savanna and swampy, mangrove wetlands. Consequently the majority of the state's three million people live either in Brisbane or along the coast in large urban sprawls like the Gold Coast, the Sunshine Coast, and the major cities of Townsville, Bundaberg, Cairns and Rockhampton.

The basic topographic variations within the state occur from east to west. Most of the coastal area is a narrow fertile strip of land that lies between the coast and the Great Dividing Range. The Great Dividing Range starts about 200km (125 miles) south of Cape York and runs in a series of low-lying ranges and tablelands all the way down the eastern coastline. In many places it rises sharply from the sea. The roads from Cairns to Kuranda and from Cairns to the Atherton Tableland are typical of these sharp rises.

Numerous spectacular waterfalls tumble over these escarpments, a number of them – notably Barron Falls near Kuranda, Tully Falls south of Cairns and

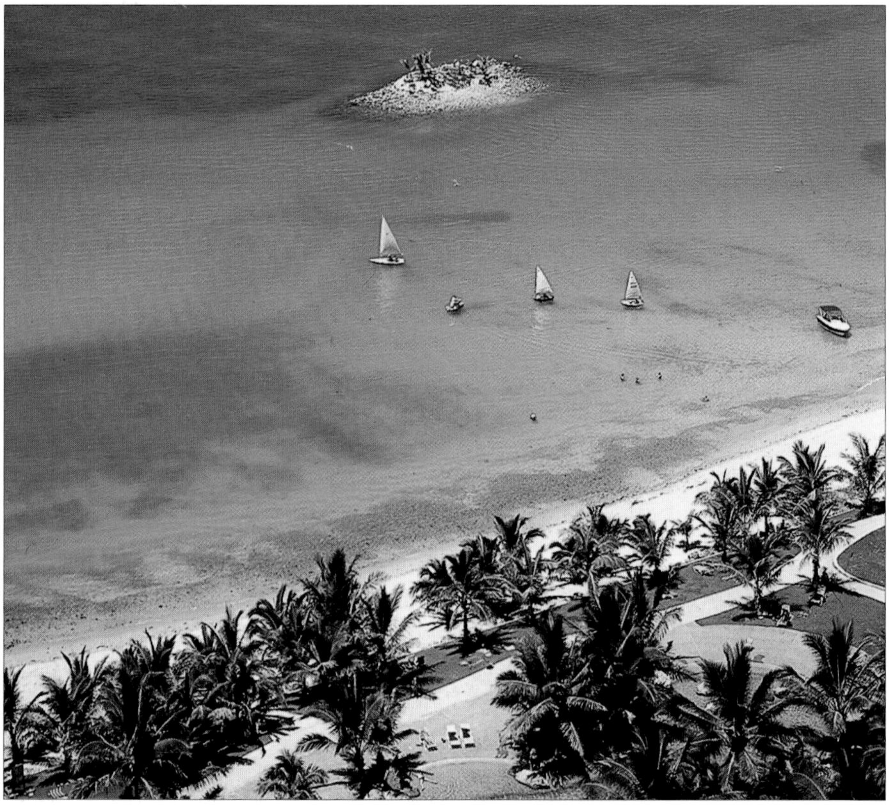

Left: *Hamilton Island is only one of the many tropical islands lying just off the coast of Queensland.*

Wallaman Falls to the west of Ingham – are very popular tourist attractions. The Wallaman Falls are the highest single-drop falls in Australia tumbling 279m (915ft) down a sheer cliff.

The tablelands and slopes that lie beyond the escarpment are agriculturally rich. Around Atherton is beef and dairy cattle country. This pattern of usage continues all the way down the coast. The Stanthorpe–Texas area of south-eastern Queensland is known for its fine beef cattle. These slopes slowly give way to the great plains of western Queensland, which become marginal lands as the rainfall drops. The area's pastoral industry is sustained by water run-off from the mighty Cooper Creek system, fed by the monsoonal rains of northern Queensland. These rains swell the river systems of western Queensland before disappearing into Lake Eyre in South Australia. The area is also sustained by the Great Artesian Basin, an underground water supply which runs from Papua New Guinea to northern Victoria. Farmers and entire communities use the hot, fresh mineral water that rises from hundreds of metres below the surface.

Queensland is also a state of great climatic variations. From the north to the south it is equally divided by the Tropic of Capricorn, which is the beginning of the true tropics, and from the east to the west it moves from coastal conditions through mild mountain temperatures to harsh desert continentality. In the south-east, the Gold Coast, Brisbane and Sunshine Coast areas, the weather in winter is mild and pleasant while the summers tend to be hot and sticky. Further north the winters are warm (certainly warm enough for swimming) but the summers are affected by cyclonic conditions. The area experiences its greatest rainfall between December and February and this is commonly associated with serious cyclonic depressions that form in the Pacific and move across the coast, laden with rain. Beyond the coast, days become much sunnier, nights become colder and rainfall decreases. The far south-west of the state experiences an average of over 10 hours of sunshine a day and less than 150mm (6in) of rainfall a year. Further east in the Darling Downs and on the low-lying mountains around Stanthorpe and Warwick the winter temperatures can drop below freezing.

Queensland is a modern, dynamic state that has built its image on its reputation as 'The Sunshine State'. For overseas visitors it is Australia's premier holiday destination and its eastern coast has been sufficiently developed for there to be abundant and diverse accommodation, excellent coastal and inland tours, and a wide variety of eating facilities available to those who want to spend their vacation enjoying a tropical holiday by the sea.

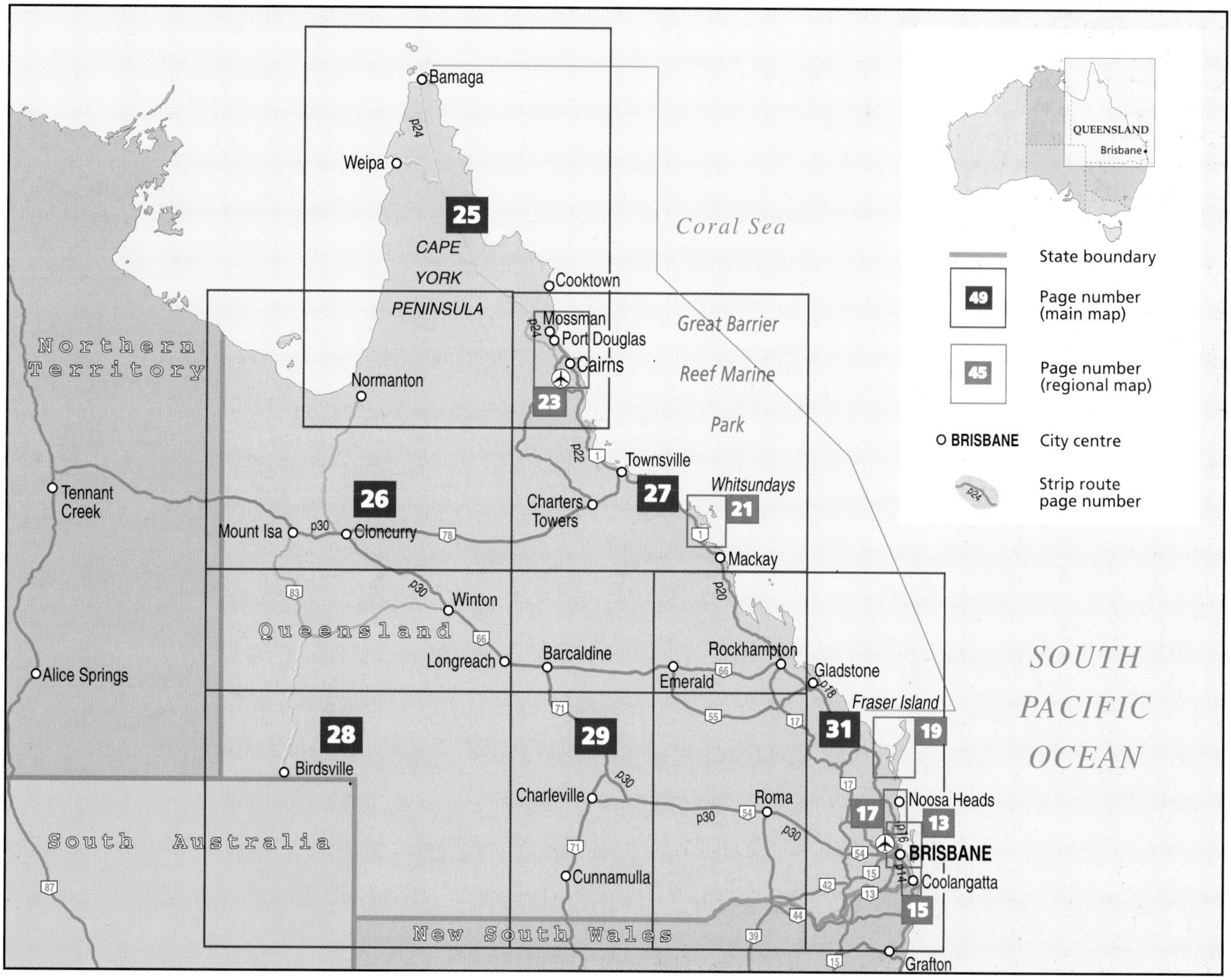

Brisbane

Brisbane is Australia's third-largest city. Its climate is subtropical with an average annual rainfall of 1090mm (43in) – most of which falls between December and March. The city receives an average of over seven hours of sunshine each day, and has a temperature range of 10°C (50°F) in winter, to 30°C (86°F) in summer. Brisbane's appeal lies in its informality, the pleasant vistas across the river and its attractive parks and gardens. There are nearly 200 parks ranging from the Mount Coot-tha Reserve, offering spectacular views of the city and Moreton Bay, to the city Botanic Gardens on the banks of the Brisbane River.

TOP ATTRACTIONS

Botanic Gardens: beautiful retreat beside the Brisbane River; rich display of tropical plants.
Government House: built in 1862 when the population of Brisbane was a mere 6000.
Mt Coot-tha Botanic Gardens: superb tropical gardens in a pleasant suburban setting.
Queensland Cultural Centre: on the South Bank of the Brisbane River comprised of the **John Oxley Library**; the **Queensland Museum** with two million items, including Bert Hinkler's tiny 'Avian Cirrus' aeroplane; a number of restaurants, and the **Performing Arts Complex** with the Lyric Theatre, Concert Hall and Cremorne Studio Theatre.

CALENDAR OF EVENTS

MARCH: Garden Spectacular.
APRIL: Pioneers Dinner at the Queensland Horse Expo & Travel Fair.
MAY: Biennial International Music Festival.
JUNE: The Big Green held on World Environment Day.
AUGUST: Brisbane Royal National Show.
SEPTEMBER: Chelsea Flower Show.
NOVEMBER: Dame Mary Durack Outback Crafts Show.
ALL YEAR: Plays, musicals and operas at the Queensland Performing Arts Complex. Exhibitions at the Queensland Art Gallery. The South Bank Parklands (seating for 3000) stages family shows throughout the year. For details contact Brisbane's Visitors & Convention Bureau on (07) 3221 8411, fax: 3229 5126.

BRISBANE	J	F	M	A	M	J	J	A	S	O	N	D
AV. TEMP. °F	77	77	75	71	66	61	59	61	65	69	73	76
AV. TEMP. °C	25	25	24	21	19	16	15	16	18	21	23	24
DAILY SUN hrs	8	7	7	7	6	7	7	8	9	8	8	9
RAINFALL in	6	7	6	4	3	3	3	2	1	4	4	5
RAINFALL mm	161	177	144	93	86	73	65	43	33	102	95	124
RAINFALL days	13	14	14	11	10	8	7	7	7	10	10	11

WHERE TO STAY

Abbey Hotel, Roma St, tel: (07) 3236 1444, fax: 3236 1134.
Heritage Hotel, cnr Margaret & Edward sts, tel: (07) 3221 1999, fax: 3221 6895.
Chifley on George, George St, tel: (07) 3221 6044, fax: 3221 7474.
Centra Brisbane Hotel, Roma St, tel: (07) 3238 2222, fax: 3238 2288.
Brisbane Hilton, Elizabeth St, tel: (07) 3231 3131, fax: 3231 3199.
Mercure Hotel, North Quay, tel: (07) 3236 3300, fax: 3236 1035.
Alatai Quest Inn, Wickham Terrace, tel: (07) 3831 5388, fax: 3839 0060.
Quest Brisbane North Quay, North Quay, tel: (07) 3236 1440, fax: 3236 1582.

Above: *The Story Bridge spans the Brisbane River and sheds its glowing reflection onto the water each night.* **Below:** *Skyscrapers in the heart of Brisbane tower like titans above the Riverside Centre where ferries berth.* **Right:** *Until 1910, Brisbane's Old Government House was used as the Governor's official residence.*

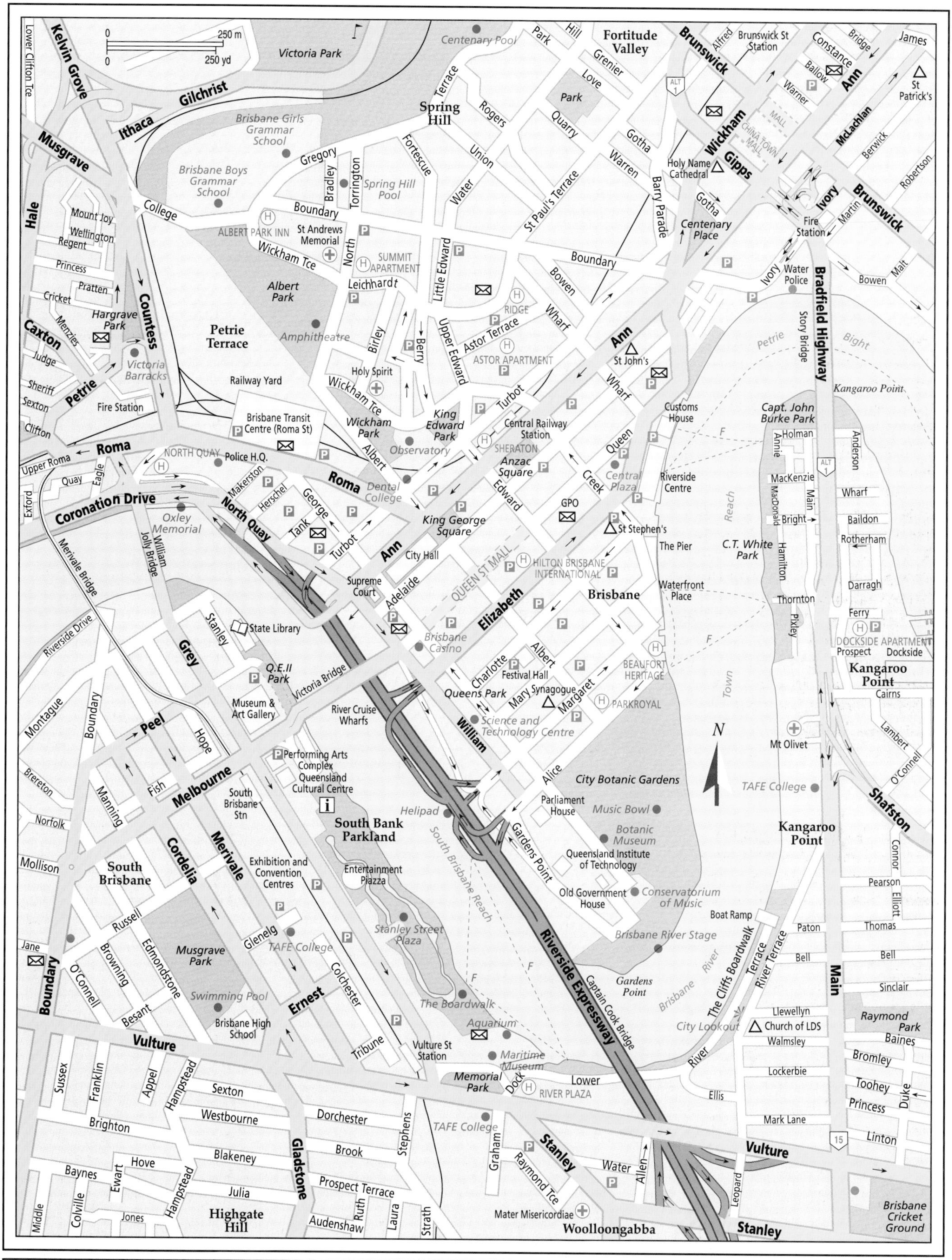

St Patrick's	Place of worship		Bus terminus		Post office
	Hotel		Police station	Market	Place of interest
	Information		Parking		Lookout

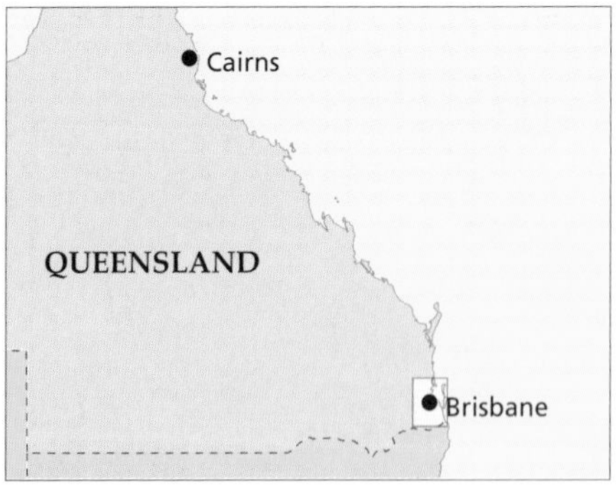

Brisbane Daytrips

Brisbane is surrounded by areas which provide a diverse selection of interesting daytrips. Possible activities include fishing, swimming, bushwalking and sight-seeing. To the west of the city, Toowoomba perches dramatically on the edge of a plateau. To the east is Moreton Bay with the historic settlement of Redcliffe as well as the delightful islands in the bay, and to the north is Bribie Island, a peaceful retreat from the city. In the hills to the north-west of Brisbane are a series of very attractive parks that offer excellent views over the city and provide wonderful walks through expansive forests.

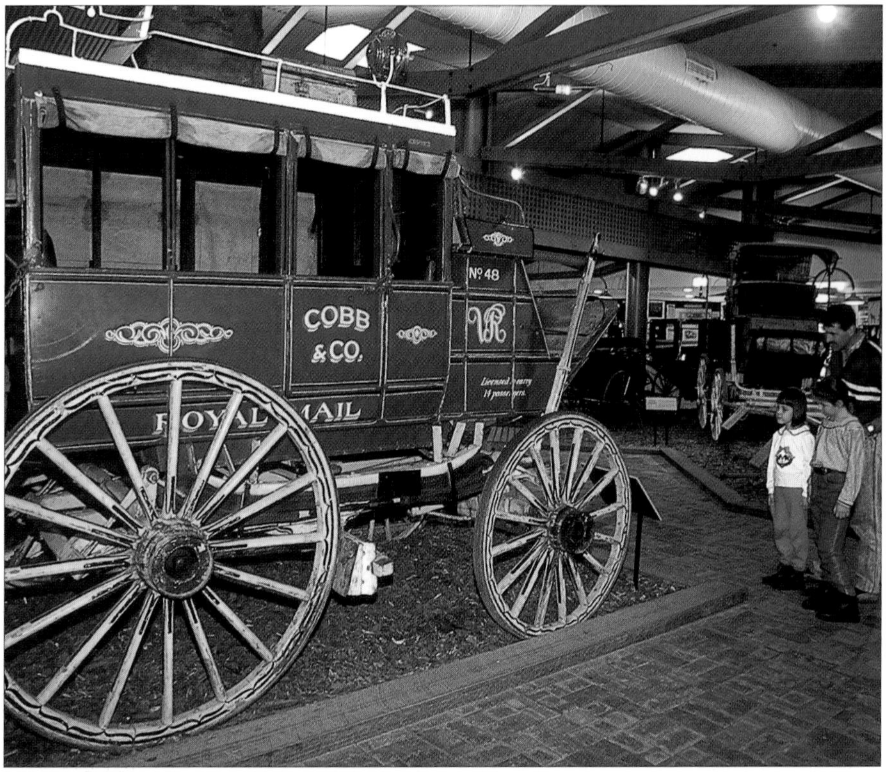

TOP ATTRACTIONS

Camp Mountain State Forest Park: offers some of the best views over Brisbane and its environs.
Ipswich: has some of the very finest domestic architecture in all of Queensland.
Moreton Island: some 192 600ha (475 915 acres) of beautiful, virtually untouched wilderness sand island.
Mount Coot-tha Botanic Gardens and Reserve: has Australia's largest display of subtropical flora.
North Stradbroke Island: long white beaches and a rich diversity of flora including several beautiful wild orchids.
Toowoomba: dramatically located city the eastern perimeter of which rests on the edge of a plateau that rises some 600–800m (2000–2600ft) above sea level.

APPROX. DISTANCES IN KM FROM BRISBANE	
Adelaide	2068
Alice Springs	3009
Cairns	1720
Canberra	1262
Darwin	3412
Melbourne	1690
Mt Isa	1817
Rockhampton	649
Perth	4350
Sydney	1021
Townsville	1384

Above, left: *Toowoomba's Cobb & Co Museum celebrates the horse-drawn coach, a major 19th-century transportation mode.*
Left: *The splendid Tropical Dome at Mt Coot-tha Botanic Gardens houses a rich diversity of Queensland's tropical plants.*

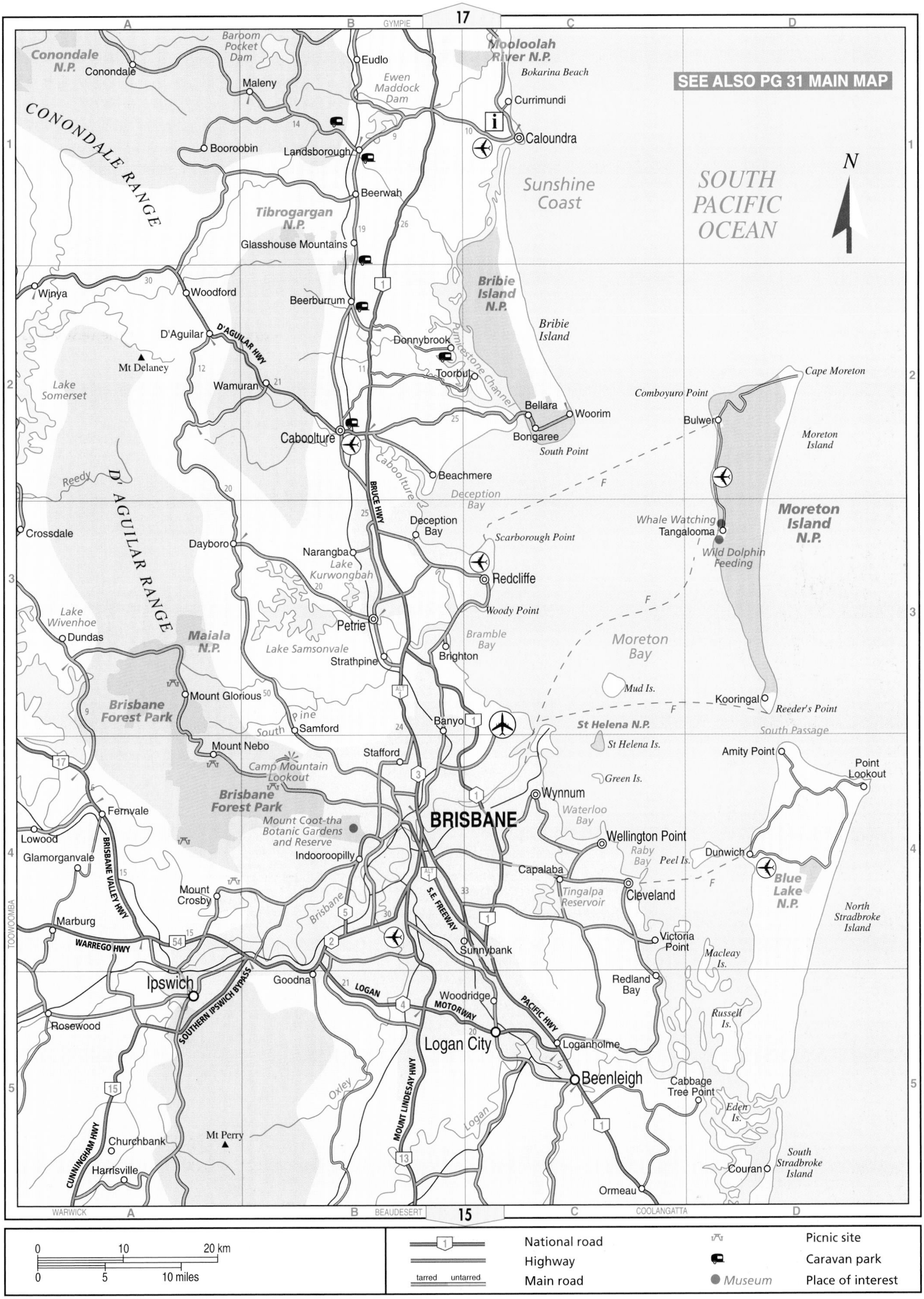
SEE ALSO PG 31 MAIN MAP
17
GYMPIE
15
BEAUDESERT
WARWICK
COOLANGATTA
TOOWOOMBA
SOUTH PACIFIC OCEAN
N
Conondale N.P.
Conondale
Baroom Pocket Dam
Maleny
Eudlo
Ewen Maddock Dam
Mooloolah River N.P.
Bokarina Beach
Currimundi
Caloundra
CONONDALE RANGE
Booroobin
Landsborough
Beerwah
Sunshine Coast
Tibrogargan N.P.
Glasshouse Mountains
Winya
Woodford
Beerburrum
Bribie Island N.P.
Bribie Island
D'Aguilar
D'AGUILAR HWY
Mt Delaney
Donnybrook
Pumicestone Channel
Toorbul
Lake Somerset
Wamuran
Cape Moreton
Comboyuro Point
Bellara
Woorim
Bulwer
Caboolture
Bongaree
South Point
Moreton Island
Reedy
D'AGUILAR RANGE
Beachmere
Deception Bay
BRUCE HWY
Moreton Island N.P.
Whale Watching
Tangalooma
Crossdale
Deception Bay
Scarborough Point
Wild Dolphin Feeding
Dayboro
Narangba
Lake Kurwongbah
Redcliffe
Woody Point
Lake Wivenhoe
Dundas
Maiala N.P.
Petrie
Bramble Bay
Moreton Bay
Lake Samsonvale
Brighton
Strathpine
Mud Is.
Mount Glorious
Brisbane Forest Park
Kooringal
Reeder's Point
Pine
Banyo
St Helena N.P.
South
Samford
St Helena Is.
South Passage
Mount Nebo
Stafford
Amity Point
Point Lookout
Camp Mountain Lookout
Green Is.
Fernvale
Brisbane Forest Park
Wynnum
BRISBANE
Waterloo Bay
Lowood
Mount Coot-tha Botanic Gardens and Reserve
Wellington Point
Glamorganvale
BRISBANE VALLEY HWY
Indooroopilly
Raby Bay
Peel Is.
Dunwich
Capalaba
Blue Lake N.P.
Mount Crosby
S.E. FREEWAY
Tingalpa Reservoir
Cleveland
North Stradbroke Island
Brisbane
Marburg
WARREGO HWY
Sunnybank
Victoria Point
Macleay Is.
SOUTHERN IPSWICH BYPASS
Ipswich
Goodna
LOGAN MOTORWAY
Redland Bay
Woodridge
PACIFIC HWY
Russell Is.
Rosewood
Logan City
Loganholme
Beenleigh
Oxley
Cabbage Tree Point
MOUNT LINDESAY HWY
Eden Is.
Logan
CUNNINGHAM HWY
Churchbank
Mt Perry
South Stradbroke Island
Harrisville
Couran
Ormeau
0 10 20 km
0 5 10 miles
National road
Highway
Main road
tarred untarred
Picnic site
Caravan park
Museum
Place of interest

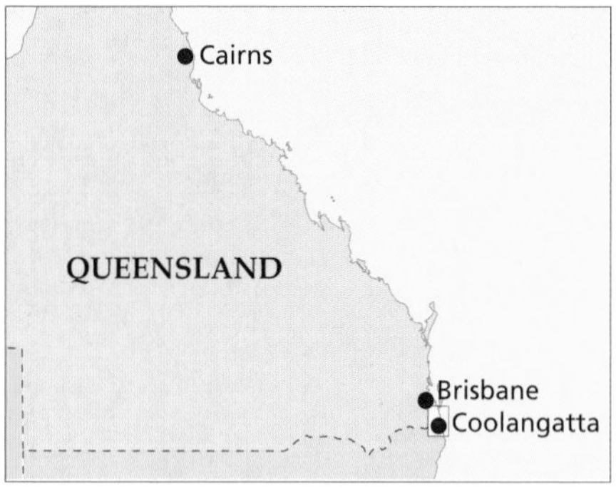

Gold Coast

The Gold Coast combines beautiful surf beaches and major tourist attractions with a hinterland of rainforest and tiny settlements that are characterised by tea-houses and art and craft shops. From humble beginnings in the 1950s the area has grown to a stretch of almost non-stop motels, hotels, eateries, a casino, and top attractions including Warner Bros Movie World, Dreamworld and Sea World. It is a place where visitors from all over the globe come to enjoy the sun, the relaxed lifestyle and 42km (26 miles) of fabulous beaches; all visitors need is their swimming gear.

WHERE TO STAY

COOLANGATTA
Beach House Seaside Resort, 52–58 Marine Parade, tel: (07) 5536 7466, fax: 5574 2810.
Beachcomber International Resort, 122 Griffith St, tel: (07) 5536 5566, fax: 5574 2810.
Carool Luxury Apartments, 5 Eden Ave, tel: (07) 5536 7154, fax: 5536 7204.
SOUTHPORT
Park Regis, 2 Barney St, tel: (07) 5532 7922, fax: 5532 0195, toll free: 1 800 644 851.
Sheraton Mirage, Sea World Drive, Main Beach, tel: (07) 5591 1488, fax: 5591 2299, toll free: 1 800 073 535.
SURFERS PARADISE
ANA Gold Coast, 22 View Ave, tel: (07) 5579 1000, fax: 5570 1260, toll free: 1 800 074 440.
Marriott Resort, tel: (07) 5592 9800, fax: 5592 9888, toll free: 1 800 809 090.

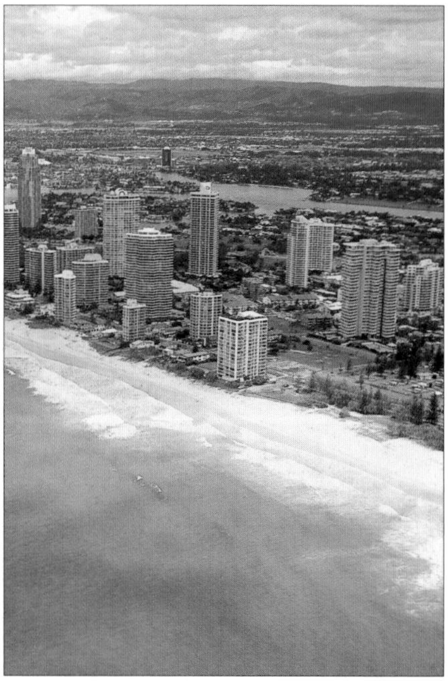

TOP ATTRACTIONS

Currumbin Sanctuary: noted for the rainbow lorikeets that flock to the sanctuary at feeding time, and its kangaroos, koalas, wallabies and emus.
Fleay's Fauna Centre: observe the native fauna of the area in their natural habitat with crocodiles, cassowaries, and brolgas being among the attractions.
Warner Bros Movie World: combination of theme park and film studios like the Universal City Studio in Hollywood.
Sea World: 25-ha (62-acre) park, the largest in Australia, with performing dolphins and whales, aqua-ballet routines and fun rides on the Three Loop Corkscrew and Lasseter's Lost Mine.

Above: *Sea World on The Broadwater at Southport is one of the premier commercial attractions on the Gold Coast.*
Left: *The Gold Coast with its stretch of golden beaches and exuberant nightlife is Queensland's most popular tourist destination.*

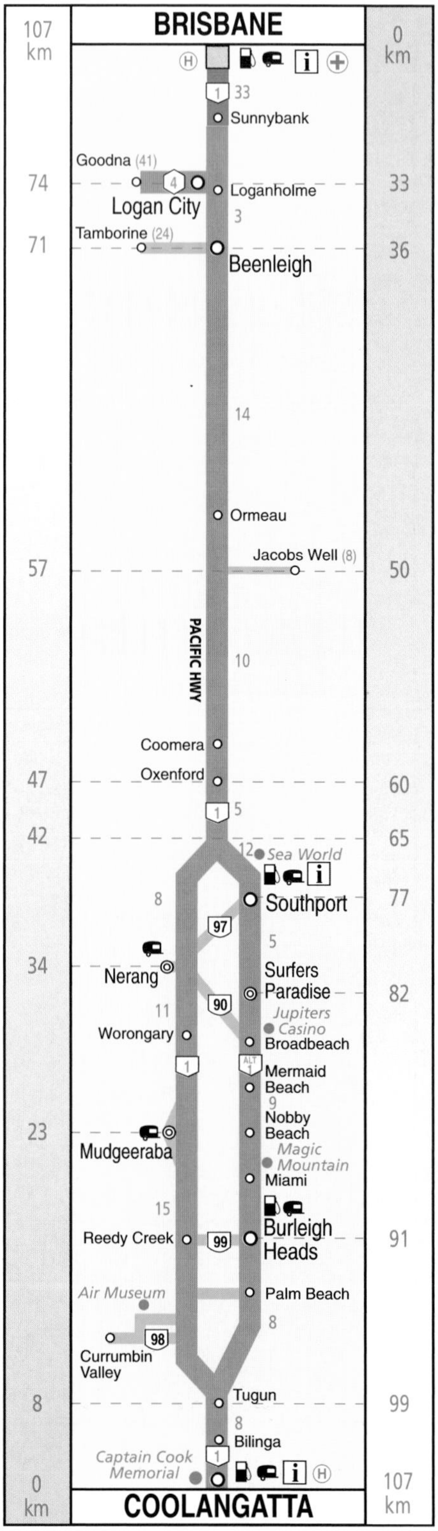

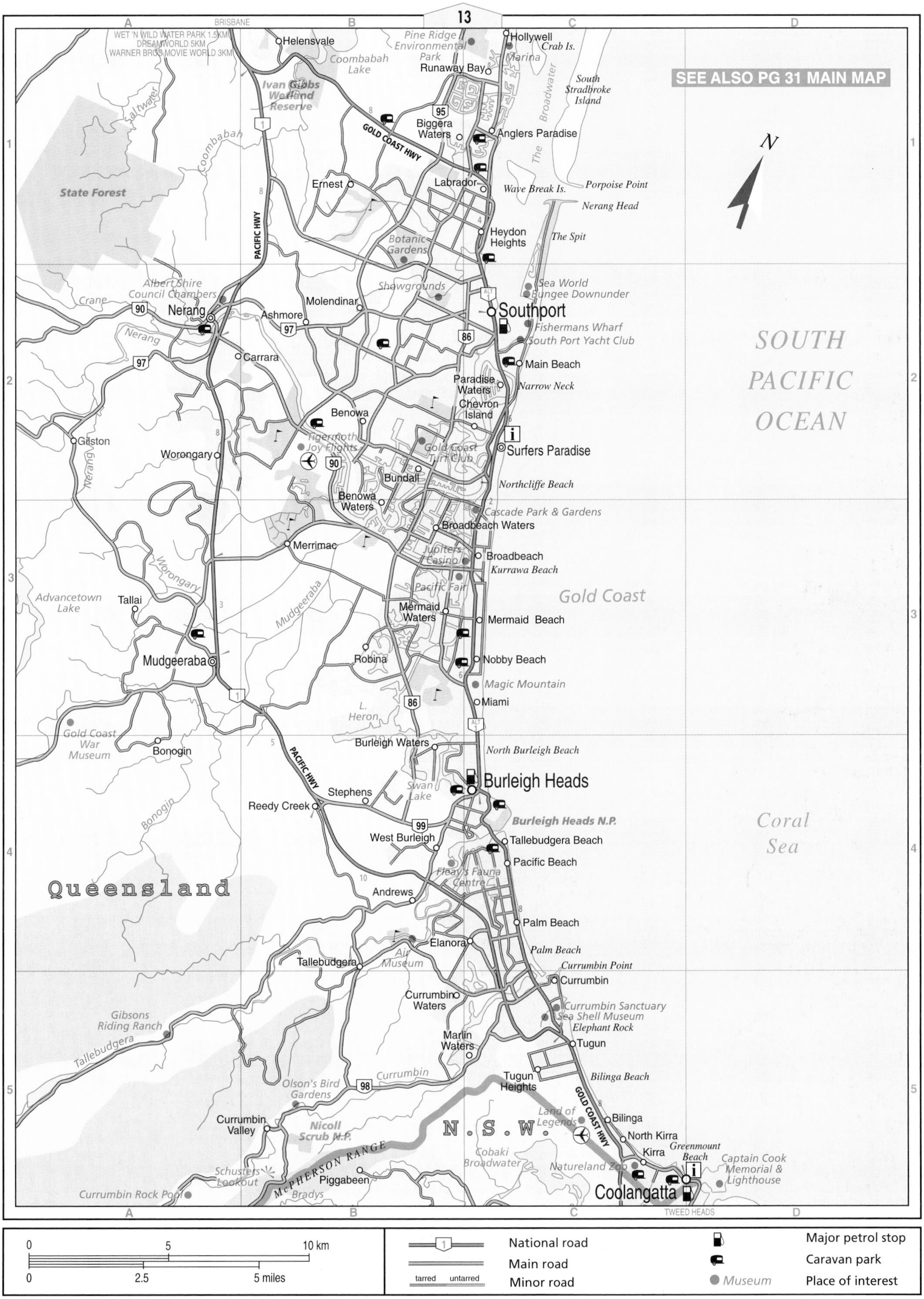

13
SEE ALSO PG 31 MAIN MAP
N
A
B
C
D
1
2
3
4
5
BRISBANE
WET 'N WILD WATER PARK 1.5KM
DREAMWORLD 5KM
WARNER BROS MOVIE WORLD 3KM
Helensvale
Pine Ridge Environmental Park
Coombabah Lake
Runaway Bay
Hollywell
Crab Is.
Marina
South Stradbroke Island
The Broadwater
Ivan Gibbs Wetland Reserve
Saltwater
Coombabah
Biggera Waters
GOLD COAST HWY
Anglers Paradise
State Forest
PACIFIC HWY
Ernest
Labrador
Wave Break Is.
Porpoise Point
Nerang Head
Heydon Heights
The Spit
Botanic Gardens
Showgrounds
Sea World
Bungee Downunder
Albert Shire Council Chambers
Crane
Nerang
Ashmore
Molendinar
Southport
Fishermans Wharf
South Port Yacht Club
Carrara
Main Beach
Paradise Waters
Narrow Neck
Chevron Island
Benowa
Tigermoth Joy Flights
Gilston
Worongary
Surfers Paradise
Gold Coast Turf Club
Bundall
Northcliffe Beach
Benowa Waters
Cascade Park & Gardens
Broadbeach Waters
Merrimac
Jupiters Casino
Broadbeach
Kurrawa Beach
Worongary
Pacific Fair
Gold Coast
Advancetown Lake
Tallai
Mudgeeraba
Mermaid Waters
Mermaid Beach
Robina
Nobby Beach
Magic Mountain
Miami
L. Heron
Gold Coast War Museum
Bonogin
Burleigh Waters
North Burleigh Beach
Swan Lake
Burleigh Heads
Stephens
Reedy Creek
Burleigh Heads N.P.
West Burleigh
Tallebudgera Beach
Pacific Beach
Fleay's Fauna Centre
Queensland
Andrews
Palm Beach
Elanora
Palm Beach
Currumbin Point
Tallebudgera
Air Museum
Currumbin
Currumbin Waters
Currumbin Sanctuary
Sea Shell Museum
Elephant Rock
Gibsons Riding Ranch
Tallebudgera
Marlin Waters
Tugun
Currumbin
Tugun Heights
Bilinga Beach
Olson's Bird Gardens
Currumbin Valley
Nicoll Scrub N.P.
N.S.W.
Land of Legends
Bilinga
North Kirra
Kirra
Greenmount Beach
Cobaki Broadwater
Natureland Zoo
Captain Cook Memorial & Lighthouse
Schusters Lookout
McPHERSON RANGE
Piggabeen
Currumbin Rock Pool
Bradys
Coolangatta
TWEED HEADS
SOUTH PACIFIC OCEAN
Coral Sea
0
5
10 km
0
2.5
5 miles
National road
Main road
tarred
untarred
Minor road
Major petrol stop
Caravan park
Museum
Place of interest

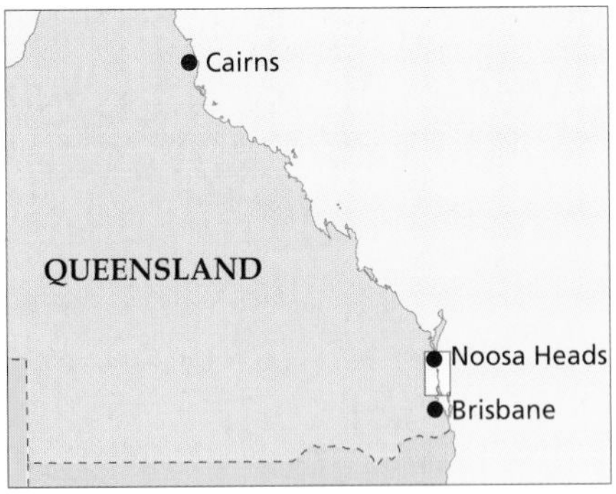

Sunshine Coast

The Sunshine Coast is an area of beaches and hinterland lying about 100km (62 miles) north of Brisbane. Major tourist attractions like the Big Pineapple (a theme park based around pineapple production), join the natural wonders (the volcanic plugs known as the Glasshouse Mountains, the peaceful beauty of the Noosa Heads National Park and a string of excellent beaches starting at Caloundra and culminating at Noosa Heads) to make the area one of the most desirable holiday destinations on the Queensland coast. Inland from the coast are even more parks with walking trails and waterfalls, as well as sleepy Queensland towns with inviting tea-houses.

TOP ATTRACTIONS

Glasshouse Mountains: a series of volcanic plugs of rhyolite and trachyte estimated to be about 25 million years old.
Gympie Gold and Mining Museum: restored buildings from historic gold-mining days.
Gympie Woodworks Forestry and Timber Museum: pit and cross-cut sawing displays, a timber cutter's bark hut, a shed with shingle roof, a blacksmith's shop and a steam-driven sawmill.
Noosa and Noosa Heads National Park: 382ha (945 acres) of native flora, bushwalk trails, picnic spots, and a refuge for birds and small mammals.
The Sunshine Plantation: tourist theme park centred on the Big Pineapple and pineapple production.

WHERE TO STAY

CALOUNDRA
Gemini Resort, Golden Beach, tel: (07) 5492 2200, fax: 5492 1000.
Oasis Resort, Golden Beach, tel: (07) 5491 0333, fax: 5491 0300, toll free: 1 800 072 096.
GYMPIE
Great Eastern Motor Inn, 27 Geordie Rd, tel: (07) 5482 7288, fax: 5482 6445.
Gympie Muster Inn, 21 Wickham Street, tel: (07) 5482 8666, fax: 5482 8601.
MAROOCHYDORE
Chateau Royale, cnr Alexandra Pde & Memorial Ave, tel: (07) 5443 0300, fax: 5443 0371.
NOOSA HEADS
Contact **Accommodation Centre**, 12 Hastings St, tel: (07) 5447 4011.

Below: *The Big Pineapple, a prominent landmark at Nambour located near the Bruce Highway.*

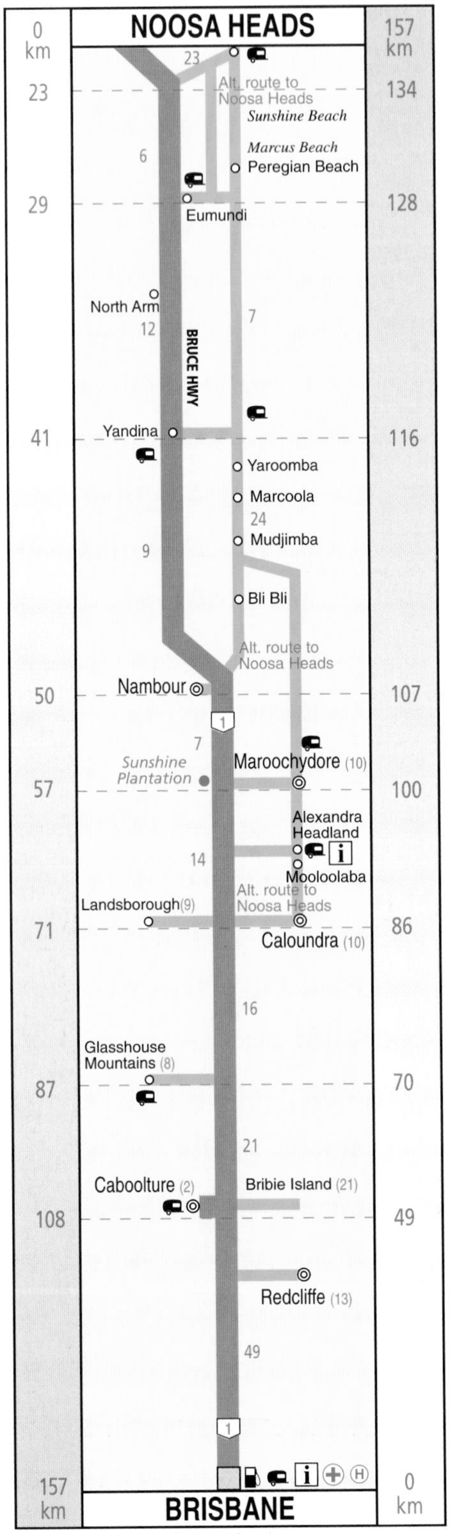

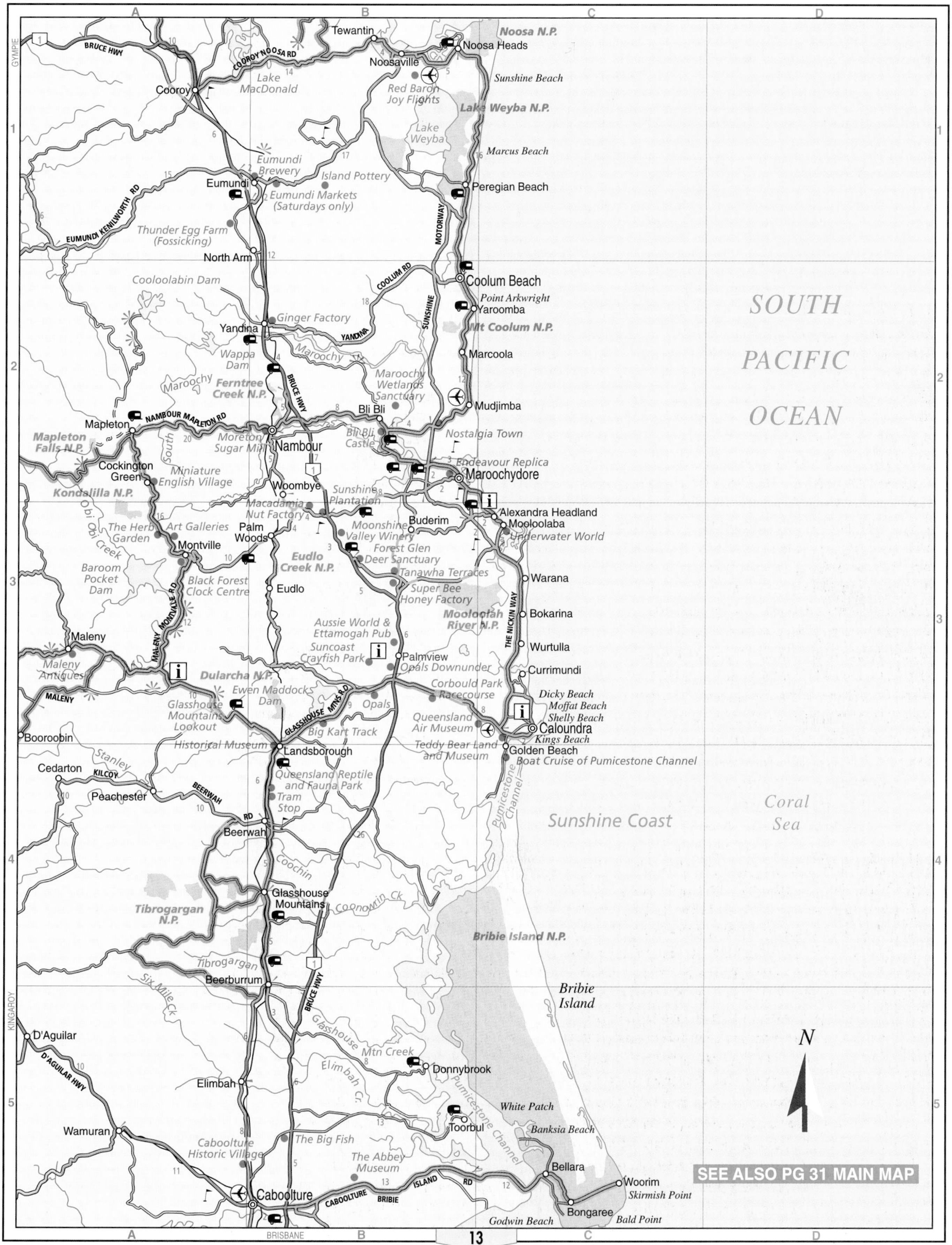

0	5	10	15	20 km
0	5	10 miles		

National road
Main road
Minor road (tarred / untarred)
Lookout
Caravan park
Museum — Place of interest

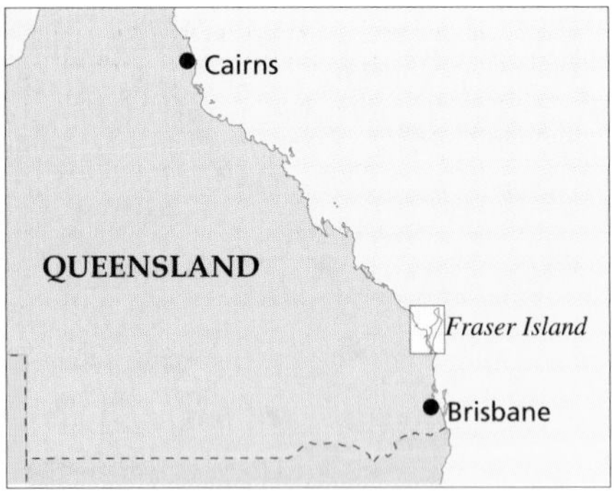

Fraser Island

Fraser Island is the world's largest sand island and lies just off the coast from Hervey Bay. It is 125km (77 miles) long and varies in width from 7–22km (4.5–14 miles). It covers 184 000km² (71 000 sq miles) and its famous sand dunes rise to a height of 240m (787ft). The only way to travel around Fraser Island is by 4WD, but there are a number of tours, among them one that starts at Kingfisher Bay Resort and includes the tranquil waters of Eli Creek, the wreck of the Maheno, *the Pinnacles and the rainforest at Central Station which flourishes despite the island's sandy base.*

WHERE TO STAY

Fraser Island Retreat, Happy Valley, tel: (07) 4127 9144. Comfortable with well-equipped bungalows. Perfect location for the many activities on the beautiful east coast of Fraser Island.
Kingfisher Bay Resort, North White Cliffs, tel: (07) 4120 3333, fax: 4120 9333, toll free: 1 800 072 555. The ultimate in resort living, offering luxury accommodation, fine dining, and tours of the island.
Department of Environment for camping areas, tel: (07) 5486 3160. There are many beautiful camping spots on this unspoilt island, but they must be booked in advance. Further information can be obtained from the National Parks and Wildlife Service.

ON THE ROAD

4WDs can be hired at Hervey Bay, Brisbane, Noosa Heads and Maryborough, and there are vehicular barges between the mainland and the island. It is sensible to fill up with petrol before leaving the mainland, however, the Kingfisher Bay and Happy Valley resorts both have petrol available. On the island keep to established tracks and avoid driving on the beaches when the tide is coming in.

TOP ATTRACTIONS

Central Station and **Woongoolbver Creek:** the creek carries clear water through the island's tranquil rainforest at Central Station.
Eli Creek: largest freshwater stream on the island's eastern coast; the whole area is exceptionally beautiful.
Lakes: there are a number of freshwater lakes on the island including **Lake Bowarrady,** 120m (394ft) above sea level, **Lake McKenzie, Lake Boomanjin** (reputedly the world's largest perched lake – it sits atop a sand dune), **Ocean Lake, Hidden Lake,** and the **Coomboo.**
The *Maheno*: a cruise ship which ran aground on the beach at Fraser Island in 1935.
The Pinnacles and **The Cathedrals:** coloured sand cliffs that have been sculpted by the wind and rain blowing in off the Pacific Ocean.

Below: *The* Maheno *chose an incredible resting place on the east coast of the world's largest sand island – Fraser Island.*

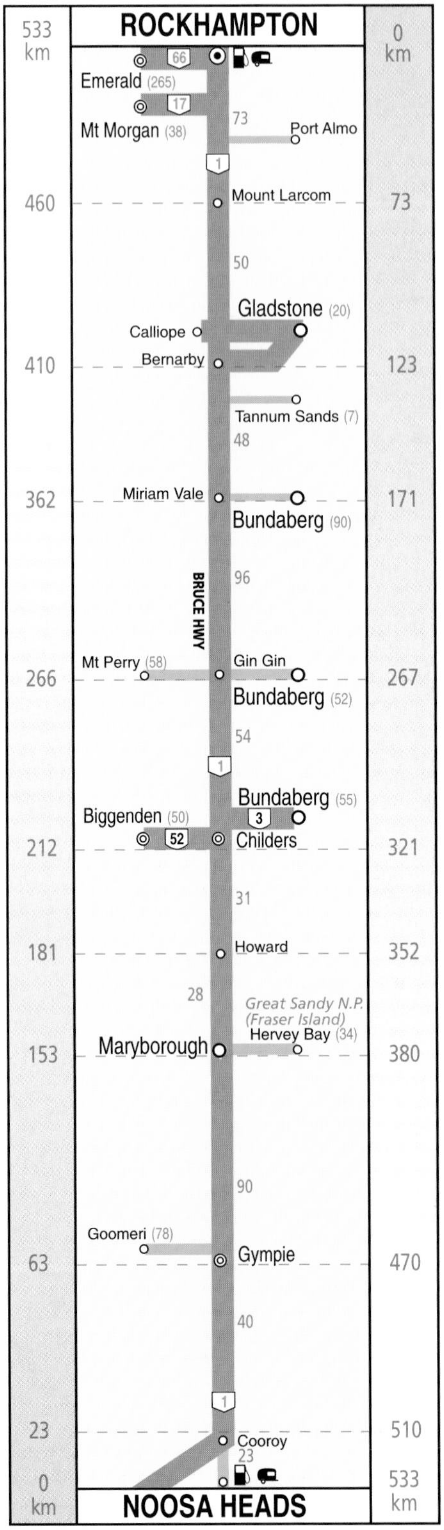

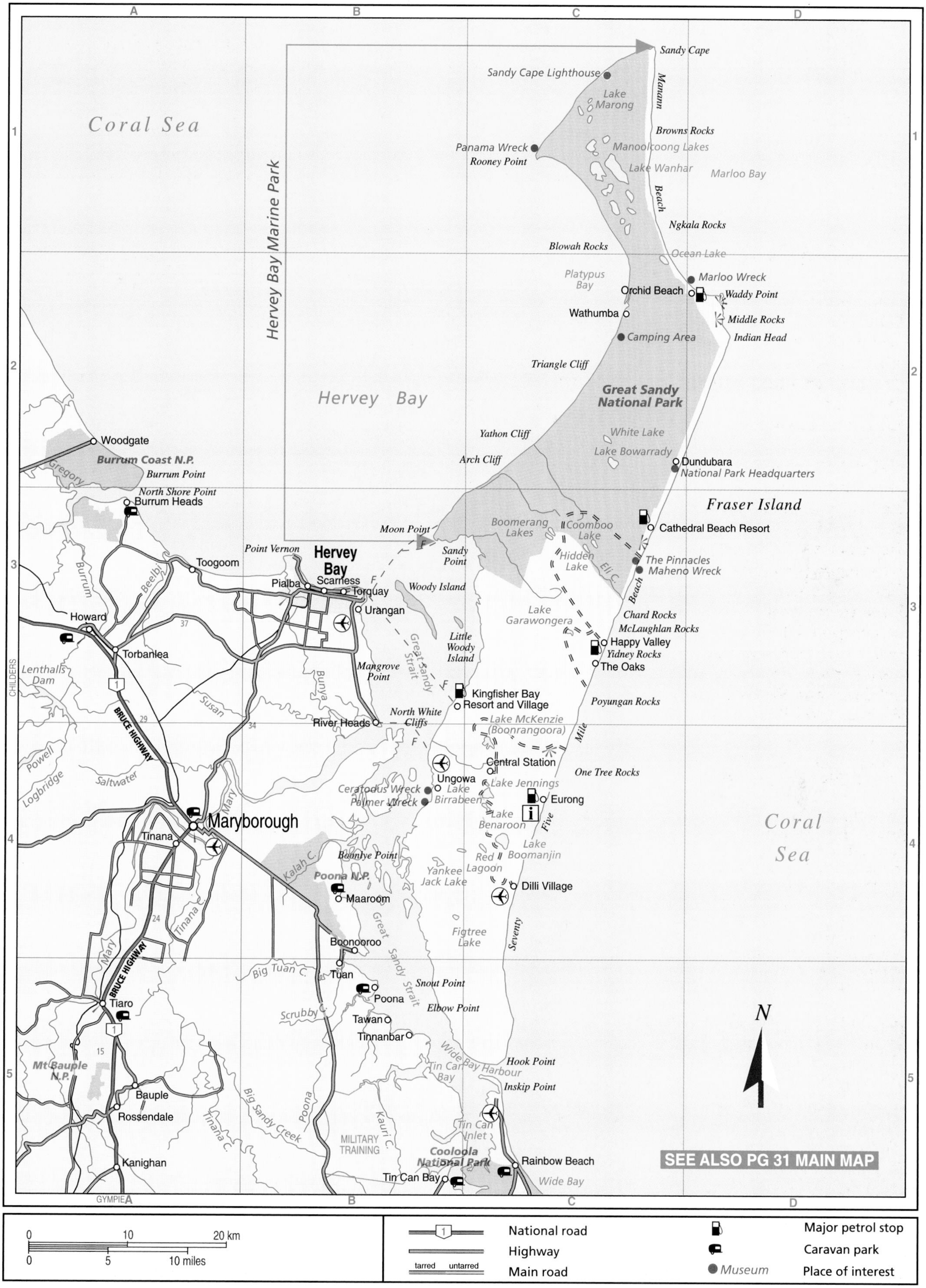

Sandy Cape
Sandy Cape Lighthouse
Lake Marong
Manann
Browns Rocks
Panama Wreck
Rooney Point
Manoolcoong Lakes
Lake Wanhar
Marloo Bay
Beach
Ngkala Rocks
Coral Sea
Hervey Bay Marine Park
Blowah Rocks
Ocean Lake
Platypus Bay
Marloo Wreck
Orchid Beach
Waddy Point
Wathumba
Middle Rocks
Indian Head
Camping Area
Triangle Cliff
Great Sandy National Park
Hervey Bay
Yathon Cliff
White Lake
Lake Bowarrady
Arch Cliff
Dundubara
National Park Headquarters
Woodgate
Burrum Coast N.P.
Burrum Point
Gregory
North Shore Point
Burrum Heads
Fraser Island
Boomerang Lakes
Coomboo Lake
Cathedral Beach Resort
Moon Point
Point Vernon
Hervey Bay
Sandy Point
Hidden Lake
Eli C.
The Pinnacles
Maheno Wreck
Toogoom
Pialba
Scarness
Torquay
Urangan
Woody Island
Burrum
Beelbi
Howard
Lake Garawongera
Chard Rocks
McLaughlan Rocks
Happy Valley
Yidney Rocks
The Oaks
Torbanlea
Little Woody Island
Great Sandy Strait
Lenthalls Dam
Mangrove Point
Bunya
Kingfisher Bay Resort and Village
Poyungan Rocks
Susan
River Heads
North White Cliffs
Lake McKenzie (Boonrangoora)
BRUCE HIGHWAY
Mile
Powell
Central Station
Logbridge
Saltwater
One Tree Rocks
Ungowa
Lake Jennings
Ceratodus Wreck
Lake Birrabeen
Eurong
Palmer Wreck
Mary
Maryborough
Lake Benaroon
Five
Tinana
Coral Sea
Lake Boomanjin
Boonlye Point
Red Lagoon
Kalah C.
Yankee Jack Lake
Poona N.P.
Dilli Village
Maaroom
Tinana
Great
Figtree Lake
Seventy
Boonooroo
Mary
Big Tuan C.
Tuan
Snout Point
Sandy Strait
Poona
Tiaro
Scrubby C.
Elbow Point
Tawan
Tinnanbar
N
Mt Bauple N.P.
Wide Bay Harbour
Hook Point
Tin Can Bay
Inskip Point
Bauple
Rossendale
Big Sandy Creek
Poona
Kauri C.
Tin Can Inlet
Tinana C.
MILITARY TRAINING
Cooloola National Park
Kanighan
Rainbow Beach
Tin Can Bay
Wide Bay
SEE ALSO PG 31 MAIN MAP
CHILDERS
GYMPIE
0 10 20 km
0 5 10 miles
National road
Highway
tarred untarred
Main road
Major petrol stop
Caravan park
Museum
Place of interest

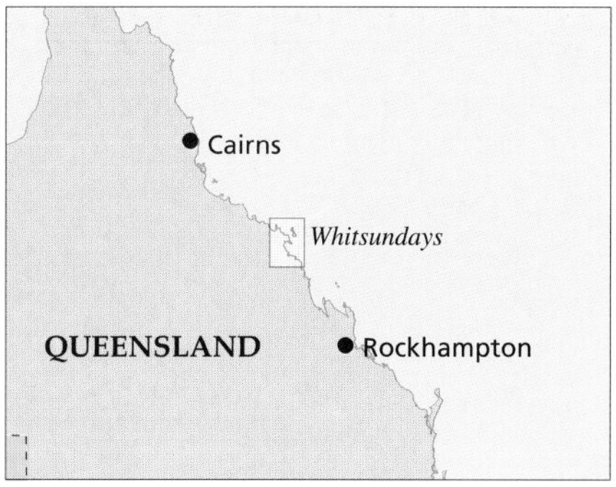

Whitsundays

The Whitsundays encompass the mainland settlements of Airlie Beach, Cannonvale and Shute Harbour, the Whitsunday Islands, the surrounding waterway, and the reef. Airlie Beach is the centre of the region and has a distinctly tropical flavour with a myriad gift shops, pubs, restaurants and shops catering for the needs of holiday-makers. The network of 74 islands, seven of which have resort facilities, are all 'drowned' mountains that were once part of the mainland. The uninhabited islands are controlled by National Parks and Wildlife. One of the highlights of a trip to the Whitsundays is a visit to the nearby reef which is part of the vast Great Barrier Reef.

Right: *Whitehaven Beach on Whitsunday Island is a picture of perfection. The whole island is protected as a national park.*

TOP ATTRACTIONS

The Whitsundays offer an array of activities from sailing, scuba diving, snorkelling and swimming to golf, bushwalking, tennis or simply relaxing at a resort.
Conway Range National Park: covers over 19 000ha (47 000 acres) and is the largest coastal national park in Queensland.
Outer Reef: cruises take visitors to a platform on the western side of the reef where they can snorkel, travel in a semi-submersible vessel, visit the underwater observatory and enjoy a smorgasbord lunch.
The resorts: the major islands (Daydream, Dent, Hamilton, Hayman, Hook, Lindeman, Long and South Molle) all have resorts with full facilities.

ON THE ROAD

The roads around the mainland are all sealed and, although they wind around the hills near the coast, they are accessible to conventional vehicles. Petrol is available at both Shute Harbour and Airlie Beach.There are no vehicular ferries across, thus a holiday on one of the islands means that the visitor is at the mercy of the available transportation which includes bicycles and walking.

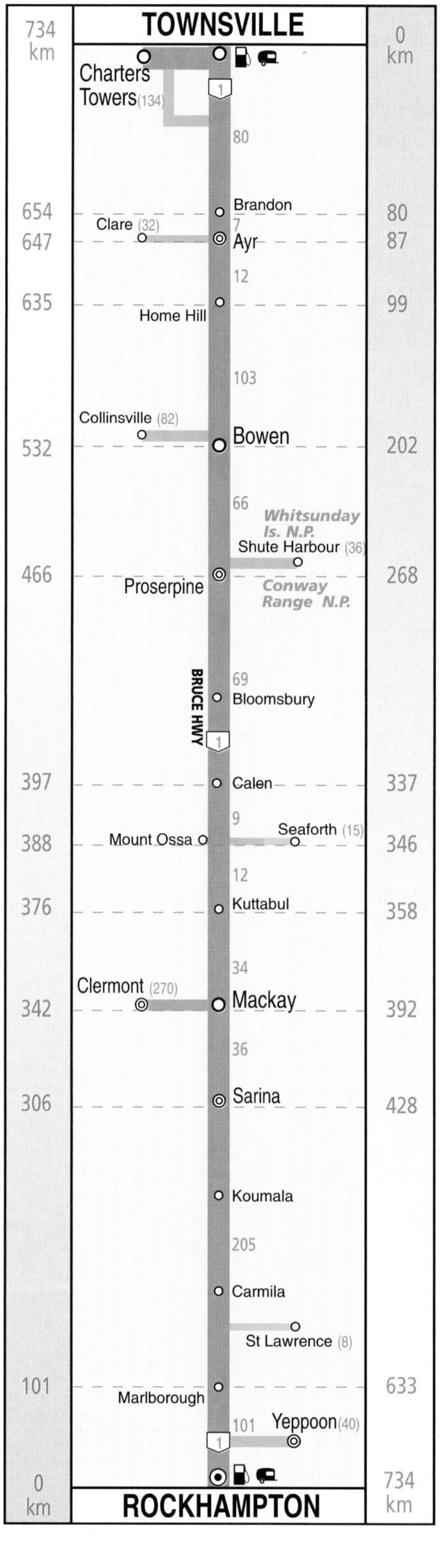

WHERE TO STAY

AIRLIE BEACH
Whitsunday Vista Quest Resort, 1 Hermitage Drive, tel: (07) 4946 7007, 1 800 671 172.
Club Crocodile Whitsunday, Shute Harbour Rd, tel: (07) 4946 7155, fax: 4946 6007, toll free: 1 800 075 151.
Whitsunday Terrace and Village Resort, Golden Orchard Drive, toll free: 1 800 075 062, tel/fax: (07) 4946 7128.
ISLAND RESORTS
Club Crocodile, Long Island, tel: (07) 4946 9400.
Daydream Island Resort, tel: (07) 4948 8488.
Hamilton Island Resort, tel: (07) 4946 9999.
Hayman Island Resort, tel: (07) 4940 1234.
Hook Island Nature Park & Coral Reef Resort, tel: (07) 4946 9380.
Lindeman Island Resort, tel: (07) 4946 9433.
Palm Bay Resort, Long Island, tel: (07) 4946 9233.
South Molle Island Resort, tel: (07) 4946 9380.

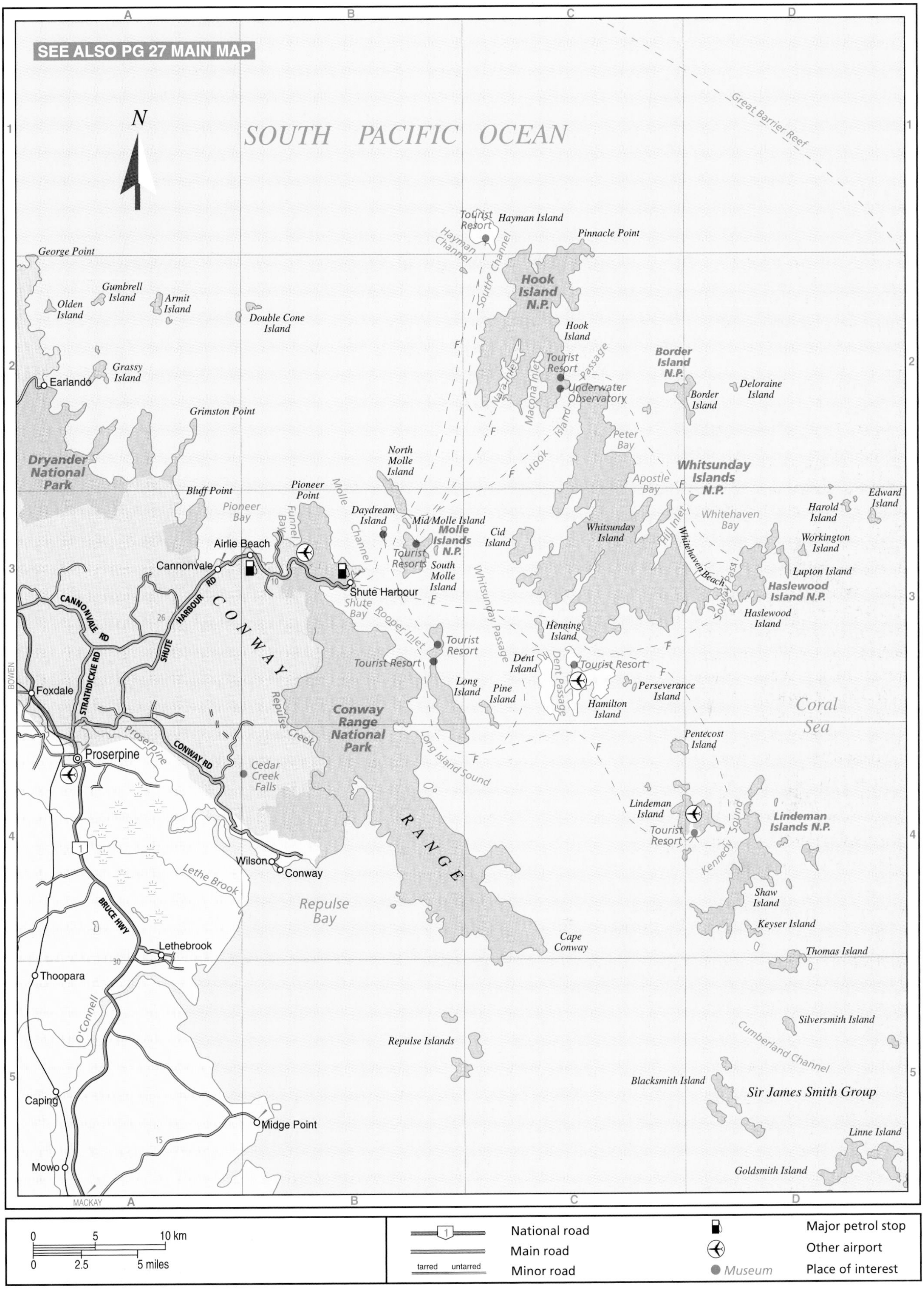
SEE ALSO PG 27 MAIN MAP
N
SOUTH PACIFIC OCEAN
Great Barrier Reef
Coral Sea
Tourist Resort
Hayman Island
Pinnacle Point
Hayman Channel
South Channel
Hook Island N.P.
Hook Island
Nara Inlet
Macona Inlet
Underwater Observatory
Hook Island Passage
Border Island N.P.
Border Island
Deloraine Island
George Point
Gumbrell Island
Olden Island
Armit Island
Double Cone Island
Grassy Island
Earlando
Grimston Point
Dryander National Park
North Molle Island
Bluff Point
Pioneer Point
Pioneer Bay
Funnel Bay
Molle Channel
Daydream Island
Mid Molle Island
Molle Islands N.P.
Cid Island
Airlie Beach
Cannonvale
Tourist Resorts
South Molle Island
Shute Harbour
Shute Bay
Rooper Inlet
Whitsunday Passage
Peter Bay
Apostle Bay
Whitsunday Islands N.P.
Whitehaven Bay
Whitsunday Island
Hill Inlet
Whitehaven Beach
Solway Pass
Harold Island
Edward Island
Workington Island
Lupton Island
Haslewood Island N.P.
Haslewood Island
Henning Island
Dent Island
Dent Passage
Tourist Resort
Perseverance Island
Hamilton Island
Long Island
Pine Island
CANNONVALE RD
SHUTE HARBOUR RD
STRATHDICKIE RD
CONWAY RD
CONWAY RANGE
Conway Range National Park
Repulse Creek
Proserpine
Cedar Creek Falls
Long Island Sound
Pentecost Island
Lindeman Island
Lindeman Islands N.P.
Kennedy Sound
Foxdale
BOWEN
Lethe Brook
BRUCE HWY
Wilson
Conway
Repulse Bay
Shaw Island
Keyser Island
Cape Conway
Thomas Island
Lethebrook
Thoopara
O'Connell
Silversmith Island
Cumberland Channel
Repulse Islands
Blacksmith Island
Sir James Smith Group
Caping
Midge Point
Mowo
Linne Island
Goldsmith Island
MACKAY
A
B
C
D
1
2
3
4
5
0
5
10 km
2.5
5 miles
National road
Main road
tarred
untarred
Minor road
Major petrol stop
Other airport
Museum
Place of interest

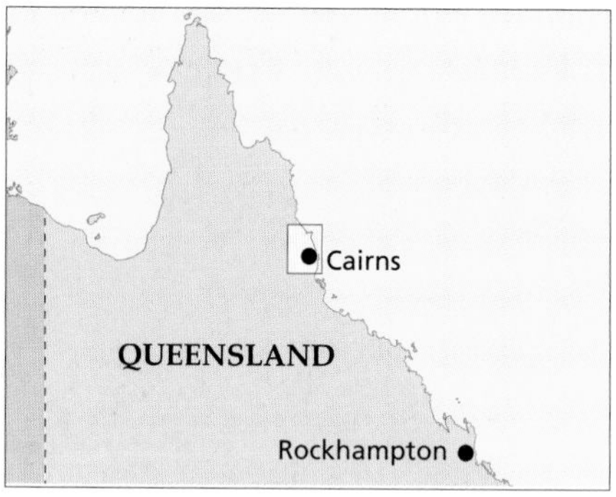

Cairns

Cairns has become a tourist magnet and boasts extensive holiday facilities. Its greatest appeal is its proximity to the Great Barrier Reef as well as the Atherton Tableland, Kuranda, Port Douglas and the Daintree and Cape Tribulation national parks. As the heart of a tropical paradise Cairns is characterised by palm-fringed beaches, balmy days, easy living, spectacular rainforest, exotic fauna and flora, and dramatic waterfalls. It is also a city of efficient transport, shopping malls, sophisticated hotels, restaurants and nightclubs, with attractions ranging from visits to the reef and snorkelling to Aboriginal artefacts and culture.

TOP ATTRACTIONS

Daintree and **Cape Tribulation national parks:** beautiful dense rainforest with a bewildering variety of flora and fauna.
Green Island and **Outer Reef:** experience the unique beauty of the Great Barrier Reef.
Kuranda Railway: scenically beautiful railway line running across the Stony Creek Falls and around the hillside, through no fewer than 15 tunnels.
Skyrail: a 7.5-km (5-mile) journey over the rainforest; this is a memorable experience.
Tjapukai Cultural Theme Park: next to the Caravonica Lakes Station in north Cairns, the venue offers a unique experience of Aboriginal culture.

Above: *Cairns is one of the best places from which to explore the Great Barrier Reef, either by boat or by plane.*

ON THE ROAD

Roads around Cairns are sealed and there are plenty of service stations. Once you cross the Daintree River, the road becomes dirt and service facilities are limited. Similarly, beyond the major Atherton Tableland towns, roads become unreliable. As a general principle, conventional vehicles should stay on the major roads, beyond these limits it is 4WD territory.

APPROX. DISTANCES IN KM FROM CAIRNS	
Alice Springs	2325
Brisbane	1720
Charleville	1392
Darwin	2750
Mackay	740
Melbourne	3052
Mt Isa	1124
Rockhampton	1084
Sydney	2544
Tennant Creek	1818
Townsville	351

WHERE TO STAY

CAIRNS
Cairns Hilton, Wharf St, tel: (07) 4052 1599, fax: 4052 1370, toll free: 1 800 222 266.
Cairns International Hotel, 17 Abbott St, tel: (07) 4031 1300, fax: 4031 1465.
Mercure Hotel Harbourside, 209–217 the Esplanade, toll free: 1 800 079 131, tel: (07) 4051 8999, fax: 4051 0317.
PORT DOUGLAS
Radisson Port Douglas, Port Douglas Rd, toll free: 1 800 333 333.
Sheraton Mirage, Port Douglas Rd, tel (07) 4099 5888.
Ti Tree Resort, Barrier St, tel: (07) 4099 34444, fax: 4098 5025.
TRINITY BEACH
Costa Royal, 59–61 Vasey Esp, 1 800 805 708, fax: (07) 4057 6577.

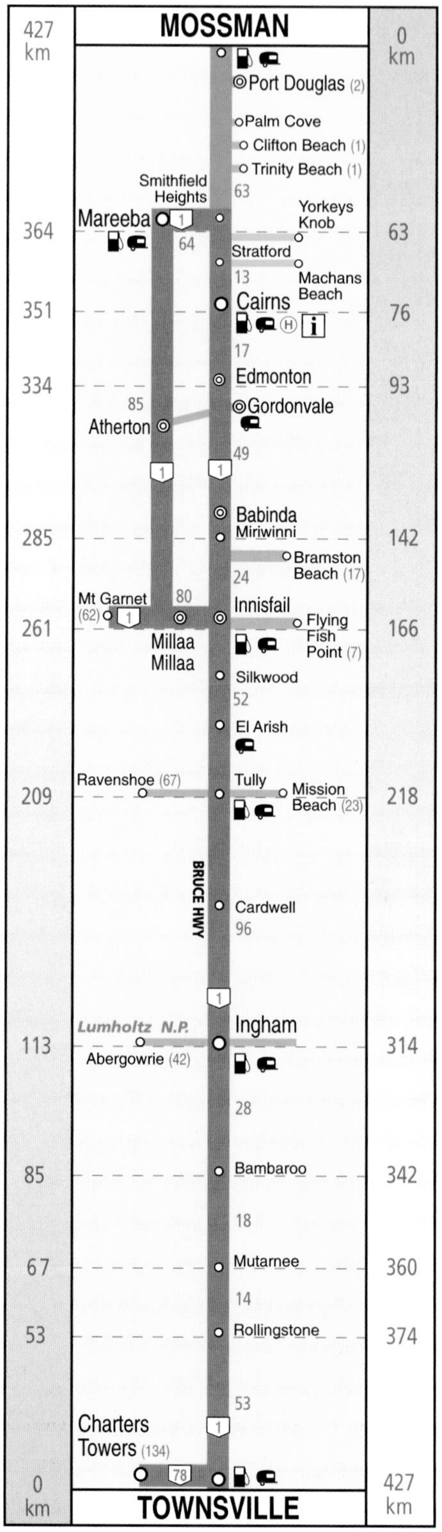

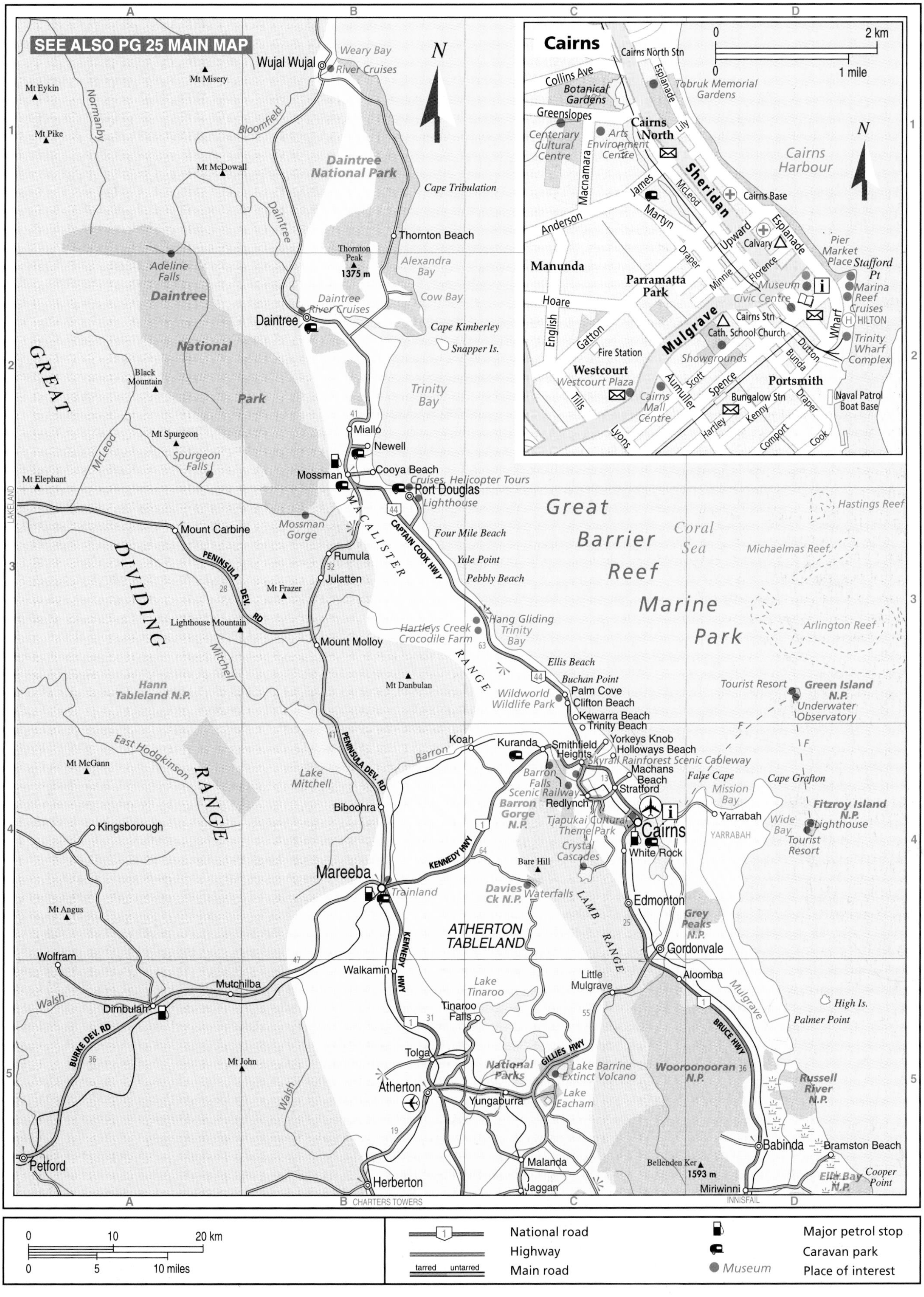
SEE ALSO PG 25 MAIN MAP
A
B
C
D
1
2
3
4
5
N
Mt Eykin
Mt Misery
Wujal Wujal
Weary Bay
River Cruises
Normanby
Mt Pike
Bloomfield
Mt McDowall
Daintree National Park
Cape Tribulation
Daintree
Thornton Beach
Adeline Falls
Daintree
Thornton Peak
1375 m
Alexandra Bay
Daintree River Cruises
Cow Bay
Daintree
Cape Kimberley
National
Snapper Is.
GREAT
Black Mountain
Park
Trinity Bay
Mt Spurgeon
Miallo
Newell
Spurgeon Falls
McLeod
Mt Elephant
Mossman
Cooya Beach
Cruises, Helicopter Tours
Port Douglas
Lighthouse
LAKELAND
Mossman Gorge
Mount Carbine
MACALISTER
CAPTAIN COOK HWY
Four Mile Beach
DIVIDING
PENINSULA DEV. RD
Rumula
Yale Point
Julatten
Pebbly Beach
Mt Frazer
Lighthouse Mountain
Hang Gliding
Trinity Bay
Mount Molloy
Hartleys Creek Crocodile Farm
RANGE
Mitchell
Ellis Beach
Hann Tableland N.P.
Mt Danbulan
Buchan Point
Palm Cove
Clifton Beach
Wildworld Wildlife Park
Kewarra Beach
Trinity Beach
East Hodgkinson
Koah
Kuranda
Smithfield Heights
Yorkeys Knob
Holloways Beach
Barron
Skyrail Rainforest Scenic Cableway
Mt McGann
RANGE
Lake Mitchell
PENINSULA DEV. RD
Barron Falls
Machans Beach
Scenic Railway
Stratford
Barron Gorge N.P.
Redlynch
Biboohra
Kingsborough
Tjapukai Cultural Theme Park
Cairns
White Rock
KENNEDY HWY
Crystal Cascades
Bare Hill
Mareeba
Trainland
Davies Ck N.P.
Waterfalls
LAMB
Mt Angus
Edmonton
ATHERTON TABLELAND
KENNEDY HWY
RANGE
Grey Peaks N.P.
Gordonvale
Wolfram
Walkamin
Little Mulgrave
Aloomba
Mutchilba
Lake Tinaroo
Walsh
Dimbulah
Tinaroo Falls
Mulgrave
BURKE DEV. RD
BRUCE HWY
Tolga
Mt John
National Parks
GILLIES HWY
Lake Barrine Extinct Volcano
Wooroonooran N.P.
Atherton
Yungaburra
Lake Eacham
Walsh
Russell River N.P.
Babinda
Bramston Beach
Petford
Malanda
Bellenden Ker
1593 m
Herberton
Jaggan
Miriwinni
Eli Bay N.P.
Cooper Point
CHARTERS TOWERS
INNISFAIL
Great Barrier Reef Marine Park
Coral Sea
Hastings Reef
Michaelmas Reef
Arlington Reef
Tourist Resort
Green Island N.P.
Underwater Observatory
False Cape
Cape Grafton
Mission Bay
Yarrabah
YARRABAH
Fitzroy Island N.P.
Lighthouse
Wide Bay
Tourist Resort
High Is.
Palmer Point
Cairns
0
2 km
1 mile
Cairns North Stn
Collins Ave
Botanical Gardens
Esplanade
Tobruk Memorial Gardens
Greenslopes
Cairns North
Lily
Centenary Cultural Centre
Arts Environment Centre
Macnamara
James
Sheridan
Cairns Harbour
McLeod
Cairns Base
Anderson
Martyn
Upward
Esplanade
Calvary
Pier Market Place
Stafford Pt
Manunda
Draper
Minnie
Florence
Museum
Marina
Parramatta Park
Civic Centre
Reef Cruises
Hoare
Cairns Stn
Wharf
HILTON
English
Gatton
Mulgrave
Cath. School Church
Dutton
Trinity Wharf Complex
Fire Station
Bunda
Westcourt
Showgrounds
Portsmith
Westcourt Plaza
Scott
Spence
Draper
Naval Patrol Boat Base
Tills
Cairns Mall Centre
Aumuller
Bungalow Stn
Kenny
Lyons
Hartley
Comport
Cook
0
10
20 km
5
10 miles
National road
Highway
tarred
untarred
Main road
Major petrol stop
Caravan park
Museum
Place of interest

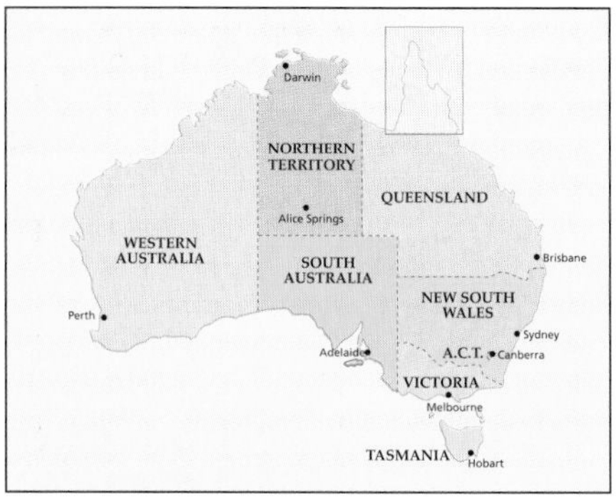

Cape York Peninsula

The vast area that comprises the Cape York Peninsula is the last refuge for seekers of true wilderness adventures. Past Cooktown there are only two towns of significance on the Cape: Weipa, a bauxite mining town located 838km (521 miles) north of Cairns, and Bamaga, the most northerly township in Queensland with a population of 2000 people, most of whom are Torres Strait Islanders. If the thought of crossing swollen rivers and travelling along roads that are hard to distinguish appeals, then this may be the trip for you. But ensure you are fully prepared before you set off, with plenty of supplies and fresh water to last a few weeks.

TOP ATTRACTIONS

Black Mountain: a strange mound of huge granite boulders blackened by lichens.
Cooktown: has six monuments to Captain Cook, including a lighthouse and museum.
Iron Range National Park: largest area of lowland rainforest remaining in Australia.
Jardine River National Park: 235 000-ha (580 450-acre) reserve near the tip of Cape York.
Quinkan Reserve: near the settlement of Laura, inland from Cooktown, and Australia's most important Aboriginal site. It is thought to contain the world's largest collection of prehistoric work and is of major cultural and historical significance.

ON THE ROAD

The road to Bamaga is over 900km (560 miles) long and is strictly for 4WD enthusiasts. Each year more and more people undertake the challenging trek but it is not a trip for the inexperienced. Be prepared: the weather is hot and sticky, so plenty of fresh water needs to be taken on the trip, the distances between communities are vast, and the rivers are home to crocodiles.

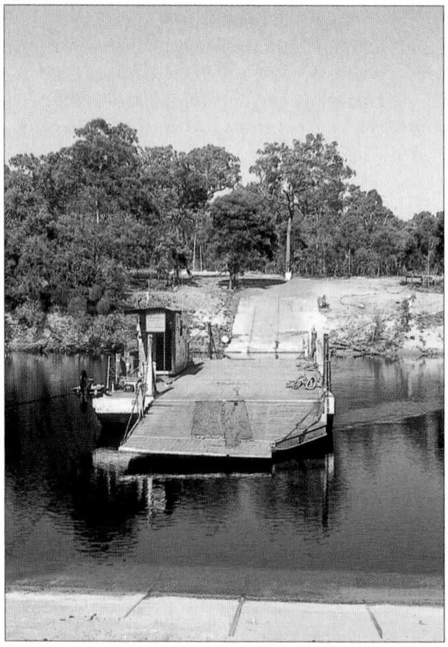

Above: *These granite boulders, 28km (17 miles) south of Cooktown, are the essence of an old Aboriginal legend.*
Right: *Most river crossings on the Cape are hazardous events, but a car ferry at Jardine River assists the adventurous traveller.*

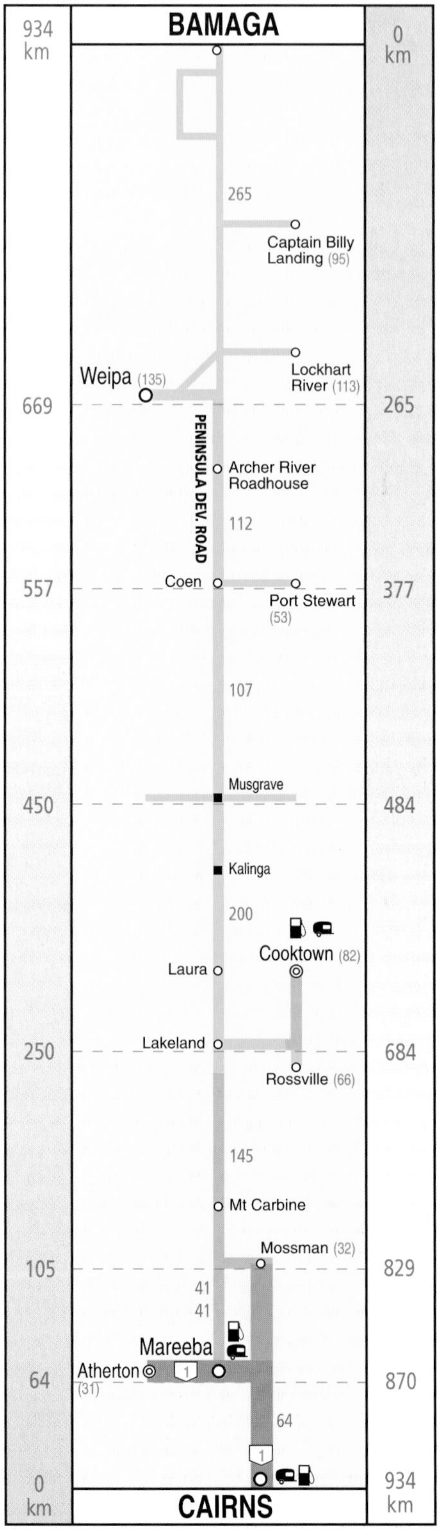

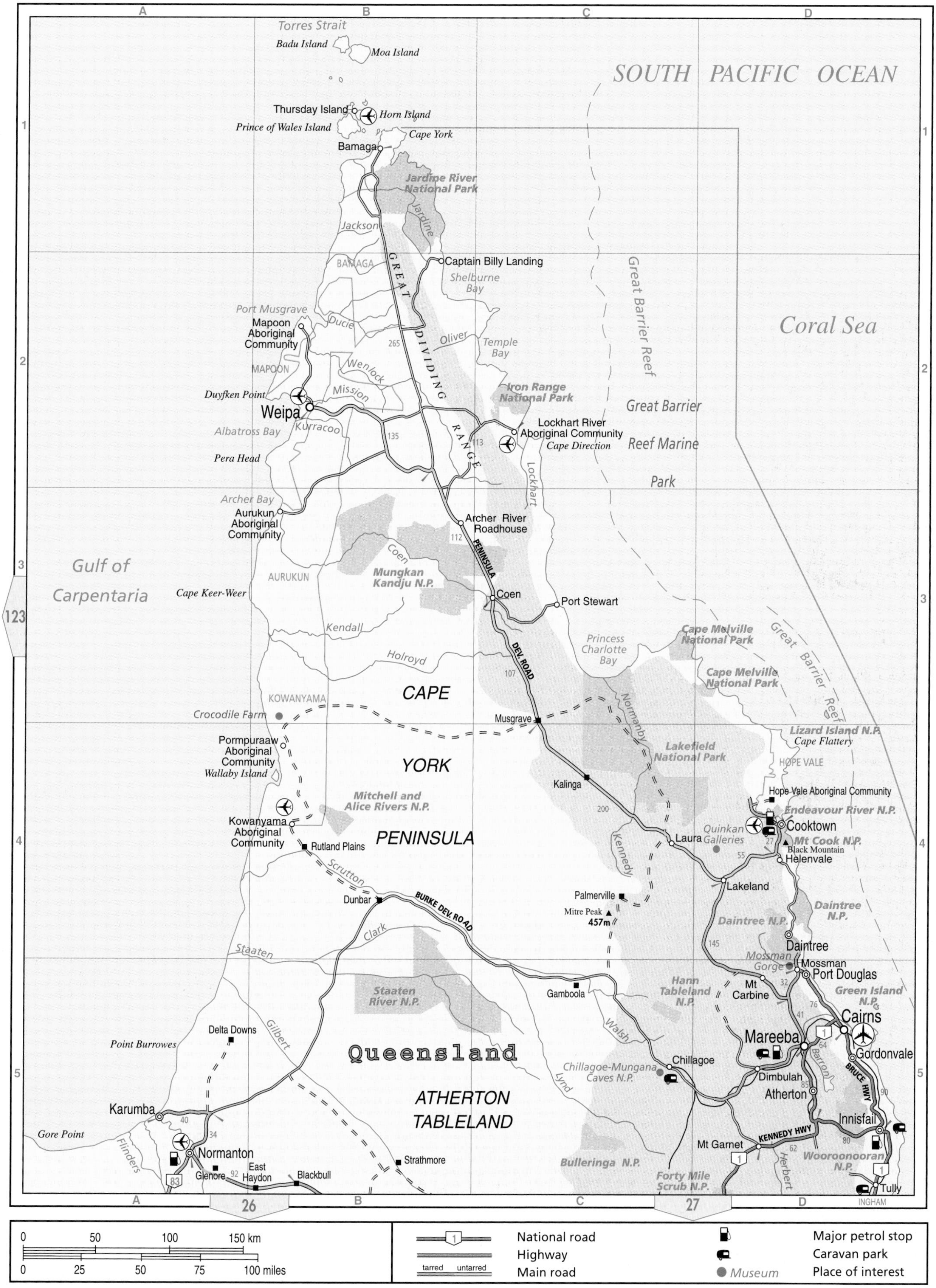
Torres Strait
Badu Island
Moa Island
Thursday Island
Horn Island
Prince of Wales Island
Cape York
Bamaga
SOUTH PACIFIC OCEAN
Jardine River National Park
Jardine
Jackson
BAMAGA
Captain Billy Landing
Shelburne Bay
GREAT DIVIDING RANGE
Port Musgrave
Mapoon Aboriginal Community
Ducie
MAPOON
Oliver
Temple Bay
Wenlock
Mission
Great Barrier Reef
Coral Sea
Duyfken Point
Weipa
Iron Range National Park
Great Barrier Reef Marine Park
Lockhart River Aboriginal Community
Cape Direction
Albatross Bay
Kurracoo
Pera Head
Lockhart
Archer Bay
Aurukun Aboriginal Community
Archer River Roadhouse
PENINSULA DEV. ROAD
Gulf of Carpentaria
Coen
Mungkan Kandju N.P.
AURUKUN
Cape Keer-Weer
Port Stewart
Kendall
Cape Melville National Park
Princess Charlotte Bay
Holroyd
KOWANYAMA
CAPE YORK PENINSULA
Crocodile Farm
Musgrave
Normanby
Lakefield National Park
Lizard Island N.P.
Cape Flattery
HOPE VALE
Pormpuraaw Aboriginal Community
Wallaby Island
Kalinga
Mitchell and Alice Rivers N.P.
Hope Vale Aboriginal Community
Endeavour River N.P.
Kowanyama Aboriginal Community
Laura
Quinkan Galleries
Cooktown
Mt Cook N.P.
Black Mountain
Helenvale
Rutland Plains
Kennedy
Scrutton
Lakeland
Dunbar
BURKE DEV. ROAD
Palmerville
Mitre Peak 457m
Daintree N.P.
Daintree
Clark
Staaten
Mossman Gorge
Mossman
Port Douglas
Staaten River N.P.
Gamboola
Hann Tableland N.P.
Mt Carbine
Green Island N.P.
Cairns
Delta Downs
Walsh
Mareeba
Point Burrowes
Gilbert
Queensland
Chillagoe-Mungana Caves N.P.
Chillagoe
Gordonvale
BRUCE HWY
Barron
Dimbulah
Lynd
ATHERTON TABLELAND
Atherton
Karumba
Innisfail
Gore Point
KENNEDY HWY
Mt Garnet
Wooroonooran N.P.
Normanton
Flinders
Strathmore
Glenore
East Haydon
Blackbull
Bulleringa N.P.
Forty Mile Scrub N.P.
Herbert
Tully
INGHAM
0 50 100 150 km
0 25 50 75 100 miles
National road
Highway
Main road
tarred untarred
Major petrol stop
Caravan park
Museum
Place of interest

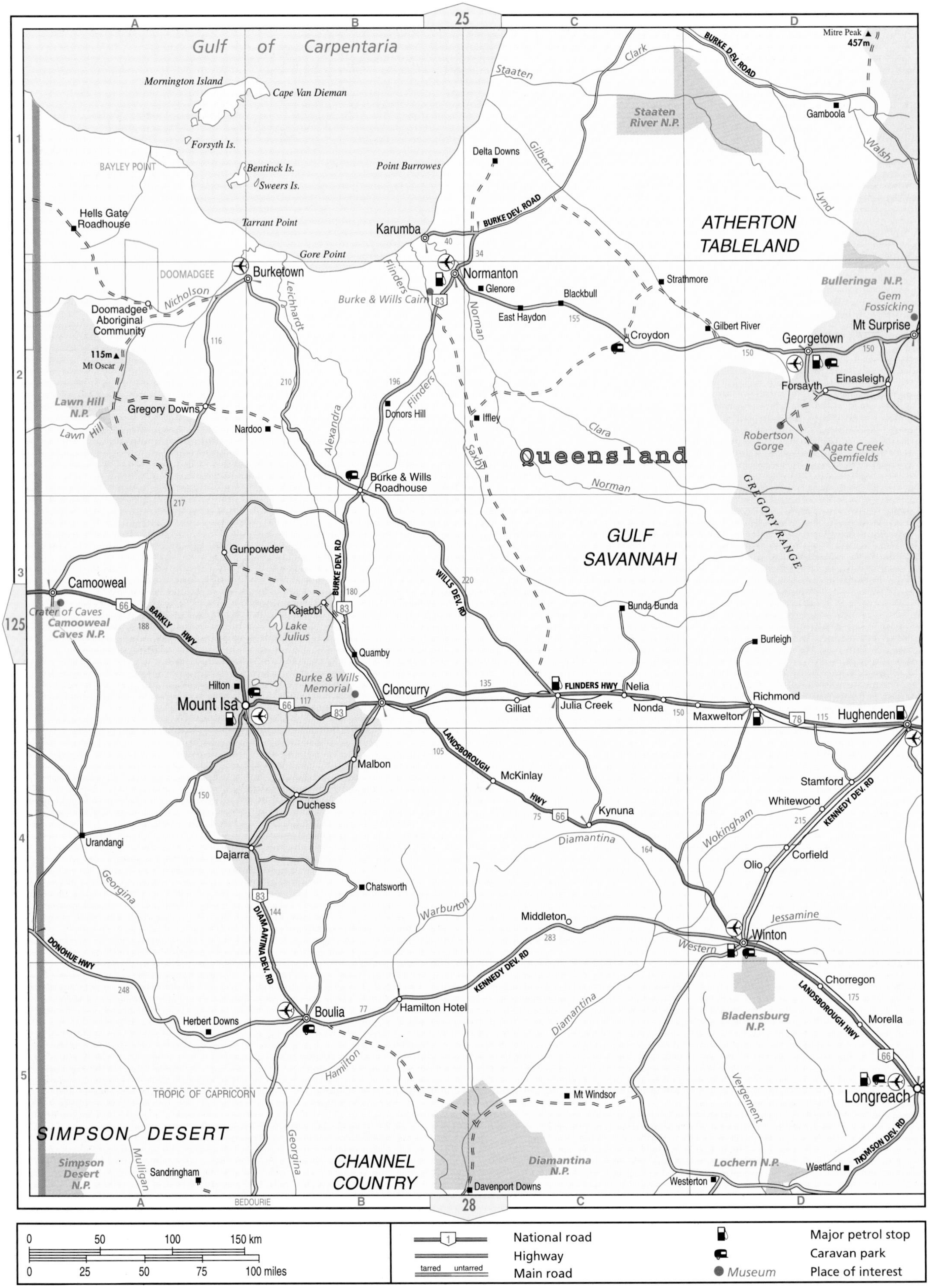

25
A
B
C
D
Gulf of Carpentaria
Mornington Island
Cape Van Dieman
Forsyth Is.
Bentinck Is.
Sweers Is.
BAYLEY POINT
Point Burrowes
Tarrant Point
Gore Point
Mitre Peak
457m
BURKE DEV. ROAD
Clark
Staaten
Staaten River N.P.
Gamboola
Walsh
Lynd
Delta Downs
Gilbert
BURKE DEV. ROAD
Karumba
Normanton
ATHERTON TABLELAND
Hells Gate Roadhouse
DOOMADGEE
Burketown
Flinders
Leichhardt
Glenore
Blackbull
East Haydon
Strathmore
Bulleringa N.P.
Gem Fossicking
Doomadgee Aboriginal Community
Nicholson
Burke & Wills Cairn
Norman
Croydon
Gilbert River
Georgetown
Mt Surprise
115m
Mt Oscar
Einasleigh
Forsayth
Lawn Hill N.P.
Gregory Downs
Lawn Hill
Nardoo
Alexandra
Flinders
Donors Hill
Iffley
Clara
Robertson Gorge
Agate Creek Gemfields
Saxby
Queensland
Norman
Burke & Wills Roadhouse
GREGORY RANGE
GULF SAVANNAH
Gunpowder
BURKE DEV. RD
WILLS DEV. RD
Camooweal
Crater of Caves
Camooweal Caves N.P.
125
BARKLY HWY
Kajabbi
Lake Julius
Bunda Bunda
Burleigh
Quamby
Burke & Wills Memorial
Hilton
Mount Isa
Cloncurry
FLINDERS HWY
Nelia
Gilliat
Julia Creek
Nonda
Maxwelton
Richmond
Hughenden
Malbon
LANDSBOROUGH
McKinlay
HWY
Stamford
Whitewood
KENNEDY DEV. RD
Duchess
Kynuna
Diamantina
Wokingham
Urandangi
Dajarra
Corfield
Olio
Georgina
Chatsworth
Warburton
Middleton
Jessamine
Winton
Western
DIAMANTINA DEV. RD
DONOHUE HWY
KENNEDY DEV. RD
Chorregon
LANDSBOROUGH HWY
Morella
Bladensburg N.P.
Boulia
Hamilton Hotel
Herbert Downs
Diamantina
Hamilton
Vergement
Longreach
TROPIC OF CAPRICORN
Mt Windsor
SIMPSON DESERT
Simpson Desert N.P.
Mulligan
Sandringham
Georgina
CHANNEL COUNTRY
Diamantina N.P.
Lochern N.P.
Westland
THOMSON DEV. RD
Westerton
Davenport Downs
BEDOURIE
28
0 50 100 150 km
0 25 50 75 100 miles
National road
Highway
Main road
tarred
untarred
Major petrol stop
Caravan park
Museum
Place of interest

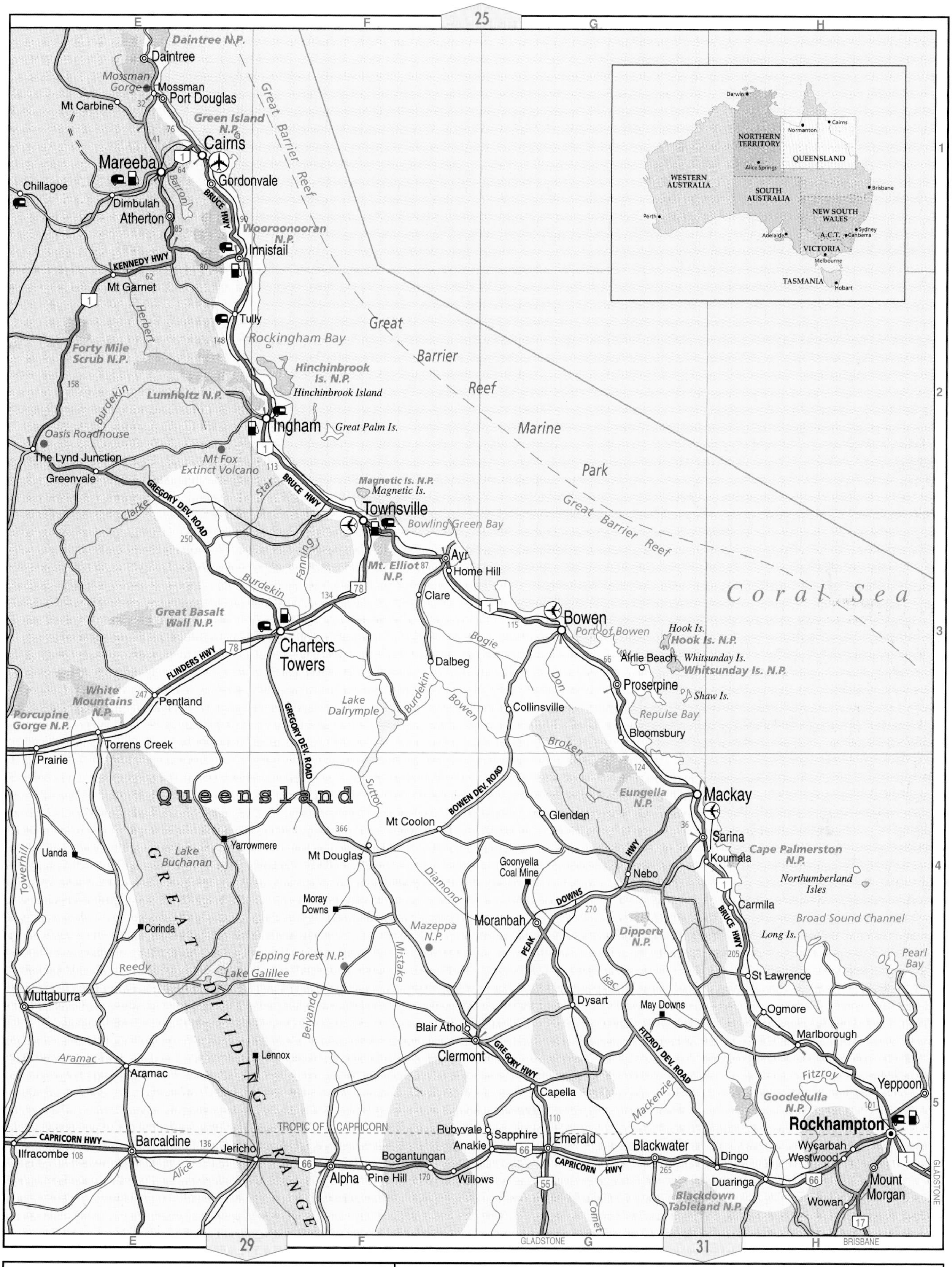
E
F
25
G
H
Daintree N.P.
Daintree
Mossman Gorge
Mossman
Port Douglas
Mt Carbine
Green Island N.P.
Cairns
Mareeba
Gordonvale
Chillagoe
Dimbulah
Atherton
Barron
BRUCE HWY
Wooroonooran N.P.
Innisfail
KENNEDY HWY
Mt Garnet
Great Barrier Reef
Tully
Herbert
Rockingham Bay
Forty Mile Scrub N.P.
Hinchinbrook Is. N.P.
Hinchinbrook Island
Great Barrier Reef Marine Park
Lumholtz N.P.
Burdekin
Oasis Roadhouse
Ingham
Great Palm Is.
The Lynd Junction
Mt Fox Extinct Volcano
Greenvale
Magnetic Is. N.P.
Magnetic Is.
GREGORY DEV. ROAD
Star
Clarke
Townsville
Bowling Green Bay
Fanning
Ayr
Home Hill
Mt. Elliot N.P.
Great Barrier Reef
Coral Sea
Clare
Great Basalt Wall N.P.
Bowen
Port of Bowen
Hook Is.
Hook Is. N.P.
Charters Towers
FLINDERS HWY
Bogie
Dalbeg
Airlie Beach
Whitsunday Is.
Whitsunday Is. N.P.
Proserpine
Shaw Is.
White Mountains N.P.
Porcupine Gorge N.P.
Pentland
Lake Dalrymple
Bowen
Don
Collinsville
Repulse Bay
Bloomsbury
Torrens Creek
Prairie
Broken
Queensland
Suttor
BOWEN DEV. ROAD
Eungella N.P.
Mackay
Glenden
Mt Coolon
Sarina
Yarrowmere
Cape Palmerston N.P.
Uanda
Lake Buchanan
Mt Douglas
Koumala
Goonyella Coal Mine
Nebo
Northumberland Isles
Towerhill
Diamond
DOWNS
Moray Downs
Carmila
Broad Sound Channel
Moranbah
Corinda
Mazeppa N.P.
PEAK
Dipperu N.P.
Long Is.
Pearl Bay
Epping Forest N.P.
Mistake
Isac
St Lawrence
Reedy
Lake Galillee
GREAT DIVIDING RANGE
Muttaburra
Dysart
May Downs
Ogmore
Belyando
FITZROY DEV. ROAD
Blair Athol
Marlborough
Clermont
GREGORY HWY
Lennox
Aramac
Aramac
Fitzroy
Yeppoon
Capella
Goodedulla N.P.
Mackenzie
Rockhampton
TROPIC OF CAPRICORN
Rubyvale
Sapphire
CAPRICORN HWY
Barcaldine
Jericho
Anakie
Emerald
Blackwater
Wycarbah
Ilfracombe
Westwood
Bogantungan
Dingo
Alice
Alpha
Pine Hill
Willows
Duaringa
Mount Morgan
Blackdown Tableland N.P.
Comet
Wowan
GLADSTONE
29
GLADSTONE
31
BRISBANE
Darwin
NORTHERN TERRITORY
Normanton
Cairns
QUEENSLAND
Alice Springs
WESTERN AUSTRALIA
SOUTH AUSTRALIA
Brisbane
Perth
NEW SOUTH WALES
Sydney
A.C.T.
Canberra
Adelaide
VICTORIA
Melbourne
TASMANIA
Hobart
0 50 100 150 km
0 25 50 75 100 miles
National road
Highway
tarred untarred
Main road
Museum
Major petrol stop
Caravan park
Place of interest

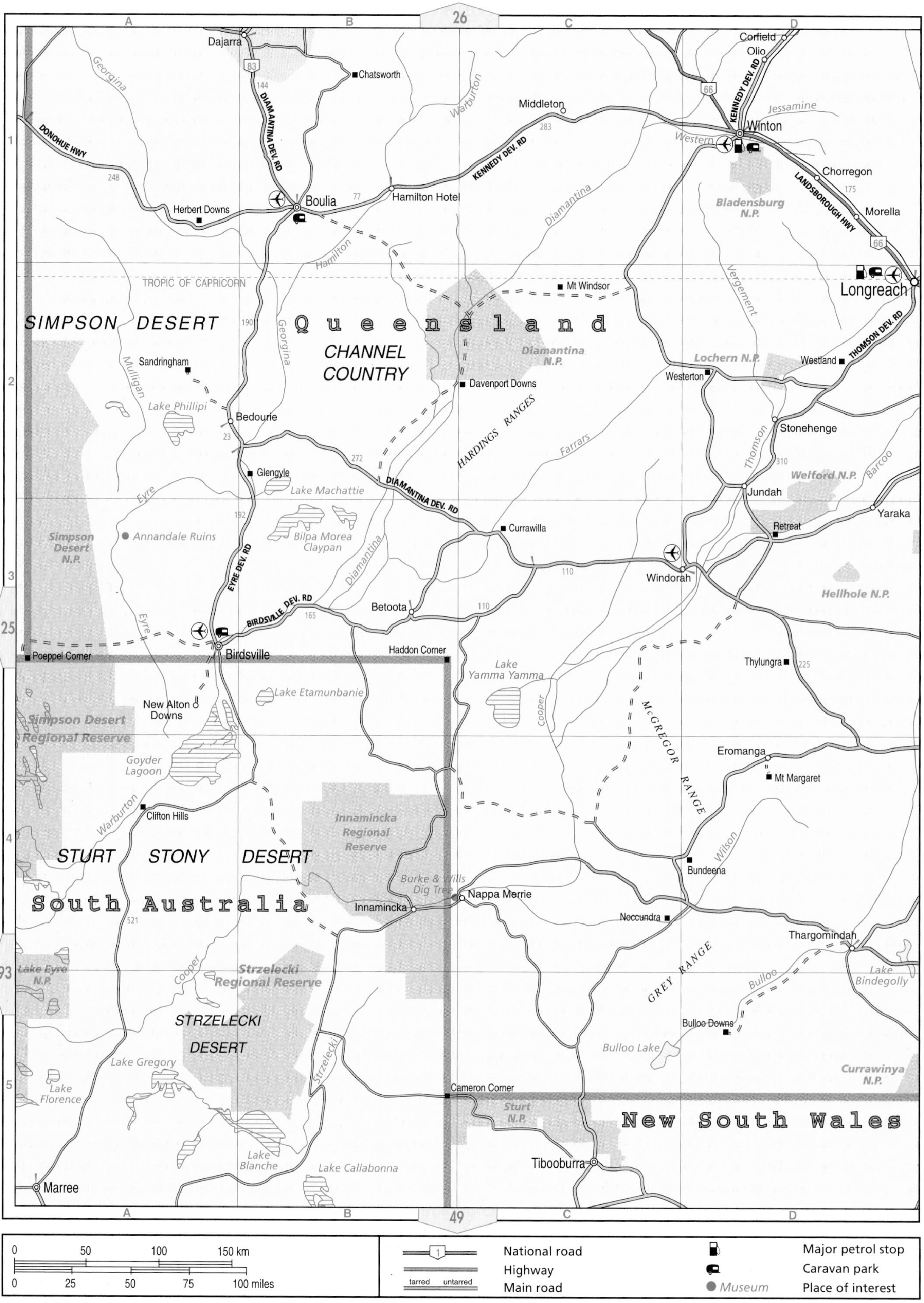
26
A
B
C
D
1
2
3
4
5
125
93
49
Dajarra
83
Chatsworth
144
DIAMANTINA DEV. RD
Georgina
DONOHUE HWY
248
Herbert Downs
Boulia
77
Hamilton Hotel
KENNEDY DEV. RD
Warburton
Middleton
283
Corfield
Olio
66
KENNEDY DEV. RD
Jessamine
Winton
Western
Chorregon
LANDSBOROUGH HWY
175
Morella
Bladensburg N.P.
Diamantina
Hamilton
TROPIC OF CAPRICORN
Mt Windsor
Longreach
Vergement
THOMSON DEV. RD
SIMPSON DESERT
190
Georgina
Queensland
CHANNEL COUNTRY
Diamantina N.P.
Lochern N.P.
Westland
Westerton
Sandringham
Mulligan
Lake Phillipi
Bedourie
23
Davenport Downs
HARDINGS RANGES
Stonehenge
Thomson
310
272
Farrars
Glengyle
Lake Machattie
Welford N.P.
Barcoo
Jundah
DIAMANTINA DEV. RD
Eyre
Yaraka
Retreat
Currawilla
192
Simpson Desert N.P.
Annandale Ruins
Bilpa Morea Claypan
Diamantina
EYRE DEV. RD
110
Windorah
Hellhole N.P.
Betoota
110
BIRDSVILLE DEV. RD
165
Eyre
Birdsville
Poeppel Corner
Haddon Corner
Thylungra
225
Lake Yamma Yamma
Lake Etamunbanie
Cooper
McGREGOR RANGE
New Alton Downs
Simpson Desert Regional Reserve
Goyder Lagoon
Eromanga
Mt Margaret
Clifton Hills
Warburton
Innamincka Regional Reserve
Wilson
Bundeena
STURT STONY DESERT
Burke & Wills Dig Tree
Nappa Merrie
South Australia
Innamincka
Noccundra
Thargomindah
521
Lake Eyre N.P.
Cooper
Strzelecki Regional Reserve
GREY RANGE
Lake Bindegolly
Bulloo
STRZELECKI DESERT
Bulloo Downs
Bulloo Lake
Lake Gregory
Strzelecki
Currawinya N.P.
Lake Florence
Cameron Corner
Sturt N.P.
New South Wales
Lake Blanche
Lake Callabonna
Tibooburra
Marree

0 50 100 150 km / 0 25 50 75 100 miles	National road		Major petrol stop
	Highway		Caravan park
tarred untarred	Main road	Museum	Place of interest

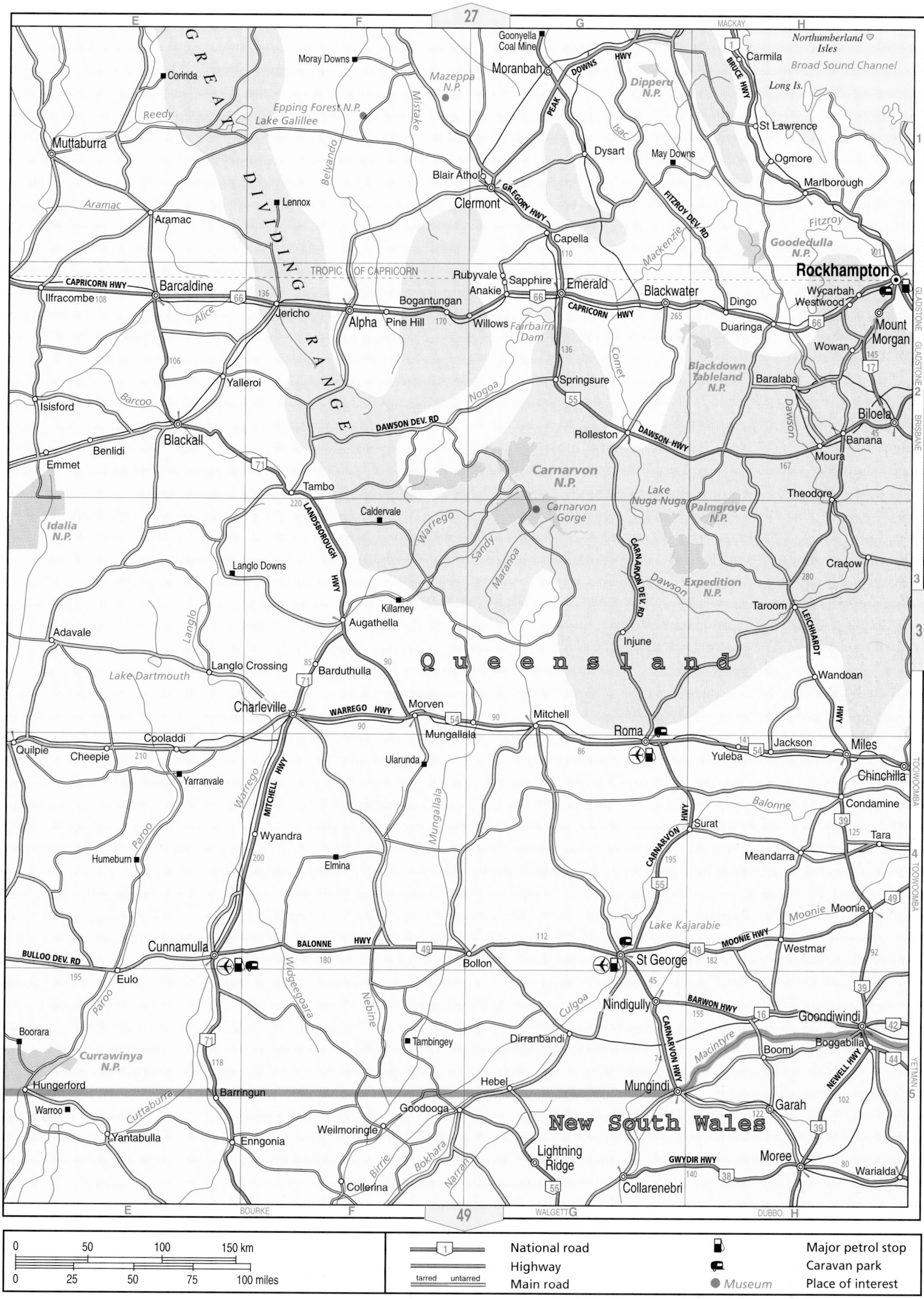

27
E
F
G
H
MACKAY
Goonyella Coal Mine
Moray Downs
Corinda
GREAT DIVIDING RANGE
Moranbah
PEAK DOWNS HWY
Dipperu N.P.
BRUCE HWY
Carmila
Northumberland Isles
Broad Sound Channel
Long Is.
Mazeppa N.P.
Epping Forest N.P.
Lake Galillee
Reedy
Mistake
Belyando
Isac
St Lawrence
Ogmore
Muttaburra
Dysart
May Downs
Marlborough
Blair Athol
Clermont
GREGORY HWY
FITZROY DEV. RD
Lennox
Aramac
Aramac
Capella
Mackenzie
Fitzroy
Goodedulla N.P.
Rockhampton
TROPIC OF CAPRICORN
CAPRICORN HWY
Barcaldine
Ilfracombe
Rubyvale
Sapphire
Anakie
Emerald
Blackwater
Dingo
Wycarbah
Westwood
Jericho
Alpha
Pine Hill
Bogantungan
Willows
Fairbairn Dam
CAPRICORN HWY
Duaringa
Mount Morgan
Alice
Wowan
Comet
Blackdown Tableland N.P.
Baralaba
Yalleroi
Springsure
Nogoa
Isisford
Barcoo
Dawson
Biloela
DAWSON DEV. RD
Rolleston
DAWSON HWY
Banana
Blackall
Benlidi
Moura
Emmet
Carnarvon N.P.
Tambo
Theodore
Lake Nuga Nuga
Palmgrove N.P.
Carnarvon Gorge
Caldervale
Idalia N.P.
LANDSBOROUGH HWY
Warrego
Sandy
Maranoa
CARNARVON DEV. RD
Langlo Downs
Dawson
Expedition N.P.
Cracow
Taroom
Killarney
Augathella
LEICHHARDT HWY
Adavale
Langlo
Injune
Queensland
Langlo Crossing
Barduthulla
Lake Dartmouth
Wandoan
Charleville
WARREGO HWY
Morven
Mitchell
Roma
Mungallala
Cooladdi
Quilpie
Cheepie
Jackson
Miles
Yuleba
Ularunda
Chinchilla
Yarranvale
MITCHELL HWY
Warrego
Balonne
Condamine
Paroo
Wyandra
CARNARVON HWY
Surat
Tara
Humeburn
Meandarra
Elmina
Mungallala
Moonie
Moonie
Lake Kajarabie
MOONIE HWY
BALONNE HWY
Cunnamulla
BULLOO DEV. RD
St George
Westmar
Bollon
Eulo
Widgeegoara
Nebine
Culgoa
Nindigully
BARWON HWY
Goondiwindi
Paroo
Boorara
Tambingey
Dirranbandi
Macintyre
Boomi
Boggabilla
Currawinya N.P.
NEWELL HWY
Hungerford
Hebel
Mungindi
Barringun
Warroo
Cuttaburra
Goodooga
Garah
New South Wales
Yantabulla
Weilmoringle
Enngonia
Lightning Ridge
Birrie
Bokhara
Narran
GWYDIR HWY
Moree
Warialda
Collerina
Collarenebri
BOURKE
49
WALGETT
DUBBO
GLADSTONE
BRISBANE
TOOWOOMBA
YETMAN
31
0 50 100 150 km
0 25 50 75 100 miles
National road
Highway
Main road
tarred untarred
Major petrol stop
Caravan park
Museum
Place of interest

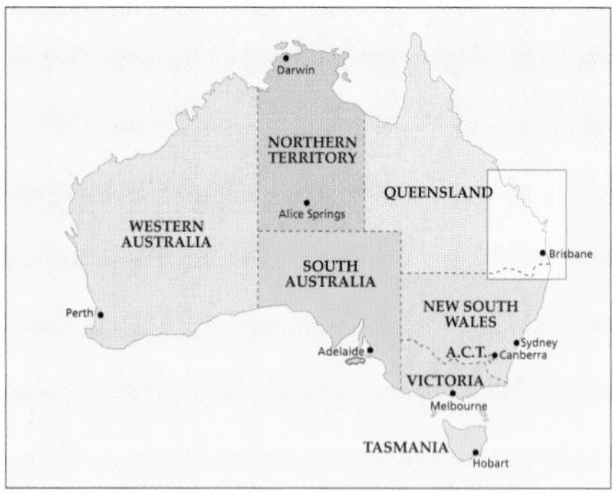

South-east Queensland

South-east Queensland not only consists of Brisbane and the Gold and Sunshine coasts, it also extends to include the Darling Downs stretching from the Great Dividing Range west to the flatlands of western Queensland, the Capricornia Coast around Rockhampton, and the central-western district of the state. The area is characterised by its tourist development on the coast, and mining and agriculture inland. The Downs is an attractive area of rich black soils, pleasant country towns and gently undulating plains, while the central west includes the beautiful Carnarvon National Park.

TOP ATTRACTIONS

Carnarvon Gorge: contains some of the finest Aboriginal art.
Mon Repos Environmental Park: protected beach and foreshore area near Bundaberg where turtles come ashore to lay eggs between November and March.
Mount Morgan: 19th-century town with an open-cut mine.
Olsen's Capricorn Caves: near Rockhampton, comprises 16 caves first discovered by Norwegian migrant John Olsen in 1882.
Rockhampton: an elegant 19th-century city on the Fitzroy River.
Stanthorpe: pretty Darling Downs town with wineries.

ON THE ROAD

The roads around south-east Queensland are consistently good. All the major townships have at least one service station where petrol and other supplies are available. A 4WD vehicle is preferable in the Carnarvon Gorge National Park as some of the roads can traverse difficult terrain. Travellers who drive off the beaten track may also find poor-quality roads; visitors choosing to remain on main roads should be fine. Contact the RACQ outlets listed in local phone books for any road assistance.

Above: *The Tropic of Capricorn divides Queensland almost in half; a column stands where it crosses the coastline near Rockhampton.*
Below: *The open-cut mine at Mount Morgan has been worked for over a century, yielding copper and gold.*

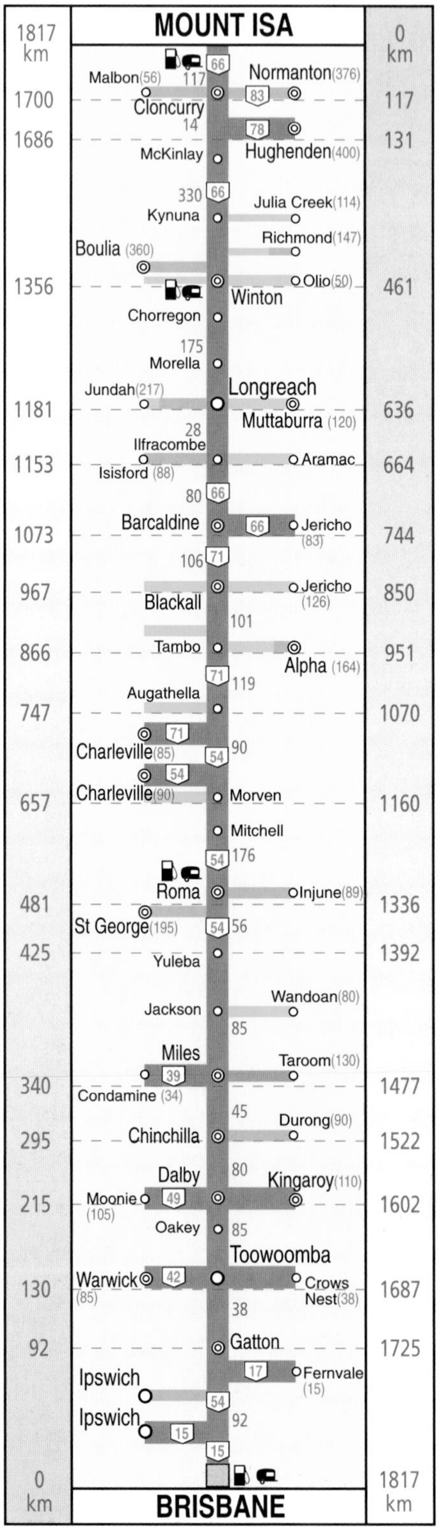

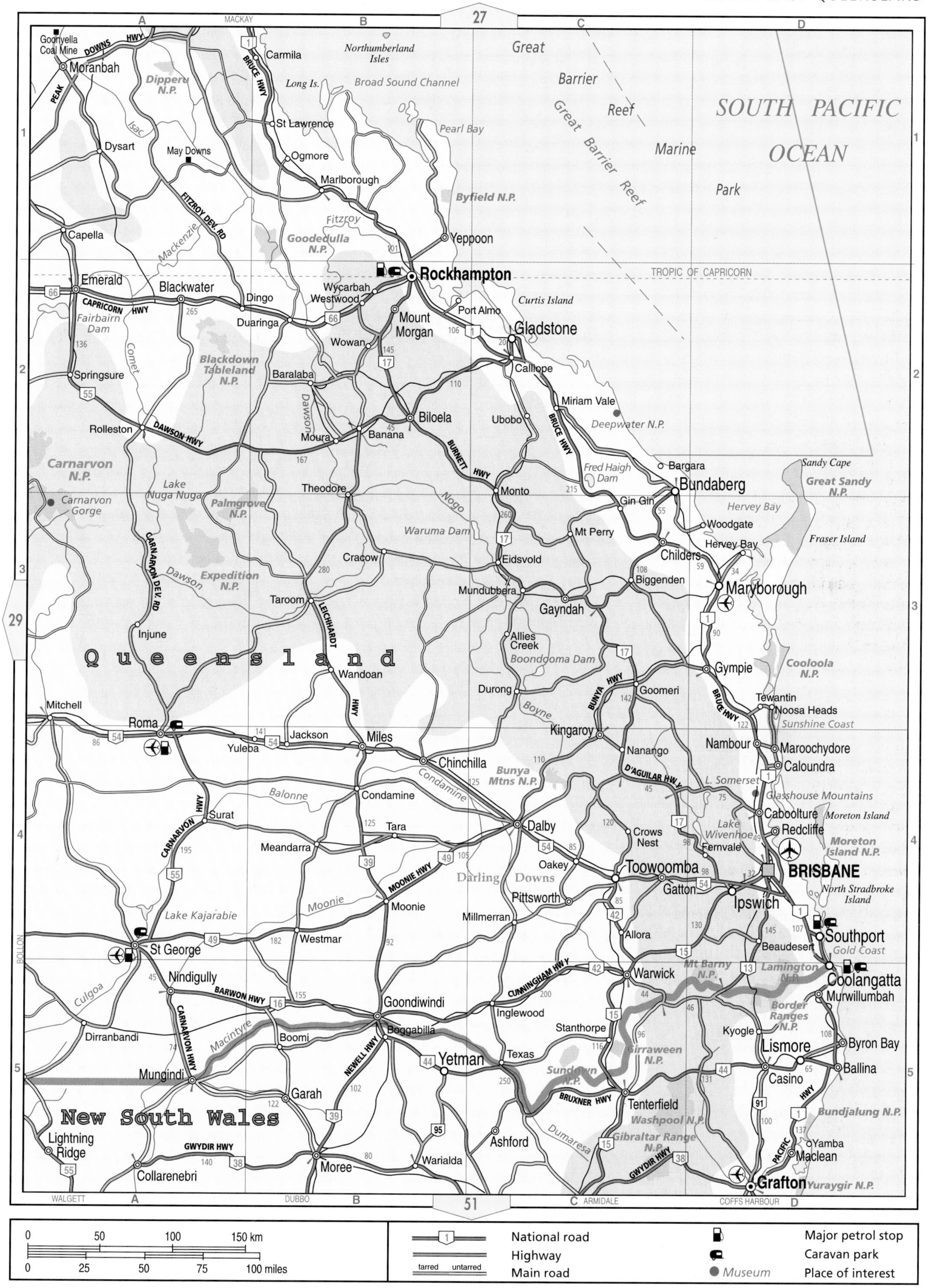
27
MACKAY
Goonyella Coal Mine
Moranbah
Dipperu N.P.
Carmila
Northumberland Isles
Long Is.
Broad Sound Channel
Great Barrier Reef Marine Park
Great Barrier Reef
SOUTH PACIFIC OCEAN
St Lawrence
Pearl Bay
Dysart
May Downs
Ogmore
Marlborough
Byfield N.P.
Capella
Goodedulla N.P.
Yeppoon
Rockhampton
TROPIC OF CAPRICORN
Emerald
Blackwater
Dingo
Wycarbah
Westwood
Curtis Island
Port Alma
Fairbairn Dam
Duaringa
Mount Morgan
Gladstone
Wowan
Blackdown Tableland N.P.
Springsure
Baralaba
Calliope
Miriam Vale
Deepwater N.P.
Rolleston
Biloela
Ubobo
Moura
Banana
Carnarvon N.P.
Bargara
Sandy Cape
Fred Haigh Dam
Bundaberg
Great Sandy N.P.
Carnarvon Gorge
Lake Nuga Nuga
Palmgrove N.P.
Theodore
Monto
Gin Gin
Hervey Bay
Woodgate
Waruma Dam
Mt Perry
Fraser Island
Cracow
Eidsvold
Childers
Expedition N.P.
Biggenden
Maryborough
Taroom
Mundubbera
Gayndah
Injune
Allies Creek
Boondooma Dam
Queensland
Wandoan
Gympie
Cooloola N.P.
Durong
Goomeri
Tewantin
Noosa Heads
Sunshine Coast
Mitchell
Roma
Kingaroy
Jackson
Miles
Yuleba
Nambour
Maroochydore
Nanango
Chinchilla
Caloundra
Bunya Mtns N.P.
L. Somerset
Glasshouse Mountains
Condamine
Surat
Caboolture
Moreton Island
Tara
Dalby
Crows Nest
Lake Wivenhoe
Redcliffe
Meandarra
Fernvale
Moreton Island N.P.
Oakey
Toowoomba
BRISBANE
Darling Downs
Gatton
Ipswich
North Stradbroke Island
Pittsworth
Moonie
Lake Kajarabie
Millmerran
Southport
Westmar
Allora
Gold Coast
St George
Beaudesert
Mt Barny N.P.
Lamington N.P.
Coolangatta
Nindigully
Warwick
Murwillumbah
Border Ranges N.P.
Goondiwindi
Inglewood
Dirranbandi
Boggabilla
Stanthorpe
Kyogle
Boomi
Girraween N.P.
Lismore
Byron Bay
Mungindi
Yetman
Texas
Sundown N.P.
Ballina
Casino
Garah
Tenterfield
New South Wales
Washpool N.P.
Bundjalung N.P.
Lightning Ridge
Ashford
Gibraltar Range N.P.
Yamba
Maclean
Warialda
Collarenebri
Moree
Grafton
Yuraygir N.P.
WALGETT
DUBBO
51
ARMIDALE
COFFS HARBOUR
BOLLON
29
PEAK DOWNS HWY
BRUCE HWY
FITZROY DEV. RD
CAPRICORN HWY
DAWSON HWY
BURNETT HWY
CARNARVON DEV. RD
LEICHHARDT HWY
BUNYA HWY
D'AGUILAR HWY
CARNARVON HWY
MOONIE HWY
BARWON HWY
CUNNINGHAM HWY
NEWELL HWY
BRUXNER HWY
GWYDIR HWY
PACIFIC HWY
0
50
100
150 km
25
75
100 miles
National road
Highway
tarred
untarred
Main road
Major petrol stop
Caravan park
Museum
Place of interest

NEW SOUTH WALES

New South Wales was where the first permanent European settlement of Australia began in 1788 with the arrival of the First Fleet. Today, it is still the most important and influential state in Australia with a population of over 6 million people. It is a state of extraordinary appeal ranging from the state capital city, Sydney, which is regarded as one of the most beautiful cities in the world, through to the dry, harsh outback deserts that lie beyond Bourke, Cobar and Broken Hill. New South Wales has a diversity of landform, climate and vegetation that is richer and more complex than any other state, with tropical rainforest in the north, alpine ski slopes in the south, seemingly endless beaches on the coast and deserts in the west. The state's premier tourist attractions lie mostly within a day's drive of Sydney and include the Blue Mountains, a series of box canyons to the west, the beautiful Royal National Park to the south of Sydney and the historic 'Macquarie towns' which lie on the north-western outskirts of the city.

New South Wales covers an area of 801 428km^2 (309 350 sq miles) including Lord Howe Island, which makes it Australia's fourth-largest state. It is positioned midway along the eastern coast of the continent and juts roughly in a rectangular shape towards the deserts of central Australia. This means that it experiences most of the country's climatic conditions and has most of its vegetation forms, and is capable of sustaining a variety of agriculture and industry despite only covering 10.4 per cent of Australia's landmass. With its population of over six million, more than 75 per cent of whom live in Sydney, Newcastle and Wollongong, it is also, not surprisingly, the most heavily industrialised and most highly urbanised state.

Geographically the state falls naturally into four distinct regions running north to south, with the Great Dividing Range, which runs the length of the eastern region, forming a natural division. Between the range and the eastern seaboard lies the fertile coastal plain. Next are the tablelands of the Great Dividing Range, followed by the range's western slopes. Finally there are the dry western plains that run from these western slopes to New South Wales' western border, where it meets the arid inland deserts.

The majority of the western plains are a vast marginal wasteland where a driver can travel on a straight road at 100kph (62mph) for over two hours and see nothing other than the occasional kangaroo (none too occasional at dusk when they become a major road hazard) and endless plains of scrub and bush. The distances are vast and communities sparse. The only stopping points on the Mitchell and Barrier highways are tiny isolated townships that exist merely to provide service to travellers and 'nearby' property owners.

There is nothing wrong with the soils of the western plains, it is merely a question of abysmally low rainfall and unreliable rivers. The rains, which could make the western plains agriculturally rich, simply never arrive. They are blocked from the east by the Great Dividing Range and dissipated from the south and the west by the vast and barren deserts. However, the southern section of the plains is much richer agriculturally because of technological assistance. The rivers of the Riverina were greatly boosted when the Snowy Mountains Scheme, a hydro-electrical project which sends water from the melting snows down the river system, was completed. The result is a region of farms where oranges, grapes, rice, grapefruit and a variety of other crops prosper through irrigation.

The western plains are also a fascinating mixture of old Australia and new values. White Cliffs, for example, is a town that exists almost entirely underground. Local opal miners (it was the opals which first brought Europeans to this inhospitable terrain), in attempts to avoid temperatures of over 40°C (104°F) in summer, have dug homes for themselves 10m (33ft) below the surface. These underground dwellings are so vast they would be considered mansions if they were above the surface. White Cliffs also boasts a solar energy source that supplies the town with electricity.

The western slopes create the belt of land falling away from the Great Dividing Range's tablelands, and still enjoy adequate rainfall. These slopes are sub-divided into three separate areas from north to south. The northern division includes the major centres, like Tamworth, Gunnedah, Narrabri and Warialda; the central area embraces the cities of Dubbo and Forbes; while the southern slopes lie between the Snowy Mountains and the dry plains of the Riverina.

All three regions are basically good sheep- and cattle-grazing country as the rainfall is high and regular enough to guarantee continuous feed. This is also an area of extensive cropping, particularly wheat. In the Namoi Valley wool gives way to fat lambs, pigs and fodder crops. Cotton is grown around Wee Waa, and the Murrumbidgee area has been successful with rice, citrus fruit and grape cultivation. The slopes are also known for their cold-climate orchards. Cherries, apples and pears, for example, are grown around Batlow and Bathurst.

The tablelands of the Great Dividing Range have led some people to describe Australia as the oldest continent on earth. What this means is that the range stabilised at its peak millions of years ago and over the millennia, erosion has weathered it down into a series of low-lying plateaux. At their narrowest point the tablelands are only 50–60km (30–37.5 miles) wide. At their widest they stretch for 160km (100 miles). In the north the range has an average elevation of about 750m (2460ft); an exception to this are the New England Ranges which rise to over 1200m (3937ft). In the south the tablelands form the Snowy Mountains, the highest range in Australia. It is here that the highest peak, Mount Kosciuszko, rises to 2228m (7310ft).

The economy of the tablelands depends mainly on wool and cattle, though there is some timber cutting. Tourism is gaining in importance and a number of the larger towns – notably Bathurst, Armidale and Goulburn – have become important educational centres.

The eastern seaboard is where the majority of the state's population lives. This coastal plain is only 30km (18 miles) wide in the south, 80km (50 miles) near the Queensland border. Fed by high orographic rainfall and a number of substantial river systems, it is home to the bulk of the state's dairy industry, vegetable production and tropical fruit plantations. Its agriculture shifts from the bananas, macadamias, pineapples and avocados of the north to gentle slopes dotted with Friesian cows, typical of the south coast.

New South Wales' greatest asset is its 1900-km (1180-mile) coastline, the state's eastern perimeter. There are superb beaches but few natural harbours, the notable exception being Port Jackson. It was into Port Jackson that the First Fleet sailed over 200 years ago, thereby launching not only European settlement of Australia, but the creation of one of the world's most beautiful cities. Sydney Harbour and its famous Harbour Bridge and Opera House are icons that sum up Australia in the minds of people worldwide.

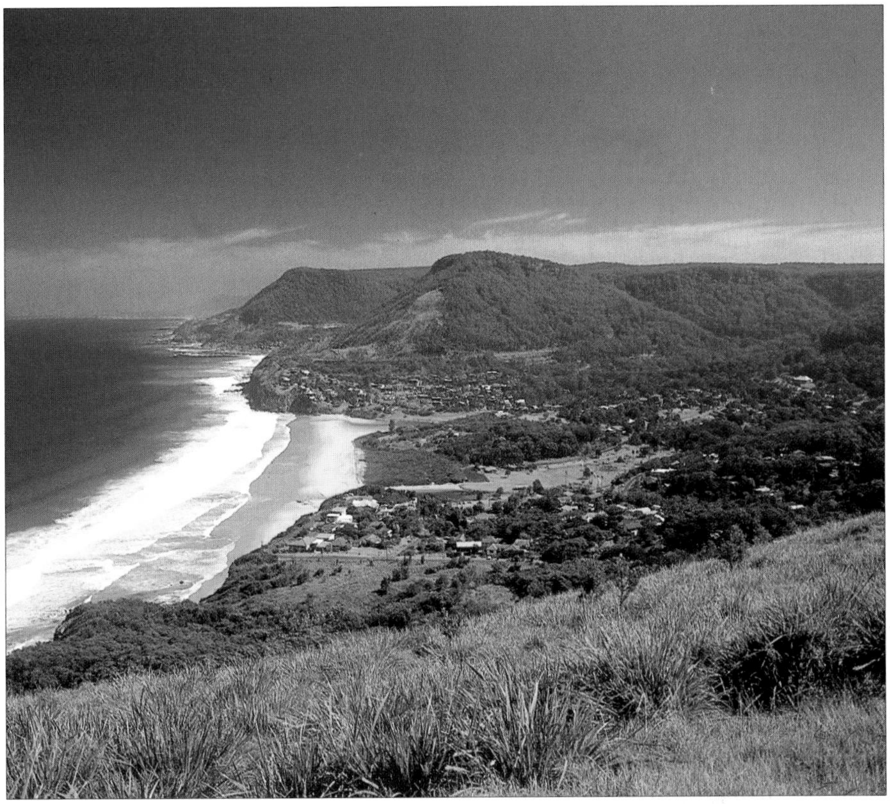

Right: *The state's eastern perimeter has inviting beaches like this one near the South Coast town of Stanwell Park.*

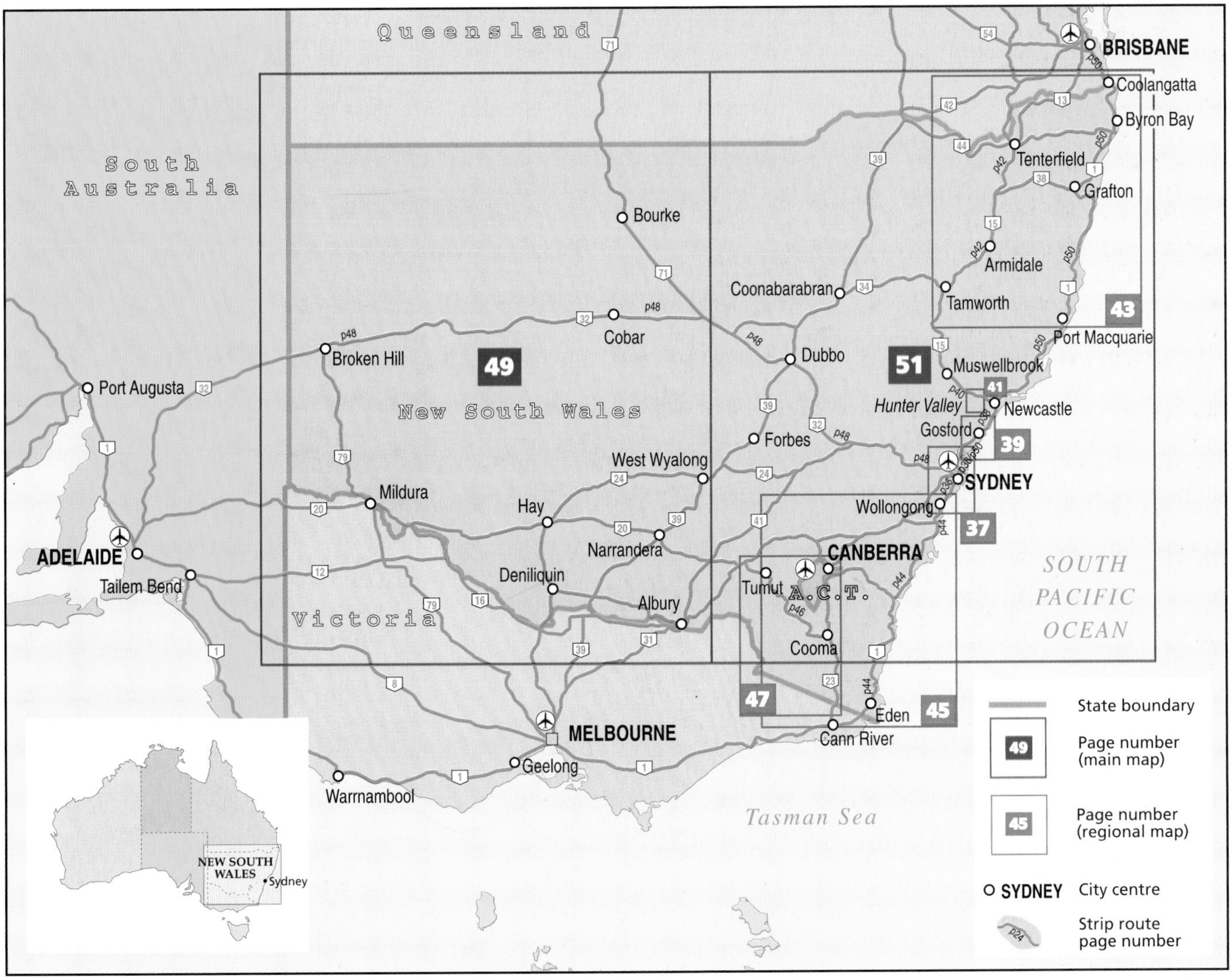

Sydney

Sydney is one of the world's great cities. The country's largest, it has a population nearing four million. Located on fabulous Port Jackson, it experiences mild temperatures, evenly distributed rainfall, and glorious, balmy, subtropical summer days of sunshine. This sprawling metropolis is contained by over 100km (62 miles) of beaches to the east, the Blue Mountains to the west, the Royal National Park to the south and the Hawkesbury River to the north. The city is famous for the Sydney Harbour Bridge and the shell-shaped Opera House, which seems to mirror the sails of the yachts racing across the harbour on weekends.

TOP ATTRACTIONS

Bondi Beach: the most popular and most famous beach in Sydney. **Sydney Tower:** provides superb 360° views of the city and environs. **Macquarie Street:** impressive 19th-century buildings which are a testament to Governor Macquarie's term of office. **Royal Botanic Gardens:** a relaxing 29ha (70 acres) of lush, green oasis where the beauty of the harbour can be appreciated. **Sydney Aquarium:** comprehensive overview of Australia's many freshwater and saltwater fish. **Sydney Harbour Bridge:** one of Australia's most distinctive constructions rises 134m (440ft) above the harbour. **Sydney Opera House:** one of the most remarkable buildings of the 20th century. **Taronga Park Zoo:** located on the harbour foreshore this is one of the world's finest zoos. **The Harbour's Heads:** provide outstanding views of the harbour, the city and the Pacific Ocean. **The Rocks:** entrée to the history of the early settlers of Sydney.

CALENDAR OF EVENTS

JANUARY: Festival of Sydney and Carnivale, Manly Surf Carnival, Australia Day, Ferrython. **FEBRUARY:** Manly Beach Iron Man Competition, Archibald, Wynne and Sulman Art Exhibitions, Chinese New Year. **MARCH:** Sydney Dragon Boat Races, Gay & Lesbian Mardi Gras. **APRIL:** Royal Easter Show. **MAY:** State of Origin Rugby League. **JUNE:** Manly Food and Wine Festival, Darling Harbour Jazz Festival, Sydney Film Festival. **JULY:** Aboriginal Week, Sydney Eisteddfod, Olympics Arts Festival. **AUGUST:** City to Surf Fun Run, Spring Racing Carnival commences. **SEPTEMBER:** Rugby League Grand Final, Spring Horse Racing Carnival, Olympics, Biennale of Sydney. **OCTOBER:** International Food & Wine Tasting Festival, Darling Harbour Fiesta. **NOVEMBER:** Kings Cross Carnival. **DECEMBER:** Sydney to Hobart Yacht Race.

SYDNEY	J	F	M	A	M	J	J	A	S	O	N	D
AV. TEMP. °F	73	73	72	66	63	57	54	57	61	64	68	72
AV. TEMP. °C	23	23	22	19	17	14	12	14	16	18	20	22
DAILY SUN hrs	8	7	7	6	6	6	7	8	8	8	8	8
RAINFALL in	4	4.5	5	5	5	5	4	3	3	3	3	3
RAINFALL mm	102	117	135	129	121	131	100	81	69	79	82	78
RAINFALL days	12	12	13	12	12	12	10	10	10	11	11	12

WHERE TO STAY

Stafford Apartments, 75 Harrington St, tel: (02) 9251 6711, fax: 9251 3458. In the heart of The Rocks, Sydney's oldest district.
Hotel Inter-Continental, Macquarie St, tel: (02) 9230 0200, fax: 9240 1240, toll free: 1 800 221 828. Partly housed in the historic treasury building.
Hyde Park Plaza Hotel, College St, tel: (02) 9331 6933, fax: 9331 6022.
Victoria Court Hotel, Potts Point, tel: (02) 9357 3200, fax: 9357 7606. Victorian-style guesthouse in a leafy, quiet suburb.
Parkroyal Darling Harbour, Day St, tel: (02) 9261 1188, fax: 9261 8766. Quality hotel opposite the Darling Harbour complex.
Regent Sydney Hotel, George St, tel: (02) 9238 8000, fax: 9251 2851. Luxury hotel, best views.
The Cambridge, Riley St, tel: (02) 9212 1111, fax: 9281 1981. Well-located, reasonably-priced.

Above: *Majestic Sydney Harbour Bridge has become an internationally recognised icon for a city that sparkles day and night.*
Below: *The Sydney Opera House is poised upon Bennelong Point between the Royal Botanic Gardens and Circular Quay.*

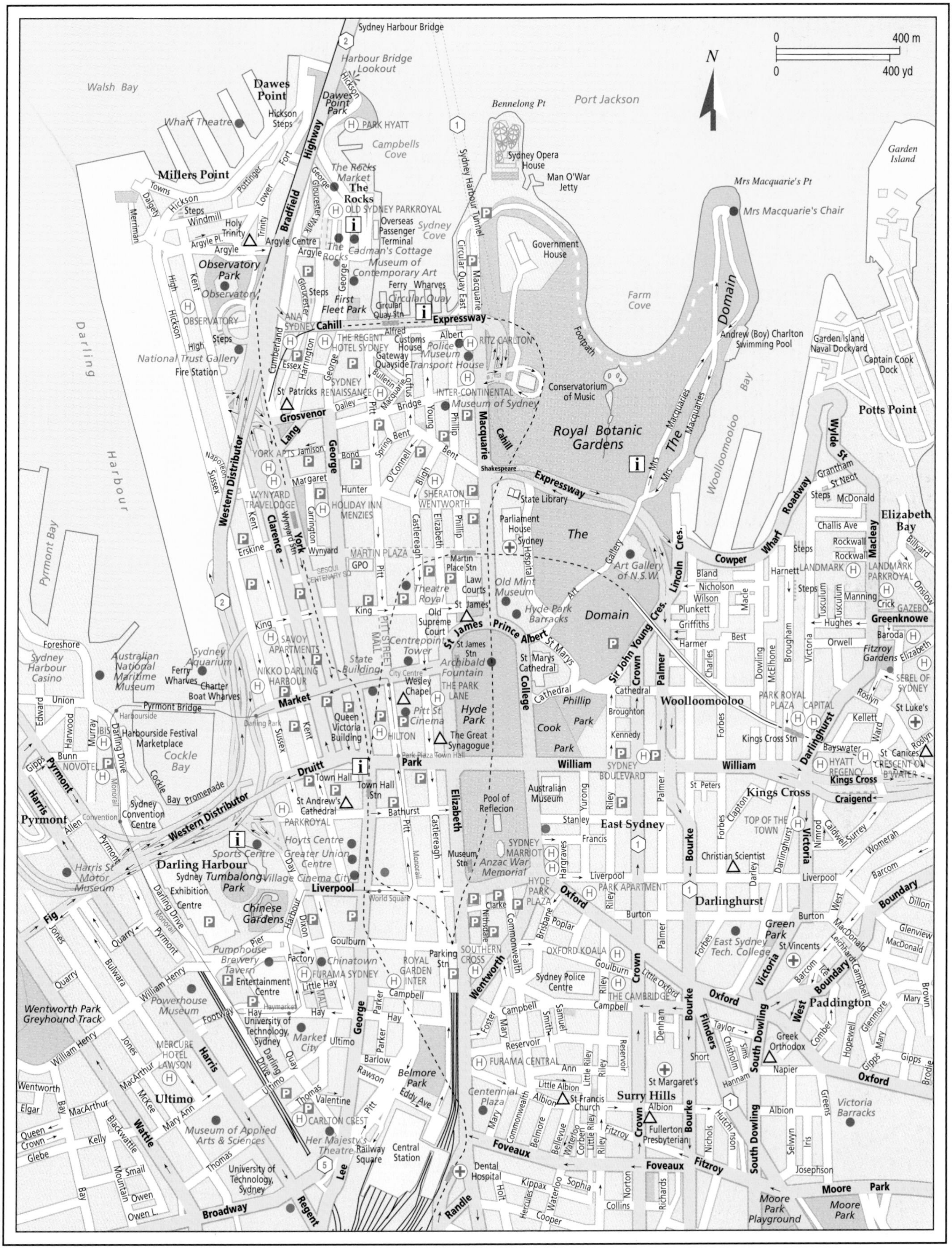

△ St Patrick's	Place of worship	Bus terminus		✉	Post office
Ⓗ	Hotel	●	Police station	● *Market*	Place of interest
i	Information	P	Parking	⊕	Hospital

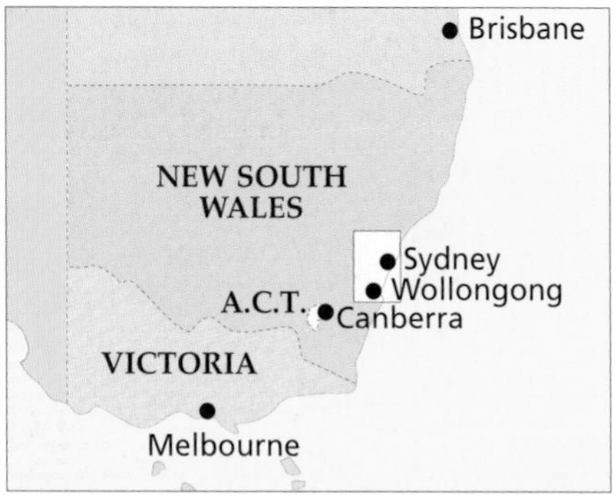

Sydney Daytrips

Most of the attractions of New South Wales are located within 200km (125 miles) of Sydney. There are a number of interesting daytrips. The Blue Mountains to the west of Sydney offer spectacular views and excellent bushwalking. The air is bracing – in fact it is quite common for Katoomba, at 1017m (3337ft) above sea level, to have snow in winter. To the south the Royal National Park has beautiful, unspoilt beaches, fabulous coastal walks and ruggedly formed cliff faces. You may also spot some of Australia's unique wildlife. Further south, the city of Wollongong offers a variety of attractions including some of the best views on Australia's eastern coastline.

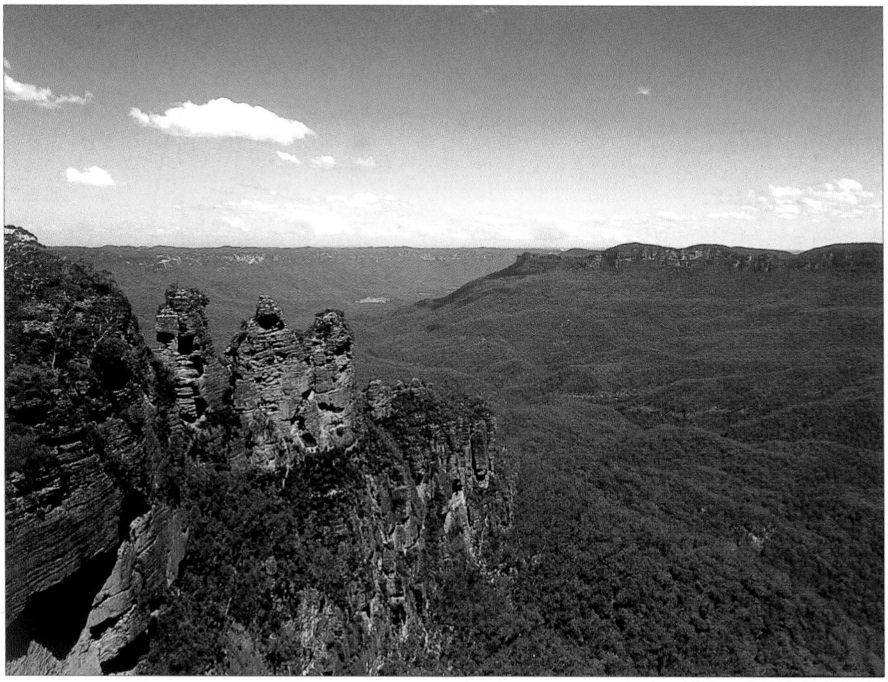

Above: *Out of Jamison Valley rise the Three Sisters, worn sandstone rock formations in the Blue Mountains.*
Below: *A delightful lagoon at Wattamolla within the Royal National Park is ideal for swimming and enjoying nature.*

TOP ATTRACTIONS

Blue Mountains: offer spectacular views across the **Grose** and **Jamison valleys** near **Katoomba**. Visitors make special visits to the **Three Sisters** on the edge of the Jamison Valley, the waterfall at **Govett's Leap**, the **Scenic Railway** at Katoomba, **Norman Lindsay's home** in Springwood and the **Jenolan Caves**.
Royal National Park: extends from the beaches of **Wattamolla** and **Garie** through the coastal wilderness to the **Hacking River**. Most people go surfing and ocean fishing, or they swim about in the saltwater lagoons at Wattamolla or Garie.
Wollongong: enjoy the breathtaking panoramic views from the escarpment above the city.

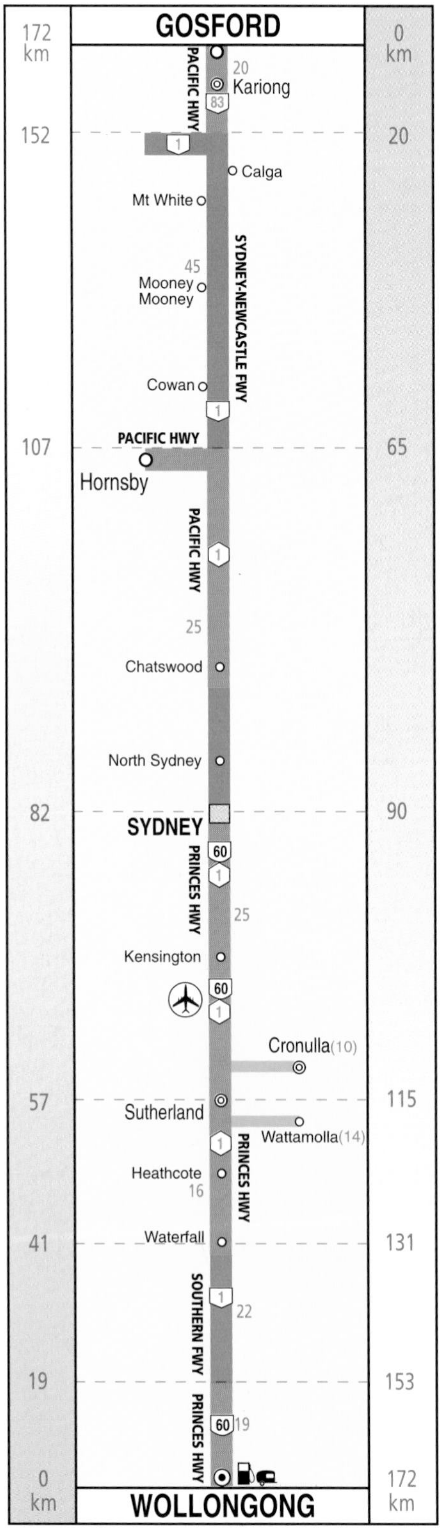

New South Wales

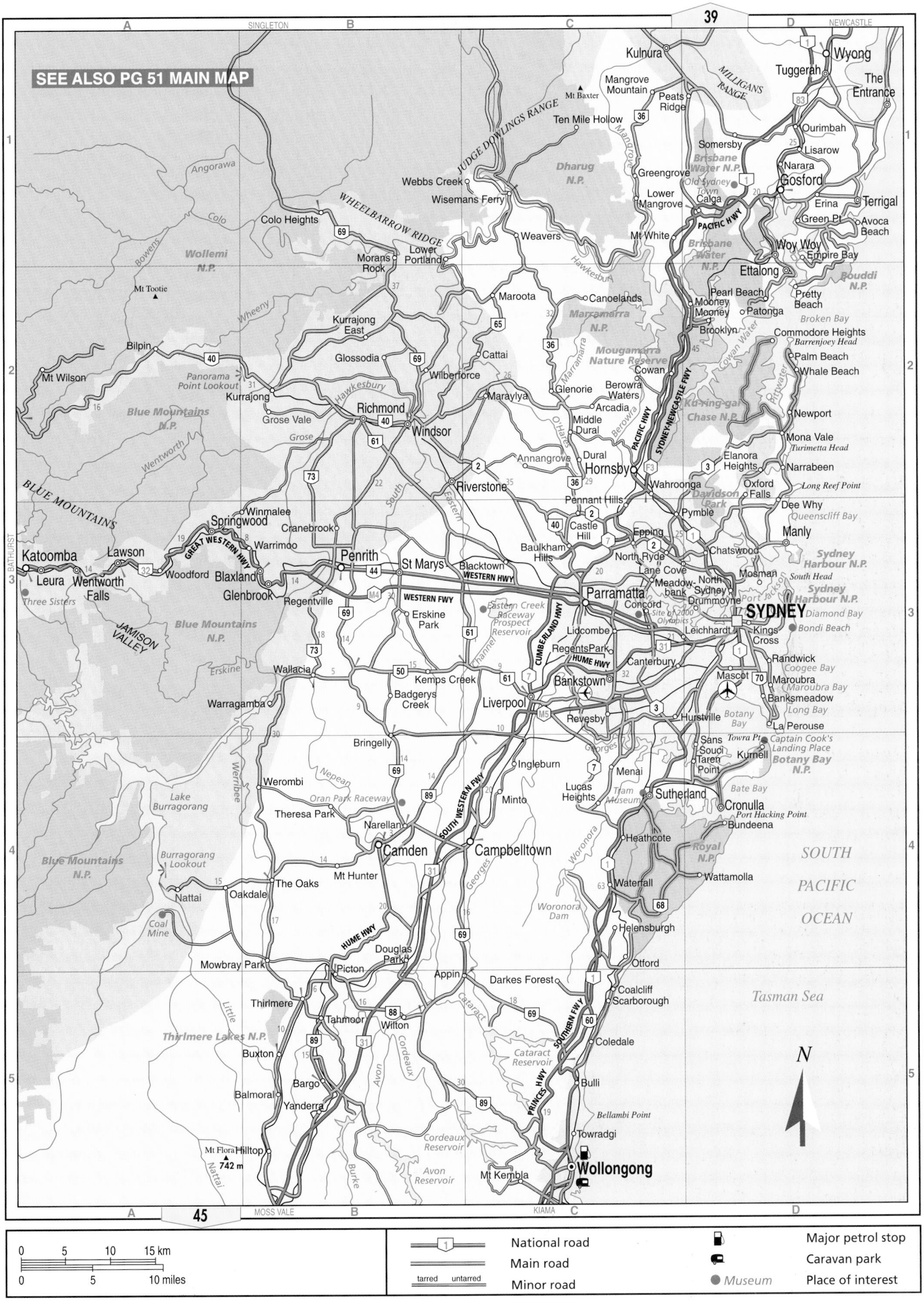

SEE ALSO PG 51 MAIN MAP
39
45
SINGLETON
NEWCASTLE
BATHURST
MOSS VALE
KIAMA
Kulnura
Wyong
Tuggerah
The Entrance
Mangrove Mountain
Peats Ridge
Mt Baxter
MILLIGANS RANGE
JUDGE DOWLINGS RANGE
Ten Mile Hollow
Ourimbah
Somersby
Lisarow
Brisbane Water N.P.
Narara
Dharug N.P.
Greengrove
Old Sydney Town
Gosford
Webbs Creek
Wisemans Ferry
Lower Mangrove
Calga
Erina
Terrigal
Angorawa
WHEELBARROW RIDGE
Colo Heights
Colo
Weavers
Mt White
PACIFIC HWY
Green Pt
Avoca Beach
Wollemi N.P.
Bowens
Morans Rock
Lower Portland
Hawkesbury
Woy Woy
Empire Bay
Ettalong
Bouddi N.P.
Mt Tootie
Maroota
Canoelands
Pearl Beach
Mooney Mooney
Patonga
Pretty Beach
Wheeny
Kurrajong East
Marramarra N.P.
Broken Bay
Brooklyn
Commodore Heights
Barrenjoey Head
Bilpin
Glossodia
Cattai
Mougamarra Nature Reserve
Cowan
Palm Beach
Whale Beach
Mt Wilson
Panorama Point Lookout
Kurrajong
Wilberforce
Maraylya
Glenorie
Berowra Waters
SYDNEY-NEWCASTLE FWY
Ku-ring-gai Chase N.P.
Pittwater
Blue Mountains N.P.
Grose Vale
Richmond
Windsor
Arcadia
Middle Dural
Newport
Grose
Wentworth
Annangrove
Dural
Hornsby
Elanora Heights
Mona Vale
Turimetta Head
Narrabeen
BLUE MOUNTAINS
Riverstone
Wahroonga
Oxford Falls
Long Reef Point
Davidson Park
Pennant Hills
Dee Why
Queenscliff Bay
Winmalee
Springwood
Cranebrook
Castle Hill
Pymble
Manly
Warrimoo
Epping
GREAT WESTERN HWY
Katoomba
Lawson
Penrith
St Marys
Baulkham Hills
North Ryde
Chatswood
Sydney Harbour N.P.
Leura
Wentworth Falls
Woodford
Blaxland
Blacktown
WESTERN HWY
Lane Cove
Mosman
South Head
Glenbrook
Regentville
WESTERN FWY
Parramatta
Meadowbank
North Sydney
Drummoyne
Port Jackson
Three Sisters
Eastern Creek Raceway
Prospect Reservoir
Erskine Park
Concord
Site of 2000 Olympics
SYDNEY
Diamond Bay
Blue Mountains N.P.
JAMISON VALLEY
CUMBERLAND HWY
Lidcombe
Leichhardt
Kings Cross
Bondi Beach
Regents Park
HUME HWY
Canterbury
Randwick
Coogee Bay
Erskine
Wallacia
Kemps Creek
Bankstown
Mascot
Maroubra
Maroubra Bay
Warragamba
Badgerys Creek
Liverpool
Banksmeadow
Long Bay
Revesby
Hurstville
Botany Bay
La Perouse
Bringelly
Sans Souci
Towra Pt
Captain Cook's Landing Place
Taren Point
Kurnell
Botany Bay N.P.
Ingleburn
Georges
Menai
Werombi
Nepean
Lucas Heights
Tram Museum
Sutherland
Bate Bay
Lake Burragorang
Werribee
Oran Park Raceway
Minto
Cronulla
Port Hacking Point
Theresa Park
Narellan
SOUTH WESTERN FWY
Bundeena
Heathcote
Camden
Campbelltown
Woronora
Royal N.P.
Blue Mountains N.P.
Burragorang Lookout
Mt Hunter
Wattamolla
PACIFIC
The Oaks
Nattai
Oakdale
Waterfall
OCEAN
Woronora Dam
Coal Mine
Helensburgh
HUME HWY
Douglas Park
Mowbray Park
Picton
Otford
Appin
Darkes Forest
Coalcliff
Scarborough
Tasman Sea
Thirlmere
Little
Tahmoor
Cataract
Wilton
SOUTHERN FWY
Thirlmere Lakes N.P.
Coledale
Cataract Reservoir
Cordeaux
Buxton
Avon
Bargo
Bulli
Balmoral
Yanderra
PRINCES HWY
Bellambi Point
Towradgi
Cordeaux Reservoir
Mt Flora
742 m
Hilltop
Nattai
Burke
Avon Reservoir
Mt Kembla
Wollongong
0 5 10 15 km
0 5 10 miles
National road
Main road
tarred untarred
Minor road
Major petrol stop
Caravan park
Museum
Place of interest

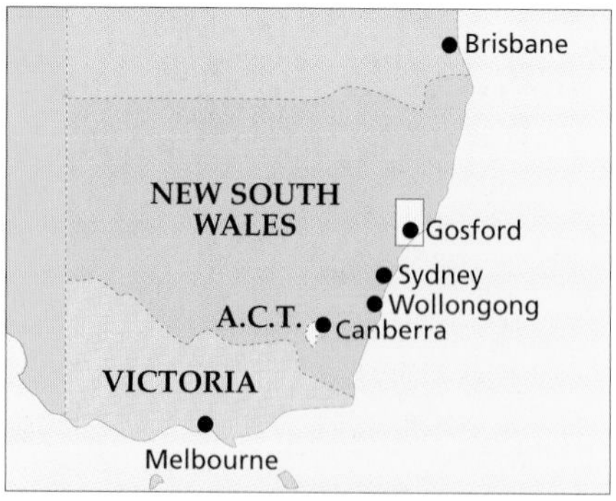

Central Coast

In the 1940s and '50s the Central Coast, north of Sydney, became the premier commuter zone for people wanting to live beyond the boundaries of the city. Development had been slow as Broken Bay isolated the region and the only easy access was by boat. In 1889, Hawkesbury Bridge linked Brisbane Water to Sydney and opened up the area. Two major post-war events, the construction of the Sydney–Newcastle freeway to Calga and the electrification of the railway line, converted this quiet backwater into a desirable beach resort–commuter belt. Today, it is the perfect place to find spacious beaches, relaxing cafés and national parks to explore.

TOP ATTRACTIONS

Avoca Beach: a popular resort which attracts people from all over Sydney. Avoca is an ideal place for a picnic, surf or run along the beach.
Brisbane Water National Park: substantial 8242-ha (20 366-acre) park characterised by rugged sandstone, open eucalyptus woodland and small pockets of temperate rainforest. The greatest attraction is the Bulgandry Aboriginal engraving site.
Old Sydney Town: an excellent recreation of Sydney, introducing the difficulties experienced by the first Europeans.
The Scenic Drive: a circular route taking in the **Bouddi National Park**.

Above: *East of Gosford lies Avoca Beach, an ever popular resort which offers camping and a golden beach.*
Below: *The Scenic Drive is a circular route through the Bouddi National park, a wilderness area of great beauty.*

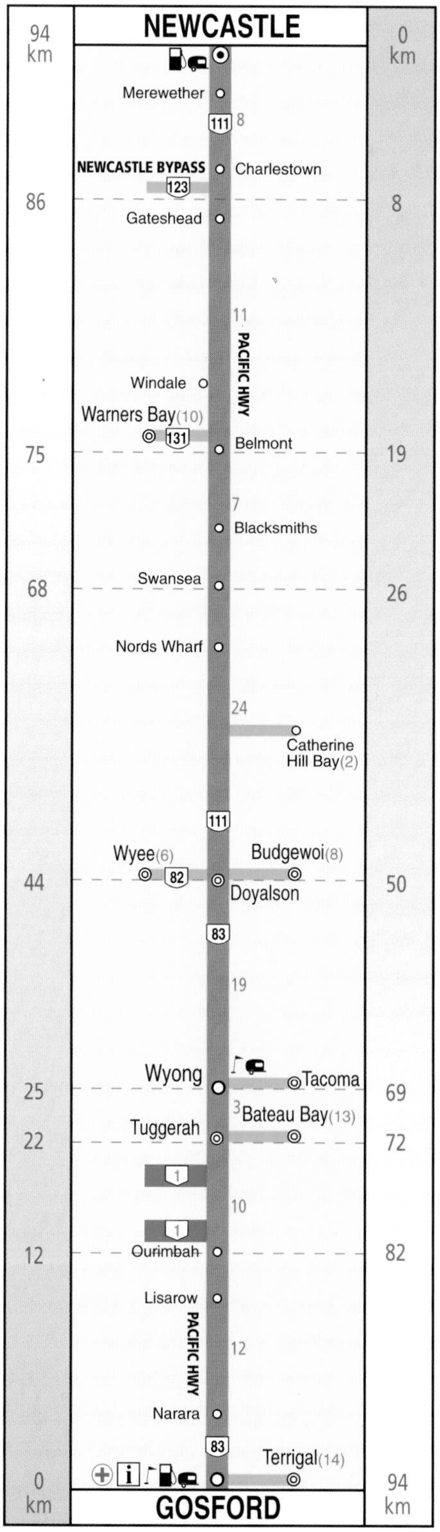

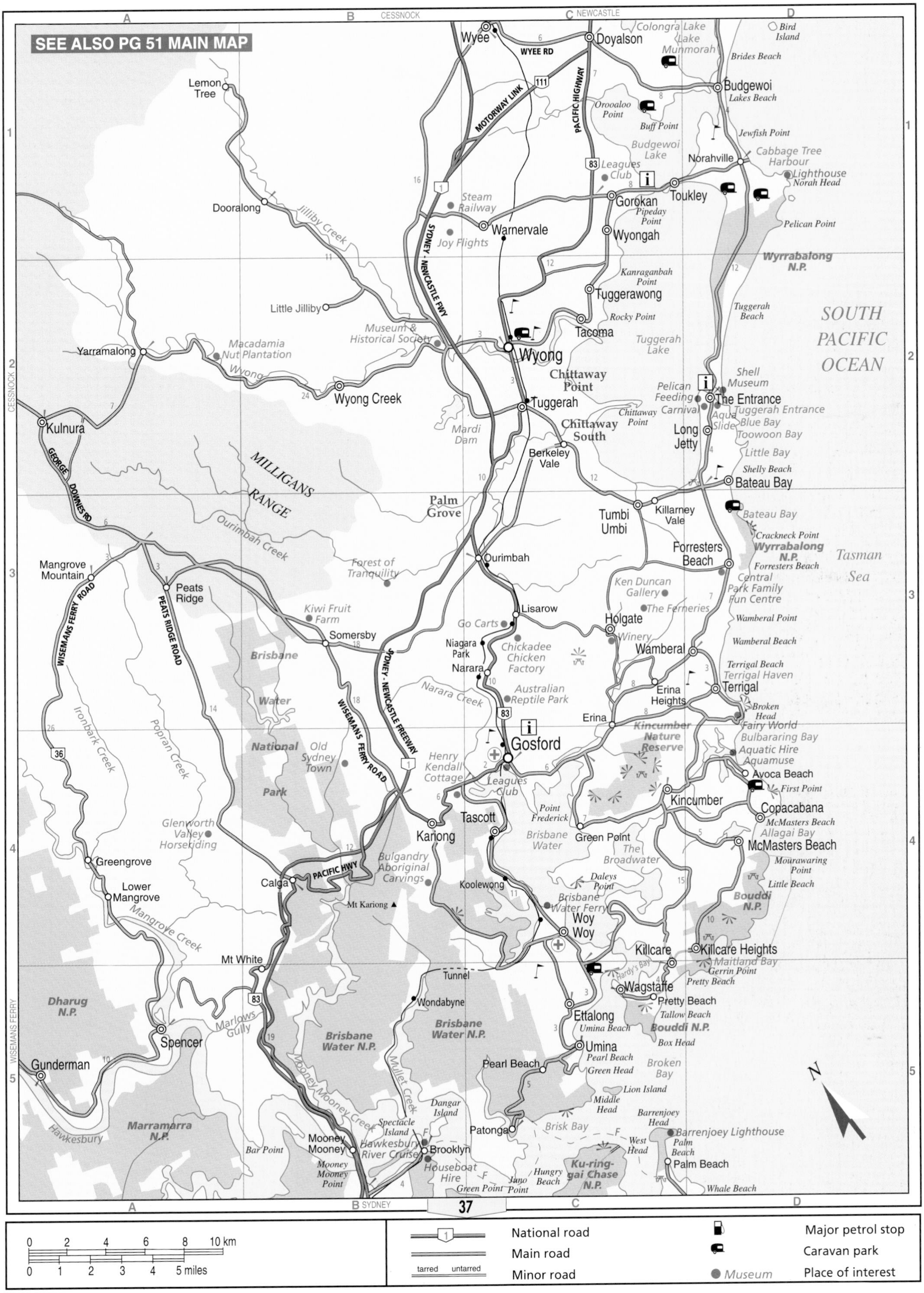
SEE ALSO PG 51 MAIN MAP
CESSNOCK
NEWCASTLE
SYDNEY
WISEMANS FERRY
37
Wyee
WYEE RD
Doyalson
Colongra Lake
Lake Munmorah
Bird Island
Brides Beach
Budgewoi
Lakes Beach
MOTORWAY LINK
PACIFIC HIGHWAY
Oroaloo Point
Buff Point
Jewfish Point
Lemon Tree
Budgewoi Lake
Norahville
Cabbage Tree Harbour
Lighthouse Norah Head
Leagues Club
Toukley
Gorokan
Steam Railway
Dooralong
Pipeday Point
Jilliby Creek
Warnervale
Wyongah
Pelican Point
Joy Flights
SYDNEY - NEWCASTLE FWY
Wyrrabalong N.P.
Kanraganbah Point
Tuggerawong
Little Jilliby
Tuggerah Beach
Rocky Point
SOUTH PACIFIC OCEAN
Museum & Historical Society
Tacoma
Macadamia Nut Plantation
Wyong
Tuggerah Lake
Yarramalong
Wyong
Chittaway Point
Shell Museum
Wyong Creek
Pelican Feeding Carnival
The Entrance
Tuggerah
Aqua Slide
Tuggerah Entrance
Blue Bay
Kulnura
Chittaway Point
Chittaway South
Mardi Dam
Long Jetty
Toowoon Bay
Little Bay
Berkeley Vale
MILLIGANS RANGE
Shelly Beach
GEORGE DOWNES RD
Bateau Bay
Palm Grove
Tumbi Umbi
Killarney Vale
Bateau Bay
Ourimbah Creek
Crackneck Point
Wyrrabalong N.P.
Forresters Beach
Tasman Sea
Ourimbah
Forest of Tranquility
Mangrove Mountain
Peats Ridge
Central Park Family Fun Centre
Ken Duncan Gallery
WISEMANS FERRY ROAD
PEATS RIDGE ROAD
Kiwi Fruit Farm
The Ferneries
Lisarow
Holgate
Wamberal Point
Go Carts
Somersby
Niagara Park
Chickadee Chicken Factory
Winery
Wamberal Beach
Wamberal
Brisbane Water National Park
Narara
Terrigal Beach
Terrigal Haven
Narara Creek
Australian Reptile Park
Erina Heights
Terrigal
Ironbark Creek
Broken Head
Poppran Creek
Old Sydney Town
Erina
Fairy World
Kincumber Nature Reserve
Bulbararing Bay
Gosford
Aquatic Hire
Aquamuse
Henry Kendall Cottage
Avoca Beach
Leagues Club
First Point
Kincumber
Copacabana
Point Frederick
McMasters Beach
Tascott
Allagai Bay
Glenworth Valley Horseriding
Kariong
Brisbane Water
Green Point
McMasters Beach
The Broadwater
Mourawaring Point
Greengrove
Bulgandry Aboriginal Carvings
Little Beach
Lower Mangrove
Calga
PACIFIC HWY
Koolewong
Daleys Point
Bouddi N.P.
Mt Kariong
Brisbane Water Ferry
Woy Woy
Mangrove Creek
Killcare
Killcare Heights
Mt White
Tunnel
Hardy's Bay
Maitland Bay
Gerrin Point
Wagstaffe
Pretty Beach
Dharug N.P.
Wondabyne
Pretty Beach
Tallow Beach
Ettalong
Bouddi N.P.
Brisbane Water N.P.
Brisbane Water N.P.
Marlows Gully
Umina Beach
Spencer
Box Head
Umina
Gunderman
Pearl Beach
Pearl Beach
Green Head
Broken Bay
Mooney Mooney Creek
Mullet Creek
Lion Island
Middle Head
Dangar Island
Marramarra N.P.
Hawkesbury
Barrenjoey Head
Spectacle Island
Patonga
Brisk Bay
Barrenjoey Lighthouse
Bar Point
Mooney Mooney
Hawkesbury River Cruise
Brooklyn
West Head
Palm Beach
Palm Beach
Mooney Mooney Point
Houseboat Hire
Green Point
Juno Point
Hungry Beach
Ku-ring-gai Chase N.P.
Whale Beach
0 2 4 6 8 10 km
0 1 2 3 4 5 miles
National road
Main road
Minor road
tarred untarred
Major petrol stop
Caravan park
Museum
Place of interest

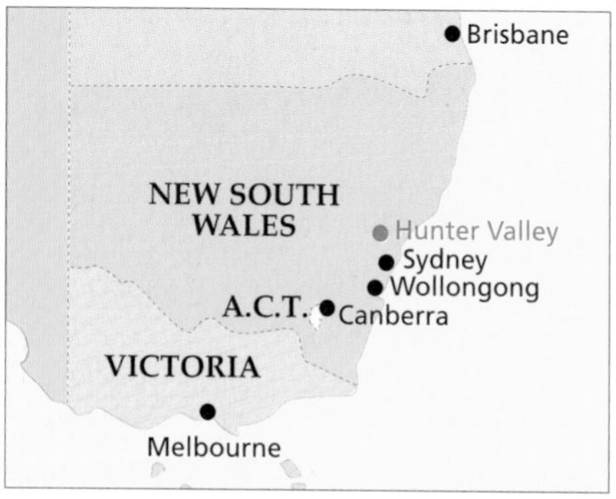

Hunter Valley

Mention the Hunter Valley and most people think of one thing – wine! This incredibly fertile region, the largest lowland plain on the New South Wales coast, has great agricultural diversity, from dairy herds of Friesians to beef and horse studs, coal mines, fodder crops, orchards, and vineyards. The first vines were planted in the Pokolbin area around Cessnock in 1832. Since then the area has developed a reputation for some of Australia's finest wines. Aboriginal rock art can be viewed at historic Wollombi, hot-air balloon trips offer extensive views, and you can get around by horse and carriage, bicycle, motorcycle, or your own car.

TOP ATTRACTIONS

Hungerford Hill Wine Village, Broke Road: picnic area, adventure playground, and a gift, souvenir and local craft shop.
Hunter Estate, Hermitage Road: beautifully landscaped gardens and wonderful views.
McWilliams Mount Pleasant Winery, Marrowbone Road: an ideal starting point to learn more about wine before buying.
Pokolbin Estate Vineyard, McDonalds Road: barbecue facilities, a small playground and a café which sells wines from a few small vineyards.
Wyndham Estate, Dalwood, Branxton: beautifully restored winery, bistro, horse-drawn coach ride to Dalwood House (circa 1828), and a picnic area with swings.

ON THE ROAD

Visits to Hunter Valley should start at the **Cessnock Tourist Information Centre**, on the corner of Mount View and Wollombi roads. The centre can arrange maps and guides, tours and accommodation for the region. Remember, if you are wine sampling you should ensure that the driver of your vehicle is *not* drinking. This will prevent fines from the police and, more importantly, keep you safe.

WHERE TO STAY

Cessnock Motel, 13 Allandale Road, tel: (02) 4990 2699, 4990 5834.
Cessnock Vintage Motor Inn, 300 Maitland Road, tel: (02) 4990 4333.
Cumberland Motor Inn, 57 Cumberland Street, Cessnock, tel: (02) 4990 6633.
Hunter Valley Motel, 30 Allandale Road, Cessnock, tel: (02) 4990 1722, fax: 4990 3025.
Elfin Hill Motel, Marrowbone Road, Pokolbin, tel: (02) 4998 7543.
Hermitage Lodge, Gillard Road, Pokolbin, tel: (02) 4998 7639.
The Hunter Resort, Hermitage Road, Pokolbin, tel: (02) 4998 7777.
Pokolbin Village Resort, Broke Road, tel: (02) 4998 7670, fax: 4998 7377.
Tallawanta Motel, Broke Road, Pokolbin, tel: (02) 4998 7854, fax: 4998 7845.

Left: *Many vineyards in the Hunter Valley, a region where excellent wines are produced, run tours of their cellars.*

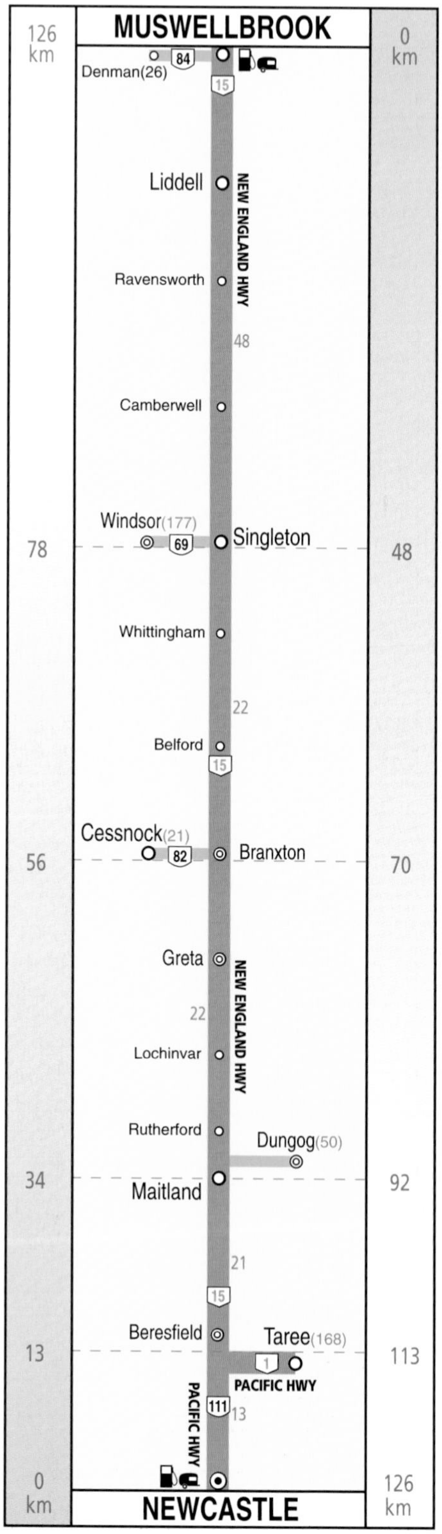

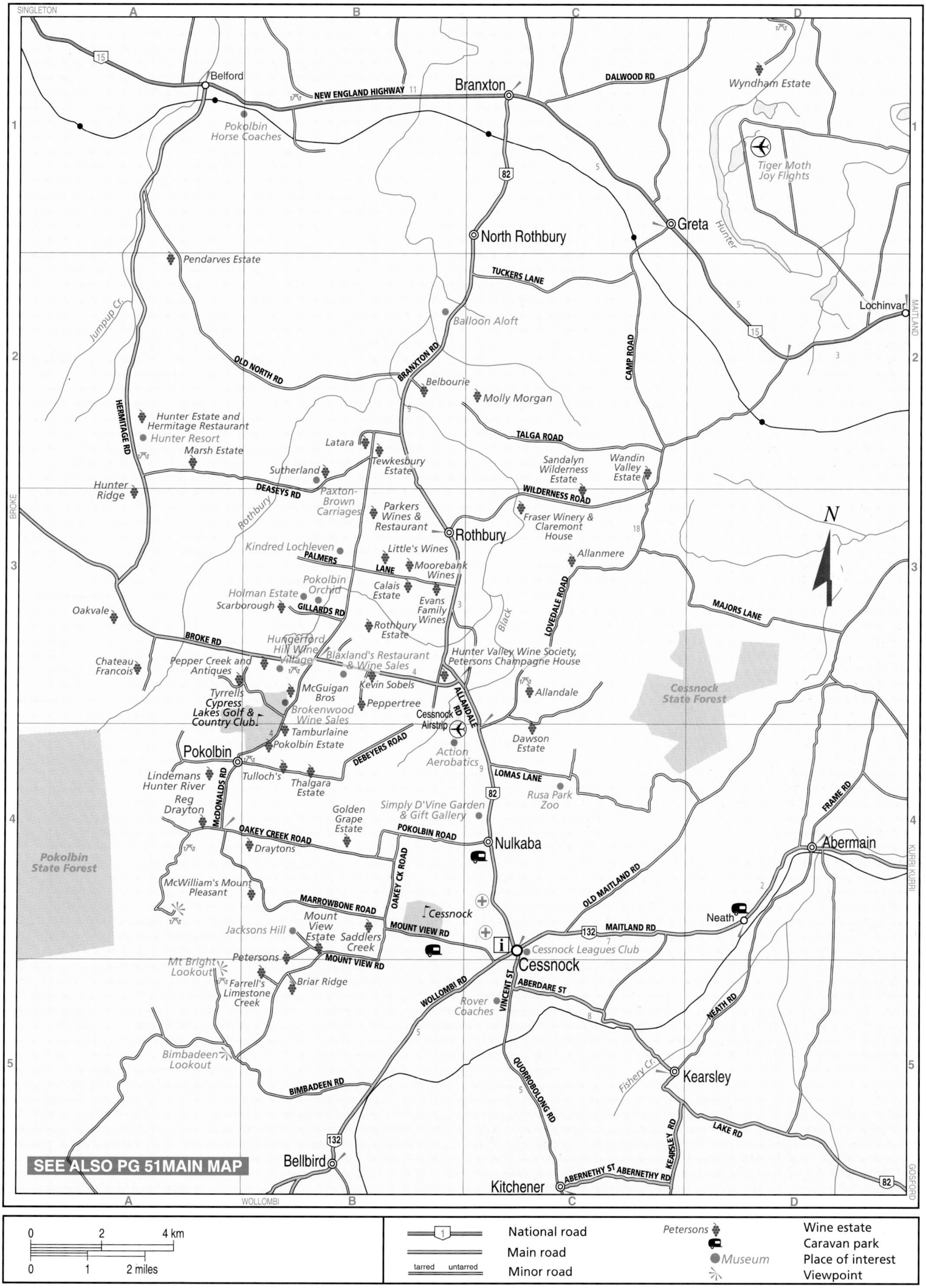
SINGLETON
A
B
C
D
1
2
3
4
5
Belford
NEW ENGLAND HIGHWAY
Branxton
DALWOOD RD
Wyndham Estate
Pokolbin Horse Coaches
82
Tiger Moth Joy Flights
North Rothbury
Greta
Hunter
Pendarves Estate
TUCKERS LANE
Jumpup Cr.
Balloon Aloft
Lochinvar
MAITLAND
CAMP ROAD
15
OLD NORTH RD
BRANXTON RD
Belbourie
Molly Morgan
HERMITAGE RD
Hunter Estate and Hermitage Restaurant
Hunter Resort
Marsh Estate
Latara
Tewkesbury Estate
TALGA ROAD
Sandalyn Wilderness Estate
Wandin Valley Estate
Sutherland
Hunter Ridge
BROKE
DEASEYS RD
Paxton-Brown Carriages
Parkers Wines & Restaurant
WILDERNESS ROAD
Fraser Winery & Claremont House
N
Rothbury
Rothbury
Kindred Lochleven
Little's Wines
Allanmere
PALMERS LANE
Moorebank Wines
Pokolbin Orchid
Holman Estate
Calais Estate
LOVEDALE ROAD
Scarborough
GILLARDS RD
Evans Family Wines
MAJORS LANE
Oakvale
Black
Rothbury Estate
BROKE RD
Hungerford Hill Wine Village
Blaxland's Restaurant & Wine Sales
Hunter Valley Wine Society, Petersons Champagne House
Chateau Francois
Pepper Creek and Antiques
Kevin Sobels
Tyrrells
McGuigan Bros
Allandale
Cessnock State Forest
Cypress Lakes Golf & Country Club
Brokenwood Wine Sales
Peppertree
ALLANDALE RD
Cessnock Airstrip
Tamburlaine
Dawson Estate
Pokolbin
Pokolbin Estate
DEBEYERS ROAD
Action Aerobatics
Lindemans Hunter River
Tulloch's
Thalgara Estate
LOMAS LANE
Rusa Park Zoo
FRAME RD
McDONALDS RD
Reg Drayton
Simply D'Vine Garden & Gift Gallery
Golden Grape Estate
OAKEY CREEK ROAD
POKOLBIN ROAD
Abermain
Pokolbin State Forest
Draytons
Nulkaba
KURRI KURRI
OAKEY CK ROAD
McWilliam's Mount Pleasant
OLD MAITLAND RD
MARROWBONE ROAD
Cessnock
Neath
Mount View Estate
MOUNT VIEW RD
MAITLAND RD
132
Jacksons Hill
Saddlers Creek
Cessnock Leagues Club
Petersons
MOUNT VIEW RD
Cessnock
Mt Bright Lookout
ABERDARE ST
Farrell's Limestone Creek
Briar Ridge
WOLLOMBI RD
VINCENT ST
NEATH RD
Rover Coaches
Bimbadeen Lookout
Fishery Cr.
Kearsley
QUORROBOLONG RD
BIMBADEEN RD
LAKE RD
KEARSLEY RD
SEE ALSO PG 51MAIN MAP
Bellbird
GOSFORD
ABERNETHY ST
ABERNETHY RD
Kitchener
WOLLOMBI
0
2
4 km
0
1
2 miles
National road
Main road
tarred
untarred
Minor road
Petersons
Museum
Wine estate
Caravan park
Place of interest
Viewpoint

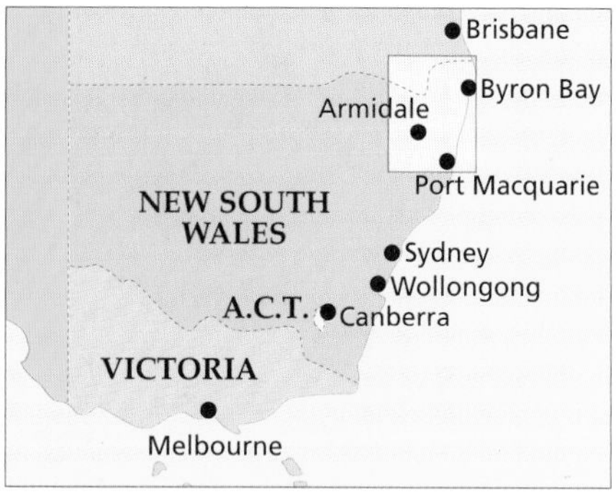

North Coast and New England

From the old river ports of Grafton and Maclean to the tumbling hills of the Great Dividing Range, this is an area of great diversity. The rich alluvial soils of the coastal plains combine with warm sunny days to produce an ideal environment for bananas, sugarcane, vegetables, avocados, kiwi fruit and macadamia nuts. Between the cultivated tracts lie valleys of dense subtropical rainforest with giant ferns, stinging trees and towering eucalypts. There are a number of resort towns along the coast, including Coffs Harbour and Port Macquarie, and the New England tableland towns include the university city of Armidale.

TOP ATTRACTIONS

Armidale: attractive city and the centre of the New England highlands district.
Byron Bay: coastal resort, excellent beaches, interesting township, and one of the coast's most dramatically located lighthouses.
Coffs Harbour: famous for the Big Banana – one of the country's oldest tourist attractions.
Nimbin: one-time dairy town that became a centre for the alternative-lifestyle set in the 1970s.
Port Macquarie: popular, family-orientated holiday town with a fascinating koala hospital.
Tamworth: centre for Australia's country music which annually celebrates the genre in a week-long festival over Australia Day weekend in January.

ON THE ROAD

The main routes through this very well-serviced and well-populated area are the inland **New England Highway** and the coastal **Pacific Highway** (which is currently being upgraded). The inland route is marginally longer and regarded as the better road, but lacks the appeal of proximity to the ocean. The towns on both routes have service stations which are able to provide both petrol and vehicle maintenance. Visitors wanting to explore the minor roads, particularly on the edge of the Great Dividing Range, will find that they can become quite winding and narrow.

Below: *Cape Byron Lighthouse is perched majestically on the end of the cape that is Australia's most easterly point.*

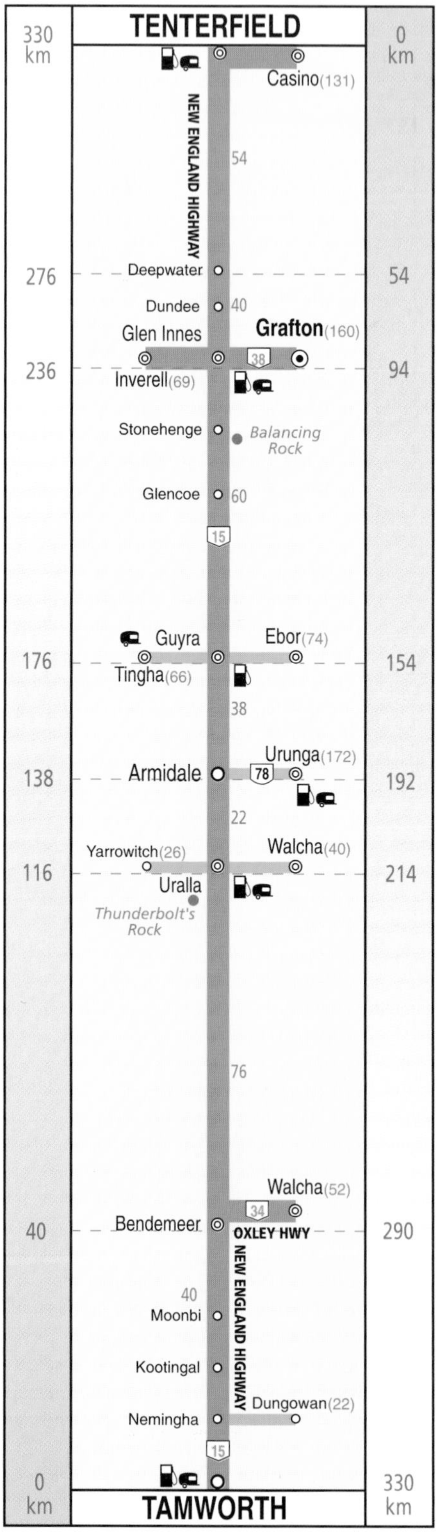

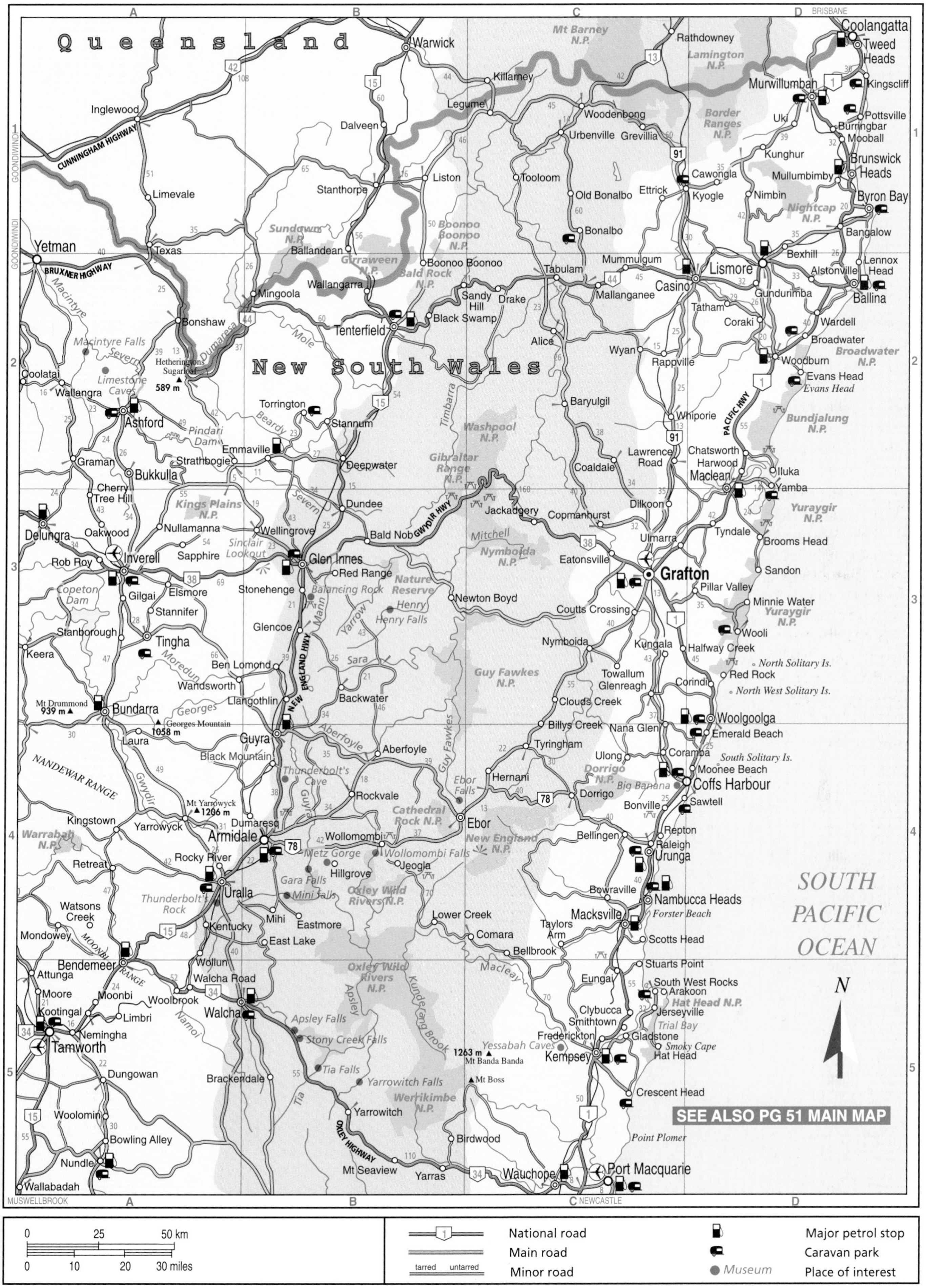
Queensland
New South Wales
SOUTH PACIFIC OCEAN
SEE ALSO PG 51 MAIN MAP
BRISBANE
GOONDIWINDI
MUSWELLBROOK
NEWCASTLE
CUNNINGHAM HIGHWAY
BRUXNER HIGHWAY
NEW ENGLAND HWY
GWYDIR HWY
PACIFIC HWY
OXLEY HIGHWAY
NANDEWAR RANGE
MOONBI RANGE
Warwick
Killarney
Legume
Dalveen
Inglewood
Limevale
Stanthorpe
Liston
Texas
Yetman
Ballandean
Wallangarra
Mingoola
Bonshaw
Tenterfield
Black Swamp
Sandy Hill
Drake
Boonoo Boonoo
Tabulam
Mummulgum
Mallanganee
Casino
Lismore
Woodenbong
Urbenville
Grevillia
Tooloom
Old Bonalbo
Bonalbo
Ettrick
Kyogle
Cawongla
Rathdowney
Coolangatta
Tweed Heads
Kingscliff
Murwillumbah
Uki
Pottsville
Burringbar
Mooball
Kunghur
Brunswick Heads
Mullumbimby
Nimbin
Byron Bay
Bangalow
Bexhill
Lennox Head
Alstonville
Ballina
Gundurimba
Tatham
Coraki
Wardell
Broadwater
Woodburn
Evans Head
Wyan
Rappville
Alice
Baryulgil
Whiporie
Chatsworth
Harwood
Maclean
Iluka
Yamba
Lawrence Road
Coaldale
Dilkoon
Ulmarra
Tyndale
Brooms Head
Sandon
Grafton
Pillar Valley
Minnie Water
Wooli
Coutts Crossing
Copmanhurst
Jackadgery
Eatonsville
Nymboida
Kungala
Halfway Creek
North Solitary Is.
Red Rock
North West Solitary Is.
Corindi
Towallum
Glenreagh
Clouds Creek
Billys Creek
Nana Glen
Woolgoolga
Emerald Beach
Tyringham
Ulong
Coramba
South Solitary Is.
Moonee Beach
Coffs Harbour
Dorrigo
Big Banana
Sawtell
Bonville
Repton
Bellingen
Raleigh
Urunga
Bowraville
Nambucca Heads
Forster Beach
Macksville
Taylors Arm
Scotts Head
Stuarts Point
South West Rocks
Arakoon
Eungai
Clybucca
Smithtown
Jerseyville
Trial Bay
Gladstone
Smoky Cape
Hat Head
Frederickton
Kempsey
Crescent Head
Point Plomer
Port Macquarie
Wauchope
Yarras
Birdwood
Mt Seaview
Yarrowitch
Mt Boss
1263 m
Mt Banda Banda
Yessabah Caves
Bellbrook
Comara
Lower Creek
Ebor
Ebor Falls
Hernani
Newton Boyd
Coolatai
Wallangra
Ashford
Hetheringtons Sugarloaf
589 m
Macintyre Falls
Limestone Caves
Pindari Dam
Torrington
Stannum
Emmaville
Strathbogie
Deepwater
Graman
Bukkulla
Cherry Tree Hill
Dundee
Delungra
Oakwood
Nullamanna
Wellingrove
Bald Nob
Inverell
Sapphire
Sinclair Lookout
Glen Innes
Red Range
Rob Roy
Copeton Dam
Gilgai
Elsmore
Stonehenge
Balancing Rock
Stannifer
Henry Falls
Glencoe
Stanborough
Tingha
Keera
Ben Lomond
Wandsworth
Llangothlin
Backwater
Mt Drummond
939 m
Bundarra
Georges Mountain
1058 m
Laura
Guyra
Black Mountain
Aberfoyle
Thunderbolt's Cave
Rockvale
Mt Yarrowyck
1206 m
Dumaresq
Kingstown
Yarrowyck
Armidale
Wollomombi
Wollomombi Falls
Metz Gorge
Hillgrove
Jeogla
Rocky River
Retreat
Uralla
Gara Falls
Mini Falls
Thunderbolt's Rock
Watsons Creek
Mihi
Eastmore
Kentucky
East Lake
Mondowey
Bendemeer
Wollun
Walcha Road
Attunga
Moore
Moonbi
Woolbrook
Kootingal
Limbri
Walcha
Apsley Falls
Stony Creek Falls
Nemingha
Tamworth
Dungowan
Brackendale
Tia Falls
Yarrowitch Falls
Woolomin
Bowling Alley
Nundle
Wallabadah
Mt Barney N.P.
Lamington N.P.
Border Ranges N.P.
Nightcap N.P.
Sundown N.P.
Girraween N.P.
Boonoo Boonoo N.P.
Bald Rock N.P.
Broadwater N.P.
Bundjalung N.P.
Washpool N.P.
Gibraltar Range N.P.
Yuraygir N.P.
Kings Plains N.P.
Mitchell
Nymboida N.P.
Nature Reserve
Guy Fawkes N.P.
Dorrigo N.P.
Cathedral Rock N.P.
New England N.P.
Oxley Wild Rivers N.P.
Hat Head N.P.
Werrikimbe N.P.
Warrabah N.P.
Macintyre
Severn
Dumaresq
Mole
Beardy
Timbarra
Mann
Sara
Yarrow
Aberfoyle
Guyra
Gwydir
Georges
Moredun
Macleay
Apsley
Kunderang Brook
Tia
Namoi
Guy Fawkes
N
0 25 50 km
0 10 20 30 miles
National road
Main road
tarred untarred
Minor road
Museum
Major petrol stop
Caravan park
Place of interest

South Coast

From Wollongong to the Victorian border the coastal strip is mostly dairy country. Behind the coastal plain lies Morton National Park where the Illawarra escarpment is notable for its spectacular waterfalls tumbling into dark, narrow valleys containing remnants of rainforest and abundant wildlife. The far south coast is a series of attractive villages where the fishing, timber and dairy industries intermingle. Eden, on the shores of Twofold Bay, was once a major whaling centre. Narooma, Bermagui, Tathra and Ulladulla all have thriving fishing fleets and towns like Bodalla and Bega are famous for their cheeses.

TOP ATTRACTIONS

Berry: charming village atmosphere with numerous eateries and gift shops.
Bodalla: famous for its cheeses; visit the factories and taste the local produce.
Eden: active fishing town, once a premier whaling station.
Jervis Bay: large, isolated and very beautiful bay with white sands and excellent bushwalking.
Kiama: attractive seaside resort noted for its Blowhole (a large fissure in the coastal rocks) and views from Saddleback Mountain.
Minnamurra Falls: rainforest and waterfall located below the Illawarra escarpment to the west of the small town of Jamberoo.
Tilba Tilba: historic timber town largely untouched since the 19th century.

ON THE ROAD

The **Princes Highway** is the coastal road from Sydney to Melbourne. From Sydney, the road is a four-lane freeway for about 100km (62 miles) until it reaches the southern outskirts of Wollongong. From there to the Victorian border it is sealed and adequate, but hardly inspiring as it winds through the coastal hinterland, rarely offering views of the ocean. There are, however, numerous attractive drives through eucalypt forests. If you decide to move off this main road, particularly if you head westward towards the Great Dividing Range, you will find the road winding steeply up the mountains.

Right: *The South Coast is noted for its peaceful lifestyle: here Friesians graze on picture-postcard pastures.*

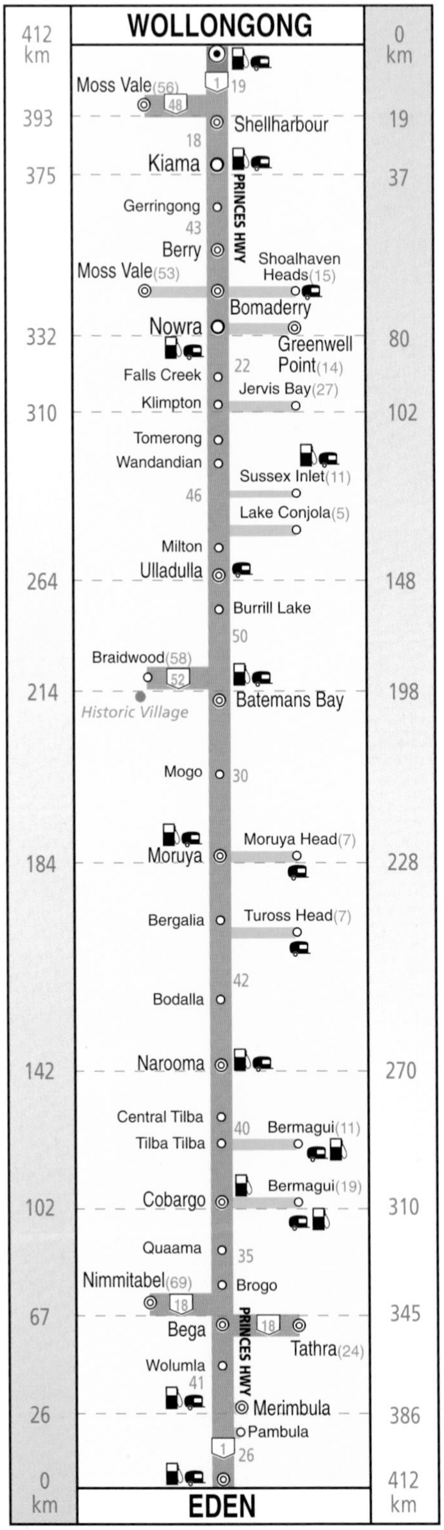

WHERE TO STAY

Bega Downs Motor Inn, cnr High & Gipps streets, Bega, tel: (02) 6492 2944, fax: 6492 2834.
Bega Village Motor Inn, Princes Highway, Bega, tel: (02) 6492 2466, fax: 6492 1851.
Bodalla Motel, Princes Highway, Bodalla, tel: (02) 4473 5201.
Bunyip Inn, 122 Queen Street, Berry, tel: (02) 4464 2064, fax: 4464 2324.
Clunes of Berry, 24 Prince Alfred Street, tel: (02) 4464 2272.
Coachmans Rest Motor Inn, Princes Highway, Eden, tel: (02) 6496 1900, fax: 6496 3398.
Green Gables Bed and Breakfast, Corkhill Dve, Tilba Tilba, tel: (02) 4473 7435, fax: 4473 7311.
Halfway Motel, Imlay Street, Eden, tel: (02) 6496 1178, fax: 6496 3316.
Jamberoo Valley Lodge, Jamberoo Mountain Road, Jamberoo, tel: (02) 4236 0269.
Kiama Terrace Motor Lodge, 51 Collins Street, tel: (02) 4233 1100.
Twofold Bay Motor Inn, 166 Imlay Street, Eden, tel: (02) 6496 3111, fax: 6496 3058.

SEE ALSO PG 51 MAIN MAP
37
69
47
SYDNEY
ORBOST
WAGGA WAGGA
CANBERRA
A.C.T.
New South Wales
GREAT DIVIDING RANGE
Victoria
SOUTH PACIFIC OCEAN
Tasman Sea
N
Young
Murringo
Wombat
Boorowa
Harden
Murrumburrah
Galong
Beggan Beggan
Binalong
Jugiong
Bookham
Yass
Bowning
Rye Park
Kangiara
Gunnary
Rugby
Binda
Laggan
Narrawa
Taralga
Crookwell
Wheeo
Bevendale
Grabben Gullen
Kialla
Bannister
Roslyn
Chatsbury
Biala
Gurrundah
Dalton
Gunning
Goulburn
Marulan
Tallong
Marulan South
Bungonia
Bungonia Caves
Wombeyan Caves
Hilltop
Colo Vale
Yerrinbool
Wollongong
Unanderra
Port Kembla
Mittagong
Berrima
Bowral
Moss Vale
Robertson
Shellharbour
Bass Point
Burrawang
Bundanoon
Minnamurra Falls
Fitzroy Falls
Jamberoo
Kiama
Penrose
Kangaroo Valley
Berry
Gerringong
Tallowa Dam
Lake Yarrunga
Bomaderry
Nowra
Shoalhaven Heads
Greenwell Point
Culburra
Morton N.P.
Falls Creek
Klimpton
Tomerong
Wandandian
Huskisson
Currarong
Jervis Bay
Sussex Inlet
Swan Haven
Cudmirrah
Bendalong
Lake Conjola
Milton
Ulladulla
Burrill Lake
Bawley Point
Kioloa
Murramarang N.P.
Durras
Nelligen
Batemans Bay
Malua Bay
Mogo
Mossy Point
Broulee
Moruya
Moruya Head
Congo
Bergalia
Coila Lake
Tuross Head
Potato Point
Bodalla
Lake Mummuga
Dalmeny
Eurobodalla
Narooma
Montague Is.
Central Tilba
Tilba Tilba
Wallaga Lake N.P.
Bermagui
Cobargo
Quaama
Brogo
Wapengo
Wapengo Lake
Mimosa Rocks N.P.
Bega
Kameruka
Tathra
Wallagoot Lake
Bournda N.P.
Candelo
Wolumla
Merimbula
Pambula
Ben Boyd N.P.
Eden
Twofold Bay
Boydtown
East Boyd
Kiah
Green Cape
Disaster Bay
Timbillica
Nadgee Nature Reserve
Gipsy Point
Genoa
Cape Howe
Croajingolong N.P.
Mallacoota
Cann River
Club Terrace
Buchan
Bellmount Forest
Collector
Murrumbateman
Burrinjuck Dam
Adjungbilly
Careys Cave
Wee Jasper
Gundaroo
Lake George
Tarago
Boro
Lake Bathurst
Nerriga
Budawang N.P.
Mt Tianjara 768 m
Sutton
Bywong
Bungendore
Doughboy
Charleyong
Currockbilly Mtn 1131 m
Tumut
Argalong
Queanbeyan
Blowering Reservoir
Kosciuszko N.P.
Talbingo
Jounama Dam
Bendora Dam
Corin Dam
Tharwa
Royalla
Captains Flat
Braidwood
Historic Village
Majors Creek
Yarrangobilly
Yarrangobilly Caves
Talbingo Res.
Tantangara Reservoir
Namadgi N.P.
Togganoggera
Araluen
Michelago
Wyanbene Caves
Deua N.P.
Kiandra
Cabramurra
Lake Eucumbene
Adaminaby
Bredbo
Peak View
Bendethera Caves
Mt Jagungal 2060 m
Eucumbene
Buckenderra
Bunyan
Avenue of Flags
Nerrigundah
Numeralla
Tuross Falls
Wadbilliga N.P.
Cooma
Bourkes Gorge
Olsens Lookout
Island Bend
Berridale
Rock Flat
Yowrie
Charlotte Pass
Perisher Valley
Lake Jindabyne
Jindabyne
2228 m Mt Kosciuszko
Thredbo
Dalgety
Mt Kydra 1236 m
Nimmitabel
Paupong
Ingebyra
Timbery Range
Holts Flat
Bemboka
Jimenbuen
Byadbo 1236 m
Rodney
Buckalong
Bibbenluke
Tingaringy
Alpine N.P.
Willis
Bombala
Cathcart
Wyndham
Suggan Buggan
Coolangubra N.P.
Yowaka N.P.
Delegate
Craigie
Wulgulmerang
Delegate River
White Rock Mtn 1093 m
Mila
Genoa N.P.
McKillops Bridge
Bendoc
Bonang
Rockton
Mt Imlay N.P.
Mt Imlay 886 m
Gelantipy
Snowy River N.P.
Errinundra N.P.
Chandlers Creek
Coopracambra N.P.
Alfred N.P.
HUME HWY
PRINCES HWY
KINGS HIGHWAY
MONARO HWY
SNOWY MOUNTAINS HWY
SNOWY MTNS HWY
CANN VALLEY HWY
BUDAWANG RANGE
KIBEYAN RANGE
COAST RANGE
SNOWY MTNS
0 20 40 60 km
0 10 20 30 miles
National road
Main road
Minor road
tarred untarred
Major petrol stop
Caravan park
Museum
Place of interest

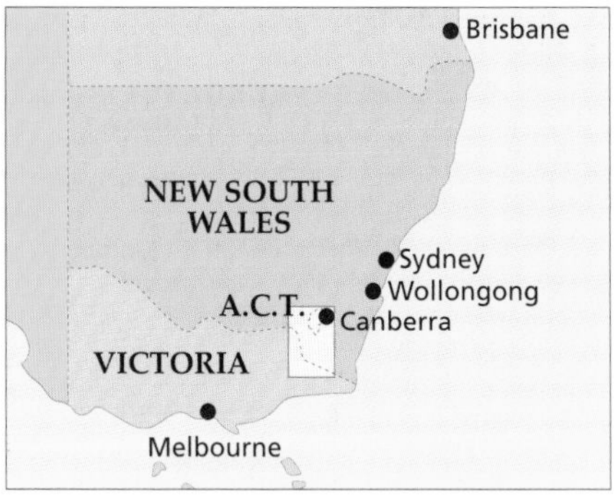

Snowy Mountains

Kosciuszko National Park lies in the heart of New South Wales snow country. This rugged, inhospitable area was first opened up to skiers in the late 1940s when a series of dams and hydro-electricity stations were constructed to harness the melt-waters from the mountains. The plan was to generate electricity and to redirect the water to the inland of New South Wales. The resulting roads and townships became the base upon which Australia's ski tourism industry was built. The Snowy Mountains are the highest mountain range in Australia, with the country's highest peak, Mount Kosciuszko, rising to 2228m (7310ft).

TOP ATTRACTIONS

Kiandra: great place to explore old gold diggings.
Mount Kosciuszko: great for bushwalking in spring and summer and skiing in winter.
Perisher Valley: widely regarded as the best ski spot in the Snowy Mountains with 30 interconnecting ski lifts, over 100 ski instructors, snow-making facilities and a wide range of accommodation.
Skitube: runs from below the snowline at Bullocks Flat through the mountains to Perisher Valley and Mount Blue Cow. The 8.5-km (5-mile) journey includes the longest railway tunnel in the country at 6.3km (4 miles).
Thredbo: pretty alpine-style village at the base of Crackenback Mountain; ski to the door of your hotel.
Yarrangobilly Caves: beautiful caves with thermal pools nearby.

ON THE ROAD

There was a time when the Snowy Mountains were a wilderness of dangerously steep ravines and narrow winding dirt roads. The dirt roads are now gone and in their place are sealed highways, a ski-tube system and high-speed ski lifts. Use chains on tyres during the snow season and drive with extreme care. There is a long dirt section between Thredbo and Khancoban, often impassable in winter.

Right: *In summer the Snowy Mountains are a hiker's paradise, while winter's thick, white blanket draws eager crowds of skiers.*

WHERE TO STAY

Accommodation on the snowfields is a large mixture of chalets, hotels and motels. Information can be obtained from the **Cooma Visitor Information Centre**, 119 Sharp Street, tel: 1 800 636 525.
Eiger Chalet, Perisher Valley, tel: (02) 6457 5209.
Alpine Gables Motel, Kosciuszko Road, Jindabyne, tel: (02) 6456 2555, 1 800 645 625.
The Station Resort, Dalgety Road, Jindabyne, tel: (02) 6456 2895, 1 800 020 808.
Thredbo Alpine Hotel and Apartments, tel: 1 800 026 333.
Thredbo Resort Centre, Friday Drive, Thredbo Village tel: (02) 6459 4294, or 1 800 020 589.
Novotel Lake Crackenback Resort, Alpine Way via Jindabyne, tel: (02) 6456 2960, fax: 6456 1008, 1 800 020 524.

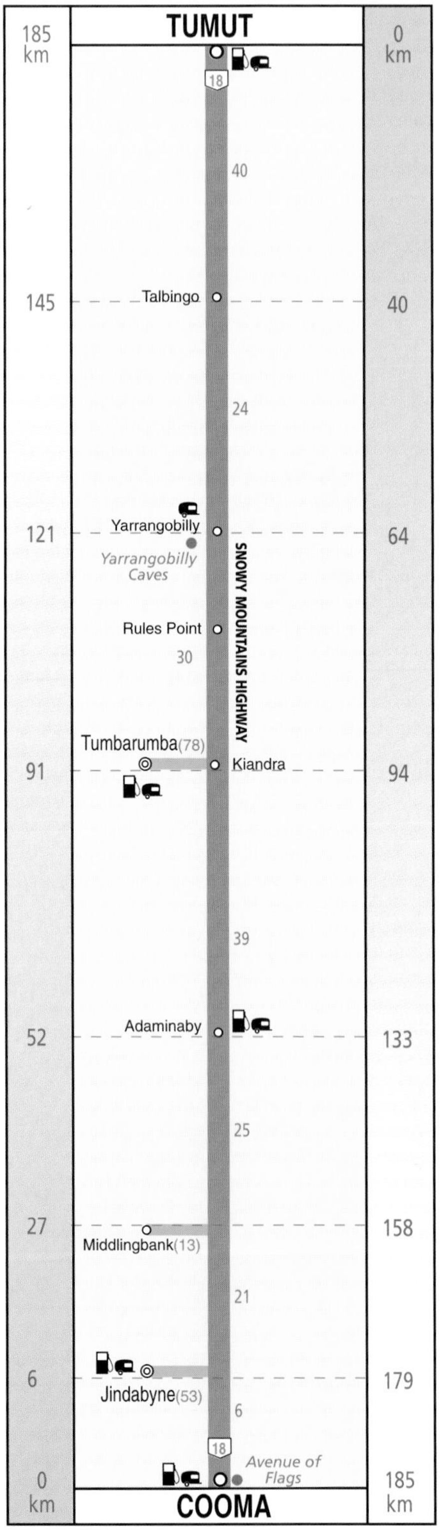

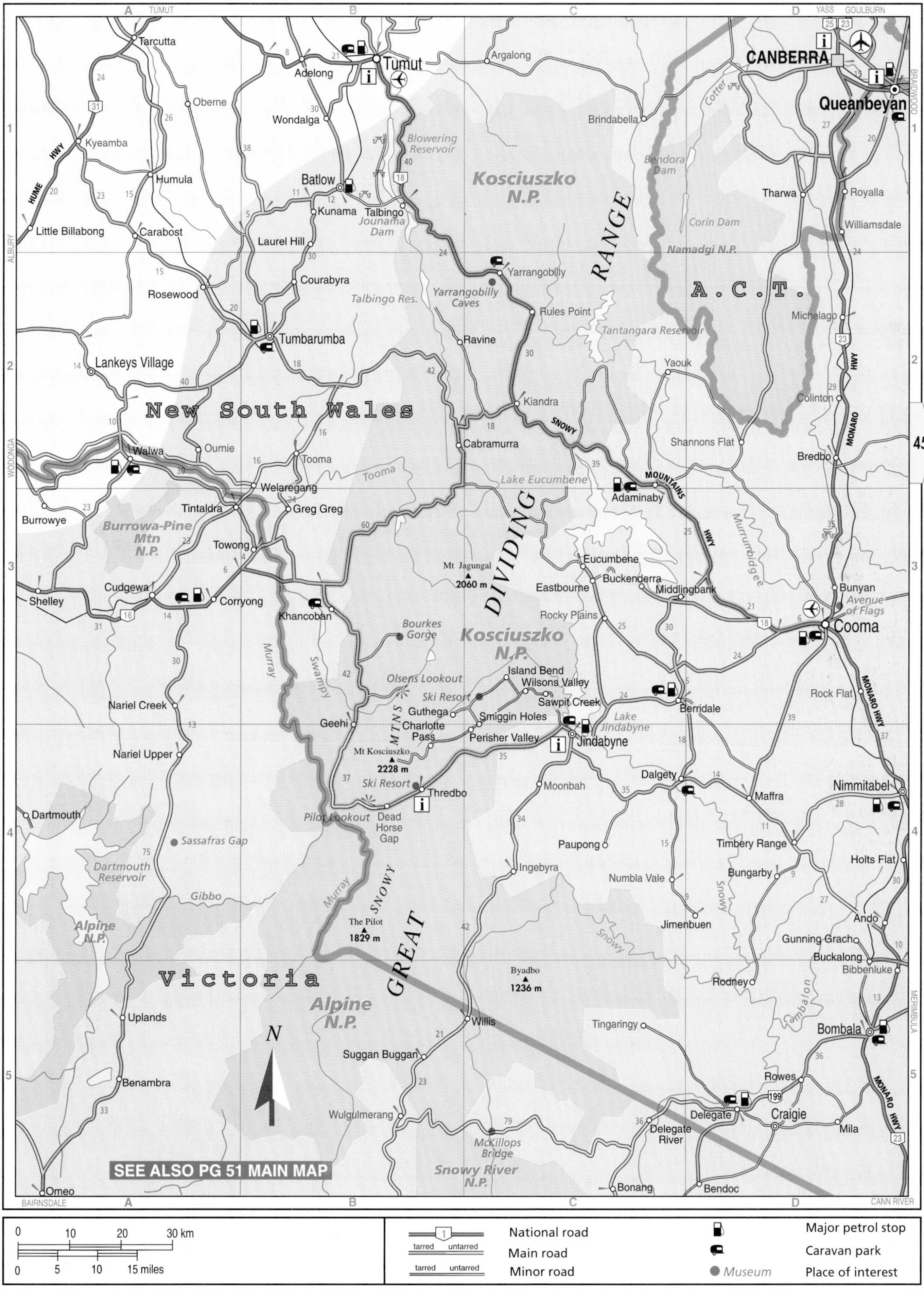
TUMUT
YASS GOULBURN
BRAIDWOOD
ALBURY
WODONGA
MERIMBULA
BAIRNSDALE
CANN RIVER
Tarcutta
Tumut
Argalong
CANBERRA
Queanbeyan
Adelong
Oberne
Wondalga
Brindabella
Kyeamba
HUME HWY
Blowering Reservoir
Kosciuszko N.P.
RANGE
Bendora Dam
Royalla
Tharwa
Humula
Batlow
Kunama
Talbingo
Jounama Dam
Corin Dam
Williamsdale
Little Billabong
Carabost
Laurel Hill
Namadgi N.P.
Yarrangobilly
Courabyra
Rosewood
Talbingo Res.
Yarrangobilly Caves
A.C.T.
Rules Point
Tantangara Reservoir
Michelago
Tumbarumba
Ravine
Lankeys Village
Yaouk
MONARO HWY
Kiandra
New South Wales
Colinton
SNOWY MOUNTAINS HWY
Shannons Flat
Bredbo
Walwa
Ournie
Cabramurra
Tooma
Welaregang
Lake Eucumbene
Adaminaby
Tintaldra
Greg Greg
Burrowye
DIVIDING
Burrowa-Pine Mtn N.P.
Towong
Murrumbidgee
Eucumbene
Mt Jagungal
2060 m
Buckenderra
Cudgewa
Eastbourne
Middlingbank
Bunyan
Shelley
Corryong
Khancoban
Avenue of Flags
Rocky Plains
Cooma
Bourkes Gorge
Murray
Swampy
Olsens Lookout
Island Bend
Wilsons Valley
Ski Resort
Sawpit Creek
Rock Flat
Nariel Creek
Guthega
Smiggin Holes
Berridale
Charlotte Pass
Lake Jindabyne
Geehi
MTNS
Perisher Valley
Jindabyne
Nariel Upper
Mt Kosciuszko
2228 m
Dalgety
Nimmitabel
Moonbah
Thredbo
Maffra
Dartmouth
Pilot Lookout
Dead Horse Gap
Sassafras Gap
Paupong
Timbery Range
Holts Flat
Dartmouth Reservoir
Ingebyra
Bungarby
Numbla Vale
Gibbo
SNOWY
Ando
Jimenbuen
Alpine N.P.
The Pilot
1829 m
Gunning Grach
Buckalong
Bibbenluke
Victoria
GREAT
Byadbo
1236 m
Rodney
Cambalong
Alpine N.P.
Willis
Tingaringy
Uplands
Bombala
N
Suggan Buggan
Benambra
Rowes
Delegate
Craigie
Wulgulmerang
Delegate River
Mila
McKillops Bridge
Snowy River N.P.
SEE ALSO PG 51 MAIN MAP
Omeo
Bonang
Bendoc
45
0 10 20 30 km
0 5 10 15 miles
National road
tarred untarred
Main road
tarred untarred
Minor road
Major petrol stop
Caravan park
Museum
Place of interest

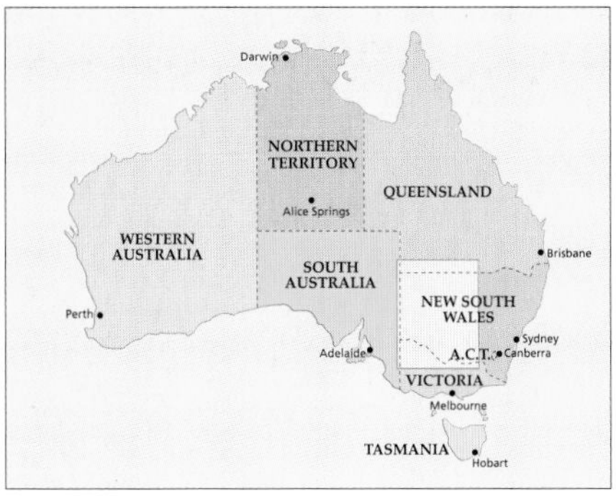

Outback New South Wales

A traveller can drive for hours out beyond the central slopes through the vast, arid western plains of outback New South Wales and see nothing of interest. However, there are many worthwhile places to visit. The north-west region is remote but contains gibber plains, the Sturt National Park, the lakes at Menindee and the prosperous mining town of Broken Hill. The Darling, Murrumbidgee and Murray rivers create an important central river system, and the dry lake beds and saltbush plains of the Mungo National Park have provided evidence of Australia's earliest known inhabitants.

TOP ATTRACTIONS

Bourke: fascinating, historic town which was once an inland port for the whole of western New South Wales and Queensland.
Broken Hill: large and hugely prosperous mining town.
Cobar: interesting old mining town with superb pubs and an excellent museum.
Menindee: very beautiful and unusual inland lakes surrounding the town which has an historic local pub.
Mungo National Park: site of important fossil finds; unusual dunes surround the dry lake and plains. A section of the park was once the Gol Gol sheep station.
Silverton: on the edge of the desert and famous as a location for Australian movies.
White Cliffs and **Lightning Ridge:** opal mining towns in the middle of the desert.
Wilcannia: barely recognisable now as the thriving late 19th-century inland port it once was.

ON THE ROAD

The main roads through the region – the Barrier Highway from Nyngan to Broken Hill, the Mitchell from Dubbo to the Queensland border, the Mid-Western from Cowra to Hay, and the Sturt from Wagga to the South Australian border – are sealed and each town has petrol stations.
Dirt roads pose no insurmountable problem (given the low rainfall and flat terrain), but services are limited.

WHERE TO STAY

Most towns in outback New South Wales have at least one motel and a couple of hotels. There is often very little to choose from and travellers will only have to make a decision between a night in the pub or in a modest motel. In larger centres, like Gunnedah, Broken Hill and Dubbo, there is an active tourist industry with a wide range of facilities, but in smaller towns, like Wilcannia and Menindee, the range is more restricted. It is sensible to book ahead. The NRMA (check telephone directory) has listings of most of the available accommodation.

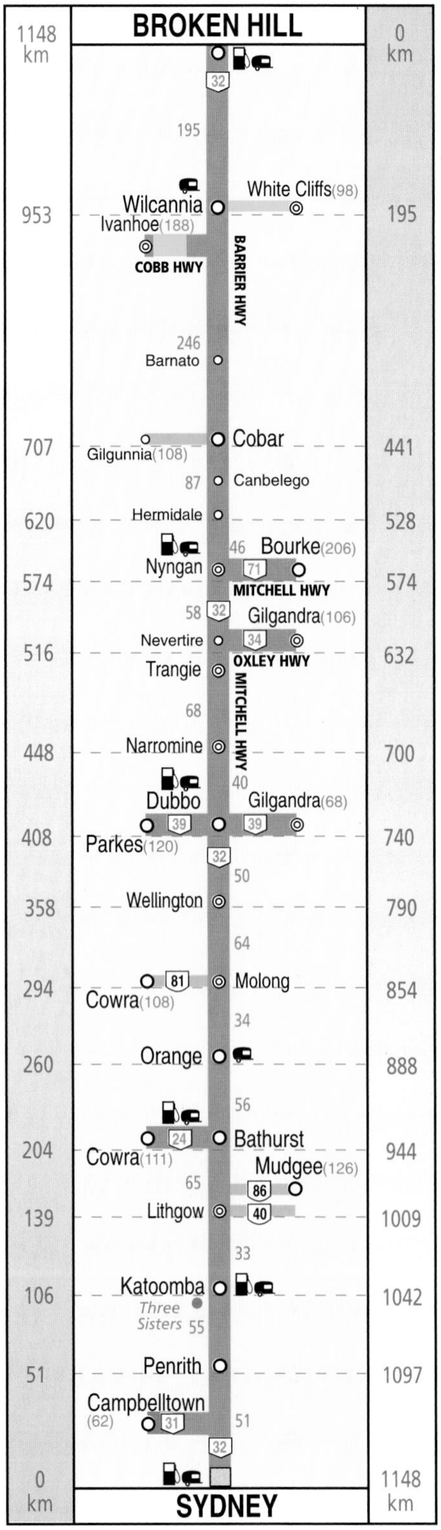

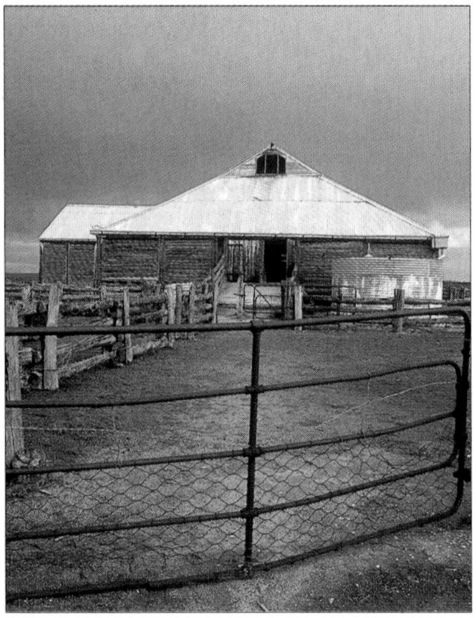

Left: *The Mungo woolshed was built by Chinese labourers in 1869 and stands beside the dry Lake Mungo basin.*

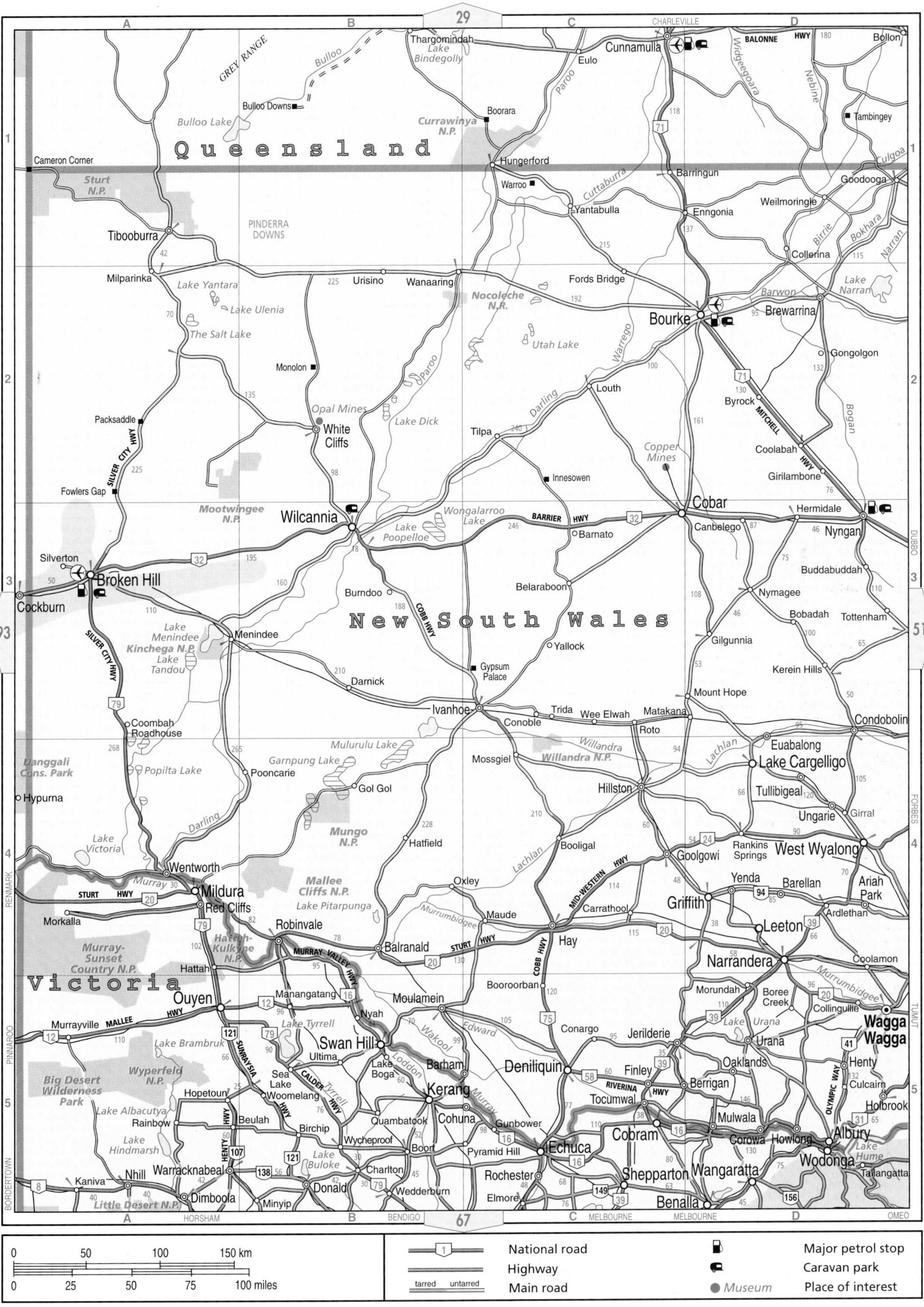

	National road		Major petrol stop
	Highway		Caravan park
tarred untarred	Main road	Museum	Place of interest

0   50   100   150 km

0   25   50   75   100 miles

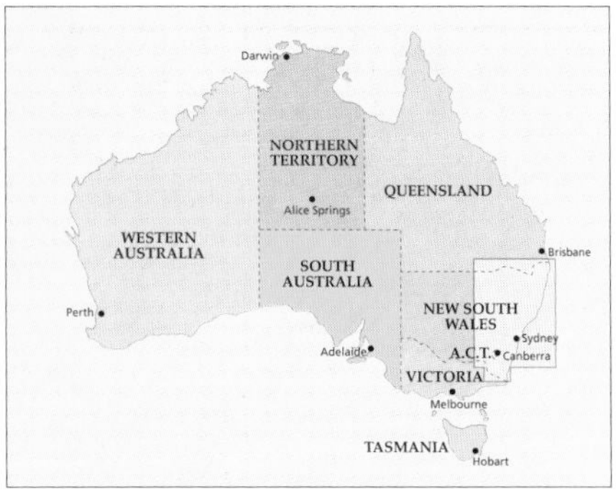

Eastern New South Wales

Most of the population of New South Wales lives along the state's eastern coast with the vast majority living in the large cities of Sydney, Newcastle and Wollongong. The coastline is characterised by a narrow, usually fertile coastal strip with attractive cliffs, headlands and beaches, sharply rising escarpments, and the rugged undulations of the low-lying Great Dividing Range. While there are many roads into the hinterland, the main road running north–south is the Pacific Highway (Sydney to Brisbane) and the Princes Highway (Sydney to the Victorian border).

TOP ATTRACTIONS

Berry: charming and fashionable village atmosphere with numerous eateries and gift shops.
Byron Bay: coastal resort, excellent beaches, interesting township and one of the country's most dramatically located lighthouses.
Jervis Bay: large, secluded bay with beautiful white sands and excellent bushwalking trails.
Royal National Park: stretches from the beaches of Wattamolla and Garie through the coastal wilderness to the quiet waters of the Hacking River.
Wollongong: fabulous views from the escarpment above the city, some of the most spectacular in Australia.

ON THE ROAD

The high concentration of residents in this region has ensured that roads are good. All the major roads are sealed, and between Sydney, Canberra, Wollongong and Newcastle they are multi-lane highways. There is also an abundance of services for cars on offer. Some of the smaller coastal roads and some of those that wind up the escarpments are quite narrow and poorly maintained. Details about these can be obtained from the local NRMA office. The phone number is available in local telephone directories.

Below: *Jervis Bay, south of Kiama, is a calm inlet with secluded beaches protected by the Beecroft Peninsula.*

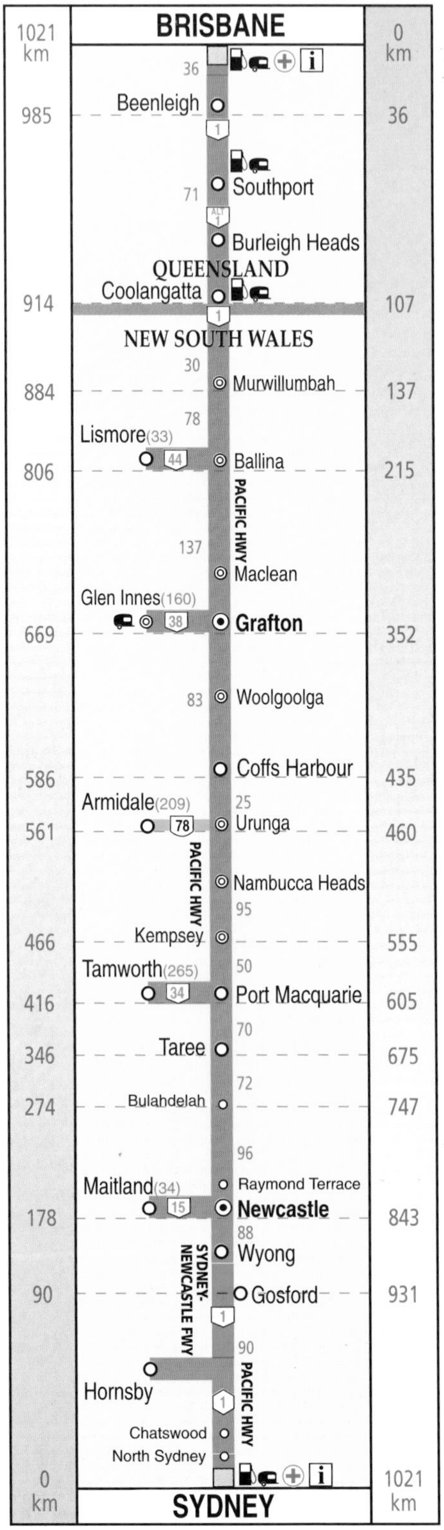

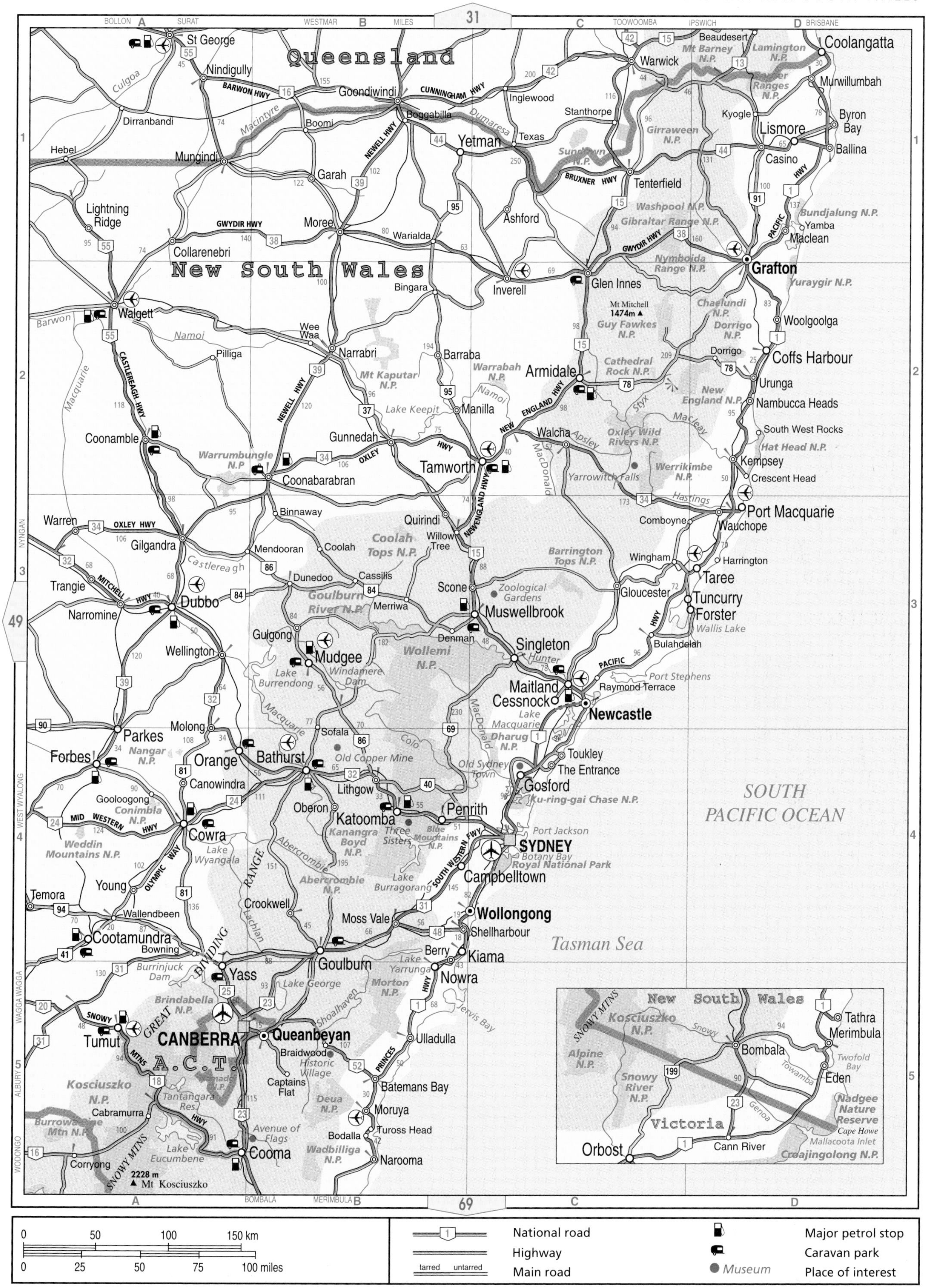

Queensland
New South Wales
South Pacific Ocean
Tasman Sea
St George
Nindigully
Goondiwindi
Boggabilla
Dirranbandi
Hebel
Mungindi
Boomi
Garah
Yetman
Texas
Inglewood
Stanthorpe
Warwick
Beaudesert
Coolangatta
Murwillumbah
Kyogle
Lismore
Byron Bay
Ballina
Casino
Tenterfield
Lightning Ridge
Collarenebri
Moree
Warialda
Ashford
Bingara
Inverell
Glen Innes
Grafton
Yamba
Maclean
Walgett
Wee Waa
Narrabri
Pilliga
Barraba
Manilla
Armidale
Dorrigo
Woolgoolga
Coffs Harbour
Urunga
Nambucca Heads
South West Rocks
Kempsey
Crescent Head
Coonamble
Gunnedah
Tamworth
Walcha
Coonabarabran
Binnaway
Quirindi
Willow Tree
Port Macquarie
Wauchope
Comboyne
Warren
Gilgandra
Mendooran
Coolah
Wingham
Harrington
Taree
Trangie
Dubbo
Narromine
Dunedoo
Cassilis
Merriwa
Scone
Muswellbrook
Gloucester
Tuncurry
Forster
Wallis Lake
Gulgong
Mudgee
Denman
Singleton
Bulahdelah
Wellington
Maitland
Cessnock
Raymond Terrace
Port Stephens
Newcastle
Parkes
Molong
Orange
Bathurst
Sofala
Forbes
Canowindra
Lithgow
Toukley
The Entrance
Gosford
Oberon
Katoomba
Three Sisters
Penrith
SYDNEY
Botany Bay
Port Jackson
Gooloogong
Cowra
Young
Temora
Campbelltown
Wollongong
Shellharbour
Kiama
Berry
Nowra
Crookwell
Moss Vale
Wallendbeen
Cootamundra
Bowning
Goulburn
Yass
Lake George
Tumut
CANBERRA
A.C.T.
Queanbeyan
Braidwood
Captains Flat
Ulladulla
Batemans Bay
Moruya
Tuross Head
Bodalla
Narooma
Cooma
Cabramurra
Corryong
Mt Kosciuszko 2228 m
Mt Mitchell 1474m
Jervis Bay
Lake Burrendong
Windamere Dam
Lake Macquarie
Lake Keepit
Lake Wyangala
Lake Burragorang
Burrinjuck Dam
Tantangara Res.
Lake Eucumbene
Yarrowitch Falls
Zoological Gardens
Old Copper Mine
Old Sydney Town
Braidwood Historic Village
Avenue of Flags
Lamington N.P.
Mt Barney N.P.
Border Ranges N.P.
Girraween N.P.
Sundown N.P.
Washpool N.P.
Gibraltar Range N.P.
Bundjalung N.P.
Nymboida Range N.P.
Yuraygir N.P.
Chaelundi N.P.
Guy Fawkes N.P.
Dorrigo N.P.
Cathedral Rock N.P.
New England N.P.
Warrabah N.P.
Mt Kaputar N.P.
Oxley Wild Rivers N.P.
Werrikimbe N.P.
Hat Head N.P.
Warrumbungle N.P.
Coolah Tops N.P.
Barrington Tops N.P.
Goulburn River N.P.
Wollemi N.P.
Dharug N.P.
Ku-ring-gai Chase N.P.
Nangar N.P.
Conimbla N.P.
Weddin Mountains N.P.
Kanangra Boyd N.P.
Blue Mountains N.P.
Royal National Park
Abercrombie N.P.
Morton N.P.
Kosciuszko N.P.
Namadgi N.P.
Burrowa-Pine Mtn N.P.
Deua N.P.
Wadbilliga N.P.
Great Dividing Range
Snowy Mtns
Barwon Hwy
Cunningham Hwy
Newell Hwy
Gwydir Hwy
Bruxner Hwy
Pacific Hwy
Castlereagh Hwy
Oxley Hwy
New England Hwy
Mitchell Hwy
Mid Western Hwy
Olympic Way
South Western Fwy
Princes Hwy
Snowy Mtns Hwy
Culgoa
Macintyre
Dumaresq
Barwon
Namoi
Macquarie
Castlereagh
Apsley
MacDonald
Macleay
Styx
Hastings
Hunter
Colo
Abercrombie
Lachlan
Shoalhaven
Bollon
Surat
Westmar
Miles
Toowoomba
Ipswich
Brisbane
Nyngan
West Wyalong
Wagga Wagga
Albury
Wodonga
Bombala
Merimbula
New South Wales
Victoria
Kosciuszko N.P.
Alpine N.P.
Snowy River N.P.
Bombala
Tathra
Merimbula
Twofold Bay
Eden
Nadgee Nature Reserve
Cape Howe
Mallacoota Inlet
Croajingolong N.P.
Orbost
Cann River
Towamba
Genoa
Snowy
0 50 100 150 km
0 25 50 75 100 miles
National road
Highway
tarred untarred
Main road
Major petrol stop
Caravan park
Museum
Place of interest

AUSTRALIAN CAPITAL TERRITORY

In the 1890s, the location of the national capital was a highly controversial debate. Federation of the states was due to occur in 1901 and the rivalry between the Sydney and Melbourne authorities was intense, neither side prepared to give way to the other. In an effort to resolve the dilemma, 2330km² (900 sq miles) of quality grazing land in southern New South Wales was set aside to become the Australian Capital Territory. On 1 January 1911 the ACT, as the territory is known, was officially handed over to the Commonwealth Government. That same year a competition for the design of a city for 25 000 people was launched and subsequently won by American landscape architect Walter Burley Griffin. His design for the national capital, Canberra, was based on a series of geometrically precise circles and axes, similar to the street patterns of Washington and Paris. The city is best seen in the autumn when the deciduous trees are in full colour, or in spring when the gardens are teeming with blooms.

The Australian Capital Territory is the area surrounding Canberra, the nation's capital. Explorers first passed through here in 1820. Encampment followed three years later, the first being called *Canberry*, the Aboriginal name for the region. The site of that town is now the location of Canberra's hospital. The western border of the territory is lined by the Brindabella Range, an extension of the slopes of the Snowy Mountains. The range then gives way to a countryside of pleasant rolling hills intersected by a number of rivers, notably the Molonglo and the Murrumbidgee. Almost half the ACT has been set aside as nature reserve, including the Namadgi National Park, and the Tidbinbilla and Gudgenby nature reserves. These unspoilt areas still indicate what the countryside must have looked like in those early days of settlement.

Canberra is a place of great style with its wide, gently curving roads, large numbers of impressive public buildings and vast areas of public parks and gardens. The city was purposely designed to be the federal capital of Australia and, as such, a showpiece for the continent. Chicago-born Walter Burley Griffin submitted a design proposal which sought to blend streets and buildings in harmony with the landscape. To achieve this he drew three axes – a land axis that runs from Mount Ainslie through to Bimberi Peak 2000m (6562ft) away, a water axis from Black Mountain through the lake, and a municipal axis which runs north of the lake – to meet at the spot he called 'Capital Hill', where the parliamentary buildings now stand. Griffin's vision, which follows the natural contours of the landscape, can best be seen from lookouts at Red Hill and Mount Ainslie, or from the roof of Parliament House.

Although Canberra's primary function is as the administrative capital of Australia, the city has developed into a major tourist attraction. Inevitably, most Australian school children make the journey to the city and are taken around Parliament House and the War Memorial. The visitor arriving in Canberra is treated with respect and affection. The city's information service is excellent and it is easy to spend a couple of days visiting the National Gallery (which boasts a superb collection of art works), the National Library, the Australian War Memorial which, with over one million visitors a year, is Australia's most visited museum, the old and new Parliament Houses, the Film and Sound Archives (which show early Australian movies) and the High Court.

The very central Parliament House was completed in 1988 and is located on top of Capital Hill. It has become the symbolic centre of the city and was designed so that visitors can walk up grassy slopes so they are, in fact, standing on top of the building. This not only keeps the contour of the hill intact, as per Burley Griffin's vision, it is also a simple demonstration of the idea that the building belongs to the people and the politicians are the servants of their public. The building contains both houses of the Australian federal parliament – the House of Representatives and the upper house, the Senate – and has an excellent art gallery. Parliament House is open to the public with free tours conducted daily. If the members are sitting, the public galleries offer an insight into Australian democracy.

Below Parliament House on King George Terrace is a stately white building. This was the house for the federal parliament from 1927, when it was officially opened (after having moved from Melbourne), to 1988 when the new Parliament House was completed. The old Parliament House, too, is open to the public and is now the home of the National Museum of Australia Exhibition, the National Portrait Gallery and the Australian Archives Gallery, and contains a café and a National Trust shop.

On the other side of the lake from both parliament houses is a broad avenue which stretches up the hill to the Australian War Memorial. This is a tribute to the country's military involvement in a number of wars, and the museum within offers excellent displays of memorabilia from those encounters.

A drive beside Lake Burley Griffin, a delightful centrepiece for the city, is also a must. An artificial lake, it was formed by the damming of the Molonglo River and has a neat shoreline that is popular with cyclists, walkers and joggers because of its marvellous network of cycleways and footpaths. It is possible to hire canoes and small boats to explore this body of water. One of its highlights is the spectacular Captain Cook Memorial Water Jet, a fine column of water shooting up to 140m (460ft) into the air. It is particularly impressive on windy days when the spray resembles a delicate curtain. A drive through Yarralumla to the west of Parliament House reveals very distinctive embassies, many built in the style of their own country's architecture.

The High Court of Australia resides on the shores of Lake Burley Griffin and is an impressive building with a gently cascading artificial waterfall. It has a popular restaurant and three major court rooms. It is the highest court in the country, hence the name.

The National Gallery of Australia is next to the High Court and houses a very comprehensive collection of Australian and overseas artists.

In recent years it has exhibited some of the finest international collections from around the world, making it a world-class gallery.

Other attractions of the territory include the Canberra Space Centre near Tidbinbilla, Mount Stromlo Observatory on the Cotter Road, the wall of the Cotter Dam, and Cockington Green, a miniature English village on the road from Yass. The areas just beyond the borders of the ACT include the beautiful Brindabella Valley and the remarkable Lake George, which has been known to disappear overnight during dry weather. Also of interest is Canberra's beautiful Botanic Gardens which display only Australian native species. The Telstra Tower on Black Mountain offers the best panoramic view of the city.

Right: *Parliament House was built into Capital Hill and the grassy slopes allow visitors to walk over the building.*

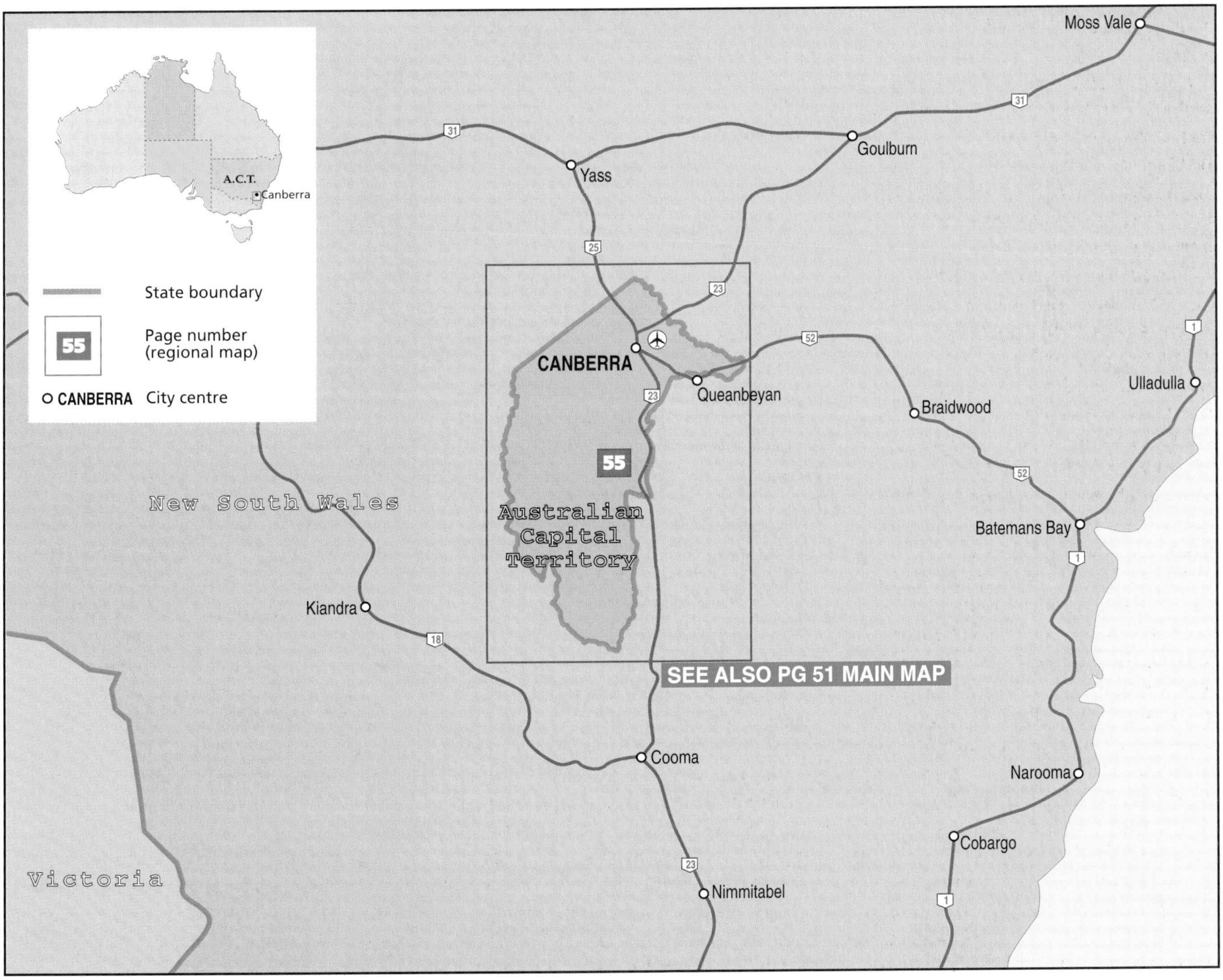

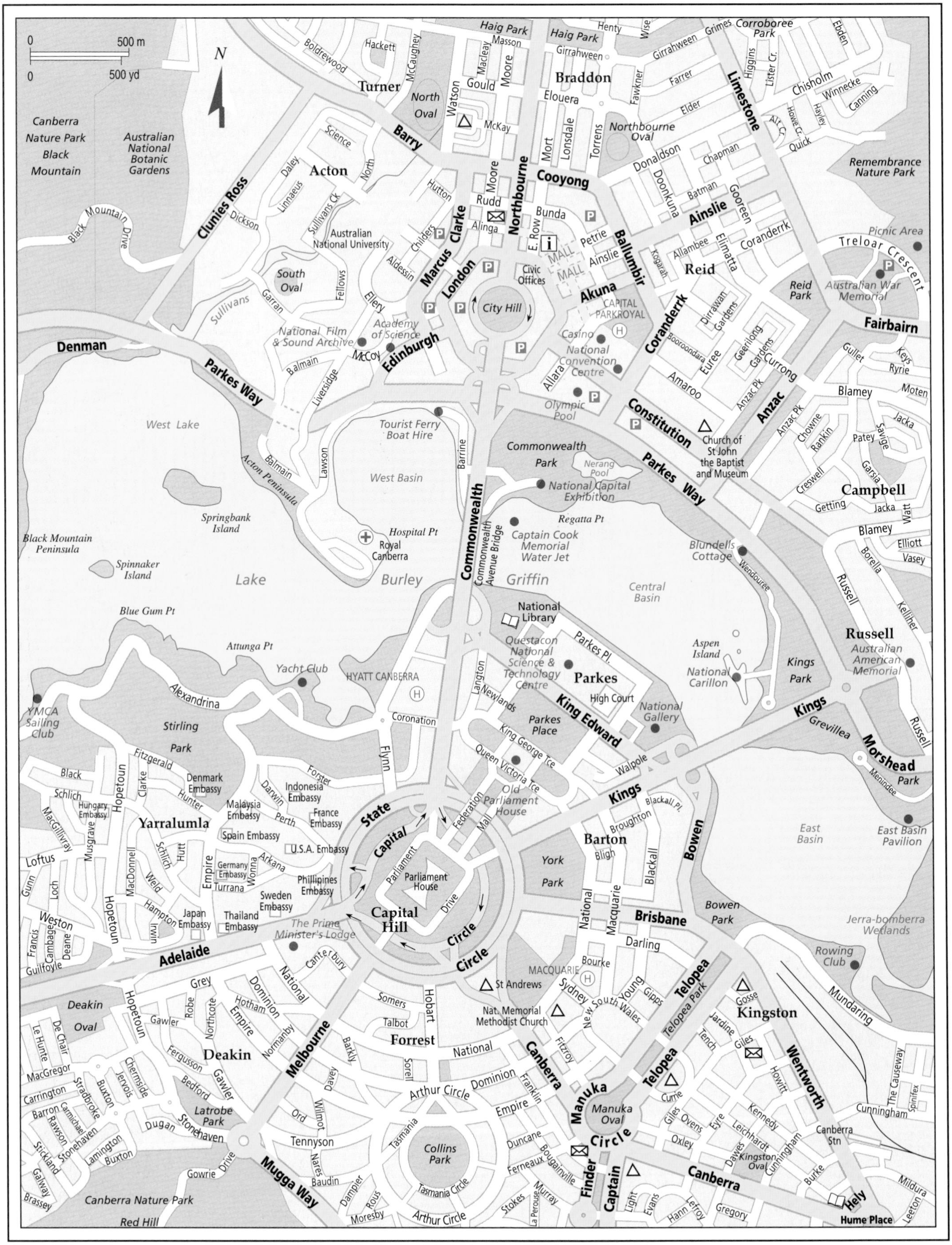

△ St Patricks	Place of worship	(bus symbol)	Bus terminus	(envelope symbol)	Post office
(H)	Hotel	●	Police station	● *Market*	Place of interest
[i]	Information	[P]	Parking	(+)	Hospital

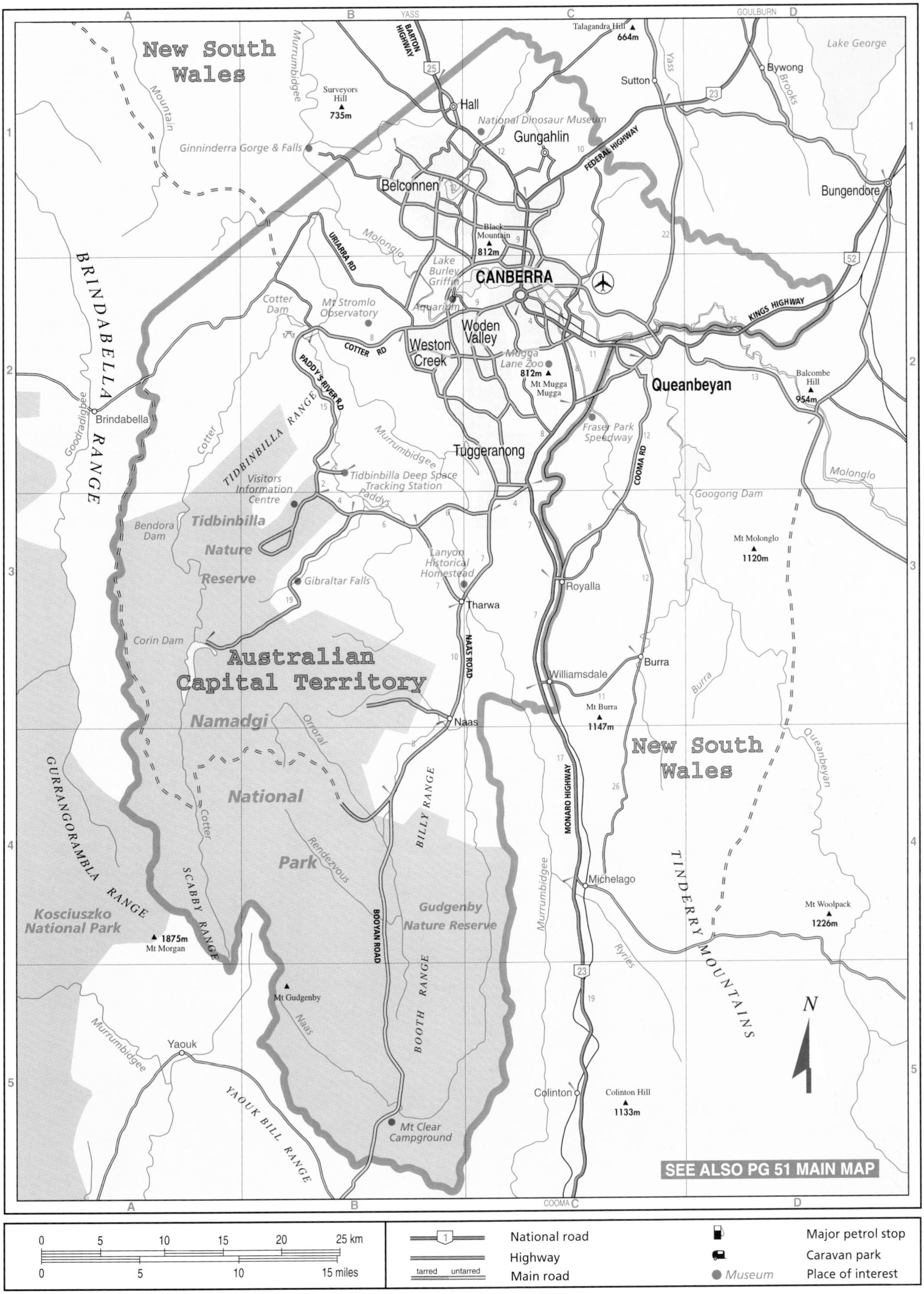
New South Wales
Australian Capital Territory
CANBERRA
Hall
Gungahlin
Belconnen
Weston Creek
Woden Valley
Tuggeranong
Queanbeyan
Sutton
Bywong
Bungendore
Lake George
Royalla
Tharwa
Williamsdale
Burra
Naas
Michelago
Colinton
Yaouk
Brindabella
BARTON HIGHWAY
FEDERAL HIGHWAY
KINGS HIGHWAY
MONARO HIGHWAY
COOMA RD
NAAS ROAD
BOOYAN ROAD
URIARRA RD
COTTER RD
PADDY'S RIVER RD
National Dinosaur Museum
Ginninderra Gorge & Falls
Mt Stromlo Observatory
Lake Burley Griffin
Aquarium
Mugga Lane Zoo
Fraser Park Speedway
Tidbinbilla Deep Space Tracking Station
Visitors Information Centre
Tidbinbilla Nature Reserve
Gibraltar Falls
Lanyon Historical Homestead
Namadgi National Park
Gudgenby Nature Reserve
Kosciuszko National Park
Mt Clear Campground
Cotter Dam
Bendora Dam
Corin Dam
Googong Dam
Surveyors Hill 735m
Talagandra Hill 664m
Black Mountain 812m
812m Mt Mugga Mugga
Balcombe Hill 954m
Mt Molonglo 1120m
Mt Burra 1147m
Mt Woolpack 1226m
Colinton Hill 1133m
1875m Mt Morgan
Mt Gudgenby
BRINDABELLA RANGE
TIDBINBILLA RANGE
GURRANGORAMBLA RANGE
SCABBY RANGE
BILLY RANGE
BOOTH RANGE
YAOUK BILL RANGE
TINDERRY MOUNTAINS
Murrumbidgee
Molonglo
Cotter
Mountain
Goodradigbee
Paddys
Orroral
Rendezvous
Naas
Ryries
Queanbeyan
Burra
Yass
Brooks
YASS
GOULBURN
COOMA
N
SEE ALSO PG 51 MAIN MAP
0 5 10 15 20 25 km
0 5 10 15 miles
National road
Highway
tarred untarred
Main road
Major petrol stop
Caravan park
Museum
Place of interest

VICTORIA

Covering 227 620km² (87 861 sq miles), only 3 per cent of mainland Australia, Victoria occupies the south-eastern corner of the continent. Australia's smallest mainland state, it contains the continent's second-largest city, possibly the country's most scenic coastline (the highlight of which is the Great Ocean Road, complete with the Twelve Apostles, an extraordinary collection of rocky outcrops), superb beaches (including Bells Beach, one of the best surfing beaches in the world), a semi-desert area, snowfields, and a river that used to be one of the country's major transport routes. No trip to Victoria is complete without visiting old gold-mining towns like Stawell, Ballarat and Bendigo (which was mined continuously for over a century). Ballarat's famous tourist attraction, Sovereign Hill, offers an opportunity to understand the way this tiny state developed both financially and socially.

Victoria is Australia's second-smallest state. Home to over 25 per cent of the country's population it is consequently the most densely populated. Victoria's greatest appeal, apart from its reputation as 'The Garden State', is that it offers a large variety of activities and differing landscapes to its visitors. The state's 1200km (745 miles) of coastline provides some of the most dramatic scenery in the country. To the west is the dry, near-desert of the Mallee, to the north are the southern edges of the Snowy Mountains with their popular ski resorts, and in the centre of the state are the beautiful Grampian Ranges.

From Swan Hill on the Murray River across to the Snowy Mountains, the north-central and north-eastern regions of Victoria encompass a wide variety of climatic, geographic and economic areas. At Swan Hill the landscape is monotonously flat. Heading south-east the terrain turns into gently undulating slopes until the mountainous region on the east coast is reached. These mountains experience significant snowfalls and sub-zero temperatures in the winter.

The Snowy Mountains form part of the Great Dividing Range, which follows the east coast from north Queensland until it swings westward in Victoria, creating a low-lying range of basalt hills and rich alluvial plains in the central highlands district, north-west of Melbourne. This region has good volcanic soils, mild temperatures and reliable rainfall. At Castlemaine, for example, the average January temperature ranges from 12.7°C (55°F) to 28.8°C (84°F), in winter it drops to between 2°C (36°F) and 12°C (54°F). Castlemaine has an annual rainfall of around 624mm (25 inches).

The central highlands were settled in the 1830s by about 70 or 80 squatters who turned the land into areas producing fat lambs and wool. Today, in spite of the state's relatively small size, Victoria has a sheep population only exceeded by that of New South Wales and Western Australia. The primary industries are lamb and fine wool, but wheat, beef and dairy products are also important to Victoria's economy. There are nearly three million beef cattle and 1.5 million dairy cattle in the state.

Victoria is rich in resources, which has resulted in a strong and productive economic base. What initially boosted the state from a small rural outpost to a major political and social power were the gold rushes of the 19th century. Gold was first discovered here as early as 1845 but it wasn't until the serious gold rushes of the 1850s that the fossickers and miners moved into the area. In 1851 gold was found at the tiny settlement of Clunes. The first major discovery occurred at Beechworth in 1852. It was quickly followed by discoveries at Omeo, Cornishtown, Myrtleford, Woolshed, Spring Creek, Yackandandah and Rutherglen. Gold was subsequently discovered at over 20 sites throughout the highlands region, including substantial strikes at Buninyong, Castlemaine, Ballarat, Bendigo, Allendale, Beaufort, Carngham, Wedderburn, Dunolly, Creswick, Moliagul and Smythesdale.

Gold fever brought tens of thousands of new settlers to the area. At its height the town of Beechworth had a population of nearly 22 500 and from 1852 to 1866 over 85 million grams (3 million ounces) of gold

Left: *The most enchanting way to explore Victoria's northern border is a paddle steamer trip along the Murray River.*

were mined in the area. Its obvious status as the centre of a vital gold-mining region led to the establishment of a hospital, telegraph office, subtreasury, courthouse and gaol. During its heyday the town had 61 hotels, four breweries and a theatre where such goldfields entertainers as the notorious Lola Montez performed. In 1911 the town's population had dropped to 3409 and now it is only a little over 3000. Today, Beechworth services the surrounding pastoral area and relies on tourism. More than 80 of its old buildings have been classified by the National Trust, making it one of the best-preserved historic gold towns in the country.

Myrtleford, south of Beechworth on the Ovens River, is another town that boomed during the 1850s then waned until after World War II, when large numbers of migrants, mostly from Italy, Spain and the former Yugoslavia, arrived in the area and established tobacco and hop farms and walnut orchards.

Similarly Rutherglen, once a gold town with a population of 25 000, is now known as a centre for viticulture. Its renowned annual wine festival, viticultural college and Vine Growers Association have helped to make it one of Victoria's most important wine-producing towns.

The entire town of Yackandandah, with its tiny population of under 500, is classified by the National Trust and consequently relies upon tourism to sustain it. At its height it supported 3000 miners, many of whom had travelled from the North American goldfields on the Klondike and in California.

Beyond the gold towns are the important Murray River towns of Swan Hill, Echuca, Yarrawonga and Wodonga. These centres were largely unaffected by the gold rushes. Surrounded by pastoralists, they gained importance with the steamer trade along the river. The first paddle steamer from South Australia reached Swan Hill in 1853 and the following year port facilities were established at Wodonga. The importance of the river ports resulted in the rapid growth of the region. Today the romantic riverboat past is recaptured with paddle steamer journeys down the Murray. The huge *Murray River Queen* still runs cruises downriver to Goolwa in South Australia.

It has been argued that the Great Ocean Road, which starts at Torquay south-west of Melbourne and winds around the coast for 250km (155 miles), affords drivers the most beautiful coastal landscape anywhere.

Dramatic coastlines create the whole southern and eastern borders of the state, from Discovery Bay near South Australia to Croajingolong National Park near the New South Wales border. Along the way there are rock arches, stacks and blowholes, nature reserves, national parks and stunning beaches, including the seemingly endless expanse of sand at Ninety Mile Beach.

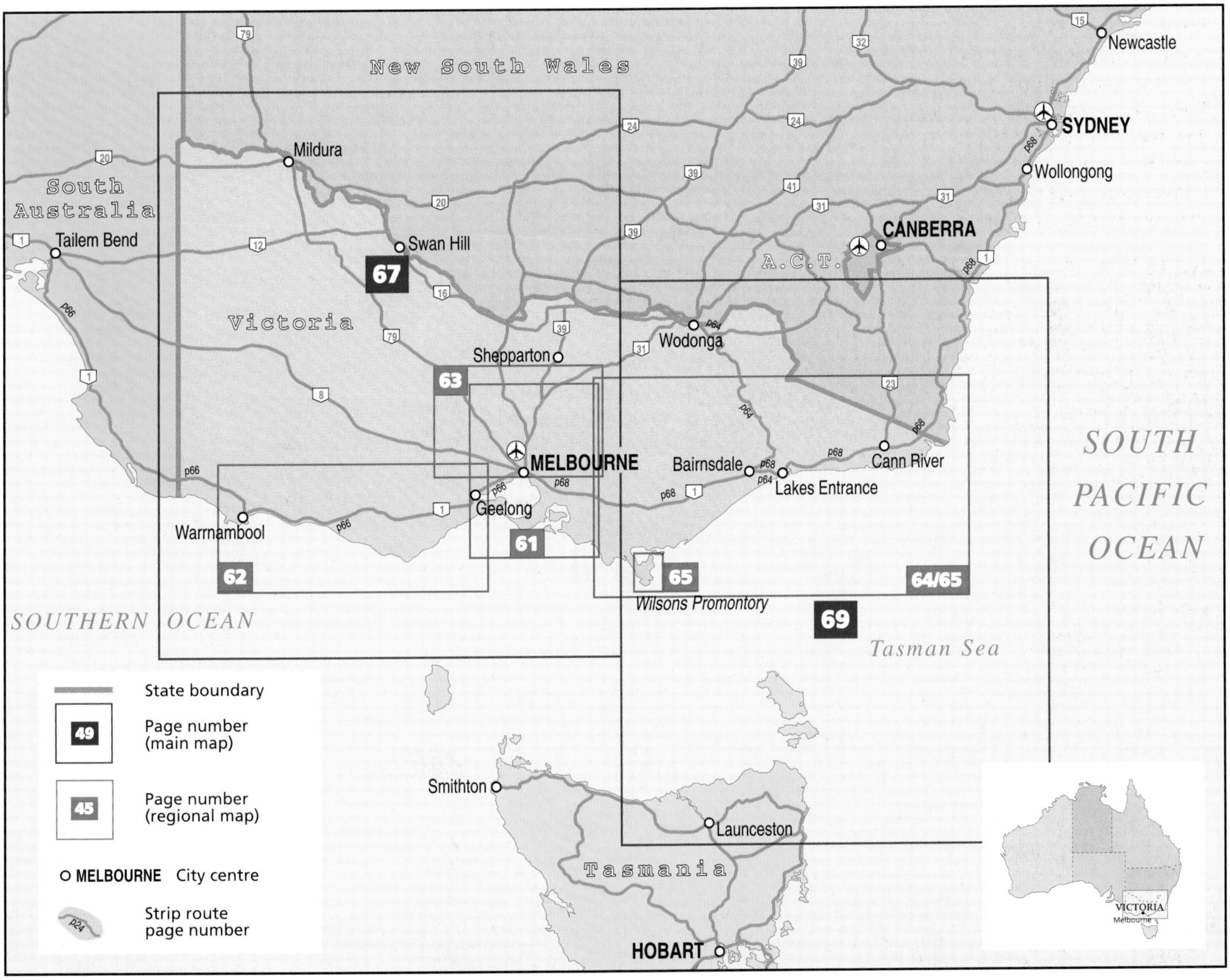

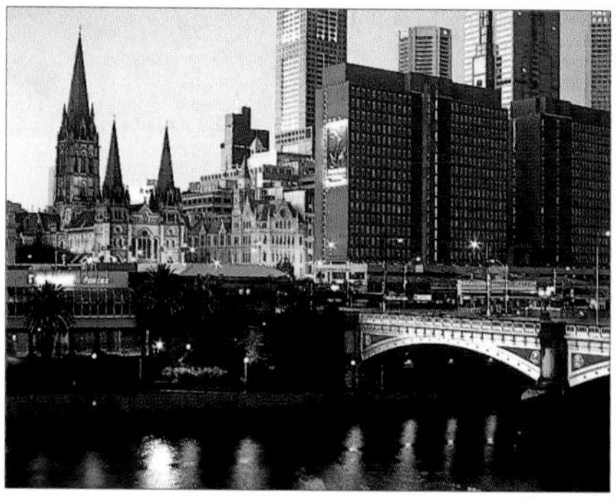

Melbourne

Melbourne, the capital of Victoria, is a sophisticated and modern city with a population that has grown to over three million and a total area of nearly 1300km^2 (500 sq miles). This cosmopolitan capital is located around the shores of Port Phillip Bay and stretches from the mouth of the Little River to the edges of the Portland Hills, the Hume Range, the Kinglake Plateau, and the Dandenong Ranges. While it was gold which made Melbourne Australia's largest city in the 1850s, it is the impressive Victorian Arts Centre and the restored 19th-century buildings that have given the city its 'culture capital' title today.

TOP ATTRACTIONS

Captain Cook's Cottage: was transported to the Fitzroy Gardens in Melbourne from Yorkshire, England.
National Gallery of Victoria: one of the finest in the country, excellent exhibitions.
Public Gardens: excellent parks, notably the **Royal Botanic Gardens**, the **King's Domain** with La Trobe Cottage (1839) and the Shrine of Remembrance, and the **Fitzroy Gardens**.
Southbank: entertainment and restaurant complex, including a casino, beside the Yarra River.
Trams: delightful way to explore Melbourne city.
Victorian architecture: Block Arcade (1892), Rialto Building (1890s), Royal Arcade (1869), Princess Theatre (1866), Exhibition Buildings (1880).
Victorian Arts Centre: contains the **National Gallery**, the **State Theatre**, drama theatres, and a 2500-seat **Concert Hall**.
Yarra River: enjoy walks along the banks or hop on a cruise.

MELBOURNE	J	F	M	A	M	J	J	A	S	O	N	D
AV. TEMP. °F	68	68	66	63	57	53	52	53	55	59	63	64
AV. TEMP. °C	20	20	19	17	14	12	11	12	13	15	17	18
DAILY SUN hrs	8	7	6	5	4	3	4	4	5	6	7	7
RAINFALL mm	48	48	52	58	58	50	49	51	59	68	60	59
RAINFALL in	2	2	2	2	2	2	2	2	2	2.5	2.5	2
RAINFALL days	8	7	9	12	14	14	15	16	15	14	12	11

Above, left: *The Yarra River flows through Melbourne, crossed by the Princes Bridge and overlooked by the spires of St Paul's.*
Above: *The Victorian Arts Centre is the central venue for Melbourne's cultural activities.*
Below: *Government House is surrounded by Melbourne's Royal Botanic Gardens, south-east of the city centre.*

WHERE TO STAY

All Seasons Premier Swanston Hotel, Swanston St, tel: (03) 9663 4711, fax: 9663 8191.
Batman Hill Hotel, Spencer St, tel: (03) 9614 6344, fax: 9614 1189.
Birches Boutique Apartments, Simpson St, tel: (03) 9417 2344, fax: 9349 1250.
Hotel Grand Chancellor, Lonsdale St, tel: (03) 9663 3161, fax: 9662 3479.
Le Meridien Melbourne, Collins St, tel: (03) 9620 9111, 1 800 331 330, fax: 9614 1219.
Magnolia Court Hotel, Powlett St, tel: (03) 9419 4222, fax: 9416 0841.
Riverside Apartments, cnr Flinders St and Highlander Lane, tel: (03) 9772 9190.
Treasury Motor Lodge, Powlett St, tel: (03) 9417 5281, fax: 9416 0893.
Windsor, Spring St, tel: (03) 9653 0653, fax: 9633 6001.

CALENDAR OF EVENTS

JANUARY: Summer in the City, Chinese New Year, Victoria Street Lunar Festival, Australian Open Tennis Championships.
FEBRUARY: Music Festival, Australian Masters Golf Tournament.
MARCH: International Motor Show in Moomba, Chinatown Food Festival, Great Melbourne Bike Ride.
APRIL: International Comedy Festival.
JULY: Great Australian Science Show, International Film Festival.
SEPTEMBER: International Festival of the Arts, Royal Melbourne Show, Exhibition of Victorian Winemakers, AFL Grand Final.
OCTOBER: Autumn Moon Lantern Festival, Caulfield Cup, Oktoberfest, Derby Day.
NOVEMBER: Melbourne Cup Day, Lygon Street Fiesta, World Weightlifting Championships.
DECEMBER: Carols by Candlelight.

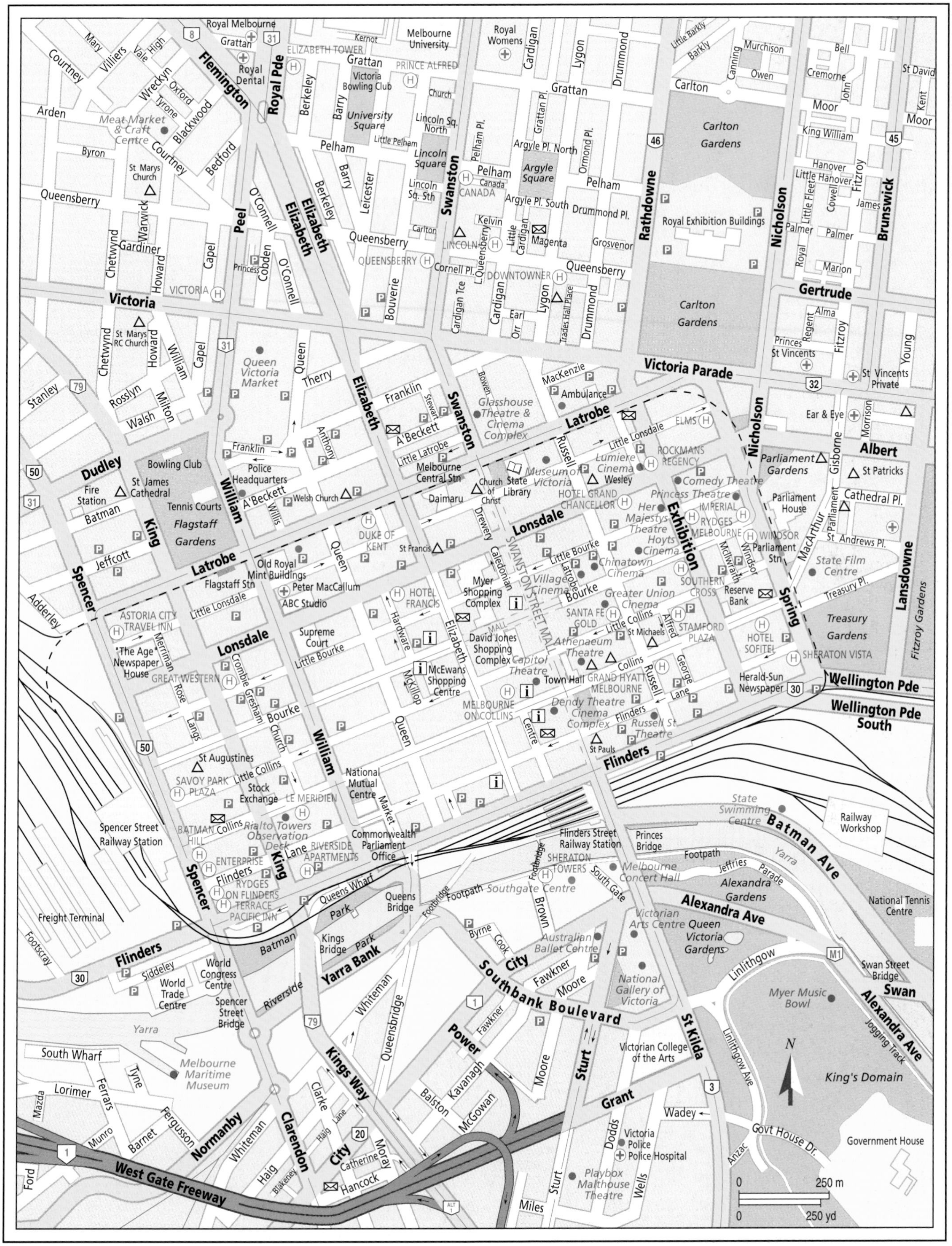

St Patricks	Place of worship		Bus terminus		Post office
	Hotel		Police station	Market	Place of interest
	Information		Parking		Tram line

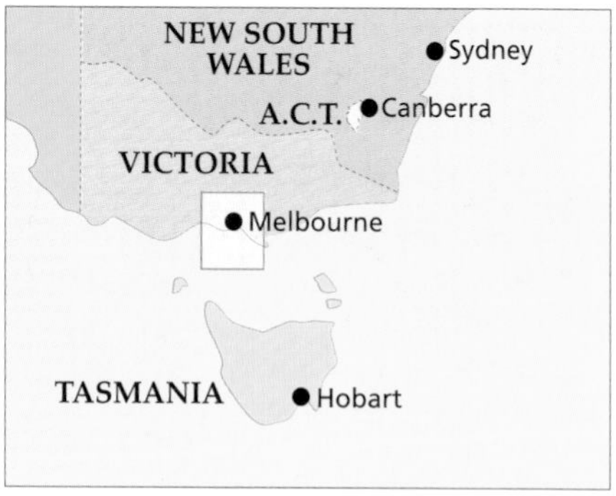

Melbourne Daytrips

It should be remembered that the relative small size of the state and the proximity of many major attractions to the capital ensures that the visitor has a number of excellent choices for daytrips, including the Great Ocean Road and Ballarat. The most popular excursion is from Melbourne to the Mornington Peninsula with its attractive seaside resort towns of Mornington, Sorrento and Portsea. The area offers a variety of things to see and do including bushwalking and water sports, as well as the option of crossing Port Phillip Bay by ferry to Queenscliff. Another popular daytrip is the Dandenong Ranges.

TOP ATTRACTIONS

Bellarine Peninsula: west of Port Phillip, Fort Queenscliff is perched on its southern extremity.
Dandenongs: temperate rain-forest mountains, abundant wildlife, including the lyrebird.
Geelong: more than 100 National Trust-classified buildings.
Mornington Peninsula: spit of land on the eastern side of Port Phillip Bay, exceptional beaches.
Phillip Island: famous for the evening parade of fairy penguins.
Puffing Billy Scenic Railway: 13-km (8-mile) journey from Belgrave to Emerald Lake Park on a restored steam train.
William Ricketts Sanctuary: filled with sculptures by the eccentric artist.

APPROX. DISTANCES IN KM FROM MELBOURNE	
Ballarat	116
Bendigo	154
Bordertown	459
Corryong	426
Geelong	75
Horsham	300
Leongatha	148
Mildura	559
Mt Gambier	482
Orbost	375
Warrnambool	266
Yarram	230

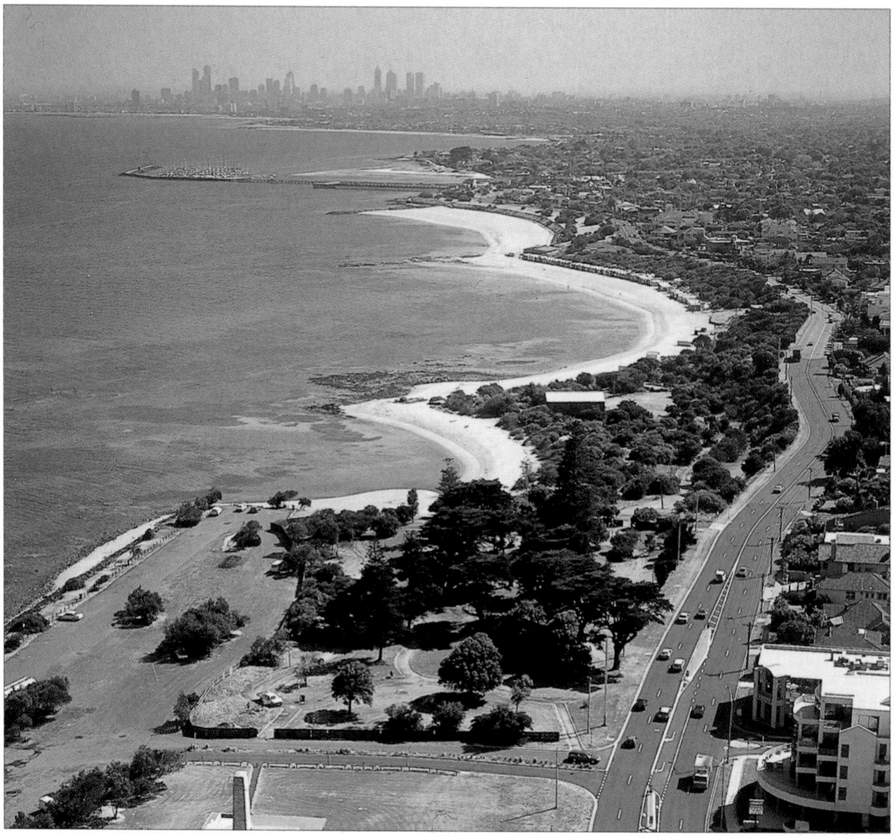

Above, right: *Puffing Billy, the oldest steam train in Victoria, has been lovingly restored and maintained by volunteers.*
Right: *Brighton Beach, on the shoreline of Port Phillip Bay, is reached from the city by the aptly named Beach Road.*

Victoria

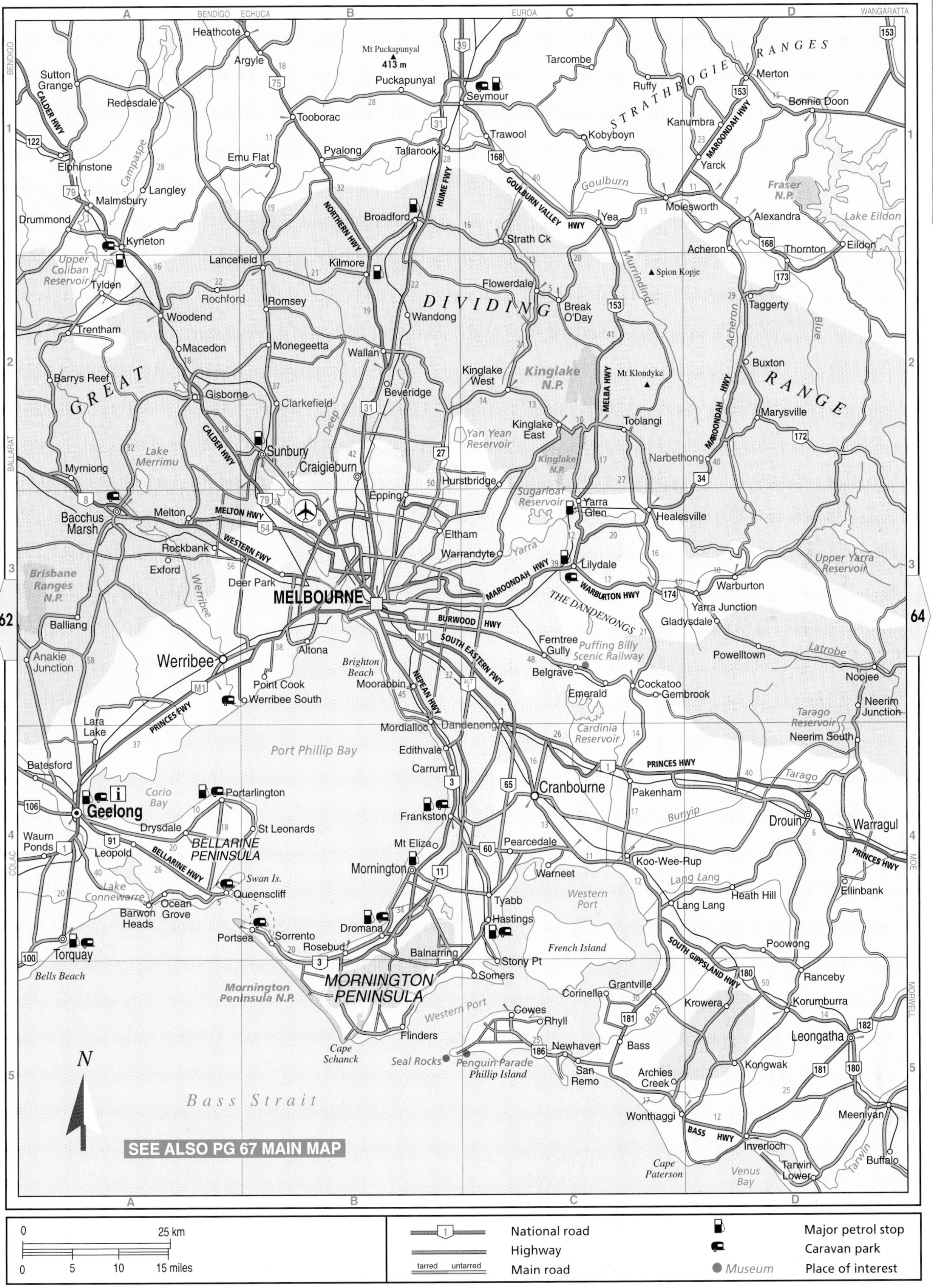
BENDIGO
ECHUCA
EUROA
WANGARATTA
BALLARAT
COLAC
MOE
MORWELL
62
64
Heathcote
Argyle
Mt Puckapunyal
413 m
Puckapunyal
Seymour
Tarcombe
Ruffy
STRATHBOGIE RANGES
Merton
Bonnie Doon
Sutton Grange
CALDER HWY
Redesdale
Tooborac
Trawool
Kobyboyn
Kanumbra
MAROONDAH HWY
Elphinstone
Emu Flat
Pyalong
Tallarook
HUME FWY
GOULBURN VALLEY HWY
Yarck
Campaspe
Langley
Malmsbury
Drummond
NORTHERN HWY
Broadford
Goulburn
Yea
Molesworth
Fraser N.P.
Alexandra
Lake Eildon
Kyneton
Strath Ck
Acheron
Thornton
Eildon
Upper Coliban Reservoir
Tylden
Lancefield
Kilmore
Murrindindi
Spion Kopje
Rochford
Romsey
Flowerdale
DIVIDING
Break O'Day
Taggerty
Woodend
Wandong
Trentham
Macedon
Monegeetta
Wallan
Blue
Acheron
Buxton
Barrys Reef
GREAT
Gisborne
Kinglake West
Kinglake N.P.
Mt Klondyke
MELBA HWY
RANGE
Clarkefield
Beveridge
Marysville
Deep
Yan Yean Reservoir
Kinglake East
Toolangi
Lake Merrimu
Sunbury
Craigieburn
Narbethong
Myrniong
Hurstbridge
Sugarloaf Reservoir
Yarra Glen
Healesville
Bacchus Marsh
Melton
MELTON HWY
Epping
Eltham
Rockbank
WESTERN FWY
Warrandyte
Yarra
Lilydale
Upper Yarra Reservoir
Exford
Brisbane Ranges N.P.
Werribee
Deer Park
MELBOURNE
MAROONDAH HWY
WARBURTON HWY
Warburton
Yarra Junction
THE DANDENONGS
Gladysdale
Balliang
BURWOOD HWY
SOUTH EASTERN FWY
Ferntree Gully
Puffing Billy Scenic Railway
Powelltown
Latrobe
Anakie Junction
Werribee
Altona
Brighton Beach
Belgrave
Noojee
Point Cook
Moorabbin
NEPEAN HWY
Cockatoo
Gembrook
Werribee South
Emerald
Neerim Junction
PRINCES FWY
Lara Lake
Mordialloc
Dandenong
Tarago Reservoir
Cardinia Reservoir
Neerim South
Port Phillip Bay
Edithvale
Batesford
Carrum
PRINCES HWY
Tarago
Corio Bay
Portarlington
Cranbourne
Pakenham
Geelong
Drysdale
St Leonards
Frankston
Bunyip
Drouin
Warragul
Waurn Ponds
BELLARINE PENINSULA
Leopold
BELLARINE HWY
Mt Eliza
Pearcedale
Koo-Wee-Rup
PRINCES HWY
Swan Is.
Mornington
Warneet
Lang Lang
Ellinbank
Lake Connewarre
Ocean Grove
Queenscliff
Western Port
Heath Hill
Barwon Heads
Tyabb
Lang Lang
Hastings
Dromana
Portsea
Sorrento
Rosebud
French Island
Poowong
Torquay
Balnarring
Stony Pt
SOUTH GIPPSLAND HWY
Bells Beach
MORNINGTON PENINSULA
Somers
Ranceby
Grantville
Mornington Peninsula N.P.
Corinella
Krowera
Korumburra
Cowes
Western Port
Bass
Rhyll
Flinders
Leongatha
Cape Schanck
Newhaven
Bass
Seal Rocks
Penguin Parade Phillip Island
San Remo
Kongwak
Archies Creek
N
Bass Strait
Wonthaggi
Meeniyan
BASS HWY
Inverloch
SEE ALSO PG 67 MAIN MAP
Cape Paterson
Venus Bay
Tarwin Lower
Tarwin
Buffalo
0
25 km
0
5
10
15 miles
National road
Highway
tarred
untarred
Main road
Major petrol stop
Caravan park
Museum
Place of interest

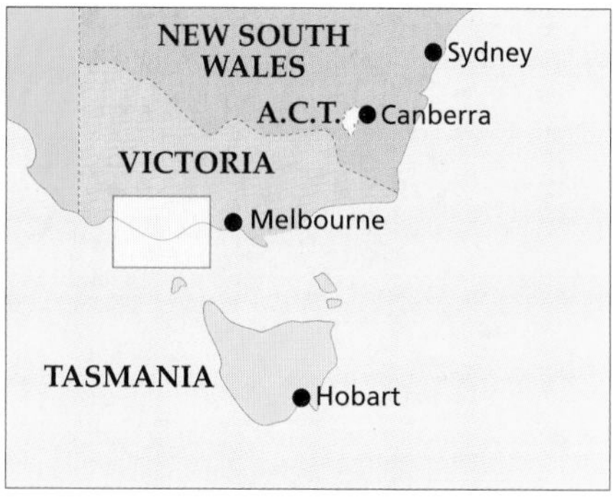

Great Ocean Road

Regarded as one of the finest scenic routes in Australia, the Great Ocean Road runs from Torquay to Peterborough and offers spectacular vistas of the sheer cliffs and wild beachfronts of the Southern Ocean. The Great Ocean Road is a memorial to the soldiers who died in World War I, and was built over a 15-year period by ex-servicemen of that time. Today it is a well-maintained sealed road winding for 300km (186 miles) around this dramatic section of coastline and it passes through the small, picturesque seaside towns of Anglesea, Lorne, Apollo Bay and Port Campbell until it reaches Peterborough.

TOP ATTRACTIONS

Apollo Bay & Cape Otway: a number of shipwrecks have occurred off the cape. Cape Otway Lighthouse is 100m (328ft) high and was built by convicts in 1848.

Port Campbell National Park: includes the famous Twelve Apostles, Loch Ard Gorge and the London Bridge, the span of which collapsed into the sea in 1990.

Torquay, Anglesea and Lorne: popular seaside resorts.

ON THE ROAD

The Great Ocean Road captivates the millions of travellers who come to marvel at the endless vistas along the coastline. The best lookout areas are clearly signposted and there are parking facilities. The isolation of the area means that breaking down can involve a wait for assistance, though all the towns along the road have some form of service station. The road that leads to Cape Otway lighthouse is a little rugged, but the trip is well worth the inconvenience.

Right: *The Twelve Apostles are rocky tors that have withstood the onslaught of the Southern Ocean.*

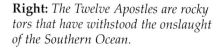

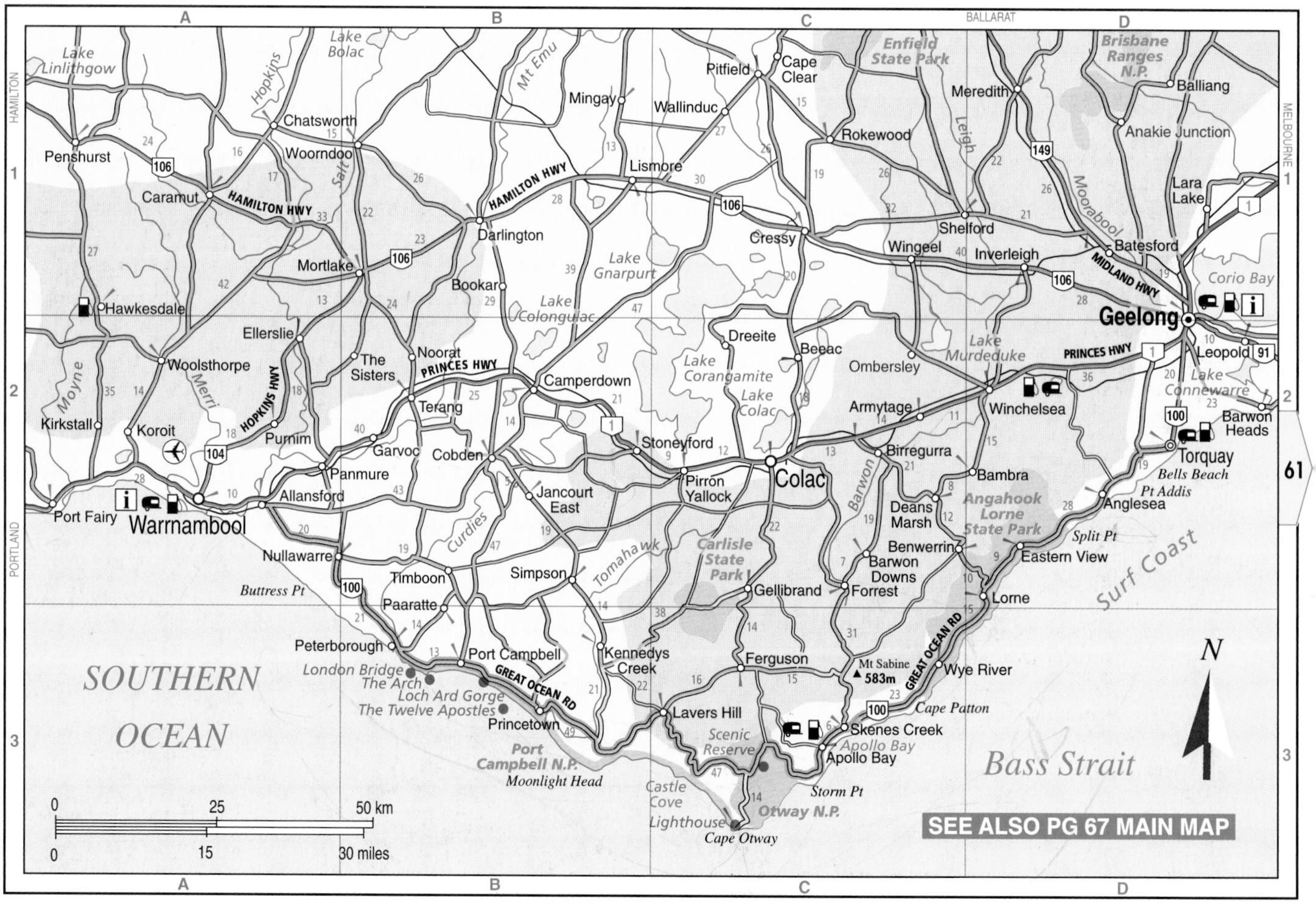

Bendigo to Ballarat

Ballarat and Bendigo are two of Victoria's premier tourist destinations. Ballarat is famous for Sovereign Hill, a fascinating and entertaining recreation of a gold rush town. It also has a Gold Museum, a memorial to the Eureka Stockade and a fine Art Gallery comprising an exceptional collection of Australian paintings. Bendigo's cosmopolitan gold rush days have left it with a rich and unusual range of attractions including a Chinese joss house, a pottery which was founded by a Scottish entrepreneur in the 1850s, a number of wineries and a mine, the Central Deborah Mine, specially opened for tourists.

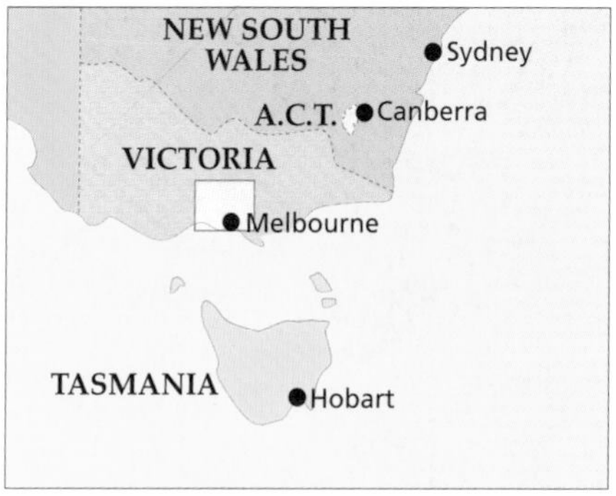

TOP ATTRACTIONS

Ballarat: largest Victorian inland city, with numerous galleries, museums and craft shops.
Bendigo: many historic buildings display the wealth that came from the goldfields.
Clunes: site of first gold find, surrounded by extinct volcanoes.
Eureka Stockade, Ballarat: site of 1854 miners' rebellion.
Sovereign Hill, Ballarat: authentic theme park of the 1850s gold-mining town.

ON THE ROAD

The journey from Bendigo to Ballarat passes through an attractive terrain of rolling hills. The area is noted for its mineral springs (Daylesford, Castlemaine) and some truly exceptional, well-preserved gold-mining towns. It is worth deviating from the main road to visit Maldon, which has changed little in the past century. The area has good services, but petrol and mechanical assistance may be difficult to get on Sundays in the smaller centres. It is possible to travel from Melbourne to both centres in a day.

Left: *Sovereign Hill re-creates the ambience of the towns that flourished during the gold rush days.*

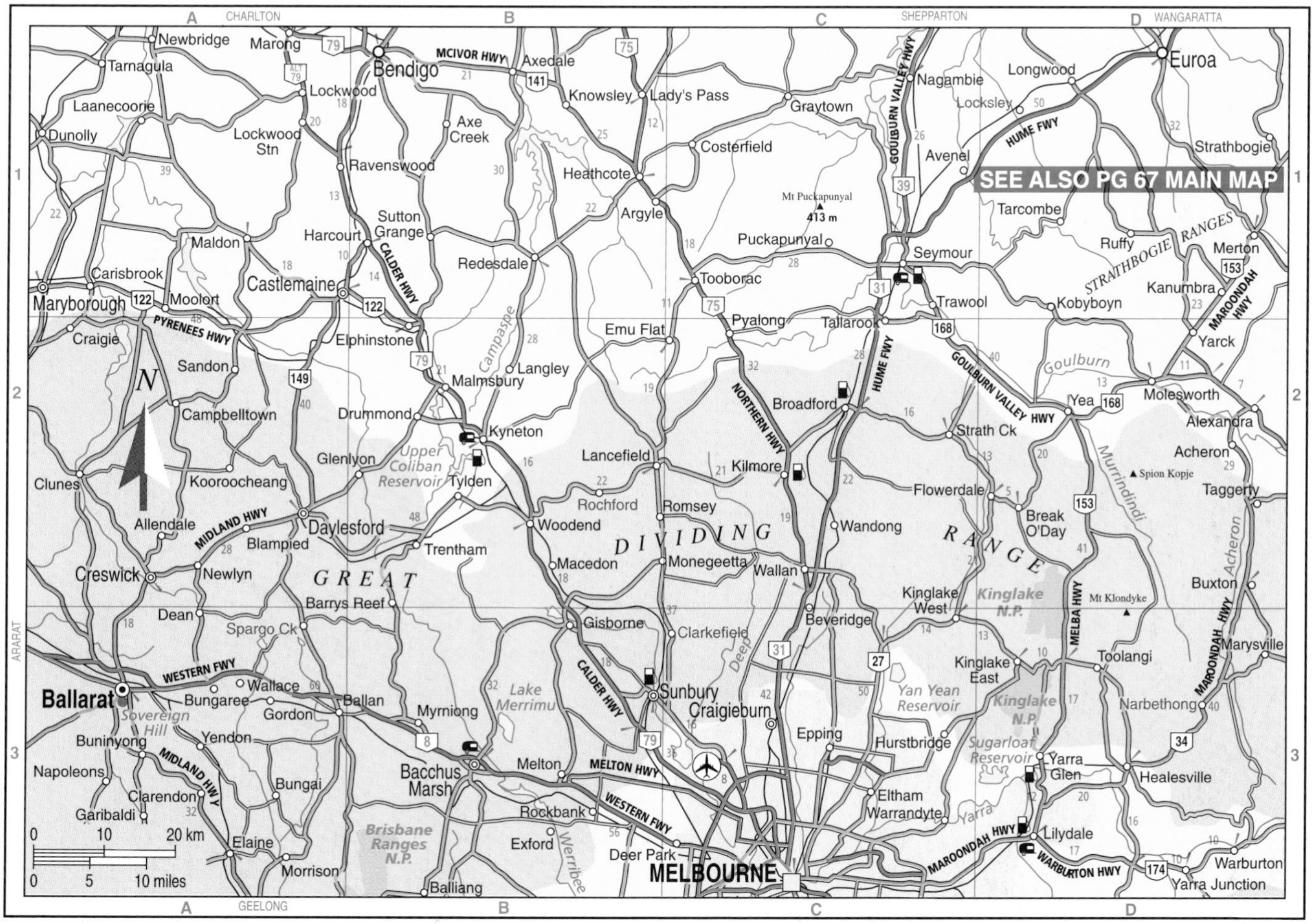

Gippsland and Alpine Country

Gippsland lies to the east of Melbourne and encompasses an area that stretches from Western Port around Wilsons Promontory and north along the coast to the New South Wales border. Inland it is bordered by the Great Dividing Range, which incorporates the Victorian Alpine Country on its southern tip. The Great Dividing Range is bleak, heavily forested and inhospitable, and even today is sparsely populated. The popular alpine mountains (with some of the best skiing in Australia) rise sharply from the plains, which stretch from Ninety Mile Beach and encompass the lakes lying between Bairnsdale and Sale.

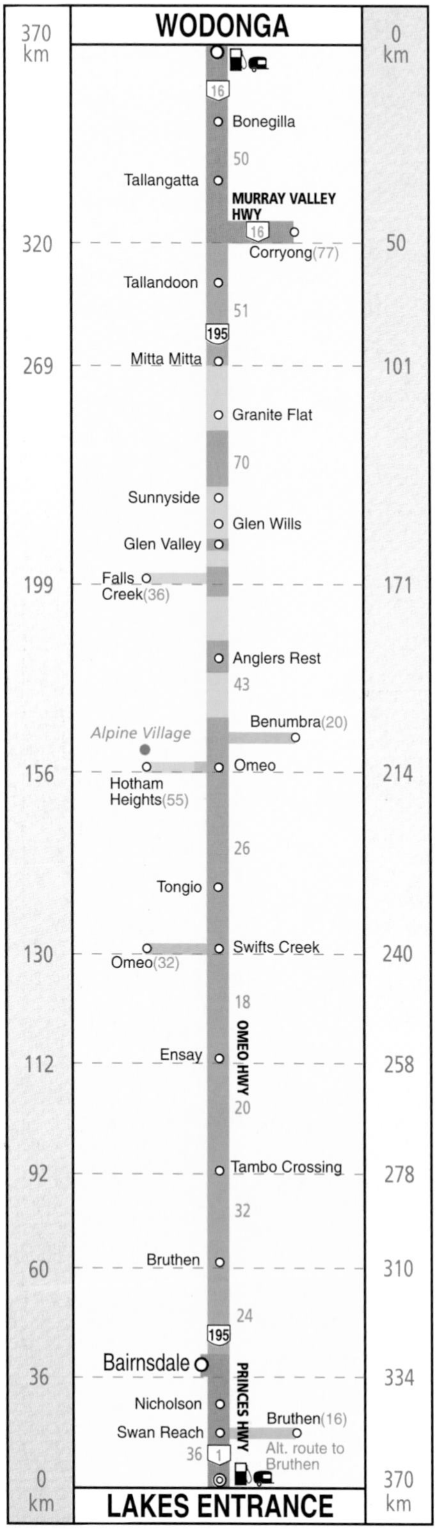

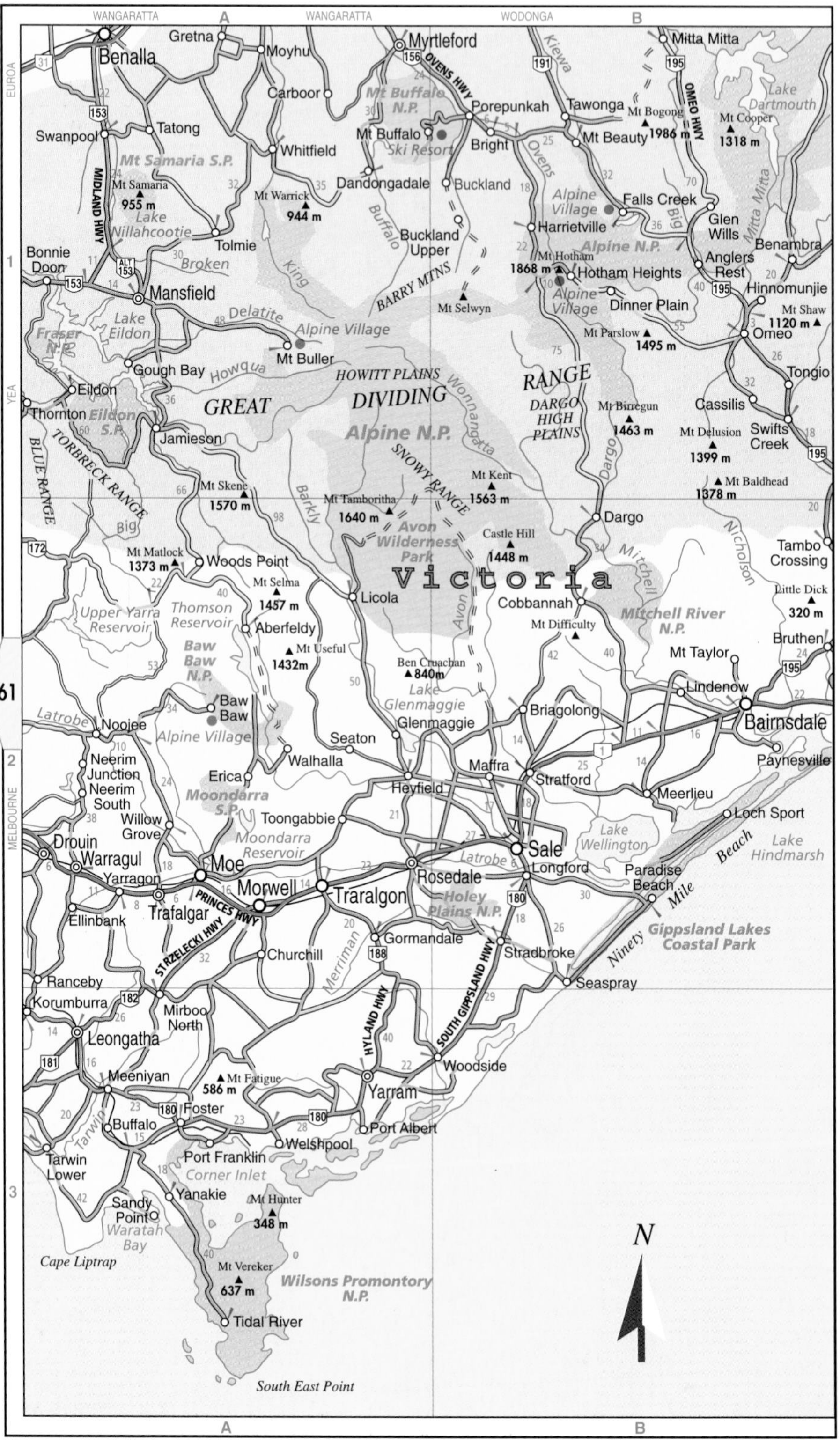

TOP ATTRACTIONS

Croajingolong National Park: 100km (62 miles) of unspoilt beaches and headlands.
Korumburra: Coal Creek Historical Park with a re-created coal-mining town from the 1890s.
Port Welshpool: excellent and isolated beaches.
Wilsons Promontory: some of the best coastal scenery in Victoria, ideal for walking and exploring.

SKI RESORTS

Falls Creek Alpine Village: over 3500 beds and nearly 20 ski lifts make this one of the most popular ski destinations in Australia.
Mt Buffalo: family ski resort.
Mt Buller: largest ski resort in Australia with over 6000 beds and nearly 30 ski lifts.
Mt Hotham Alpine Village: the highest ski resort in Australia with excellent facilities.

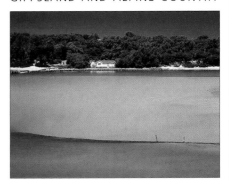

Above: *A stunning place to visit is Lakes entrance, Victoria.*

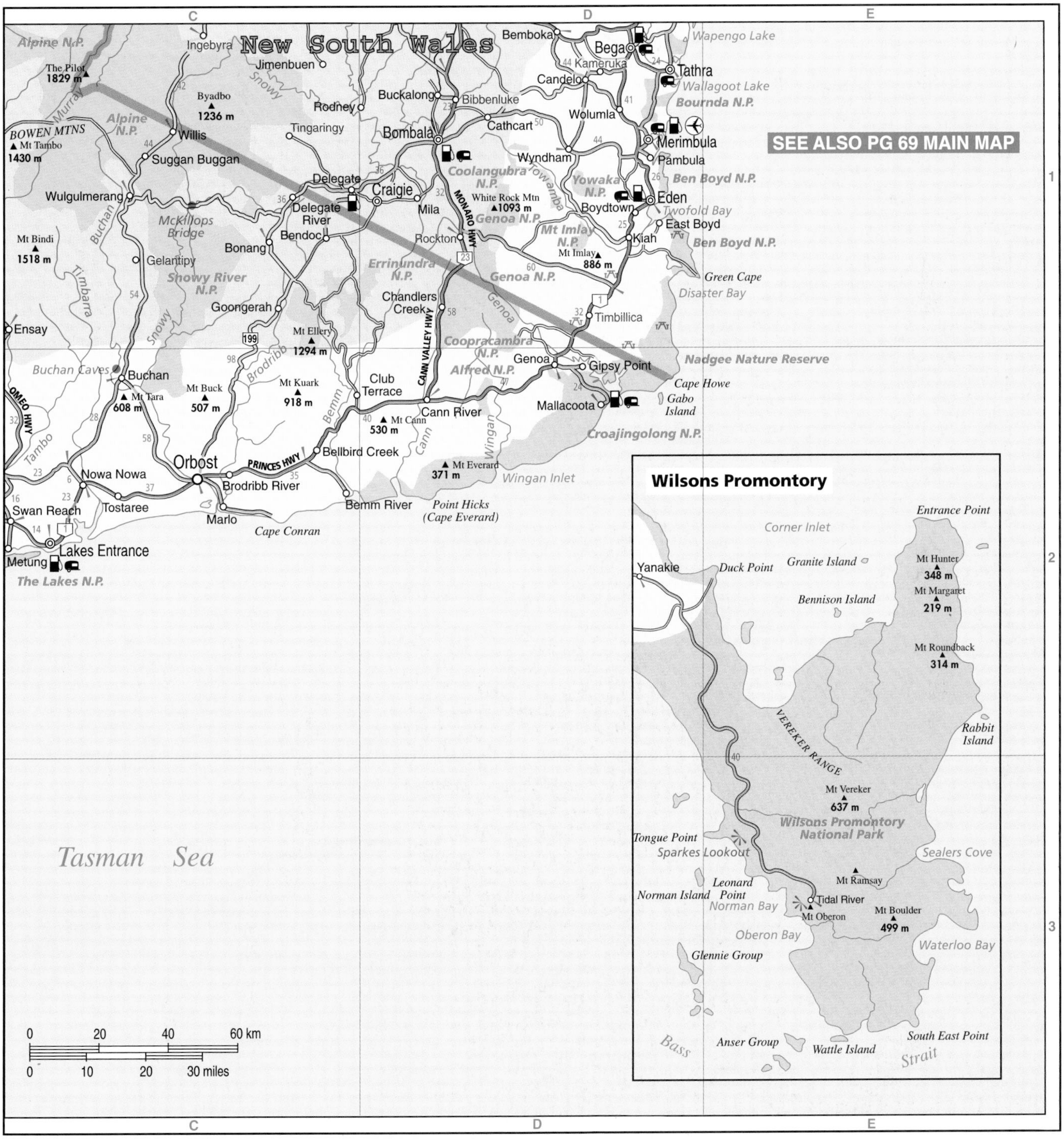

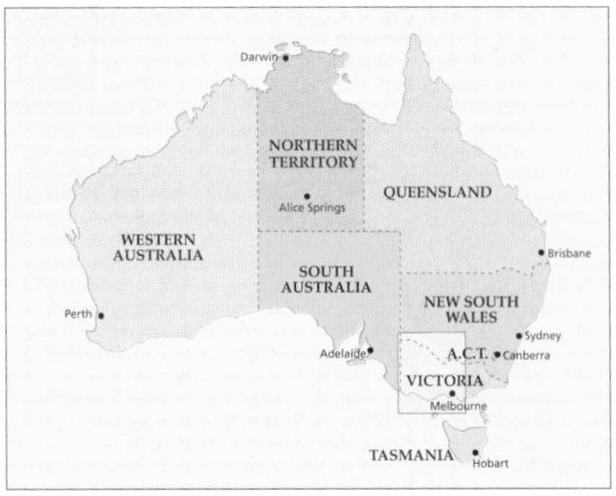

Western Victoria

The Western District stretches west of Melbourne, including the southern coast of Victoria around Port Phillip Bay, to the South Australian border. It comprises the major regional centres of Geelong, Portland, Port Fairy and Warrnambool. Also included in the west are the dramatic Grampian Ranges and the western deserts. The region is mostly characterised by low, undulating terrain, which forms one of the largest basaltic plains in the world. Fat lambs, fine wool, dairy farming, hay and clover, barley, oats, wheat and domestic vegetables have made the Western District one of Australia's richest agricultural areas.

TOP ATTRACTIONS

Grampians (Gariwerd) National Park: in the south-western extremity of the Great Dividing Range, this dramatic set of sandstone ridges is ideal for bushwalking. It is an area noted for its wildflowers and superb vistas.
Little Desert National Park: an unusual desert in western Victoria characterised by flowering tea-trees and mallee.
Port Fairy: a charming, old-world ambience pervades this former whaling and sealing port.
Portland: the only deepwater port between Adelaide and Melbourne, this historic town permits an insight into the wealth of Victoria's western district.

ON THE ROAD

It is hard to imagine Victoria having a substantial semi-arid region but the area to the north-west of the Grampians and bounded by the South Australian border and the Murray River is dry, marginal country, which can only sustain wheat and sheep. While the roads are good, the settlements are isolated and the country can be exceptionally hot and dry in the summer months. The towns, most of which are service centres for the pastoral areas, have tried to strengthen their fragile economic bases by establishing small rural secondary industries like canneries, meat-freezing works and flour mills. Services are adequate but don't expect too many places to be open on Sundays. If you experience any problems contact the RACV, the local branches of which are listed in telephone books.

Below: *The Balconies are protruding rocks that overhang the Victoria Valley near Reid Lookout in the Grampians (Gariwerd) National Park.*

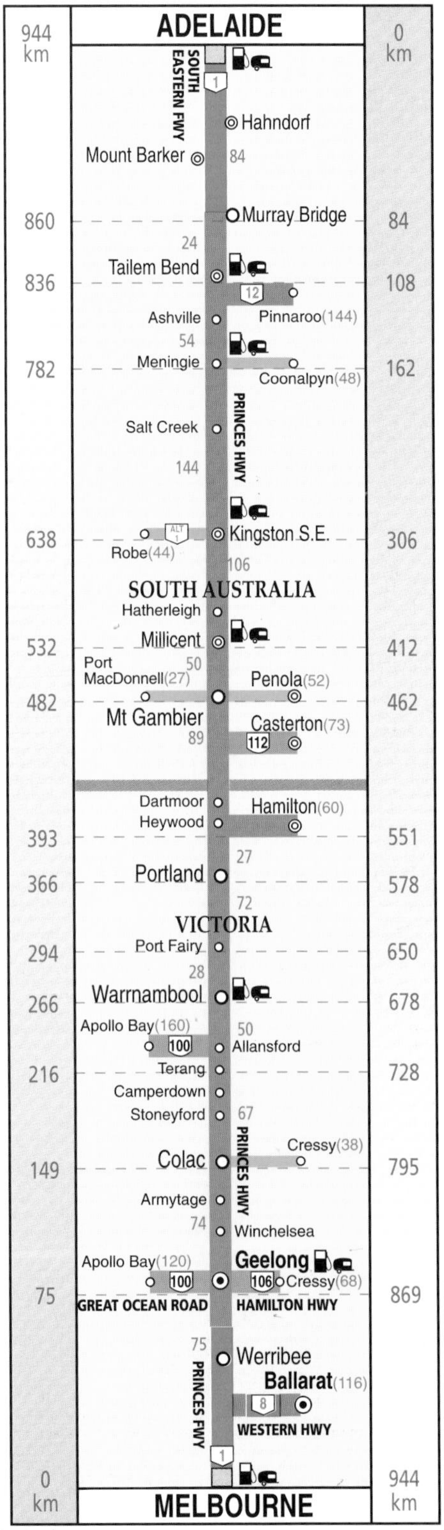

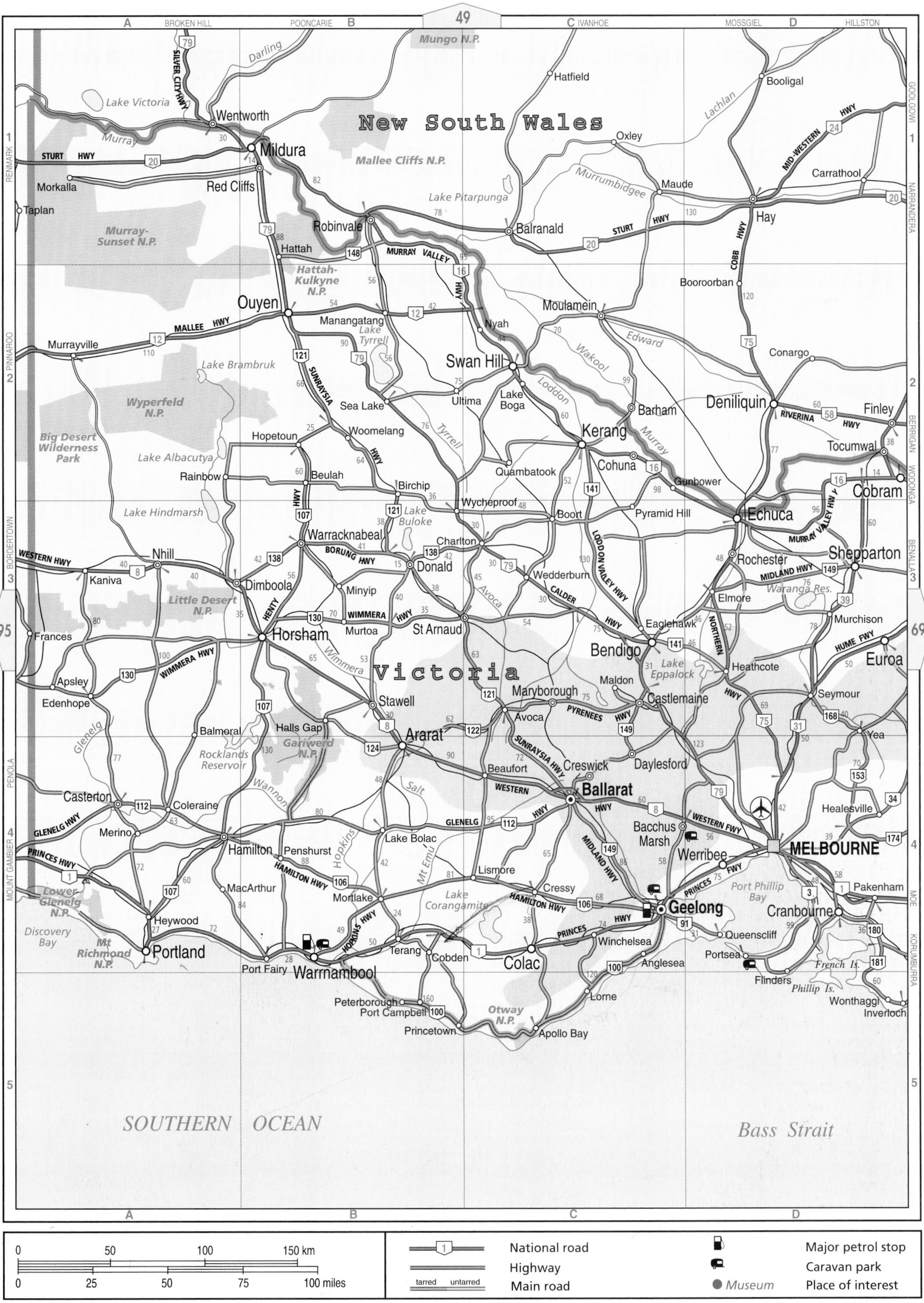
49
BROKEN HILL
POONCARIE
IVANHOE
MOSSGIEL
HILLSTON
GOOLGOWI
NARRANDERA
BERRIGAN
WODONGA
BENALLA
MOE
KORUMBURRA
RENMARK
PINNAROO
BORDERTOWN
PENOLA
MOUNT GAMBIER
95
69
New South Wales
Victoria
Mungo N.P.
Mallee Cliffs N.P.
Murray-Sunset N.P.
Hattah-Kulkyne N.P.
Wyperfeld N.P.
Big Desert Wilderness Park
Little Desert N.P.
Gariwerd N.P.
Lower Glenelg N.P.
Mt Richmond N.P.
Otway N.P.
Lake Victoria
Lake Pitarpunga
Lake Tyrrell
Lake Brambruk
Lake Albacutya
Lake Hindmarsh
Lake Buloke
Rocklands Reservoir
Lake Corangamite
Lake Eppalock
Waranga Res.
Darling
Murray
Lachlan
Murrumbidgee
Edward
Wakool
Loddon
Tyrrell
Avoca
Wimmera
Glenelg
Wannon
Hopkins
Mt Emu
Salt
Wentworth
Mildura
Red Cliffs
Morkalla
Taplan
Robinvale
Hattah
Ouyen
Murrayville
Manangatang
Nyah
Swan Hill
Sea Lake
Ultima
Lake Boga
Kerang
Barham
Cohuna
Gunbower
Hopetoun
Woomelang
Rainbow
Beulah
Birchip
Quambatook
Wycheproof
Boort
Pyramid Hill
Echuca
Warracknabeal
Charlton
Donald
Nhill
Kaniva
Dimboola
Minyip
Wedderburn
Frances
Horsham
Murtoa
St Arnaud
Eaglehawk
Bendigo
Maldon
Castlemaine
Apsley
Edenhope
Stawell
Maryborough
Avoca
Balmoral
Halls Gap
Ararat
Creswick
Daylesford
Beaufort
Ballarat
Casterton
Coleraine
Merino
Hamilton
Penshurst
Lake Bolac
Lismore
Cressy
Bacchus Marsh
Werribee
MacArthur
Mortlake
Heywood
Portland
Discovery Bay
Port Fairy
Warrnambool
Terang
Cobden
Colac
Winchelsea
Geelong
Anglesea
Lorne
Peterborough
Port Campbell
Princetown
Apollo Bay
Hatfield
Booligal
Oxley
Maude
Carrathool
Hay
Balranald
Booroorban
Moulamein
Conargo
Deniliquin
Finley
Tocumwal
Cobram
Rochester
Shepparton
Elmore
Murchison
Heathcote
Euroa
Seymour
Yea
Healesville
MELBOURNE
Pakenham
Cranbourne
Queenscliff
Portsea
Port Phillip Bay
Flinders
French Is.
Phillip Is.
Wonthaggi
Inverloch
SILVER CITY HWY
STURT HWY
MALLEE HWY
MURRAY VALLEY HWY
COBB HWY
MID-WESTERN HWY
SUNRAYSIA HWY
RIVERINA HWY
HENTY HWY
BORUNG HWY
WESTERN HWY
WIMMERA HWY
CALDER HWY
LODDON VALLEY HWY
NORTHERN HWY
MIDLAND HWY
HUME FWY
PYRENEES HWY
GLENELG HWY
PRINCES HWY
HAMILTON HWY
HOPKINS HWY
WESTERN FWY
PRINCES FWY
SOUTHERN OCEAN
Bass Strait
A
B
C
D
1
2
3
4
5
0
50
100
150 km
25
75
100 miles
National road
Highway
tarred
untarred
Main road
Major petrol stop
Caravan park
Museum
Place of interest

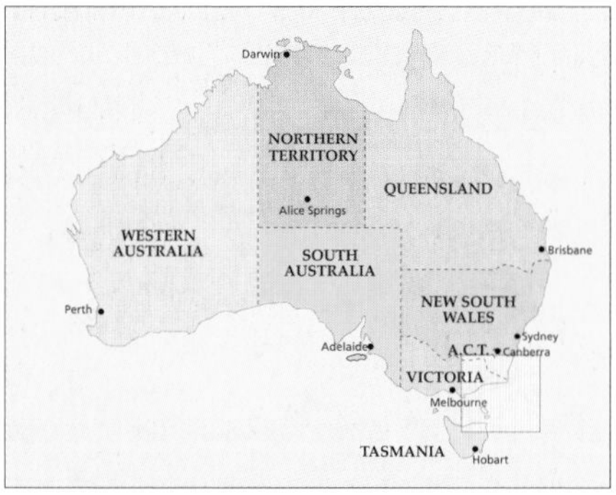

Eastern Victoria

Eastern Victoria includes the area stretching from Western Port around Wilsons Promontory and north along the coast to the New South Wales border as well as the Victorian end of the Snowy Mountains and the southern tip of the Great Dividing Range. Noted for its quiet seaside villages, the area has changed little in the past 50 years. People come here to get away from the more tourist-orientated southern coastal areas. Towns like Bairnsdale and Lakes Entrance are sustained by their fishing fleets. Attractions around the area include the Gippsland Lakes, Ninety Mile Beach and the Croajingolong and Lakes national parks.

Above: *Ninety Mile Beach stretches along the south-eastern coast of Victoria, between Lakes National Park and the sea.*

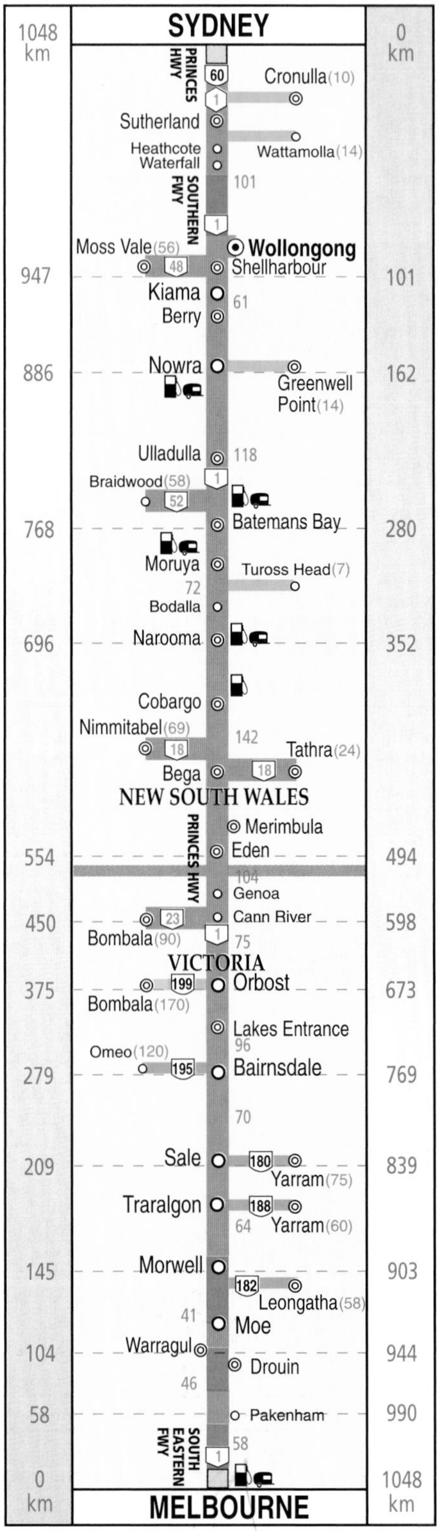

TOP ATTRACTIONS

Alpine National Park: contains a number of popular ski resorts like Mt Buller and Mt Buffalo.
Croajingolong National Park and **The Lakes National Park:** delightful escapes for people keen on coastal bushwalking.
Lakes Entrance: coastal town with a sleepy and unspoilt charm, entrance to Gippsland Lakes.
Mallacoota Inlet: remote and peaceful lakeside resort near Croajingolong wildlife area.
Ninety Mile Beach: easily accessible, a long flat beach that is ideal for walking.
Wilsons Promontory National Park: noted for its beautiful white beaches, rugged coastline and excellent bushwalking.

ON THE ROAD

The main coastal roads through Eastern Victoria are sealed and easy to navigate. However, the appeal of the area is based on getting off the beaten track and often travellers will find themselves on poor, sandy dirt roads. Behind the coast the Great Dividing Range is desolate, heavily forested and forbidding. The roads through this area are often closed by snow in winter and frequented by timber trucks, thus making them quite dangerous. They often start as sealed surfaces only to become dirt roads as they move further and further into the hinterland. Roads like the route from Buchan to Suggan Buggan are difficult and isolated. People unsure of routes, or needing mechanical assistance, should contact the RACV, which is listed in the local telephone directory. It is unlikely that the smaller centres will have many facilities open on Sundays.

51
TUMUT B
TUMUT C
CANBERRA
SYDNEY
SHEPPARTON
EUROA
MELBOURNE
Cobram
Mulwala
Corowa
Yarrawonga
Howlong
Albury
Wodonga
Wangaratta
Benalla
HUME FWY
Lake Hume
MURRAY VALLEY HWY
Tallangatta
Corryong
Burrowa-Pine Mtn N.P.
Cabramurra
SNOWY MTNS HWY
Lake Eucumbene
Avenue of Flags
Cooma
MONARO HWY
Deua N.P.
Moruya
Tuross Head
Bodalla
Narooma
PRINCES HWY
Wadbilliga N.P.
Kosciuszko N.P.
▲ 2228 m
Mt Kosciuszko
RANGE
New South Wales
DIVIDING
GREAT
SNOWY MTNS
Snowy
Tathra
Merimbula
Twofold Bay
Eden
Towamba
Bombala
Myrtleford
OVENS HWY
Bright
Mt Beauty
Dartmouth Dam
Alpine N.P.
Mt Buffalo N.P.
Whitfield
Merton
Mansfield
Mt Buller
Lake Eildon
Eildon
Jamieson
Marysville
Omeo
Swifts Creek
OMEO HWY
Dargo
Victoria
Snowy River N.P.
Genoa
Nadgee N.R.
Cape Howe
Mallacoota Inlet
Cann River
Croajingolong N.P.
Orbost
Marlo
Nowa Nowa
Bruthen
Tambo
Bairnsdale
Lakes Entrance
The Lakes N.P.
Ninety Mile Beach
Warburton
BawBaw N.P.
Noojee
Heyfield
Latrobe
PRINCES HWY
Sale
Traralgon
Drouin
Warragul
Moe
Morwell
Korumburra
MIRBOO NORTH
Leongatha
SOUTH GIPPSLAND HWY
Yarram
GIPPSLAND HWY
Seaspray
Gippsland Lakes Coastal Park
Inverloch
Welshpool
Corner Inlet
Wilsons Promontory N.P.
Tidal River
South East Point
Tasman Sea
Bass Strait
67
Palana
Flinders Island
Emita
Furneaux Group
Whitemark
Lady Barron
Cape Barren Island
Cape Barren Is.
Clarke Island
Banks Strait
Cape Portland
Mt William N.P.
Eddystone Point
Bay of Fires
Tasmania
Wynyard
Somerset
Burnie
Ulverstone
Devonport
Port Sorell
Beaconsfield
Latrobe
George Town
Bridport
Derby
Scottsdale
St Helens
South Esk
Launceston
HOBART
81
0 50 100 150 km
0 25 50 75 100 miles
National road
Highway
tarred untarred
Main road
Major petrol stop
Caravan park
Museum
Place of interest

TASMANIA

Tasmania is Australia's smallest and most mountainous state. Unlike the mainland it is not dry, sunny or hot, but it is a well-watered, lush area of natural wilderness. The southern coastline is noted for its ragged inaccessible cliffs, and the centre of the island is a plateau broken by glacial lakes and a number of mountains, notably Mount Ossa, Ben Lomond, Cradle Mountain and Eldon Park, all of which rise above 1400m (4600ft). These features mean that the island has large tracts of pristine wilderness in the west and south. It is really only the north coast and the valleys of the Tamar, Derwent and Huon rivers that have been developed. Tasmanian fauna and flora are also of importance for their rarity and uniqueness. The beautiful Huon pine, for example, can grow for well over 2000 years. The Tasmanian devil, once an inhabitant of mainland Australia, is now found only on the island state, and the Tasmanian tiger, thought to be extinct, may still be hiding somewhere in the state's unexplored wilderness.

Tasmania is European in its climate and temperament. This is the smallest of Australia's states, an area of great beauty, much of which is still undiscovered. A mere 67 800km^2 (26 170 sq miles), including King, Flinders and a number of lesser islands in Bass Strait, support a population of 473 500 (2.7 per cent of Australia's total population), 195 500 of which lived in Hobart in 1997. To understand just how small Tasmania is in relation to the rest of the country, it is worth noting that the state's entire population is roughly equal to that of Newcastle in NSW and less than half that of Adelaide or Perth.

In broad terms the island can be divided into three regions. There is Hobart and the south-east corner, Launceston and the north-east, and the broad, sparsely populated region of the west and north-west coast.

The island is Australia's most mountainous state, its surface features scoured and carved into wild, romantic peaks by the force of slow-moving ancient glaciers. The southern coastline, which has no permanent settlements, is a series of ragged and inaccessible cliffs. The centre of the island is a plateau with a series of glacial lakes. This highland terrain is rugged, covered in dense forest and dotted with trout-filled lakes – deep valleys echo with the sound of bird calls. Mount Ossa is the island's highest peak at 1617m (5300ft). Most of this mountainous terrain remains in its natural state.

The island's agricultural land is concentrated along the north coast and in the valleys of the Tamar, Derwent and Huon rivers.

In total, Tasmania has over 2 million hectares (5 million acres) of land under agriculture. There are nearly 6000 farms on the island and they directly employ over 11 000 people.

Around Hobart and in the valleys of the Derwent and Huon rivers are the state's orchards. Here the bulk of the state's apples are grown, as well as apricots and lucrative crops of essential oils, poppies and hops. The orchards are rarely larger than 20ha (50 acres). For decades the apple was the symbol of the state, firstly because the island's shape resembles that of an apple, and secondly because for many mainland Australians, apples were commonly associated with Tasmania.

Mixed farming, the most common of the state's agricultural endeavours and an activity that tends to give large areas of Tasmania a distinctly English appearance, usually occurs on farms ranging in size from 40–200ha (100–500 acres). Livestock often consists of a small dairy herd as well as some pigs and fat lambs, while spare land supports crops of potatoes, various other vegetables and small areas of barley and wheat. These farms form the backbone of the state's economy.

The north-west coastal strip running from Smithton and Stanley across to Devonport is widely regarded as the best land on the island. The soils are rich and volcanic, rainfall averages around 960mm (38in) and the average temperatures are mild, from a summer maximum of 19°C (66°F) to a winter minimum of 7°C (45°F).

The northern and north-eastern coastal strip from Devonport across the estuary of the Tamar River to Scottsdale and Gladstone, and around the coast to St Helens and Scamander, is heavily cropped, producing sub-

Left: *Port Arthur is a reminder of Tasmania's brutal past as a convict penal settlement.*

stantial harvests of potatoes, wheat and barley. There are some apple orchards, and hay and fodder crops are grown with some success.

In recent times King Island to the north-west of Tasmania has gained an extraordinary reputation for its choice dairy products. King Island butters, cheeses and creams (particularly the clotted cream) have found their way into trendy suburban delicatessen shops on the mainland and have become a byword for dairy quality.

The most important pastoral area in Tasmania lies in the valley created by the confluence of the South Esk, Macquarie and Tamar rivers. This rich flat valley, with Launceston as its main centre, is traversed by the main north–south road which joins Launceston and Hobart, and is the state's most important wool and beef area.

Tasmania boasts four other major industries – timber, mining, hydro-electricity production and tourism, all of which can potentially harm the island's fragile environment. In Tasmania the environmental issue is an extremely complex one. On the one side there is the push to exploit the state's abundant natural resources, and on the other are the environmentalists who wish to preserve the uniqueness of the Tasmanian wilderness – particularly the central mountains and the south-west corner.

Large areas of Tasmania, because of their location and inhospitable terrain, have resisted the encroachment of human beings. Indeed, the south-western corner of the island has no permanent settlement whatsoever and has often been marked on maps with a label that signifies desolation: the word 'unexplored'.

The flora confined to this island is exceptional and unique. Celery-top pines contrast with flower-covered alpine meadows, while the bleak highland moors are far removed from the unspoilt sandy beaches of the east coast. The wildlife is equally fascinating, from the fierce little Tasmanian devil, to the elusive Tasmanian tiger (*thylacine*) which may still roam the remote wilderness.

Tasmania is a traveller's delight. For environmentally conscious bushwalkers and backpackers it offers walking paths, mountain climbing and whitewater rafting to challenge even the most hardy and committed. For families it offers a diversity of entertainment – from watching Tasmanian devils at Cradle Mountain and cruising across Macquarie Harbour to exploring the island's convict past at Port Arthur.

Tasmania is a land of pastoral gentleness with an almost Celtic wildness in its national parks and mountains. It has a modern capital, but has retained most of the early colonial buildings which lend charm to the city centre. It is an island state of extraordinary contrast and breathtaking beauty.

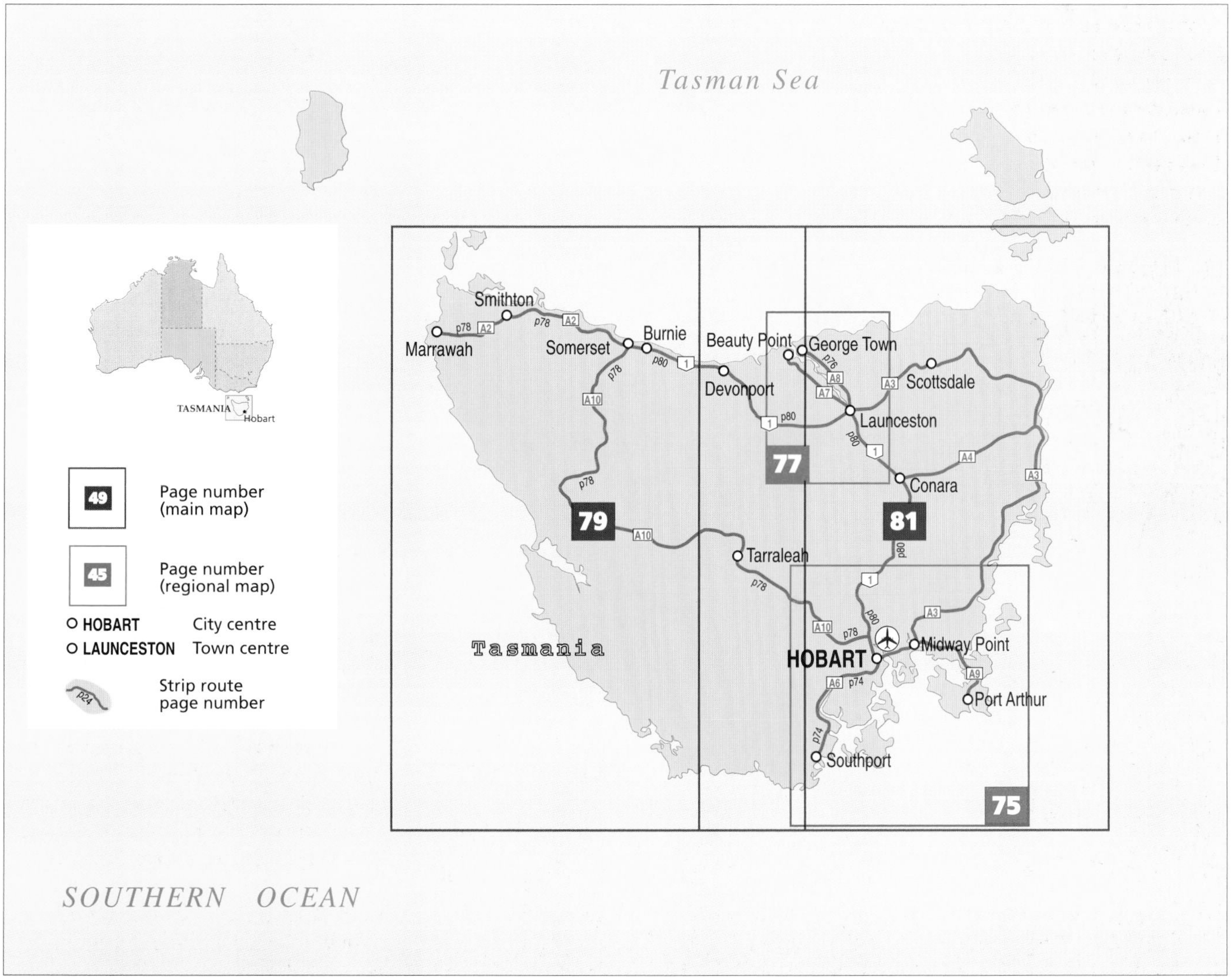

Hobart

Hobart is predominantly a 19th-century colonial city, beautifully located on either side of the Derwent River. It is partially protected from the full force of the westerly winds by Mount Wellington, which dominates the city's landscape, and by Mount Nelson to the south. The visitor will find the city immensely appealing as it has a straggling, irregular appearance, and a distinctive old-world charm maintained by its docklands and port. It is into this port that victors of the Sydney to Hobart Yacht Race sail at the turn of each New Year. The city centre has a number of modern buildings, but its particular essence remains 19th century.

TOP ATTRACTIONS

Anglesea Barracks: built in 1814, oldest military establishment still in use in Australia.
Battery Point: elegant 'suburb' with an extraordinary concentration of beautifully preserved 19th-century houses. Walk up Kelly's Steps from Salamanca Place and start wandering through the winding streets.
Cadbury's factory: a chocolate factory, upriver at Claremont.
Historic buildings: Bond Store (1824), Tasmanian Museum and Art Gallery (1863), Town Hall (1864), Theatre Royal (1837), Commissariat Store (1808–10).
Royal Tasmanian Botanical Gardens: imported and native species, includes historic Arthur Wall, Rossbank Observatory, a Conservatory, Rosarium, Floral Clock, Fern House and Tropical Glasshouse.
Salamanca Place: weekend markets and finishing line for Sydney to Hobart Yacht Race.
Wrest Point Casino: Australia's first casino, located on the banks of the Derwent River.

CALENDAR OF EVENTS

JANUARY: Taste of Tasmania, Prince Phillip Cup, National Sabot Sailing Championships, 'King of the Derwent' Yacht Race, Vintage/Classic Boat Race.
FEBRUARY: Hobart Regatta.
APRIL: Targa Tasmania (motor rally).
SEPTEMBER: Australia vs New Zealand Golf Tournament, Australian Amateur Golf Championships, Tulip Festival.
OCTOBER: Oliebollen Festival.
NOVEMBER: Sea-Summit Half Marathon.
DECEMBER: Melbourne to Hobart and Sydney to Hobart Yacht races.

Above, left: *Battery Point has preserved its ambience for over 100 years with its lovingly maintained buildings and village green.*
Above: *Wrest Point Casino is perfectly located for views over the waterway.*

HOBART	J	F	M	A	M	J	J	A	S	O	N	D
AV. TEMP. °F	70	70	68	62	57	53	53	55	59	63	64	68
AV. TEMP. °C	21	21	20	17	14	12	12	13	15	17	18	20
DAILY SUN hrs	8	7	6	5	4	4	4	5	6	6	7	7
RAINFALL ins	2	1.5	2	2	2	2	2	2	2	2.5	2	2
RAINFALL mm	48	40	47	52	49	56	54	52	52	64	55	57
RAINFALL days	11	10	11	12	14	14	15	15	15	16	14	13

WHERE TO STAY

Battery Point Guest House, 'Mandalay', McGregor St, tel: (03) 6224 2111. Converted from an old coach house and stables.
Fountainside Motor Inn, cnr Brooker Hwy & Liverpool St, tel: (03) 6234 2911, fax: 6231 0710. Modern motel which is reasonably priced and centrally located.
Innkeepers Lenna of Hobart, Runnymede St, tel: 1 800 030 633, fax: 6224 0112. Victorian charm with modern conveniences, overlooking the Derwent River.
Salamanca Inn, Gladstone St, tel: (03) 6223 3300, fax: 6223 7167. Modern hotel integrated with the old warehouses, located in a prime city spot.
Sandy Bay Motor Inn, Sandy Bay Rd, tel: (03) 6225 2511, fax: 6225 4354. Reasonably priced, modern accommodation, located near the casino.
Hotel Grand Chancellor, Davey St, tel: (03) 6235 4535, fax: 6223 8175. First-class hotel with all modern comforts.
Wrest Point Hotel Casino, Sandy Bay Rd, tel: (03) 6225 0112, fax: 6225 3909. First-class hotel with great riverside views, attached to the casino complex.

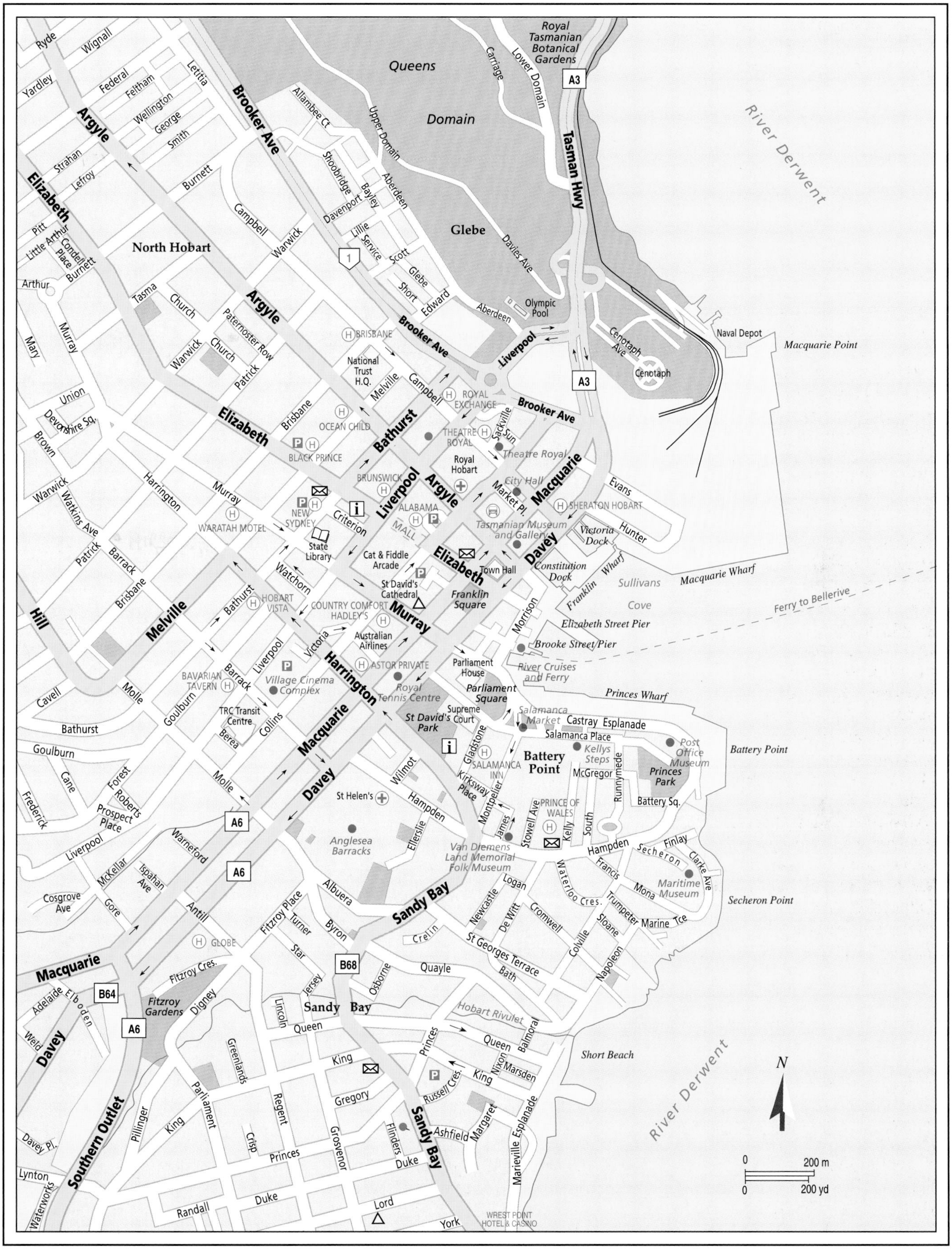

△ St Patricks	Place of worship	Ⓗ (bus)	Bus terminus	✉	Post office
Ⓗ	Hotel	●	Police station	● Market	Place of interest
i	Information	P	Parking	B68	Route number

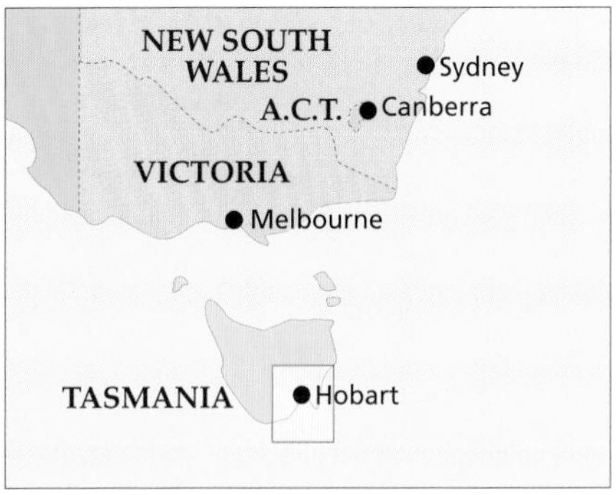

Hobart Daytrips

The area around Hobart offers visitors an exciting range of attractions. A visit to Mount Wellington, a dormant volcano, offers a superb view across the Derwent River and down the D'Entrecasteaux Channel. To the north of the city are the charming 19th-century villages of Ross and Richmond. To the east lies the infamous penal colony of Port Arthur with its restored historic showpiece, the Model Prison. To the south and west there is a pleasant daytrip along the coast through Snug and Cygnet, returning to Hobart through Huonville, a picturesque area where hops and apples are grown.

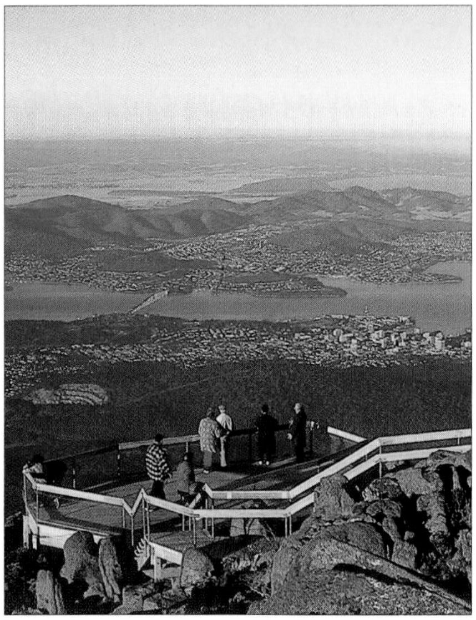

Above: *A trip to Mount Wellington allows the visitor spectacular vistas over Hobart and the Derwent River.*
Below: *Richmond Bridge can probably lay claim to being the most picturesque bridge in Australia, as well the oldest.*

TOP ATTRACTIONS

Huon Valley: lately settled by potters, woodworkers and crafts-people who sell their wares in the gift shops in the city centre.
Mount Wellington: dormant volcano, 1270m (4165ft) high.
Port Arthur: magnificently preserved penal colony where 12 500 hardened criminals were sent between 1830 and 1877. Most visitors board the ferry to the **Isle of the Dead**, the burial place for the colony which was established not long after the settlement and almost immediately divided into free settler and convict burial grounds.
Ross and Richmond: among the finest preserved 19th-century villages in Australia.

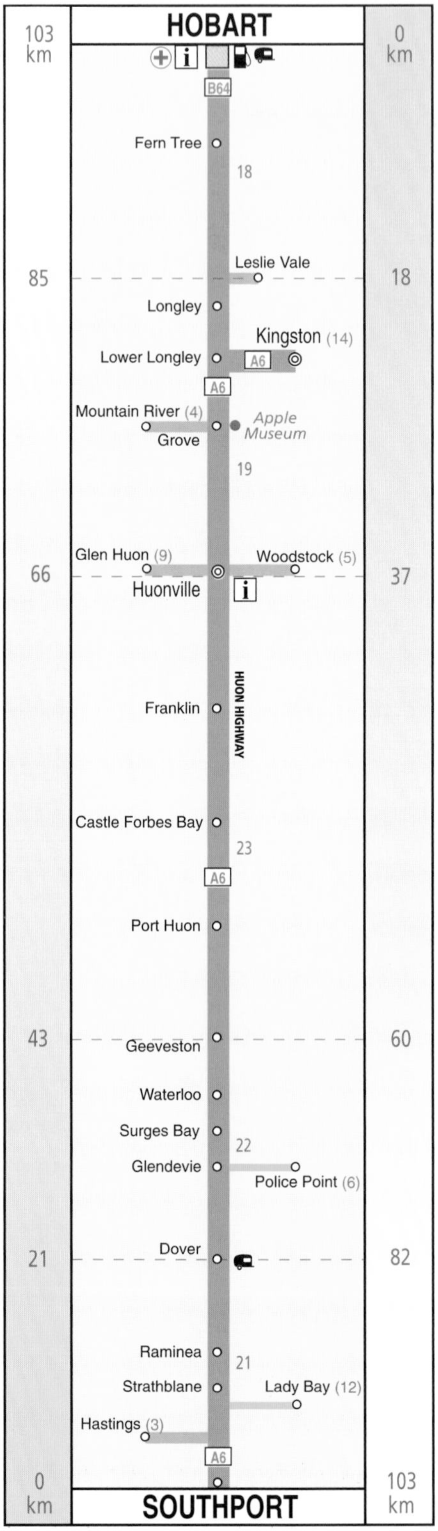

LAUNCESTON
LITTLE SWANPORT
Thorpe Water Mill
Bothwell
Ruins
Jericho
Stonor
Stonehenge
Baden
Whitefoord
Lake Tiberias
Mt Reid 477 m
Melton Mowbray
Rhyndaston
Tunnack
Boltons Beach Coastal Reserve
MIDLAND HWY
Woodsdale
Bluff
Triabunna
317 m
Okehampton
Historic Town
Hamilton
Hollow Tree
Kempton
900 m
Eldon
Colebrook
Levendale
Pt Horne Lookout
Orford
Spring Beach
Darlington
Ruins
Jordan
Chauncy Vale Wildlife Sanctuary
Dysart
Elderslie
Brown Mtn 792 m
White Kangaroo
Coal
Buckland
Maria Island
TASMAN HWY
Rheban
Meadowbank Lake
LYELL HWY
Broadmarsh
Bagdad
Mangalore
Campania
Runnymede
Wildlife Sanctuary
Maria Island N.P.
Westerway
Pontville
Historic Town
647 m
Sandspit
Riedle Bay
Gretna
Brighton
Passage
Glenora
Macquarie Plains
Black Hills
Wildlife Park
Historic Town
Orielton
Pawleena
Nugent
Mercury
Dromedary
Bridgewater
Richmond
Cape Bernier
Cape Peron
Plenty
Magra
Boyer
Granton
Old Beach
Salmon Ponds
Uxbridge
New Norfolk
Cadbury's Factory
Risdon Vale
Midway Point
Sorell
Forcett
Kellevie
404 m Ragged Tier
Marion Bay
Feilton
Copping
Mount Lloyd
Lachlan
Cambridge
Lewisham
Dodges Ferry
Carlton
Museum
Glenorchy
Tasman Memorial
North Bay
Plenty
Collins Cap
HOBART
Bellerive
Seven Mile Beach
Carlton
Dunalley
Cape Frederick Hendrick
Wellington Park
Howrah
Mt Wellington
Primrose Pt
Primrose Sands
FORESTIER PENINSULA
Fern Tree
Rokeby
Lauderdale
Derwent
Mountain River
Mountain
Sandford
Frederick Henry Bay
Lime Bay Nature Reserve
Smooth Is.
ARTHUR HWY
Lonnavale
Crabtree
Murdunna
Macgregor Peak 591 m
Longley
Cremorne
Coal Mines Historic Site
Cape Surville
Apple Museum
HUON
Leslie Vale
Shot Tower
Judbury
Grove
Kingston
Opossum Bay
Norfolk Bay
Ranelagh
North West Head
Pirates Bay
Kaoota
Blackmans Bay
Deer Point
Tessellated Pavement
Eaglehawk Neck
Huonville
Saltwater River
Glen Huon
Margate
Tasmanian Devil Wildlife Park
Blowhole
HUON VALLEY
South Arm
Premaydena
Taranna
Tasman Arch & Devils Kitchen
Betsey Is.
Arve
Woodstock
Snug
Tinderbox
Dennes Point
Mt Communication 344 m
Franklin
Mt Grey 831 m
Auk Point
Nubeena
Oakwood
Cradoc
Oyster Cove
Storm Bay
Wedge Bay
TASMAN PENINSULA
Hippolyte Rocks
Castle Forbes Bay
Kettering
Roberts Point
Barnes Bay
Wedge Is.
Fortescue Bay
Cygnet
CHANNEL
Port Huon
North Bruny Island
Port Arthur
Isle of the Dead
Cape Hauy
Wildlife Park
Woodbridge
Geeveston
Wattle Grove
Cape Raoul State Reserve
Cape Pillar State Reserve
Birchs Bay
Stormlea
Gardners Bay
Variety Bay
Munroe Bight
Waterloo
Lymington
Salters Point
Remarkable Cave
Blowhole
Great Bay
Surges Bay
Huon
Garden Is. Creek
Mt Raoul 462 m
Maingon Bay
Cape Pillar
Glendevie
Bruny Island Neck Game Reserve
Raoul Bay
Esperance
Middleton
Isthmus Bay
Cape Raoul
HWY
Police Point
Tasman Island
HUON HWY
Gordon
Hartz Mountains National Park
Simpsons Bay
Huon Is.
Adventure Bay
D'Entrecasteaux Channel
Ramine
Dover
Alonnah
Adamsons Pk 1225 m
Strathblane
Adventure Bay
Tasman Sea
Hastings Cave
Lunawanna
Captain Cook's Landing Place
Cookville
Cape Connella
570 m
Bligh Museum
Lady Bay
Thermal Pool
Hastings
Partridge Is.
South Bruny Island
Lune River
Southport
Great Taylors Bay
Mangana Bluff
Ida Bay
Scenic Railway
Cloudy Bay
N
Southport Lagoon
Southwest National Park
Cape Bruny
Mt Bruny
Boreel Head
Tasman Head
Recherche Bay
Catamaran
Fishers Pt
Cockle Creek
SEE ALSO PG 81 MAIN MAP
Whale Head
0 5 10 15 km
0 2.5 5 7.5 10 miles
National road
Highway
tarred untarred
Main road
Major petrol stop
Caravan park
Museum
Place of interest

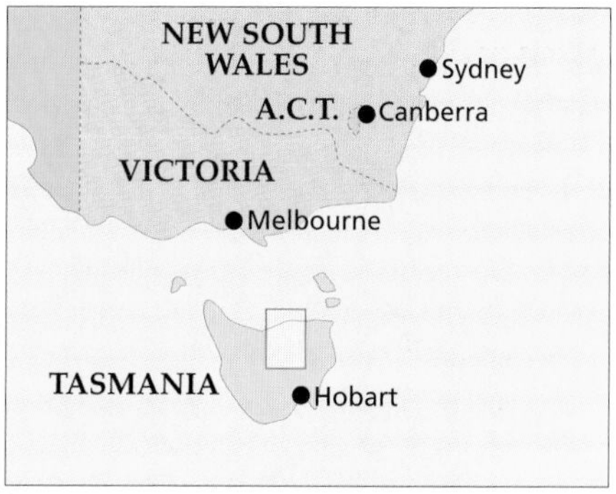

Launceston and Tamar Valley

Launceston is Tasmania's second-largest city. Lying 199km (124 miles) north of Hobart on the River Tamar, the city's population is approximately 65 000. It has retained the ambience of a large country town but has an extraordinary history and a large number of elegant 19th-century buildings. Of particular appeal are the city's docks, Penny Royal Gunpowder Mill, Launceston's many attractive parks and gardens, and Cataract Gorge. The River Tamar flows north towards Bass Strait, where Bell Bay, home to one of the largest aluminium smelting works in the Southern Hemisphere, lies opposite George Town, site of the first settlement in northern Tasmania.

TOP ATTRACTIONS

Cataract Gorge: a delightful escape from the city centre and an ideal swimming location in summer time.
Launceston City Park: 5-ha (12-acre) park which includes a small zoo, a rhododendron garden and an attractive conservatory.
National Automobile Museum: excellent collection of historic vehicles for motoring enthusiasts.
Penny Royal World: attractive and interesting complex consisting of modern accommodation, museum, working corn mill and a restored tramway.
Stately homes in the Tamar Valley: Franklin House, Entally and Clarendon (all open daily).

ON THE ROAD

The roads radiating out from suburban Launceston and along the Tamar Valley are sealed and of good quality. In the Tamar Valley there are plenty of service stations. The main road from Launceston to Scottsdale and St Helens, although at times narrow and winding, is sealed and in good condition. Off the main roads, conditions deteriorate and they are mostly little more than dirt tracks; this is particularly the case with roads to the east of Gladstone.

Right: *Delightful gardens make Launceston beautiful to visit in the spring and summer months.*
Below: *Elegantly withstanding the test of time, gingerbread houses overlook the peaceful River Tamar.*

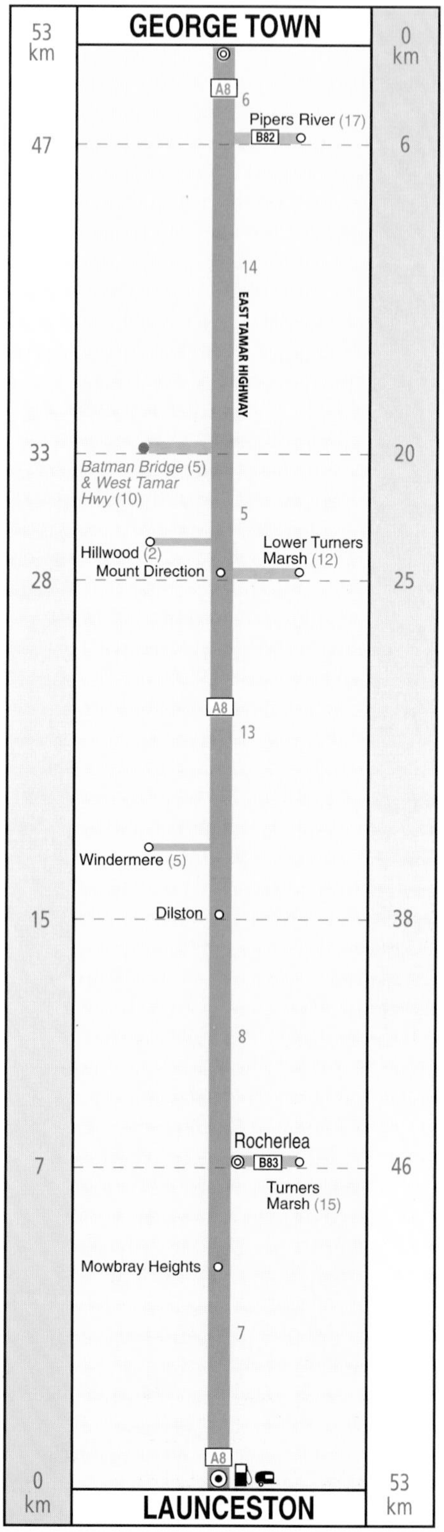

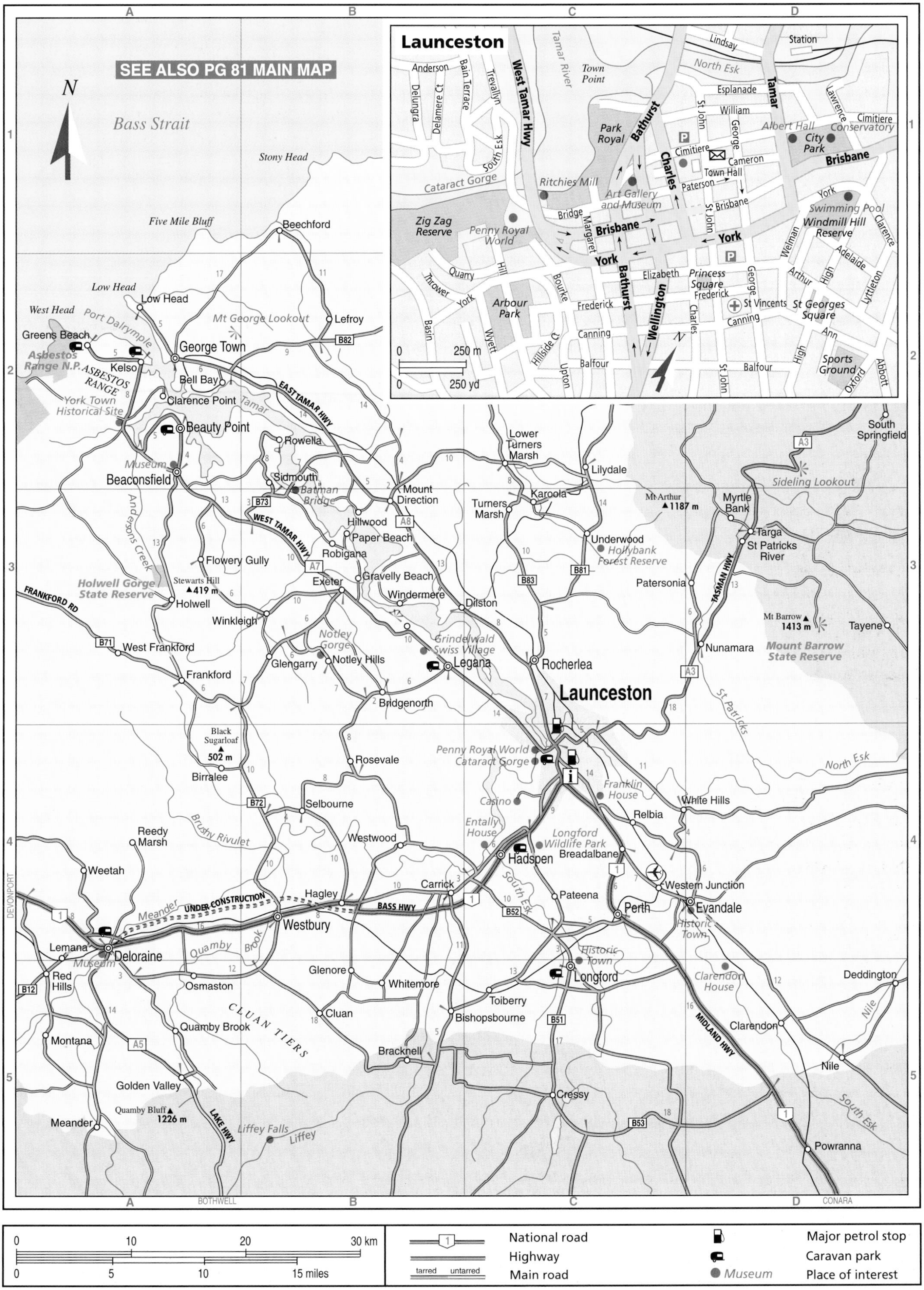
SEE ALSO PG 81 MAIN MAP
N
Bass Strait
Stony Head
Five Mile Bluff
Beechford
Low Head
West Head
Port Dalrymple
Greens Beach
Kelso
Asbestos Range N.P.
ASBESTOS RANGE
York Town Historical Site
Low Head
George Town
Bell Bay
Clarence Point
Beauty Point
Mt George Lookout
Lefroy
EAST TAMAR HWY
Tamar
Museum
Beaconsfield
Rowella
Sidmouth
Batman Bridge
Mount Direction
Hillwood
Paper Beach
WEST TAMAR HWY
Robigana
Andersons Creek
Flowery Gully
Holwell Gorge State Reserve
Stewarts Hill
419 m
Holwell
FRANKFORD RD
Exeter
Gravelly Beach
Windermere
Winkleigh
West Frankford
Frankford
Notley Gorge
Notley Hills
Glengarry
Grindelwald Swiss Village
Legana
Bridgenorth
Black Sugarloaf
502 m
Birralee
Rosevale
Selbourne
Brushy Rivulet
Reedy Marsh
Westwood
Weetah
DEVONPORT
UNDER CONSTRUCTION
BASS HWY
Hagley
Carrick
Westbury
Meander
Lemana
Deloraine
Museum
Quamby Brook
Red Hills
Osmaston
Glenore
Whitemore
CLUAN TIERS
Cluan
Montana
Quamby Brook
Golden Valley
Quamby Bluff
1226 m
Meander
LAKE HWY
Liffey Falls
Liffey
Bracknell
Bishopsbourne
Toiberry
Cressy
BOTHWELL
Lower Turners Marsh
Lilydale
Karoola
Turners Marsh
Mt Arthur
1187 m
Underwood
Hollybank Forest Reserve
Paternsonia
Dilston
Rocherlea
Launceston
Penny Royal World
Cataract Gorge
Casino
Franklin House
Entally House
Longford Wildlife Park
Hadspen
Breadalbane
Relbia
White Hills
South Esk
Pateena
Western Junction
Perth
Evandale
Historic Town
Longford
Historic Town
Clarendon House
Clarendon
MIDLAND HWY
Powranna
CONARA
South Esk
Nile
Nile
Deddington
North Esk
St Patricks
Nunamara
TASMAN HWY
Targa
St Patricks River
Myrtle Bank
Sideling Lookout
South Springfield
Mt Barrow
1413 m
Mount Barrow State Reserve
Tayene
B82
A8
A7
B73
B71
B72
B12
A5
B52
B51
B53
B81
B83
A3
1
Launceston
Anderson
Delungra
Delamere Ct
Bain Terrace
Trevallyn
West Tamar Hwy
Tamar River
Town Point
Lindsay
Station
North Esk
Esplanade
William
Park Royal
Bathurst
St John
George
Tamar
Albert Hall
Lawrence
Cimitiere
Conservatory
City Park
Brisbane
Charles
Cimitiere
Cameron
Town Hall
Paterson
South Esk
Cataract Gorge
Ritchies Mill
Art Gallery and Museum
Bridge
St John
Brisbane
York
Swimming Pool
Windmill Hill Reserve
Zig Zag Reserve
Penny Royal World
Margaret
Brisbane
York
Welman
Clarence
Adelaide
York
Quarry
Thrower
Hill
York
Bathurst
Elizabeth
Princess Square
Frederick
George
Arthur
High
Lyttleton
Arbour Park
Bourke
Frederick
Wellington
Charles
St Vincents
Canning
St Georges Square
Ann
Basin
Wyett
Hillside Ct
Canning
High
Sports Ground
Oxford
Abbott
Balfour
Upton
St John
Balfour
0
250 m
250 yd
0
10
20
30 km
0
5
10
15 miles
tarred
untarred
National road
Highway
Main road
Major petrol stop
Caravan park
Museum
Place of interest

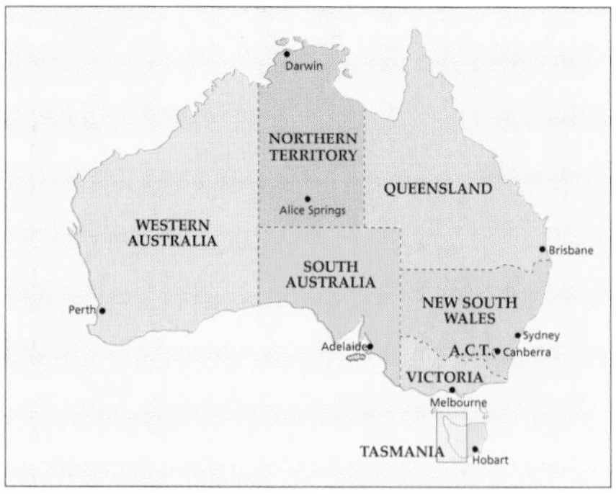

Western Tasmania

Western Tasmania comprises the townships of Queenstown, the beautiful, isolated Strahan, and the mining town of Zeehan. In 1871, a man known as Philosopher Smith discovered tin at Mount Bischoff. In the next decade, substantial deposits of silver, copper, tin and gold were found throughout the west coast area. The north-west coastal strip from Smithton and Stanley across to Devonport has an average rainfall of 960mm (38in) and mild temperatures of 7°–19°C (45°–66°F), while the South-West National Park is wild and rugged, ranging from superb glacial tarns to dense rainforest.

TOP ATTRACTIONS

Macquarie Harbour: named after Governor Lachlan Macquarie, this 50-km long (30-mile) harbour opens to the sea through the narrow eddying waters of Hell's Gates and marks the entrance to the King and Gordon rivers.
Queenstown: has the appearance of a deserted moonscape. The hills around this mining town have been totally denuded of vegetation. The surrounding undulating hills of the west coast can be intensely beautiful with dark, low clouds, which are a distinctive feature of the region's climate.
Strahan: on the west coast, seems the last outpost of civilisation. One of the loneliest places on earth, it is also very picturesque.

Above: *Strahan on the far west coast at Macquarie Harbour is the last outpost before Tasmania's wild south-west region.*
Left: *The Gordon River flows to Macquarie Harbour from the Franklin –Gordon Wild Rivers and Southwest national parks.*

ON THE ROAD

Main roads are good, but services limited. Lyell Highway is a good-quality sealed road through the Cradle Mountain–Lake St Clair National Park. The road from Queenstown to Strahan and Zeehan is well maintained. Settlements are isolated and if you experience trouble you are at the mercy of other travellers. At times there is no traffic for hours. Services and accommodation are available in Queenstown, Strahan and Zeehan, and the road from Queenstown to Burnie and Wynyard has recently been upgraded.
If you decide to travel off the main roads you are likely to experience steep gradients and deteriorating surfaces. Large numbers of trucks pass through this area.

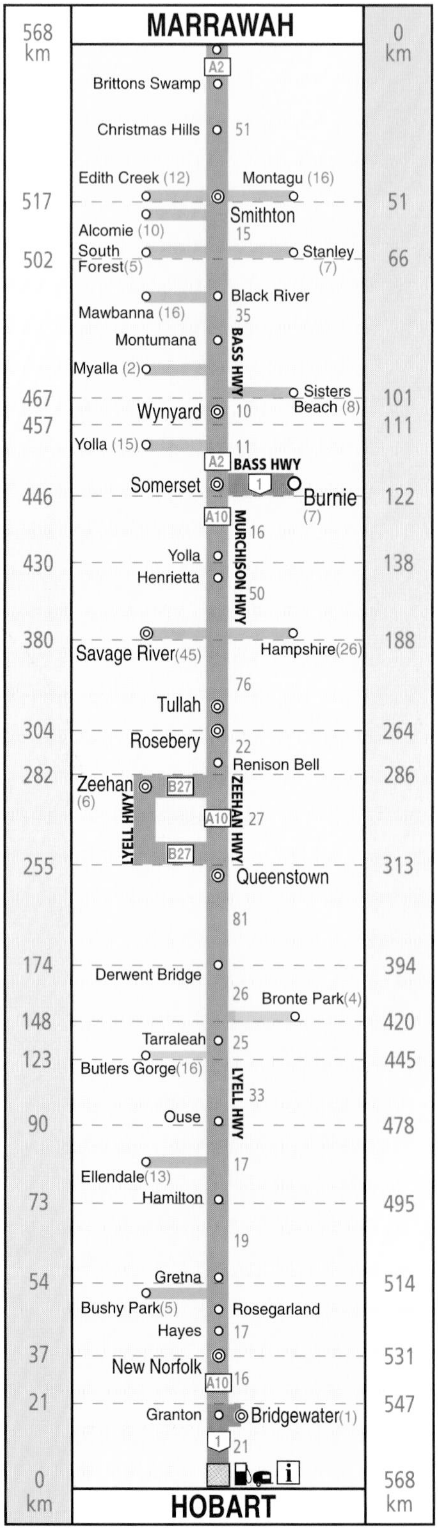

Three Hummock Island
Hope Channel
Hunter Island
Walker Island
Walker Channel
Robbins Island
Cape Grim
Bass Strait
Cape Elie
North Point
Perkins Island
Perkins Bay
Stanley
Sawyer Bay
West Montagu
Montagu
Studland Bay
Smithton
Christmas Hills
Black River
Rocky Cape N.P.
Rocky Cape
Birdlife Park
Sisters Beach
Table Cape
Wynyard
Marrawah
West Point
Brittons Swamp
South Forest
Montumana
Alcomie
Mawbanna
Edith Creek
Roger River
BASS HWY
Dip Falls
Myalla
Lower Mt Hicks
Somerset
Burnie
Arthur River
Arthur
Milkshake Hills Forest Reserve
Preolenna
Yolla
Stowport
Penguin
Ulverstone
Devonport
Port Dalrymple
Low Head
West Head
Greens Beach
Port Sorell
George Town
Asbestos Range N.P.
Beauty Point
Nelson Bay
Nelson
Meunna
Ridgley
Natone
Riana
Gawler
Forth
Port Sorell
Beaconsfield
Temma
Temma Harbour
Frankland
Rapid
Henrietta
Tewkesbury
South Riana
Spreyton
Latrobe
Flowery Gully
Holwell
Balfour
Hampshire
Sprent
Lower Barrington
Railton
Frankford
Glengarry
Arthur Pieman Protected Area
Mt Hazelton 671 m
Blythe
Loyetea
Warringa
Nietta
Wilmot
Kimberley
Sandy Cape
Donaldson
Savage
Erriba
Sheffield
Elizabeth Town
Birralee
Mt Norfolk 759 m
Lake Cethana
Moina
Lower Beulah
Deloraine
Iron-Ore Mine
Savage River
Waratah
Mt Pearse 1001 m
MURCHISON HWY
Lorinna
Mersey
Needles
Westbury
Mt Ramsey 855 m
Belvoir
Daisy Dell
King Solomon Cave
Liena
Mole Creek
Marakoopa Cave
Montana
Cluan
Golden Valley
Liffey Falls
Western Creek
Pieman
Hardwick Bay
Pieman Gorge
Corinna
Mt Livingstone 782 m
Lake Mackintosh
Waldheim Chalet
Cradle Valley
Cradle Mtn 1545 m
Ahrberg Bay
Tullah
Rosebery
Devils Gullet Lookout
Great Lake
Lake Pieman
Renison Bell
Mt Murchison 1275 m
Bluff
Lake Rowallen
Lake Augusta
GREAT PINE TIER
Zeehan
Montezuma Falls
Mt Ossa 1617 m
LAKE HWY
Cramps
Cradle Mtn-Lake St Clair N.P.
Walls of Jerusalem N.P.
Remine
Museum
Trial Harbour
ZEEHAN HWY
Mt Gould 1491 m
Flintstone
Henty
South Eldon
Miena
Shannon
Mt Lyell Mine
Queenstown
Lake Burbury
Lake St Clair
Bronte Park
Ocean Beach
LYELL HWY
Mt Owen 1146 m
Lynchford
Derwent Bridge
Waddamana
Trout Fishing
Lake Echo
Hell's Gates
Cape Sorell
Strahan
1168 m
Mt Jukes
King
LYELL HWY
Mt King William I 1324 m
Frenchmans Cap 1443 m
Lake King William
Butlers Gorge
Dee Lagoon
Hermitage
Macquarie Harbour
1144 m
Mt Sorell
Franklin-Gordon Wild Rivers N.P.
Mt King William II 1372 m
Tarraleah
Derwent
Osterley
PRINCE OF WALES RANGE
Birthday Bay
Sloop Point
Birch Inlet
Franklin
Jane
Ouse
Clyde
Hamilton
Mt Discovery 680 m
Maxwell
Denison
Hibbs Bay
Point Hibbs
Mt Lee 734 m
Ellendale
Mt Field N.P.
Mt Field East 1269 m
Russell Falls
Westerway
Old Mine
National Park
Trout Farm
Endeavour Bay
Gordon
Lake Gordon
Mt Mueller 1234 m
Maydena
High Rocky Point
Wanderer
Mt Sprent 1058 m
Strathgordon
Mt Wedge 1146 m
Mt Bowes 957 m
Styx
SOUTHERN OCEAN
FRANKLAND RANGE
Serpentine Reach
SCOTTS PEAK RD
Russell
Lewis
Lonnavale
Mt Weld 1338 m
Low Rocky Point
Elliott Bay
Giblin
Lake Pedder
Tahune Forest Reserve
Nye Bay
Davey
Crossing
ARTHUR RANGE
Huon
Southwest N.P.
Mt Hean 747 m
Spring
Mt Norold 978 m
Mt Picton 1327 m
Waratah Lookout
Hartz Peak 1255 m
Wreck Bay
Old
Hartz Mountains N.P.
Point St Vincent
Port Davey
Solly
Hastings Cave
Stephens Bay
Mine
Mt Counsel 800 m
Thermal Pool
Southwest N.P.
Ida Bay
Mt Melaleuca 595 m
New River Lagoon
Window Pane Bay
Mt Leillateah 799 m
South West Cape
De Witt Island
Ile Du Golfe
Cockle Creek
Flat Witch Island
Surprise Bay
South Cape
Maatsuyker Island
South Cape Bay
Maatsuyker Group
LAUNCESTON
HOBART
81
0 20 40 60 km
0 10 20 30 40 miles
National road
Highway
tarred untarred
Main road
Museum
Other airport
Route number
Place of interest

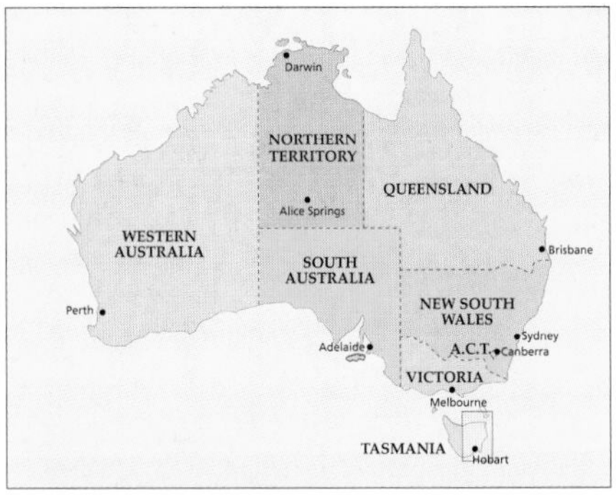

Eastern Tasmania

The northern and north-eastern coastal strip from Devonport around the coast to St Helens and Scamander, is characterised by small farming communities and their successful agricultural ventures. Substantial amounts of potatoes, wheat and barley are grown, with some apple orchards and hay and fodder crops. The greatest attractions of the area are the delightful seaside townships of St Helens and Bicheno and the stunningly beautiful, and unspoilt, Freycinet National Park. Bushwalking in Freycinet is an exceptional experience. There are some outstanding views over Great Oyster Bay and Wineglass Bay.

Top: *Binalong Bay confronts the Tasman Sea just north of St Helens, the largest town on the east coast.*
Above: *The Tasmanian devil, a carnivore marsupial, is extinct on the Australian mainland and found only in Tasmania.*

TOP ATTRACTIONS

Bicheno: attractions include the **East Coast Birdlife and Animal Park**, opportunities to see the diverse fauna of the region (Forester kangaroos, Bennett's wallabies, Tasmanian devils, Cape Barren geese, and pelicans), and the coastal trader, *Enterprise*, built at Battery Point in 1902, and now the **Sea Life Centre**.
Freycinet National Park: an area of great natural beauty with a number of excellent bushwalks and spectacular views over Wineglass Bay and Great Oyster Bay.
Scamander: quiet holiday resort, ideal for fishing.
St Helens: an attractive holiday resort with superb white beaches.
Lagoons: the road runs close to a rocky and wild coastline.

ON THE ROAD

The main road around the coast, the **Tasman Highway**, is sealed and of good quality. Most of the area's attractions can be seen from this road which offers the visitor various routes across the mountains back to the **Midland Highway** between Hobart and Launceston. Visitors wishing to explore beyond the main roads will encounter poor-quality tracks like the road along Nine Mile Beach (east of Swansea) and the roads and paths beyond Coles Bay in the Freycinet National Park. The larger centres all have petrol and mechanical services but the areas between the towns are lonely and isolated. The roads into the mountains are little more than timber tracks. As a general principle the roads in the north-east to Ansons Bay, Eddystone Point and beyond Gladstone are unsealed and of a poor quality. Travellers should check in the towns before making the journey.

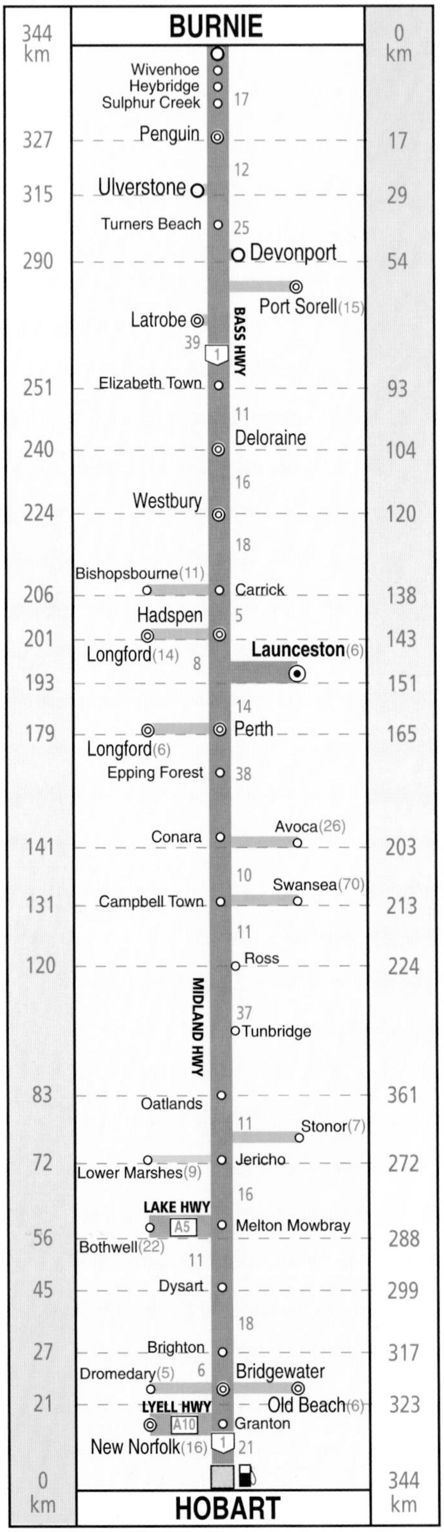

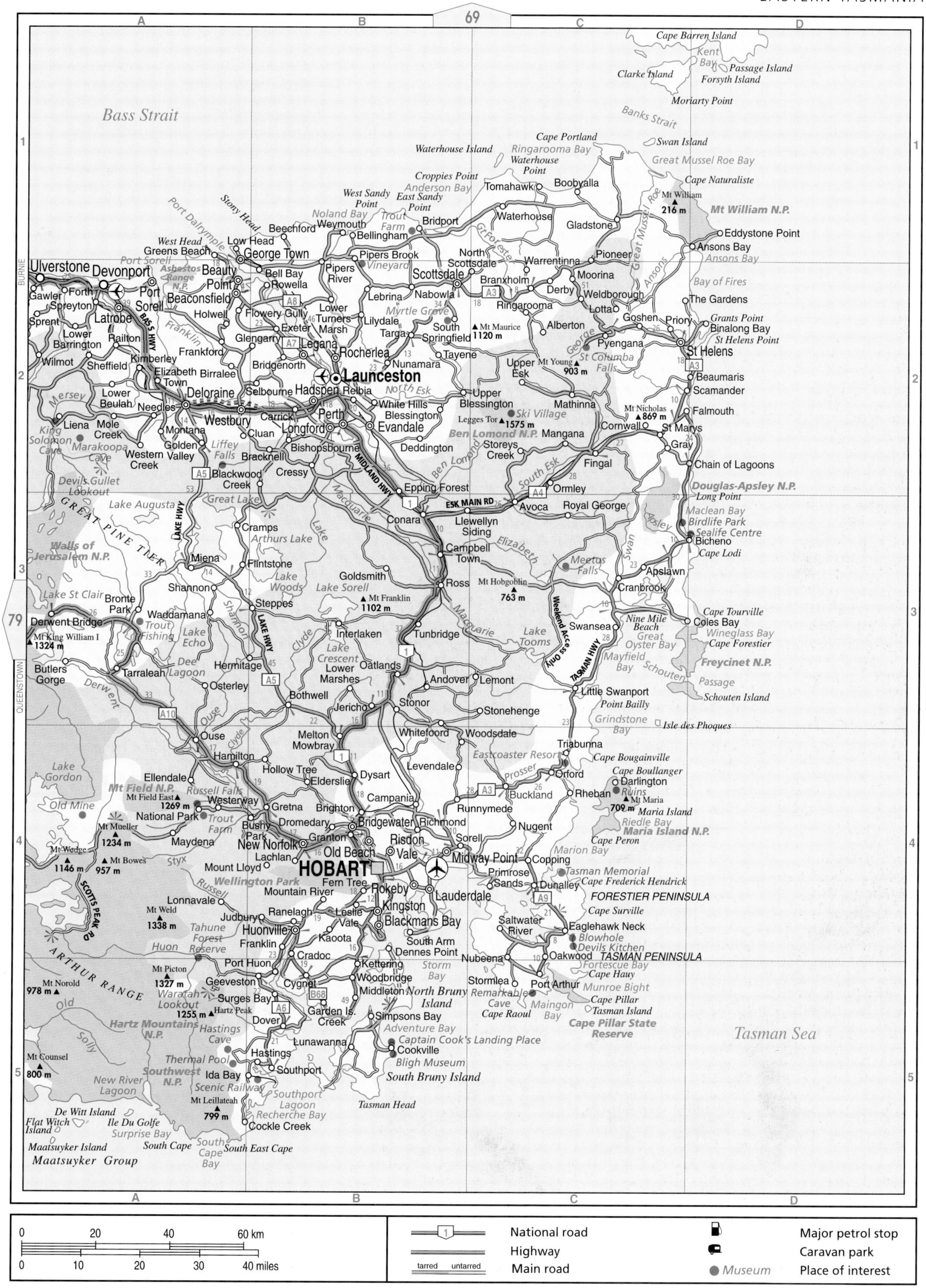
69
A
B
C
D
1
2
3
4
5
79
BURNIE
QUEENSTOWN
Cape Barren Island
Kent Bay
Passage Island
Clarke Island
Forsyth Island
Moriarty Point
Bass Strait
Banks Strait
Cape Portland
Swan Island
Waterhouse Island
Ringarooma Bay
Waterhouse Point
Great Mussel Roe Bay
Croppies Point
Cape Naturaliste
Anderson Bay
Tomahawk
Boobyalla
West Sandy Point
East Sandy Point
Mt William 216 m
Mt William N.P.
Stony Head
Noland Bay
Trout Farm
Bridport
Waterhouse
Gladstone
Eddystone Point
Port Dalrymple
Beechford
Weymouth
Bellingham
Ansons Bay
West Head
Low Head
North Scottsdale
Warrentinna
Pioneer
Greens Beach
George Town
Pipers Brook
Vineyard
Ansons Bay
Port Sorell
Asbestos Range N.P.
Beauty Point
Bell Bay
Pipers River
Scottsdale
Branxholm
Moorina
Great Mussel Roe
Ulverstone
Devonport
Rowella
Nabowla
A3
Derby
Weldborough
Bay of Fires
Gawler
Forth
Port Sorell
Beaconsfield
Lebrina
Ringarooma
Lotta
The Gardens
Spreyton
Latrobe
Holwell
A8
Flowery Gully
Lower Turners Marsh
Myrtle Grove
Alberton
Goshen
Priory
Grants Point
Sprent
Bass Hwy
Exeter
Lilydale
South Springfield
Mt Maurice 1120 m
George
Binalong Bay
Lower Barrington
Railton
Franklin
Glengarry
A7
Legana
Targa
Pyengana
St Helens Point
Wilmot
Kimberley
Frankford
Rocherlea
Tayene
St Columba Falls
St Helens
Sheffield
Elizabeth Town
Birralee
Bridgenorth
Nunamara
Upper Esk
Mt Young 903 m
A3
Mersey
Launceston
Beaumaris
Lower Beulah
Deloraine
Selbourne
Hadspen
Relbia
North Esk
Upper Blessington
Scamander
Needles
Westbury
Carrick
Perth
White Hills
Blessington
Mathinna
Mt Nicholas 869 m
Falmouth
King Solomon Cave
Liena
Mole Creek
Montana
Longford
Evandale
Ski Village
Legges Tor 1575 m
Cornwall
St Marys
Marakoopa Cave
Golden Valley
Cluan
Bishopsbourne
Deddington
Ben Lomond N.P.
Mangana
Gray
Western Creek
Liffey Falls
Bracknell
Midland Hwy
Storeys Creek
Fingal
Chain of Lagoons
Devils Gullet Lookout
A5
Blackwood Creek
Cressy
Ben Lomond
South Esk
Douglas-Apsley N.P.
Epping Forest
Ormley
Long Point
Great Pine Tier
Lake Augusta
Great Lake
Lake Hwy
Macquarie
Esk Main Rd
A4
Avoca
Royal George
Maclean Bay
Birdlife Park
Sealife Centre
Cramps
Lake
Conara
Llewellyn Siding
Apsley
Bicheno
Walls of Jerusalem N.P.
Arthurs Lake
Campbell Town
Elizabeth
Swan
Cape Lodi
Miena
Flintstone
Meetus Falls
Apslawn
Goldsmith
Ross
Mt Hobgoblin 763 m
Cranbrook
Lake St Clair
Shannon
Lake Woods
Lake Sorell
Mt Franklin 1102 m
Bronte Park
Steppes
Weekend Access Only
Nine Mile Beach
Cape Tourville
Derwent Bridge
Waddamana
Shannon
Lake Hwy
Macquarie
Swansea
Coles Bay
Mt King William I 1324 m
Trout Fishing
Lake Echo
Interlaken
Tunbridge
Lake Tooms
Great Oyster Bay
Wineglass Bay
Cape Forestier
Clyde
Lake Crescent
Tasman Hwy
Mayfield Bay
Freycinet N.P.
Butlers Gorge
Dee Lagoon
Hermitage
Lower Marshes
Oatlands
Schouten
Tarraleah
A5
Andover
Lemont
Passage
Derwent
Osterley
Little Swanport
Schouten Island
Bothwell
Point Bailly
A10
Jericho
Stonor
Stonehenge
Ouse
Grindstone Bay
Isle des Phoques
Ouse
Clyde
Melton Mowbray
Whitefoord
Woodsdale
Triabunna
Lake Gordon
Hamilton
Eastcoaster Resort
Cape Bougainville
Hollow Tree
Levendale
Prosser
Orford
Cape Boullanger
Ellendale
Dysart
Darlington
Mt Field N.P.
Russell Falls
Elderslie
Buckland
Rheban
Ruins
Mt Field East 1269 m
Westerway
Campania
Mt Maria 709 m
Old Mine
Gretna
Brighton
Runnymede
Maria Island
National Park
Trout Farm
Bushy Park
Dromedary
Bridgewater
Richmond
Riedle Bay
Mt Mueller 1234 m
Nugent
Maria Island N.P.
Maydena
New Norfolk
Granton
Risdon Vale
Sorell
Cape Peron
Mt Wedge 1146 m
Mt Bowes 957 m
Styx
Lachlan
Old Beach
Midway Point
Copping
Marion Bay
Mount Lloyd
HOBART
Primrose Sands
Tasman Memorial
Wellington Park
Fern Tree
Rokeby
Dunalley
Cape Frederick Hendrick
Scotts Peak Rd
Russell
Mountain River
Lauderdale
Forestier Peninsula
Lonnavale
Kingston
A9
Cape Surville
Mt Weld 1338 m
Judbury
Ranelagh
Leslie Vale
Blackmans Bay
Saltwater River
Eaglehawk Neck
Tahune Forest Reserve
Huonville
Kaoota
Blowhole
Huon
Franklin
South Arm
Devils Kitchen
Arthur Range
Cradoc
Dennes Point
Nubeena
Oakwood
Tasman Peninsula
Mt Picton 1327 m
Port Huon
Kettering
Storm Bay
Fortescue Bay
Mt Norold 978 m
Geeveston
Cygnet
Woodbridge
Stormlea
Port Arthur
Cape Hauy
Waratah Lookout
Surges Bay
B68
Middleton
North Bruny Island
Remarkable Cave
Munroe Bight
Old
Mt 1255 m
Hartz Peak
A6
Garden Is. Creek
Cape Raoul
Maingon Bay
Cape Pillar
Hartz Mountains N.P.
Dover
Simpsons Bay
Tasman Island
Hastings Cave
Adventure Bay
Cape Pillar State Reserve
Tasman Sea
Solly
Lunawanna
Captain Cook's Landing Place
Cookville
Mt Counsel 800 m
Thermal Pool
Hastings
Bligh Museum
Southwest N.P.
Southport
New River Lagoon
Ida Bay
Scenic Railway
South Bruny Island
Mt Leillateah 799 m
Southport Lagoon
Tasman Head
De Witt Island
Recherche Bay
Flat Witch Island
Ile Du Golfe
Cockle Creek
Surprise Bay
Maatsuyker Island
South Cape
South Cape Bay
South East Cape
Maatsuyker Group
0
20
40
60 km
0
10
20
30
40 miles
National road
Highway
tarred
untarred
Main road
Major petrol stop
Caravan park
Museum
Place of interest

SOUTH AUSTRALIA

South Australia is a fascinating mixture of desert and sophisticated agricultural endeavours. While nearly half the state is desert, the other half is famous for its excellent vineyards, fine citrus groves and highly productive wool and wheat areas. Australia's third-largest state, it covers a total of 984 400km² (380 000 sq miles) of which just under half is no more than a desert of saltbush, mulga, seemingly endless sand dunes and flat, waterless lakes. The south and south-east of the state, notably the area of the Flinders and Mount Lofty ranges, the Eyre, Yorke and Fleurieu peninsulas, the Coorong and the Murray River valley is home to more than 70 per cent of the state's population. It is here that vines, olives, figs, oranges, wheat, sheep, barley and oats are successfully farmed. Tourist attractions include the Adelaide Hills, the vineyards of the Barossa and Clare valleys, the unspoilt beaches of the Coorong, the strange blue lake at Mount Gambier, paddle steamer and houseboat trips along the Murray, and bushwalking in the beautiful Flinders Ranges.

South Australia's capital is Adelaide, with its slow-flowing River Torrens, beautiful parks and churches. The state also contains fertile vineyards and produces some of Australia's premium wines, despite the fact that just under half the state's area is not arable. Only about one-third of South Australia – the area of the Flinders and Mount Lofty ranges, the Eyre, Yorke and Fleurieu peninsulas, the Coorong and the Murray River valley – is deemed to be economically viable. Most of these areas experience a Mediterranean climate of cold, moist winters and dry hot summers. These conditions near the coast weaken further inland and degenerate into areas where annual rainfall is below 125mm (5in) and summer temperatures can soar beyond 40°C (100°F).

A low and unreliable water supply has necessitated the development of a sophisticated system of water storage and conservation. In recent times the resources of the Murray River have become a vital part of the state's economic well-being, supporting an agricultural base that accounts for most of Australia's wine production, as well as an assortment of other crops.

The gem of South Australia is its capital. There is no city in Australia quite like Adelaide. It has a country-town friendliness with an urbanity that gives it a distinctively European feel. It is a city that can still be traversed from north to south via the main street, King William Road, without having to contend with traffic jams. In the last half-century, Adelaide, like all Australian cities, has sprawled. Its suburbs now spread for nearly 40km (25 miles) to the south, reaching almost to the McLaren Vale wine-producing area. To the east they nestle upon the Adelaide Hills, and to the north they spill into the industrial town of Elizabeth.

Beyond the city are the famous Adelaide Hills, now one of South Australia's most popular holiday destinations. The small villages tucked into the hills – Birdwood, Cudlee Creek, Blackwood, Clarendon, Glen Osmond, Gumeracha, Hahndorf, Lobethal, Mount Barker – offer a mixture of tourist attractions such as museums and gift shops, and rural housing for people eager to escape the city life. Centrepiece of the area is Hahndorf – the oldest-surviving German settlement in Australia. First settled by German émigrés in 1840, Hahndorf is a popular tourist haunt with galleries, crafts, bakeries and restaurants specialising in German cuisine.

The Mediterranean climate of South Australia convinced the early settlers that this was an ideal area for vineyards and as early as 1837, less than a year after the arrival of the state's first settlers, John Barton Hack had planted grape vines in north Adelaide. Today more than half of all grapes grown in Australia are harvested in South Australia, which has over 150 wineries.

The most famous wine-producing area is the Barossa Valley, where wine has been grown commercially since the 1840s. The valley is only 30km (19 miles) long and 8km (5 miles) wide, but its soil, climate and rainfall are ideal. Over 100km (62 miles) north of the Barossa Valley, and surrounded by the Mount Lofty Ranges, is the Clare Valley. Vineyards were introduced into this area in 1848 by the Austrian Jesuit priest, Father Aloysius Kranewitter.

North of the Clare Valley, the Flinders Ranges, the most extensive mountain range in the state, stretch 500km (311 miles) from Crystal Brook to the southern edges of the Lake Eyre basin. The beauty of the ranges, particularly in spring with its clear blue days and its fields of indigenous flowers, has resulted in a dramatic increase in tourism. Wilpena Pound, especially, is popular with walkers and explorers.

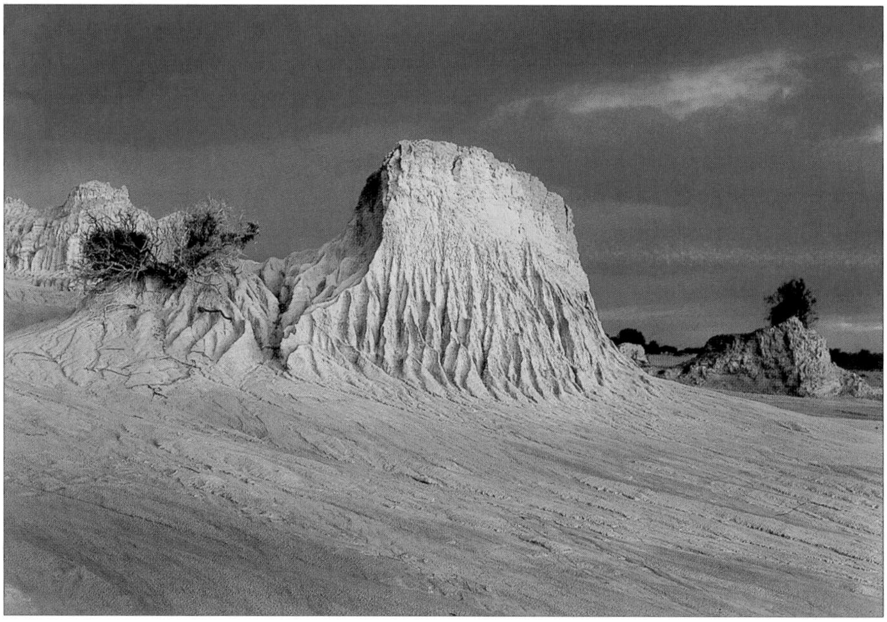

Left: *The reward of a hike to St Mary's Peak in the Flinders Ranges is a spectacular view of Wilpena Pound, so called because of the enclosing lie of the land.*

At the entrance of Gulf St Vincent is Kangaroo Island, the third-largest island off the Australian coast. The absence of predators and any large human settlement has resulted in wildlife that has never been threatened. Thus, at Seal Bay, visitors can walk among the unwary seals.

To the south-east of Adelaide lie over 145km (90 miles) of sand dunes, known as the Coorong. On the western shore of Gulf St Vincent lies a long narrow promontory known as the Yorke Peninsula. The poor quality of the vegetation and the lack of permanent water inhibited settlement and it wasn't until the 1860s, when copper was discovered, that any permanent townships were established.

The Eyre Peninsula, the western coastline of South Australia, was the first part of the state to be sighted by Europeans. In 1627 the Dutch explorer Peter Nuyts sailed across the Great Australian Bight, sighted the peninsula but, deciding not to land, turned back and headed north towards Batavia (now Indonesia). At best the Eyre Peninsula is marginal land. As a consequence, the main agricultural activities of this harsh area are sheep grazing and wheat farming. One of the peninsula's distinctive features are the clusters of wheat silos scattered over the countryside.

Port Lincoln is the home of a fish cannery. The Spencer Gulf and the Southern Ocean yield a rich harvest of bluefin and striped tuna, whiting, shark, garfish, snapper and salmon, as well as southern rock lobsters, western king prawns, abalone, scallops and Coffin Bay oysters.

To the north and west of the Eyre Peninsula is desert. In the 1950s this barrenness was deemed ideal for a rocket launching station and nuclear experiments, a ruling that totally ignored the resident indigenous population. Woomera, established in 1948, was a base for service and scientific personnel. In 1955 the nearby centre of Maralinga was established as a base for British nuclear testing.

The western strip of coastal South Australia, the southern limit of the Nullarbor Plain, is an arid flat limestone plateau which has been chewed away for millions of years by the relentless seas of the Southern Ocean. On the coast the plain falls away in a dramatic series of sheer cliffs. The Nullarbor plain experiences less than 250mm (10in) of rainfall per annum, but due to the porous nature of the limestone, rainwater drains underground so quickly that streams cannot form.

In recent years elaborate cave systems have been found under the plain's harsh exterior. Mullamullang Cave in the Madura district is now recognised as the largest in Australia. There are cave paintings and flint quarries in the region, and Koonalda Cave has evidence of Aboriginal habitation dating back 18 000 years.

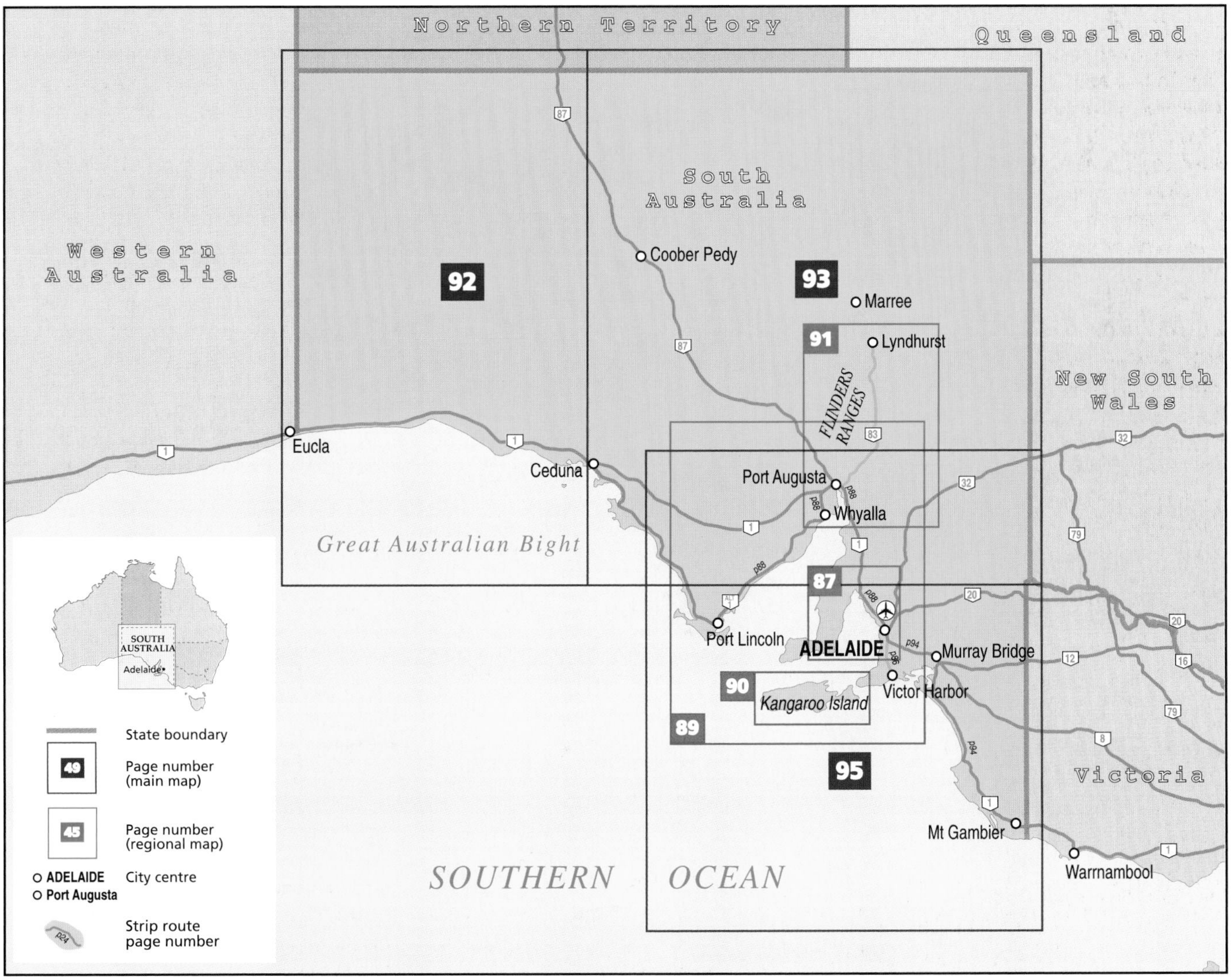

Adelaide

Adelaide, located on the flat coastal plain between Gulf St Vincent and the Mount Lofty Ranges, spreads out on either side of the Torrens River. Famed for its churches and parks, the city is small enough to have the easy charm of a country town, retaining an elegance that many other Australian cities envy. With a population of over a million people, Adelaide is the country's fourth-largest city. Its broad streets give it a sense of openness and cleanliness. Adelaide's malls, parks and the Torrens River are all conducive to leisurely walks and picnics. Every even-numbered year, the city hosts its international arts festival.

TOP ATTRACTIONS

Art Gallery: early prints and drawings of colonial Australia.
Ayers House: elegant Regency building, which was built in 1846, now houses the National Trust of South Australia.
Botanic Gardens: magnificent wisteria arbour and an avenue of Moreton Bay figs.
Festival Centre: arts complex on the banks of the Torrens River.
Glenelg: beachside town which is where Adelaide started.
Holy Trinity Church: known as the 'pioneer church of South Australia'.
St Francis Xavier's Cathedral: the centre for Roman Catholic worship in Adelaide.
Tandanya: home of the National Aboriginal Cultural Institute.

WHERE TO STAY

Adelaide's City Backpackers, Franklin St, tel: (08) 8212 7974, Simple living in a historic sandstone building situated in the city centre.
Festival Lodge Motel, North Terrace, tel: (08) 8212 7877, fax: 8211 8137. Well appointed, reasonably priced and centrally located.
Grosvenor, North Terrace, tel: (08) 8231 2961, fax: 8407 8866. Family hotel with a variety of room styles and rates.
Hilton International Adelaide, Victoria Sq, tel: (08) 8217 2000, fax: 8217 2001. Central, luxury hotel.
Hindley Parkroyal, Hindley St, tel: (08) 8231 5552, fax: 8237 3800. Well located, excellent facilities.
Ramada Grand Hotel, Glenelg, tel: (08) 8376 1222, fax: 8376 1111. Best hotel in this beautiful suburb, short tram ride to city centre.
Stamford Plaza, North Terrace, tel: (08) 8461 1111, fax: 8461 0319. Adelaide's most elegant hotel, offers service and views to match.
Mary Penfold Panorama, 17 Mary Penfold Drive, Rosslyn Park, tel/fax: (08) 8332 6684. A luxury residence that overlooks the city.

ADELAIDE	J	F	M	A	M	J	J	A	S	O	N	D
AV. TEMP. °F	75	75	72	64	59	53	52	53	57	63	68	72
AV. TEMP. °C	24	24	22	18	15	12	11	12	14	17	20	22
DAILY SUN hrs	10	9	8	6	5	4	4	5	6	7	9	9
RAINFALL in	1	1	1	2	2.5	3	2.5	2.5	2	2	1	1
RAINFALL mm	20	21	24	44	68	72	67	62	51	44	31	26
RAINFALL days	4	4	5	9	13	15	16	16	13	11	8	6

CALENDAR OF EVENTS

JANUARY: Australian Hardcourt Tennis Championships, Rio International Tennis Challenge, Greek Blessing of the Waters (Glenelg), Oom Pah Festival (Tanunda).
MARCH: Fiesta Music Festival, International Women's Day Procession, St Patrick's Week Festivities, Outback Tourism Fair, Multicultural Carnival, Glendi Greek Festival and the Essenfest at Tanunda.
APRIL: Heritage Week, Rose Festival. A number of autumn leaves festivals are held in the Adelaide Hills area.
MAY: Come Out Festival, the Barossa Balloon Festival in Seppeltsfield.
JUNE: The Riverland Country Music Festival, held at a number of venues along the Murray River.
AUGUST: Classic Gourmet Weekend held in the Barossa Valley.
SEPTEMBER: Hills Affare.
OCTOBER: Wine Bushing Festival held at McLaren Vale.
NOVEMBER: John Martin's State Bank Christmas Pageant, Port Adelaide Parade, Blumenfest at Hahndorf.

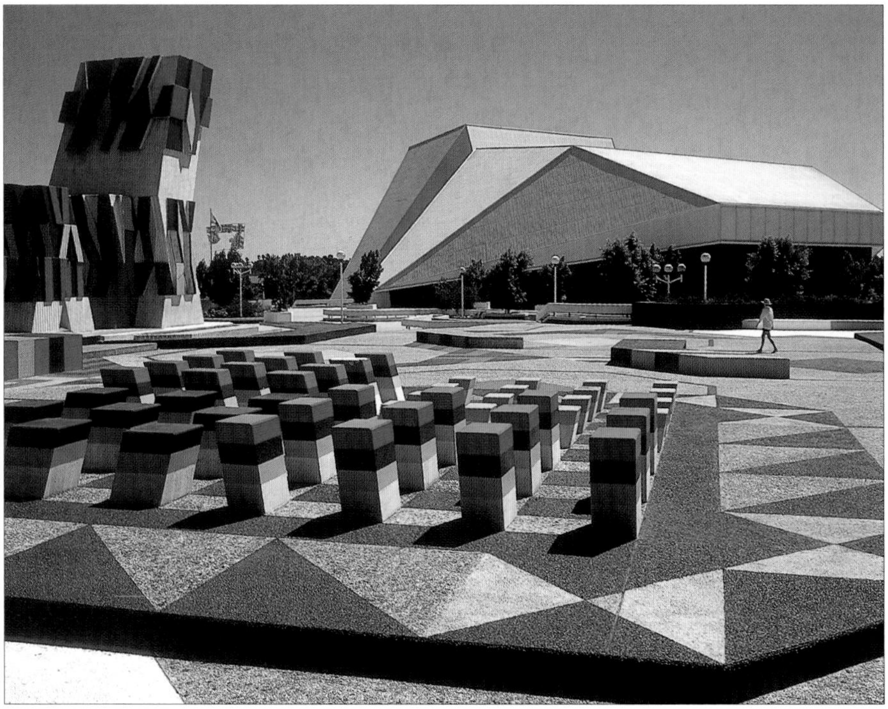

Top: *Victoria Bridge is overlooked by the Hyatt Hotel.*
Left: *The Festival Centre, heart of the Adelaide Festival of Arts held on even-numbered years.*

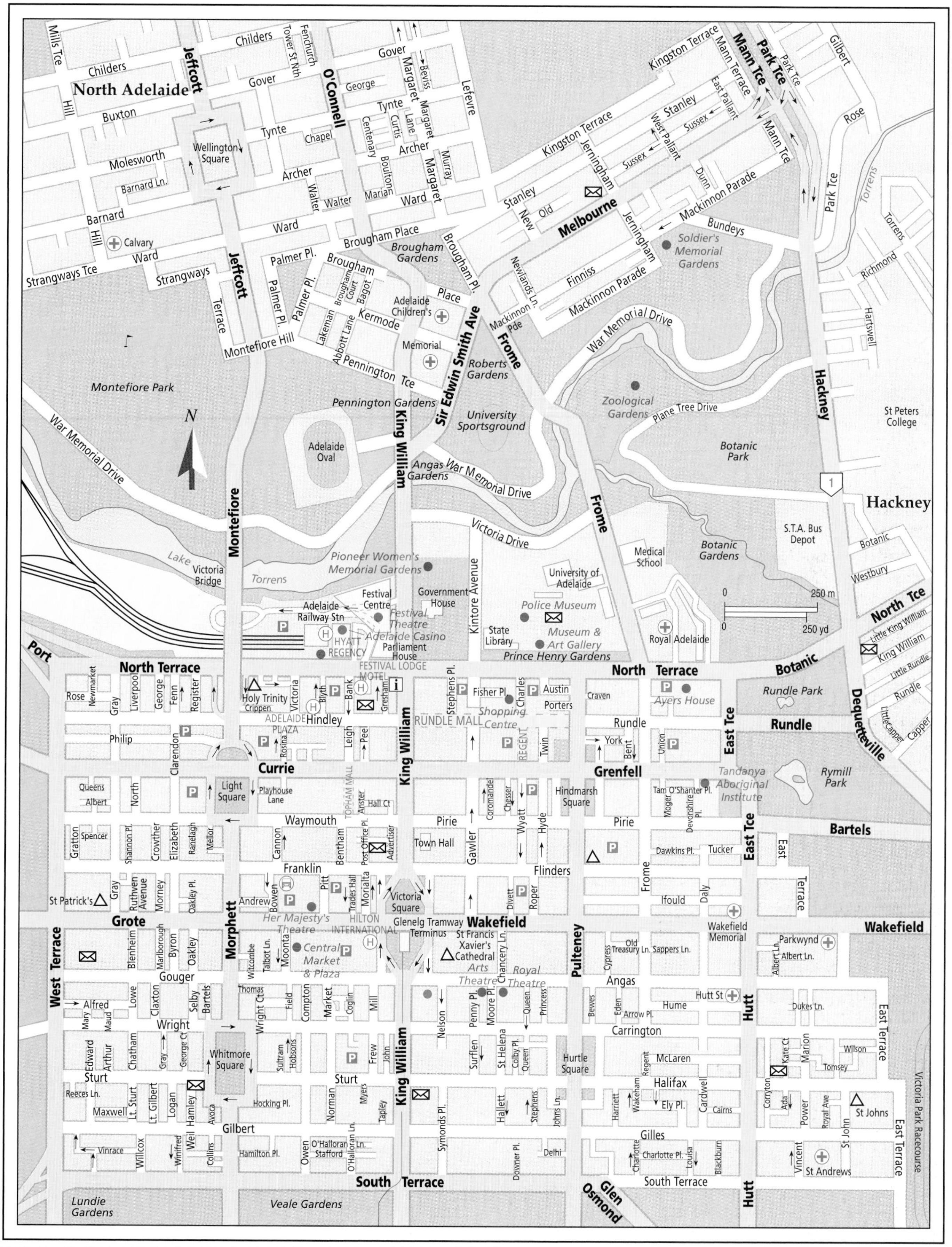

△ St Patrick's	Place of worship	(bus)	Bus terminus	✉	Post office
Ⓗ	Hotel	●	Police station	● Market	Place of interest
i	Information	P	Parking	(flag)	Golf course

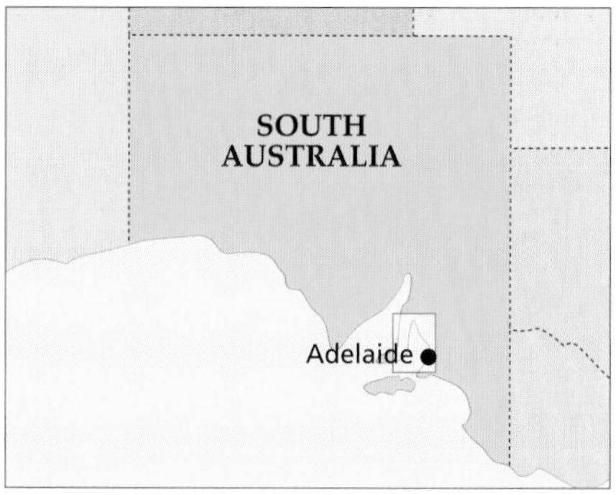

Adelaide Daytrips

The areas surrounding Adelaide, particularly the beaches of Spencer Gulf and Gulf St Vincent and the hills and valleys to the east of the city, offer an interesting range of activities combined with the region's mild weather and reliable roads. There is the luxurious charm of the Adelaide Hills, complete with tea-houses and gift shops; the vineyards of the Barossa and Clare valleys to the east, offering an opportunity to taste the local produce and inspect the wine-making facilities; the beaches, quiet villages and charming old mining towns on the Yorke Peninsula; and the peaceful, isolated beauty of the Flinders Ranges which offer excellent bushwalking.

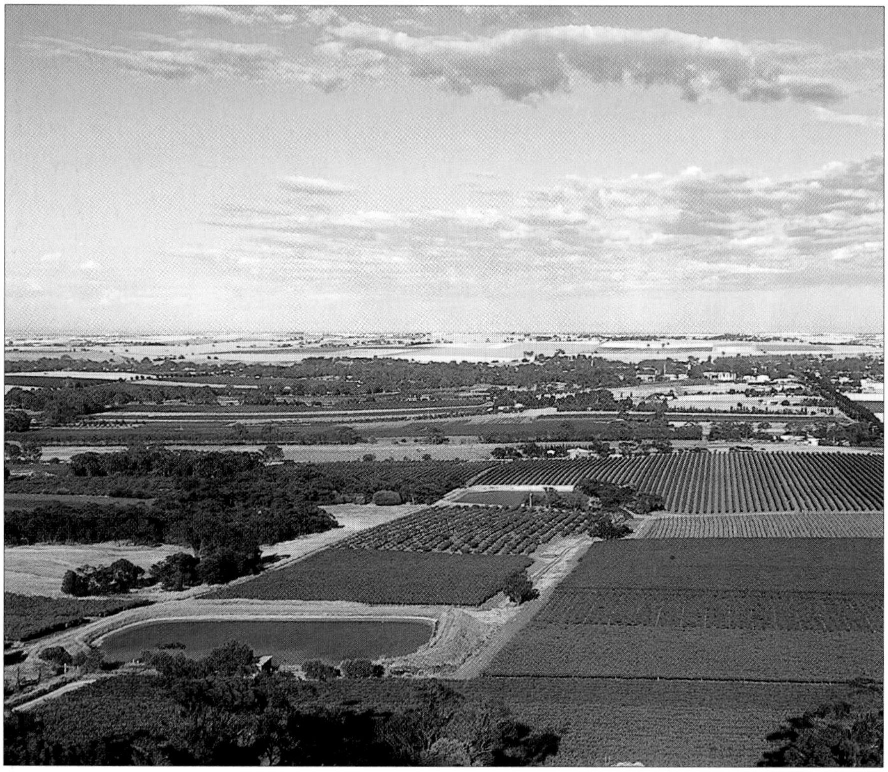

Above: *The Barossa Valley is named after the sherry region of Spain and lies 55km (34 miles) north of Adelaide.*

TOP ATTRACTIONS

Adelaide Hills: small villages with gift shops, tourist attractions and excellent restaurants, within easy reach of Adelaide.
Barossa and Clare valleys: nearly 60 per cent of all grapes grown in Australia are harvested in South Australia which boasts no fewer than 150 wineries known both locally and overseas.
Flinders Ranges: most extensive mountain range in the state, the beauty of the region has created a dramatic increase in tourism.
Wilpena Pound: within the Flinders Ranges, is of exceptional beauty and popular with walkers and explorers.
Hahndorf: the oldest-surviving German settlement in Australia.

APPROX. DISTANCES IN KM FROM ADELAIDE	
Broken Hill	517
Bordertown	274
Ceduna	783
Coober Pedy	846
Innamincka	1048
Leigh Creek	600
Mt Gambier	462
Murray Bridge	84
Pinnaroo	252
Port Augusta	318
Port Lincoln	672
Port Pirie	231
Renmark	253
Streaky Bay	708
Whyalla	392
Woomera	490

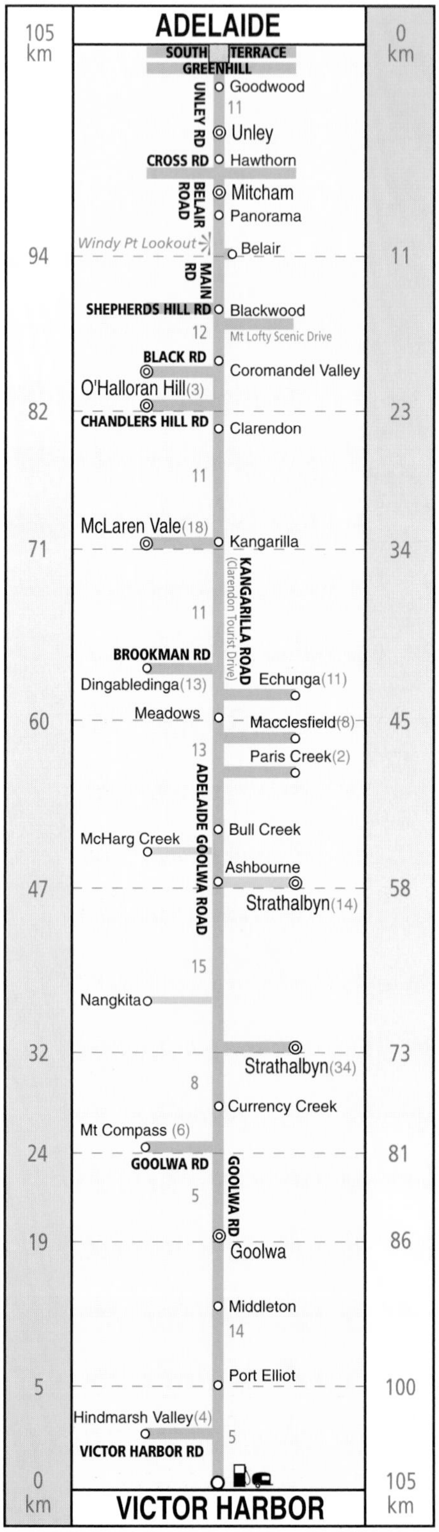

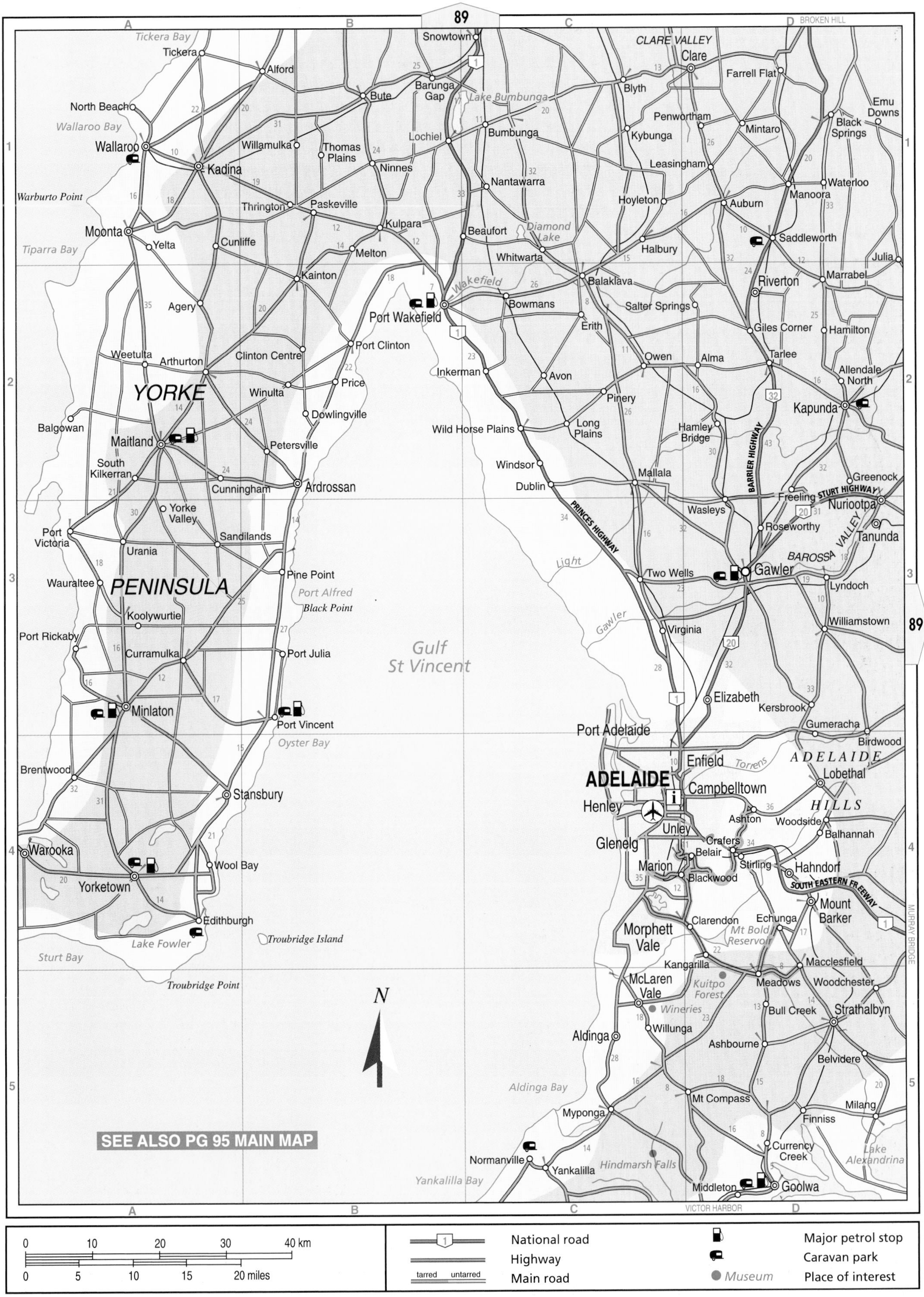
89
A
B
C
D
BROKEN HILL
Tickera Bay
Tickera
Alford
Snowtown
Barunga Gap
Lake Bumbunga
CLARE VALLEY
Clare
Farrell Flat
North Beach
Bute
Blyth
Emu Downs
Wallaroo Bay
Penwortham
Black Springs
Mintaro
Wallaroo
Willamulka
Thomas Plains
Lochiel
Bumbunga
Kybunga
Kadina
Ninnes
Leasingham
Nantawarra
Waterloo
Manoora
Warburto Point
Thrington
Paskeville
Hoyleton
Auburn
Kulpara
Moonta
Beaufort
Diamond Lake
Saddleworth
Tiparra Bay
Yelta
Cunliffe
Melton
Halbury
Whitwarta
Julia
Kainton
Wakefield
Balaklava
Marrabel
Riverton
Agery
Bowmans
Salter Springs
Port Wakefield
Erith
Giles Corner
Hamilton
Port Clinton
Weetulta
Arthurton
Clinton Centre
Owen
Alma
Tarlee
Inkerman
Avon
Allendale North
YORKE
Winulta
Price
Pinery
Kapunda
Balgowan
Dowlingville
Wild Horse Plains
Long Plains
Hamley Bridge
Maitland
Petersville
BARRIER HIGHWAY
South Kilkerran
Windsor
Greenock
Mallala
Cunningham
Ardrossan
Dublin
Freeling
STURT HIGHWAY
Nuriootpa
Yorke Valley
Wasleys
PRINCES HIGHWAY
Port Victoria
Sandilands
Roseworthy
Tanunda
Urania
BAROSSA VALLEY
Light
Pine Point
Two Wells
Gawler
Wauraltee
PENINSULA
Port Alfred
Lyndoch
Black Point
Koolywurtie
Williamstown
Gawler
Port Rickaby
Virginia
Curramulka
Port Julia
Gulf St Vincent
Minlaton
Elizabeth
Kersbrook
Port Vincent
Port Adelaide
Gumeracha
Oyster Bay
Birdwood
Enfield
Torrens
ADELAIDE
Brentwood
ADELAIDE
Lobethal
Campbelltown
Stansbury
Henley
HILLS
Ashton
Woodside
Unley
Balhannah
Warooka
Glenelg
Crafers
Belair
Stirling
Hahndorf
Wool Bay
Marion
Blackwood
SOUTH EASTERN FREEWAY
Yorketown
Mount Barker
MURRAY BRIDGE
Clarendon
Echunga
Edithburgh
Morphett Vale
Mt Bold Reservoir
Lake Fowler
Troubridge Island
Sturt Bay
Kangarilla
Macclesfield
McLaren Vale
Kuitpo Forest
Meadows
Woodchester
Troubridge Point
N
Wineries
Bull Creek
Strathalbyn
Willunga
Aldinga
Ashbourne
Belvidere
Aldinga Bay
Mt Compass
Milang
Myponga
Finniss
SEE ALSO PG 95 MAIN MAP
Currency Creek
Lake Alexandrina
Normanville
Yankalilla
Hindmarsh Falls
Yankalilla Bay
Middleton
Goolwa
VICTOR HARBOR
0 10 20 30 40 km
0 5 10 15 20 miles
National road
Highway
tarred untarred
Main road
Major petrol stop
Caravan park
Museum
Place of interest

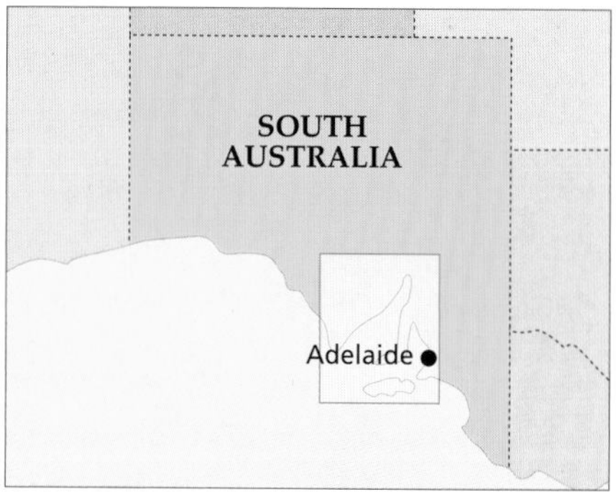

Yorke and Eyre Peninsulas

To the west of Adelaide is the Yorke Peninsula. Further west across the Spencer Gulf lies the Eyre Peninsula, which is isolated and sparsely populated. The waters of the Gulf and the Southern Ocean yield a rich harvest of fish, southern rock lobsters, western king prawns, abalone, scallops and Coffin Bay oysters. Near Port Lincoln at the foot of the Eyre Peninsula, both Coffin Bay and Lincoln national parks provide visitors with excellent bushwalking and dramatic coastal scenery. At the northern end of the peninsula, Whyalla is the centre of the state's steel industry and one of the most important steel-producing cities in the country.

TOP ATTRACTIONS

Lincoln National Park: the Flinders Monument vantage point on Stamford Hill offers magnificent views over the rugged coast. **Port Lincoln:** the National Trust's Mill Cottage Museum has an interesting collection of local memorabilia including furniture brought from England in 1839. **Whalers' Way:** excellent views of blowholes, bomboras, dramatic crevasses, capes and cliffs. The coastline is pounded by waves from the Southern Ocean and is home to substantial numbers of kangaroos and emus. **Winter Hill Lookout:** offers views across Boston Bay out to Boston and Donington islands.

Right: *Coffin Bay is a sheltered Eyre Peninsula inlet, popular for fishing and water sports.*
Below: *Winter Hill Lookout provides fabulous views of Port Lincoln and across the Spencer Gulf to the Yorke Peninsula.*

WHERE TO STAY

Port Lincoln offers a wide range of accommodation:
Boston Island Homestead, Boston Island, tel: (08) 8682 1741 or 8682 1708 .
First Landing Motel, 11 Shaen St, tel: (08) 8682 2344.
Flintstone Lodge, Cook St, tel: (08) 8682 1655.
Hilton Motel, 13 King St, tel: (08) 8682 1144.
Kingscourt Motel, 12 Tasman Terrace, tel: (08) 8682 2033.
Limani Motel, Lincoln Hwy, tel: (08) 8682 2200.
Sleaford Bay Holiday Park, Sleaford Bay, tel: (08) 8685 6002.
Westward Ho Holiday Units, London St, tel: (08) 8682 2425.

ON THE ROAD

The **Lincoln Highway** runs along the east coast of the Eyre Peninsula with the **Flinders Highway** running up the west. Both are sealed and services are offered in all the major towns. This is an area of low population and small levels of tourism, consequently the roads into the national parks and to the cliffs and beaches are often unsealed and of poor quality. The lesser roads on the peninsula are often good because the area is rather flat and the rainfall is low.

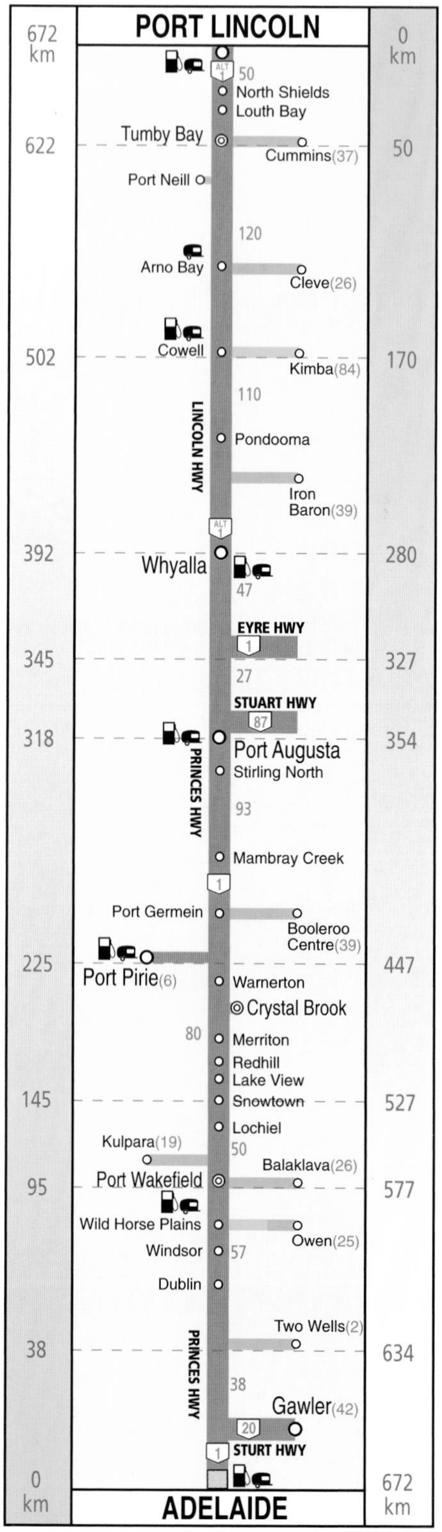

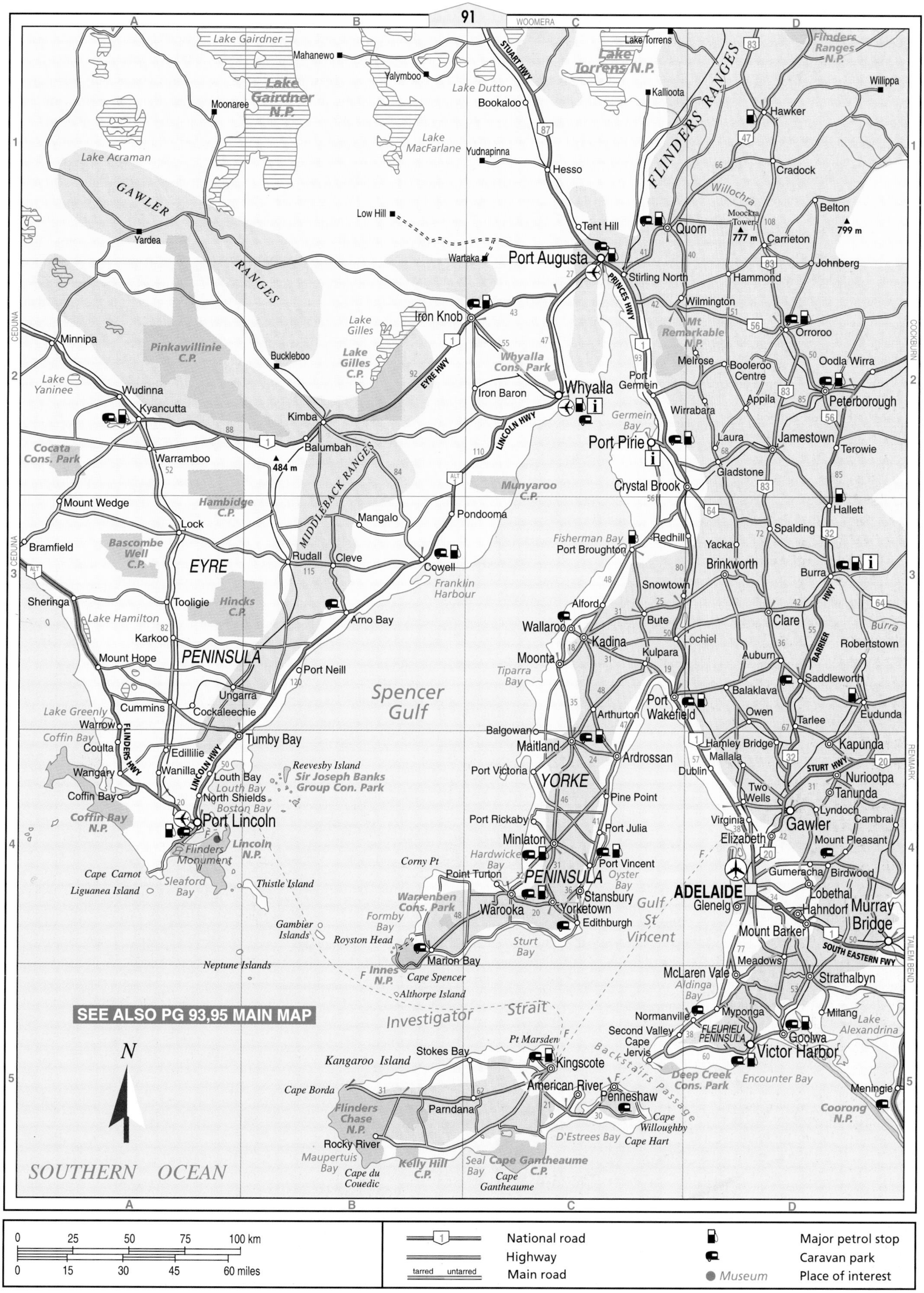
91
WOOMERA
CEDUNA
COCKBURN
RENMARK
TAILEM BEND
Lake Gairdner
Lake Gairdner N.P.
Mahanewo
Yalymboo
Lake Dutton
Bookaloo
Moonaree
Lake Torrens
Lake Torrens N.P.
Kallioota
Flinders Ranges N.P.
Willippa
Hawker
FLINDERS RANGES
Lake Acraman
Lake MacFarlane
Yudnapinna
Hesso
Cradock
Willochra
Moockra Tower
777 m
Belton
799 m
Carrieton
Johnberg
GAWLER RANGES
Yardea
Low Hill
Tent Hill
Quorn
Wartaka
Port Augusta
Stirling North
Hammond
Wilmington
STUART HWY
PRINCES HWY
Iron Knob
Lake Gilles
Lake Gilles C.P.
Whyalla Cons. Park
Mt Remarkable N.P.
Orroroo
Melrose
Oodla Wirra
Minnipa
Pinkawillinie C.P.
Buckleboo
EYRE HWY
Booleroo Centre
Lake Yaninee
Wudinna
Iron Baron
Whyalla
Port Germein
Appila
Peterborough
Kyancutta
Kimba
Germein Bay
Wirrabara
Jamestown
Terowie
Cocata Cons. Park
Warramboo
484 m
Balumbah
LINCOLN HWY
Port Pirie
Laura
Gladstone
MIDDLEBACK RANGES
Munyaroo C.P.
Crystal Brook
Mount Wedge
Hambidge C.P.
Mangalo
Pondooma
Hallett
Lock
Redhill
Spalding
Bramfield
Bascombe Well C.P.
Fisherman Bay
Port Broughton
Yacka
Rudall
Cleve
Cowell
Brinkworth
EYRE
Franklin Harbour
Burra
Sheringa
Tooligie
Hincks C.P.
Snowtown
Alford
Lake Hamilton
Arno Bay
Bute
Clare
Karkoo
Wallaroo
Kadina
Lochiel
Robertstown
Burra
BARRIER HWY
Mount Hope
PENINSULA
Moonta
Kulpara
Auburn
Port Neill
Tiparra Bay
Saddleworth
Spencer Gulf
Ungarra
Port Wakefield
Balaklava
Lake Greenly
Cummins
Cockaleechie
Arthurton
Owen
Eudunda
Warrow
Tarlee
Coffin Bay
Coulta
FLINDERS HWY
Tumby Bay
Balgowan
Maitland
Ardrossan
Hamley Bridge
Kapunda
Edillilie
Mallala
STURT HWY
Wangary
Wanilla
Reevesby Island
Sir Joseph Banks Group Con. Park
Port Victoria
Dublin
Nuriootpa
YORKE
Two Wells
Tanunda
Coffin Bay
Louth Bay
North Shields
Boston Bay
Pine Point
Lyndoch
Coffin Bay N.P.
Port Lincoln
Port Rickaby
Gawler
Cambrai
Lincoln N.P.
Virginia
Port Julia
Elizabeth
Minlaton
Mount Pleasant
Flinders Monument
Hardwicke Bay
Port Vincent
Cape Carnot
Corny Pt
Gumeracha
Birdwood
Liguanea Island
Sleaford Bay
Thistle Island
Point Turton
PENINSULA
Oyster Bay
ADELAIDE
Lobethal
Warrenben Cons. Park
Stansbury
Gulf St Vincent
Glenelg
Hahndorf
Murray Bridge
Warooka
Yorketown
Formby Bay
Gambier Islands
Edithburgh
Mount Barker
Royston Head
Sturt Bay
SOUTH EASTERN FWY
Meadows
Marion Bay
Neptune Islands
Innes N.P.
Cape Spencer
McLaren Vale
Aldinga Bay
Strathalbyn
Althorpe Island
SEE ALSO PG 93,95 MAIN MAP
Investigator Strait
Normanville
Myponga
Milang
Lake Alexandrina
Second Valley
FLEURIEU PENINSULA
Cape Jervis
Goolwa
Pt Marsden
Victor Harbor
N
Stokes Bay
Kangaroo Island
Kingscote
Backstairs Passage
Deep Creek Cons. Park
Encounter Bay
Cape Borda
American River
Penneshaw
Meningie
Flinders Chase N.P.
Parndana
Cape Willoughby
Coorong N.P.
D'Estrees Bay
Cape Hart
Rocky River
Maupertuis Bay
Cape du Couedic
Kelly Hill C.P.
Seal Bay
Cape Gantheaume C.P.
Cape Gantheaume
SOUTHERN OCEAN
0
25
50
75
100 km
0
15
30
45
60 miles
tarred
untarred
National road
Highway
Main road
Museum
Major petrol stop
Caravan park
Place of interest

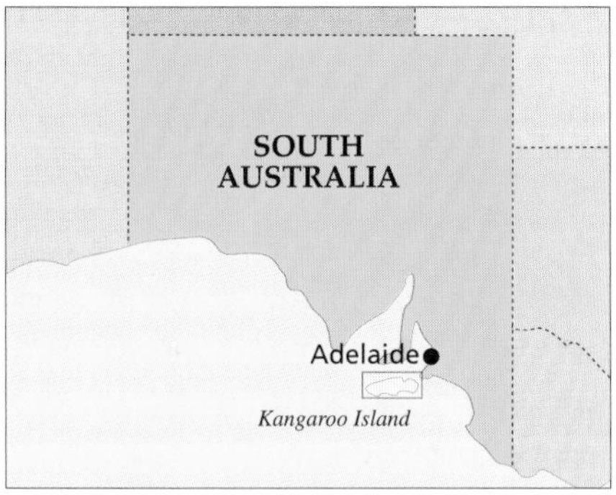

Kangaroo Island

Kangaroo Island, at the entrance of Gulf St Vincent, is Australia's third-largest island and recognised as one of the best natural attractions in South Australia. The absence of predators and any large, permanent human settlement has resulted in a rich variety of wildlife, which is unthreatened by the presence of people. At Seal Bay visitors can walk among the mammals and at the western end of the island the 60 000-ha (148 260-acre) Flinders Chase National Park is home to a wealth of flora and fauna. Other attractions include Kingscote, the largest town on the island, Remarkable Rocks, Kelly Hill Caves and many isolated beaches.

TOP ATTRACTIONS

Remarkable Rocks and Cape du Couedic: island's most south-westerly tip, unusual and impressive natural rock formations.
Cape Willoughby Lighthouse: built of limestone.
Flinders Chase National Park: 803km² (310 sq miles) set aside to protect the island's wildlife.
Hanson Bay: rugged cliffs and safe swimming bays.
Kelly Hill Caves: interesting cave formations.
King George Beach: excellent fishing on a shingle beach.
Little Sahara Desert: white sand dunes with spectacular views.
Seal Bay: it is possible to walk among this large seal colony.

Above: *The sea lions on Kangaroo Island are so used to humans that they are not perturbed by visitors to the beach. The island has always been a sanctuary for wildlife. Since settlement, people have continued to protect the fauna and flora.*

ON THE ROAD

There is no public transport on the island. The island's only sealed road runs between Penneshaw, Kingscote and Parndana, many others are little more than dirt tracks, although they are well maintained. There are very few petrol, food and accommodation outlets on the western side. No fuel or food is available in the island's parks.

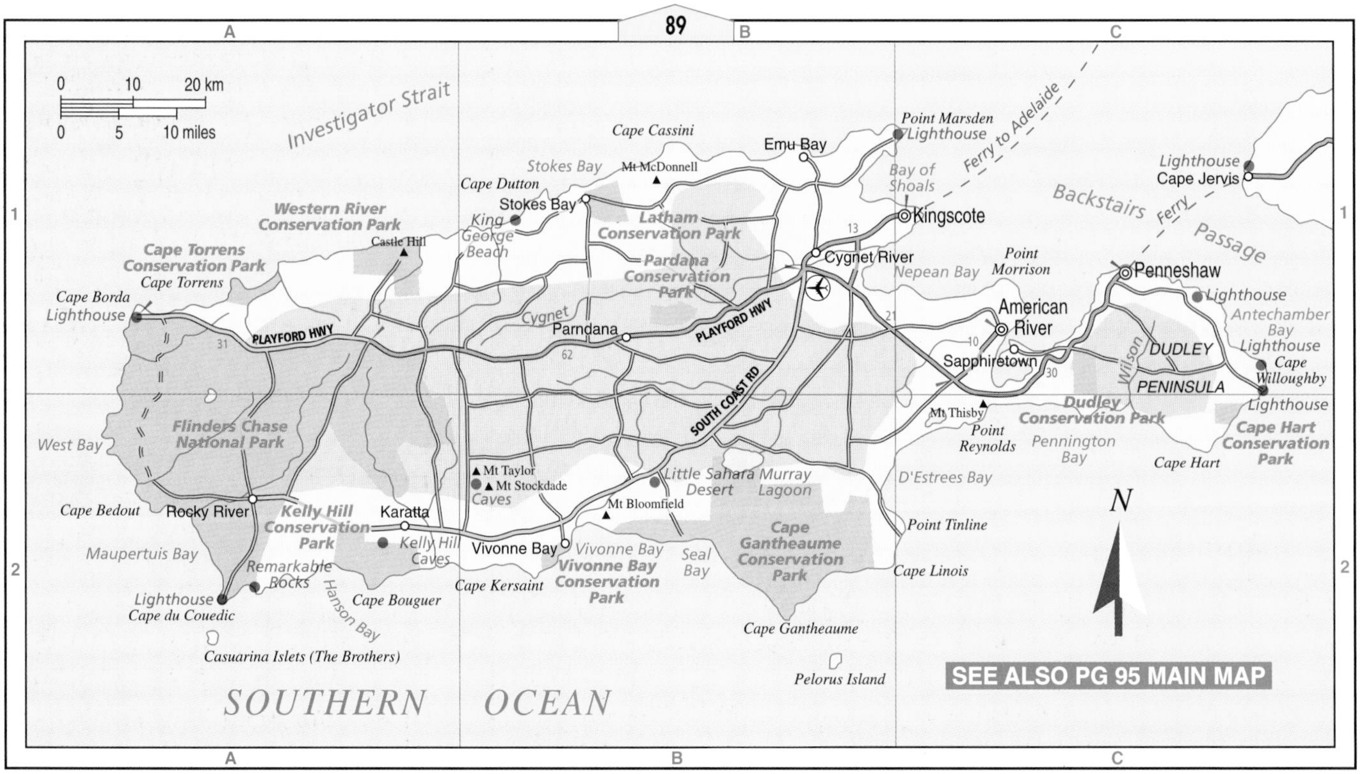

Port Augusta and Flinders Ranges

The northern half of South Australia is nothing more than desert – sand dunes, searing summer temperatures, and a scrubby, inhospitable terrain. The Flinders Ranges are the most extensive mountain range in the state. They stretch 500km (311 miles) from Crystal Brook, near Port Pirie to the Lake Eyre Basin. About 650 million years ago the range formed part of the sea bed. Its subsequent uplift revealed fossilised sea creatures – trilobites and worms – in the rock formations. These are generally recognised as being the oldest fauna fossils on earth and they are surrounded by an incredibly beautiful, rugged terrain.

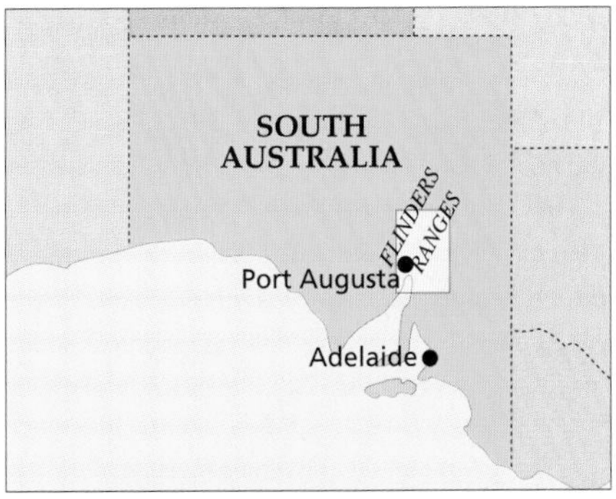

TOP ATTRACTIONS

Flinders Ranges: the Flinders Ranges National Park (1972) and Gammon Ranges National Park (1970), offer bushwalking and a chance to appreciate the beauty of this ancient, hilly landscape.
Lyndhurst: on the edge of the desert, a small town with a few buildings at the crossroads of the Strzelecki and Oodnadatta tracks.
Port Augusta: the Tourist Centre provides excellent information on both the Flinders Ranges and the Stuart Highway which runs from Port Augusta to Darwin.
Wilpena Pound: a 'pound' is a synclinal basin; Wilpena Pound, an area of great beauty, has become popular with both walkers and explorers.

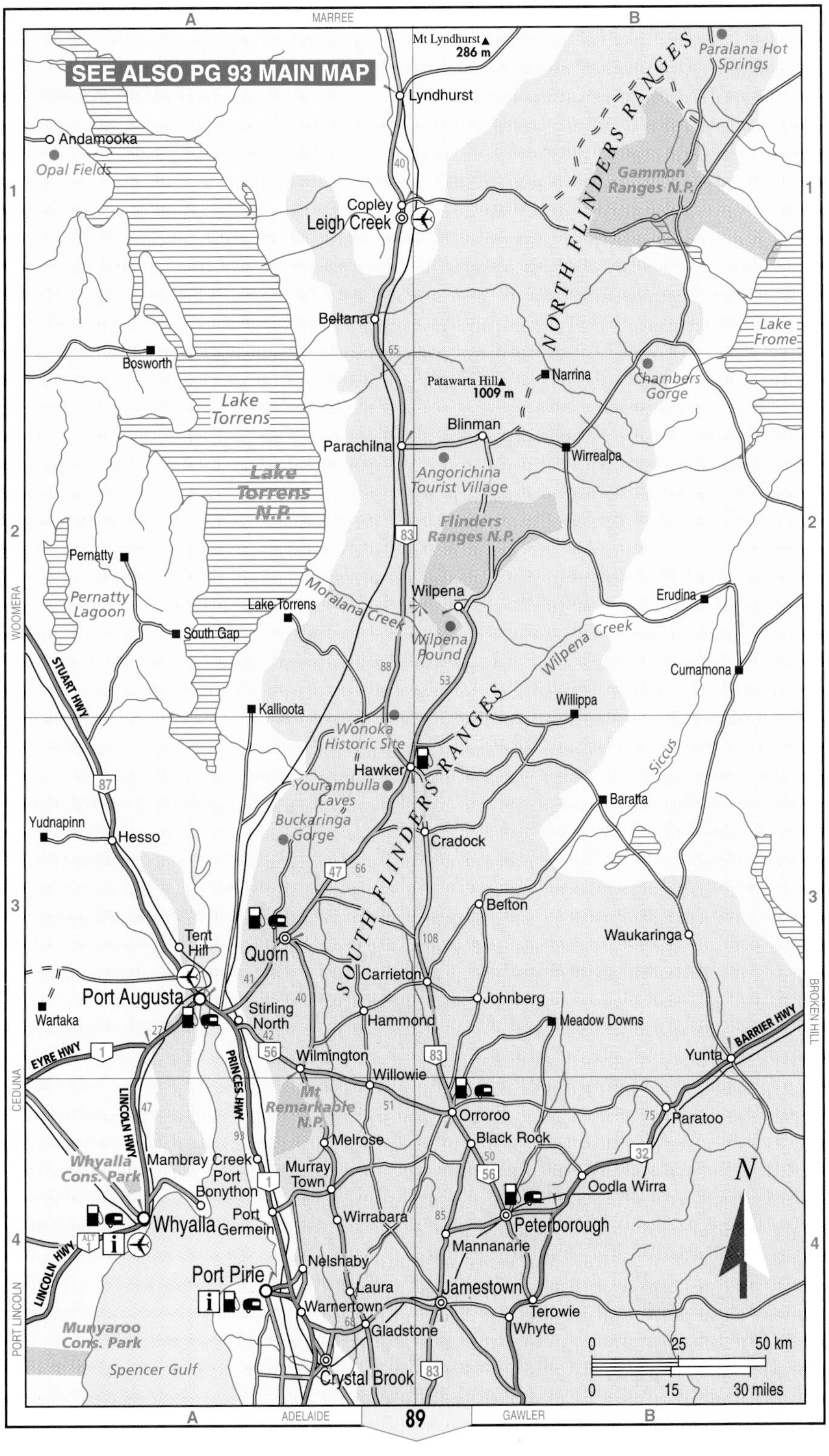

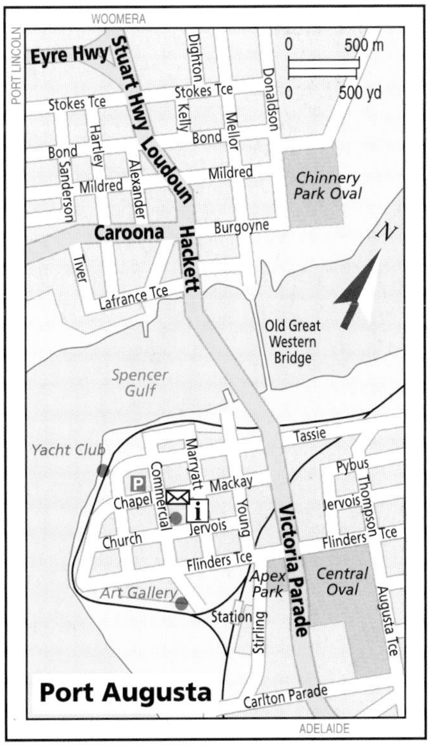

Outback South Australia

After leaving Port Augusta the road is flanked by salt lakes, scrubby dry country and occasional mesas rising from the flat landscape. However, strange settlements allow travellers to experience the frontier lifestyle of the Australian outback – and to spend a night in an underground motel. Woomera is an interesting space-research township. Modern Roxby Downs mines copper, gold, silver and uranium, while in opal-mining towns like Coober Pedy and Andamooka most of the population live underground due to the heat.

ON THE ROAD

The **Stuart Highway** is the main sealed road through outback South Australia. Townships and roadhouses appear at regular intervals, providing food, accommodation and motoring services. Beyond the highway the roads are unsealed and dangerous for those unfamiliar with desert driving. The distances are great and there are few vehicles on the road. Fill your tank before you leave the main road and stay with your vehicle if it breaks down, particularly in the hot summer months.

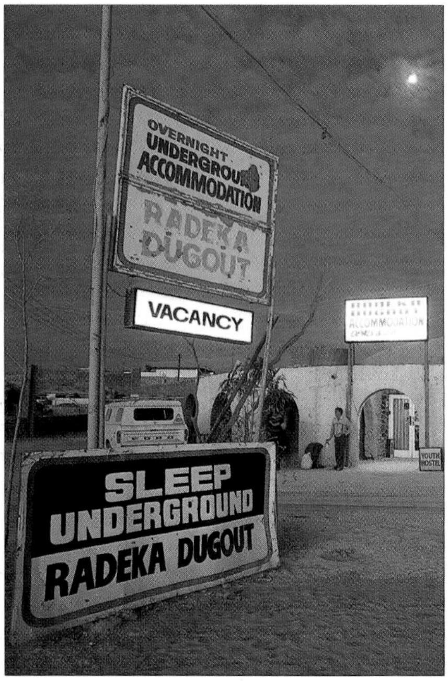

Above: *Radeka hostel provides travellers with a taste of living life underground at the eccentric outback town of Coober Pedy.*

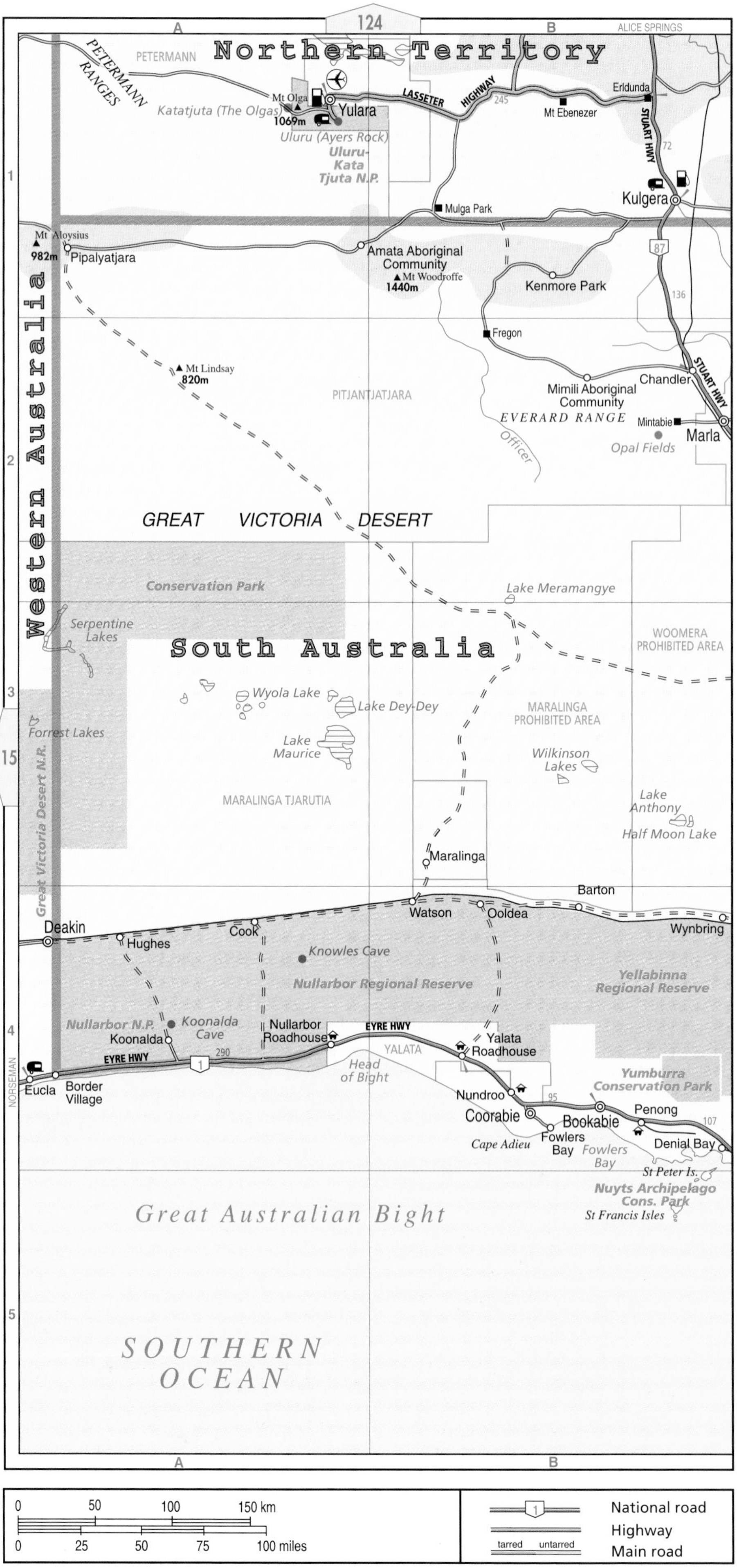

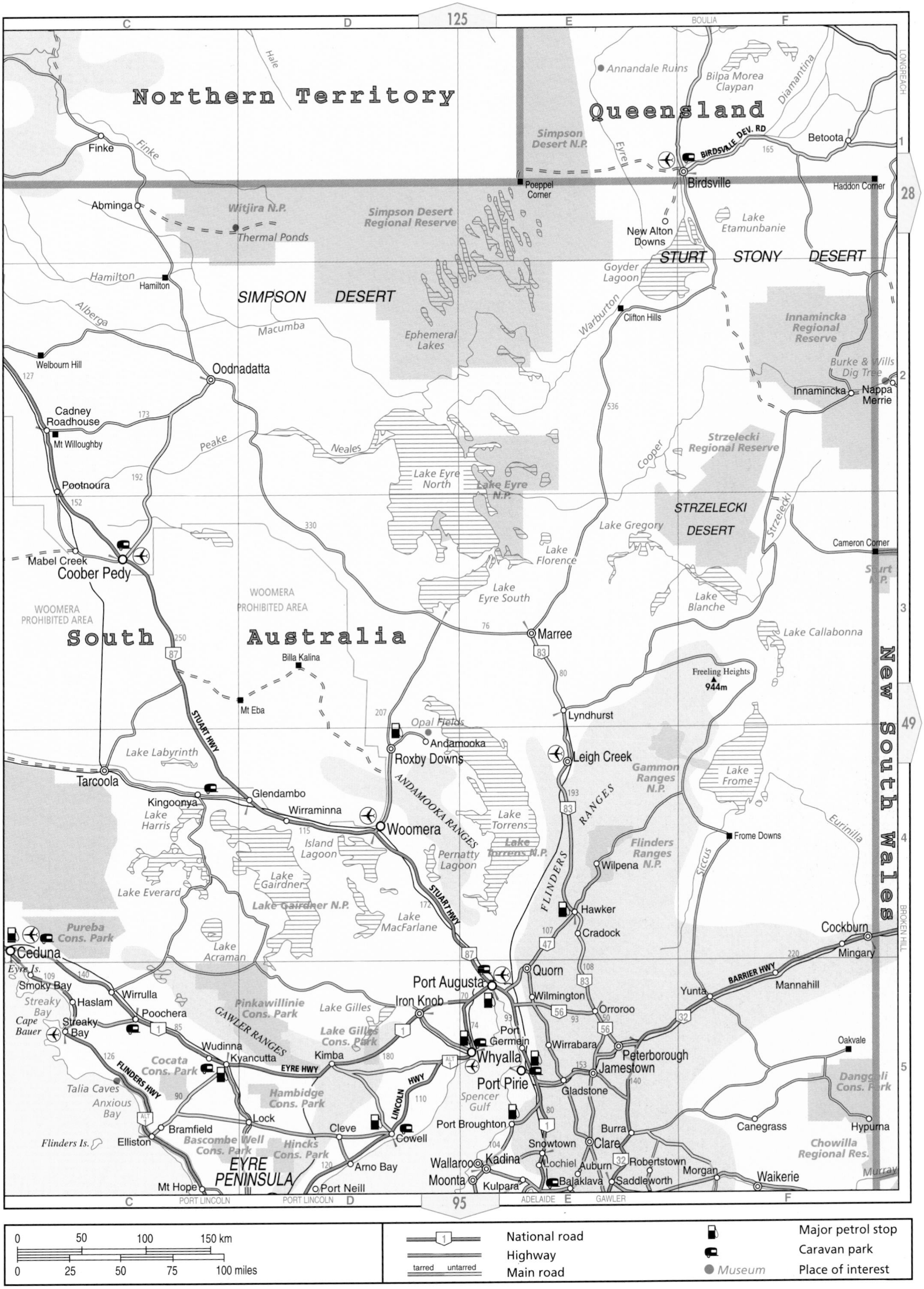
Northern Territory
Queensland
South Australia
New South Wales
SIMPSON DESERT
STURT STONY DESERT
STRZELECKI DESERT
Simpson Desert N.P.
Simpson Desert Regional Reserve
Witjira N.P.
Innamincka Regional Reserve
Strzelecki Regional Reserve
Lake Eyre N.P.
Flinders Ranges N.P.
Gammon Ranges N.P.
Lake Torrens N.P.
Lake Gairdner N.P.
Pureba Cons. Park
Pinkawillinie Cons. Park
Lake Gilles Cons. Park
Cocata Cons. Park
Hambidge Cons. Park
Bascombe Well Cons. Park
Hincks Cons. Park
Danggali Cons. Park
Chowilla Regional Res.
Sturt N.P.
WOOMERA PROHIBITED AREA
Finke
Abminga
Thermal Ponds
Hamilton
Welbourn Hill
Oodnadatta
Cadney Roadhouse
Mt Willoughby
Pootnoura
Mabel Creek
Coober Pedy
Birdsville
Betoota
Poeppel Corner
Haddon Corner
Annandale Ruins
Bilpa Morea Claypan
New Alton Downs
Goyder Lagoon
Clifton Hills
Burke & Wills Dig Tree
Innamincka
Nappa Merrie
Lake Etamunbanie
Ephemeral Lakes
Lake Eyre North
Lake Eyre South
Lake Gregory
Lake Florence
Lake Blanche
Lake Callabonna
Cameron Corner
Marree
Freeling Heights 944m
Lyndhurst
Leigh Creek
Lake Frome
Frome Downs
Billa Kalina
Mt Eba
Opal Fields
Andamooka
Roxby Downs
Tarcoola
Lake Labyrinth
Kingoonya
Glendambo
Wirraminna
Woomera
Lake Harris
Island Lagoon
Lake Torrens
Pernatty Lagoon
Lake Gairdner
Lake Everard
Lake MacFarlane
Lake Acraman
Wilpena
Hawker
Cradock
Quorn
Wilmington
Orroroo
Port Augusta
Iron Knob
Port Germein
Wirrabara
Peterborough
Jamestown
Whyalla
Port Pirie
Gladstone
Cockburn
Mingary
Mannahill
Yunta
Oakvale
Canegrass
Hypurna
Ceduna
Eyre Is.
Smoky Bay
Haslam
Streaky Bay
Cape Bauer
Wirrulla
Poochera
Wudinna
Kyancutta
Kimba
Lake Gilles
Talia Caves
Anxious Bay
Flinders Is.
Elliston
Bramfield
Lock
Cleve
Cowell
Arno Bay
Port Neill
Mt Hope
EYRE PENINSULA
Spencer Gulf
Port Broughton
Wallaroo
Kadina
Moonta
Kulpara
Snowtown
Lochiel
Balaklava
Auburn
Clare
Burra
Robertstown
Saddleworth
Morgan
Waikerie
STUART HWY
BIRDSVILLE DEV. RD
BARRIER HWY
EYRE HWY
FLINDERS HWY
LINCOLN HWY
GAWLER RANGES
ANDAMOOKA RANGES
FLINDERS RANGES
Finke
Hale
Alberga
Macumba
Peake
Neales
Warburton
Eyre
Diamantina
Cooper
Strzelecki
Siccus
Eurinilla
Murray
BOULIA
LONGREACH
BROKEN HILL
PORT LINCOLN
ADELAIDE
GAWLER
125
28
49
95
0 50 100 150 km
0 25 50 75 100 miles
National road
Highway
tarred untarred
Main road
Major petrol stop
Caravan park
Museum
Place of interest

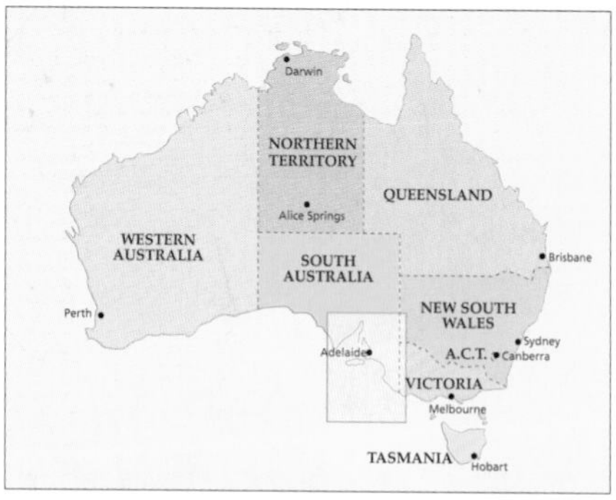

South-east South Australia

The south-eastern corner of South Australia stretches from Lake Alexandrina (the mouth of the Murray River) down the Coorong to Mount Gambier. The beautiful wilderness area of the Coorong is one of South Australia's premier national parks. In 1908, the poet Will Ogilvie captured its essence when he wrote: 'It is sunset in the Coorong, the ribbon of blue water that divides the ninety mile desert from the sea. . . Great flocks of wild-fowl sweep and settle again with strange, discordant cries, and the white beach gleams.' Mount Gambier is famous for its volcanic lakes which are intensely and mysteriously blue.

Above: *Pelicans are common in most Australian waterways, but they are nowhere as abundant as in the Coorong wetland area on the South Australian coast.*
Below: *In one of the craters of a long-extinct volcano, Blue Lake, near Mount Gambier in South Australia, mysteriously changes colour from grey to this brilliant blue for a few months of each year*

ON THE ROAD

The **Princes Highway** is the main road through south-eastern South Australia, running from the Victorian border to Adelaide. There are numerous roads leading off the **Dukes Highway** to the Coorong National Park, passing over the flat regions behind huge sand dunes. There are tracks onto the beach but they are only passable with a 4WD vehicle and, even then, it is quite possible to become bogged down in the sand, so care should always be taken. Services in the area adequately cater for the needs of tourists and travellers.

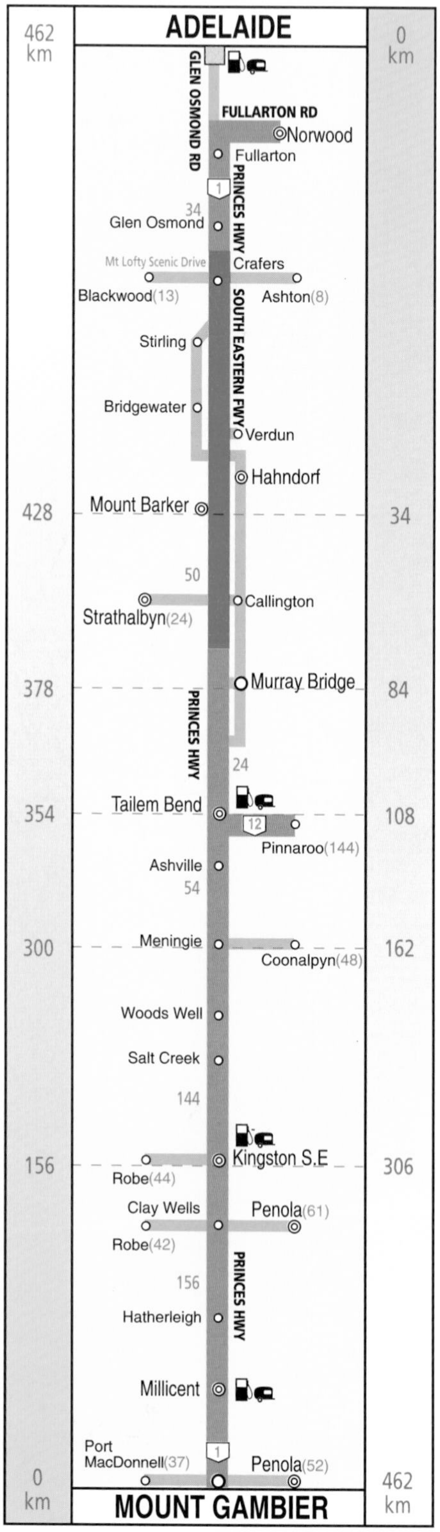

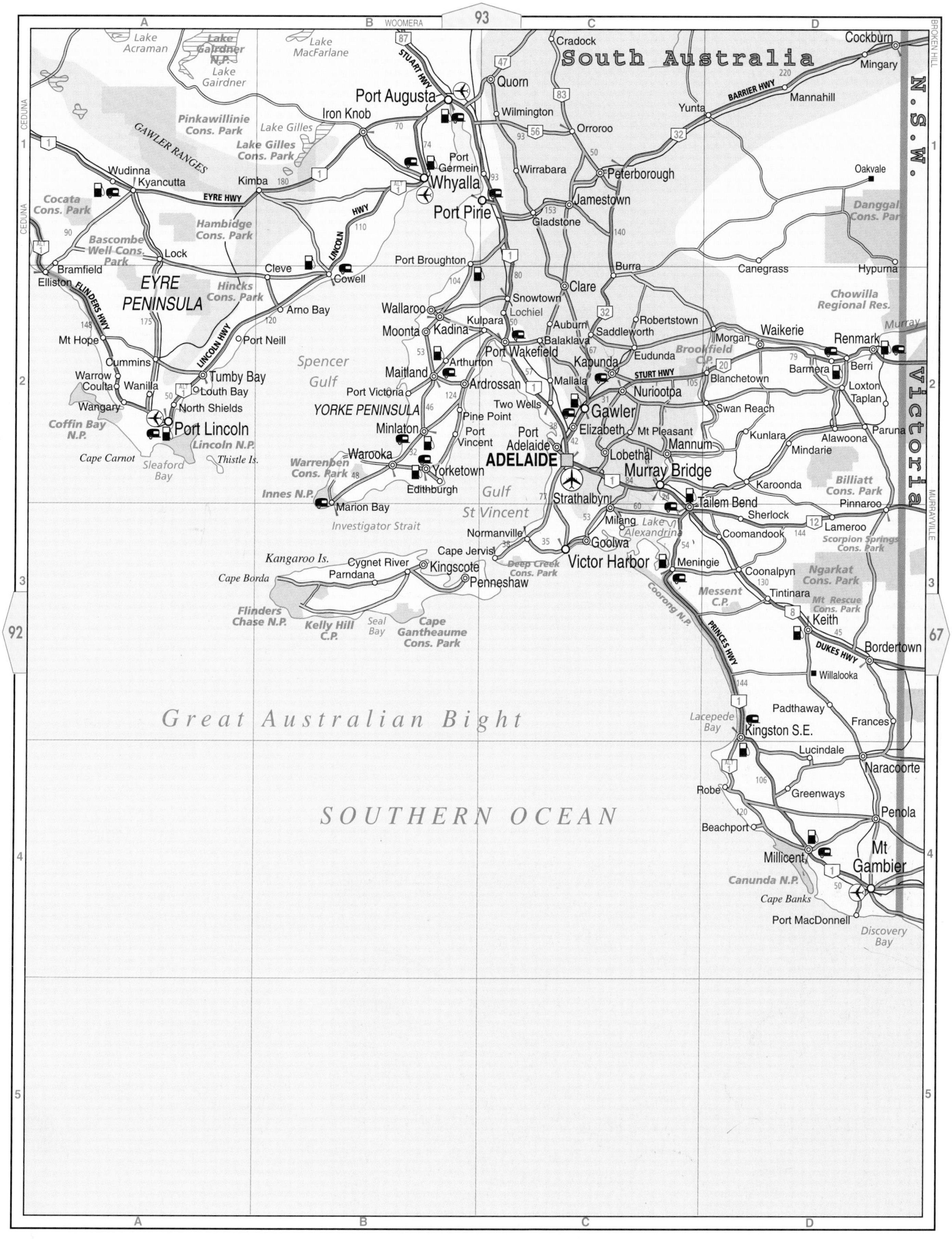

0 50 100 150 km

0 25 50 75 100 miles

National road

Highway

tarred untarred

Main road

Major petrol stop

Caravan park

Museum

Place of interest

WESTERN AUSTRALIA

Australia's largest state, Western Australia covers 2 525 500km² (974 843 sq miles) and has over 7000km (4350 miles) of coastline. Physically it is a vast low-lying plateau that rarely rises above 600m (1970ft). This plateau is broken by the Stirling Ranges in the south, the Hamersley Range in the north-west and a narrow coastal plain running down the west coast from Broome to Albany. The distances may be vast but the state's attractions range from the spectacular cliffs at the edge of the Nullarbor Plain to the tropical paradise of Broome. Visitors to the state can spend a day in the beautiful wine-growing area around Margaret River, visit Shark Bay where the dolphins come to the shore to be fed twice a day, marvel at the tall jarrah and karri trees of the southern forests, go walking around the granite coastline at Albany, gasp at the whiteness of the beaches along the southern coast or visit the famous gold mines at Kalgoorlie and Coolgardie, the country's leading gold producers in the 1890s.

Western Australia was first explored by Europeans in the 17th and 18th centuries when the Dutch, seeking a new route to Batavia (now Indonesia), harnessed the Roaring Forties and headed straight across the Indian Ocean. They kept bumping into the barren Western Australian coastline. Every Australian child knows the story of Dirk Hartog who, on 25 October 1616, nailed a pewter plate to a post at Cape Inscription and how, 80 years later, another sailor, Willem de Vlamingh, took it down and returned it to the Netherlands.

The state wasn't settled until the 19th century, after the British had colonised the east coast. A series of isolated outposts were established, including Broome in the far north-west which was to became a major pearl fishing port. It was a wild colonial settlement, where luggers sailed out to sea and men were lowered to the ocean floor to search for pearls. The stories told of pearl divers who died of 'the bends', of the Japanese cemetery (the largest in Australia), and of the storms that blew up out of nowhere and decimated the pearling fleet, all added to the romance. Other pioneering legends were the Durack family, who carved a cattle empire out of the wild, fertile lands of the Kimberleys, and Paddy Hannan, the compulsive gold fossicker, who literally tripped over a nugget and founded Kalgoorlie, one of the greatest gold-mining towns in the world.

It wasn't until the 1940s and '50s that the state really started to grow. The Australian Government's post-war immigration policy saw a huge influx of migrants, nearly all of them from Britain, in the period from 1947–70. In the early 1980s the state boasted the remarkable population profile of having 1.3 million people, 72 per cent of whom were Australian born and 15 per cent who were British immigrants.

Australia's largest state is actually a low-lying plateau which rarely rises above 600m (1970ft). The monotonous topography of Western Australia is broken only by the narrow coastal plain which runs down the west coast from Broome to Albany, the low-lying Stirling Ranges in the south and the Hamersley Range in the north-west. Mount Meharry in the Hamersleys is the state's highest peak at 1244m (4080ft).

The state's climate ranges from tropical in the north to arid desert in the west and mild Mediterranean in the south. In the north the monsoonal wet season sweeps across Wyndham, the Kimberley and the Broome area between December and March. The mean annual temperature in Wyndham is 30°C (86°F). The south-west corner of the state enjoys a classic Mediterranean climate of cool, wet winters and warm, dry summers. Albany has a mean annual temperature of 15°C (59°F) and Geraldton, further up the coast, reaches 19°C (66°F). To the east of Port Hedland lies the town of Marble Bar, recognised as Australia's hottest place. From 31 October 1923 to 17 April 1924 a blistering 38°C (100°F) was recorded for every single day, in the longest heat wave ever recorded in Australia.

Beyond the coastal plain the state degenerates into endless desert. Few people who fly from Sydney to Asia will forget the sight from the windows of the plane of the endless, uninhabited corrugations that are the vast sand dunes of the Great Sandy Desert. In the centre of the state lies the Gibson Desert and in the south, the Great Victoria Desert and Nullarbor Plain sprawl across from South Australia.

This vast desert wasteland means that, in spite of the state's vast area, most Western Australians cling to the coast. Less than 15 per cent of the state's population lives in rural areas

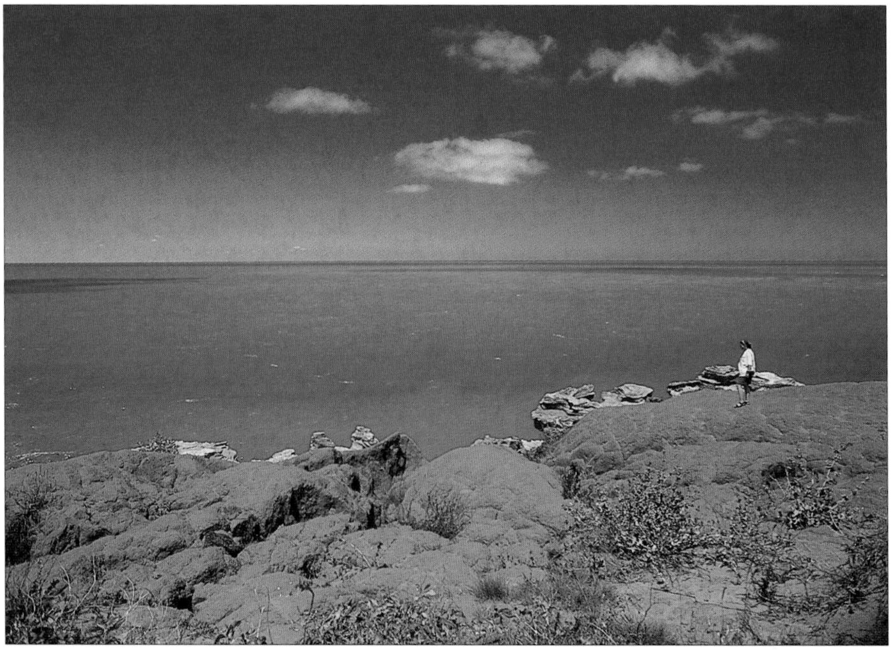

Left: *Gantheaume Bay near Broome in the north of Western Australia is where the inland red meets the blues of the sea.*

and over 90 per cent lives in the fertile south-west, which encompasses both Perth and Fremantle.

Perth, the capital of Western Australia, is located on the Swan River. The city was first settled in 1929, and after a number of years of constant struggle, convict labour was introduced in the 1950s. This provided the fledgling settlements with a much-needed workforce, and today Perth is a modern city with a population of nearly 1.3 million.

The arc of coastal land which surrounds Perth and runs from Geraldton to Esperance is the state's grain belt. Mild temperatures, adequate rainfall and good soil result in large crops of barley, oats and over 5 million tonnes of wheat each year. It was to this area that the British rural workers came in their thousands during the 1950s. The area also produces quality wines and fruit. Vegetables too are grown, but mainly for the local populations of Perth and Fremantle.

Beyond the narrow coastal plains, between the deserts and the intensive agricultural area, lies the state's sheep belt. Sheep are raised not only for local wool and meat, but also for export, particularly to the Islamic countries of the Middle East. In the far north the huge holdings of the Kimberleys are the centre of the state's cattle production. The animals are slaughtered in local abattoirs and most of the meat is exported. Dairy farming and pig raising have become part of a mixed farming pattern increasingly common in the far south-west. Western Australia is also known for its quality timber. Most of this industry is located in the south-west corner of the state.

Iron ore forms the basis of the state's mineral wealth. In the early 1950s significant deposits were found at Yampi Sound off the north-west coast and at Koolyanobbing in the desert, between Perth and Kalgoorlie. These deposits, however, were dwarfed by the vast amounts subsequently discovered in the Pilbara region. Over the next two decades iron-ore mining started at Mount Goldsworthy, Shay Gap, Mount Whaleback, Mount Tom Price, Paraburdoo (opened in 1970 by Hamersley Iron), Pannawonnica and Koolanooka.

In the 1960s both oil and gas were discovered off the north-west shelf of the continent. The early 1960s also saw the discovery of bauxite in the Darling Ranges south of Perth, which subsequently led to the establishment of alumina refineries at Pinjarra and Kwinana.

Nickel has been found around Kalgoorlie at Agnew, Kambalda and Mount Windarra, which resulted in the establishment of a nickel smelter at Kalgoorlie. The state's economy is also boosted by significant deposits of mineral beach sands, like ilemnite, leucoxine, rutile, zircon, mangazite and zenotime.

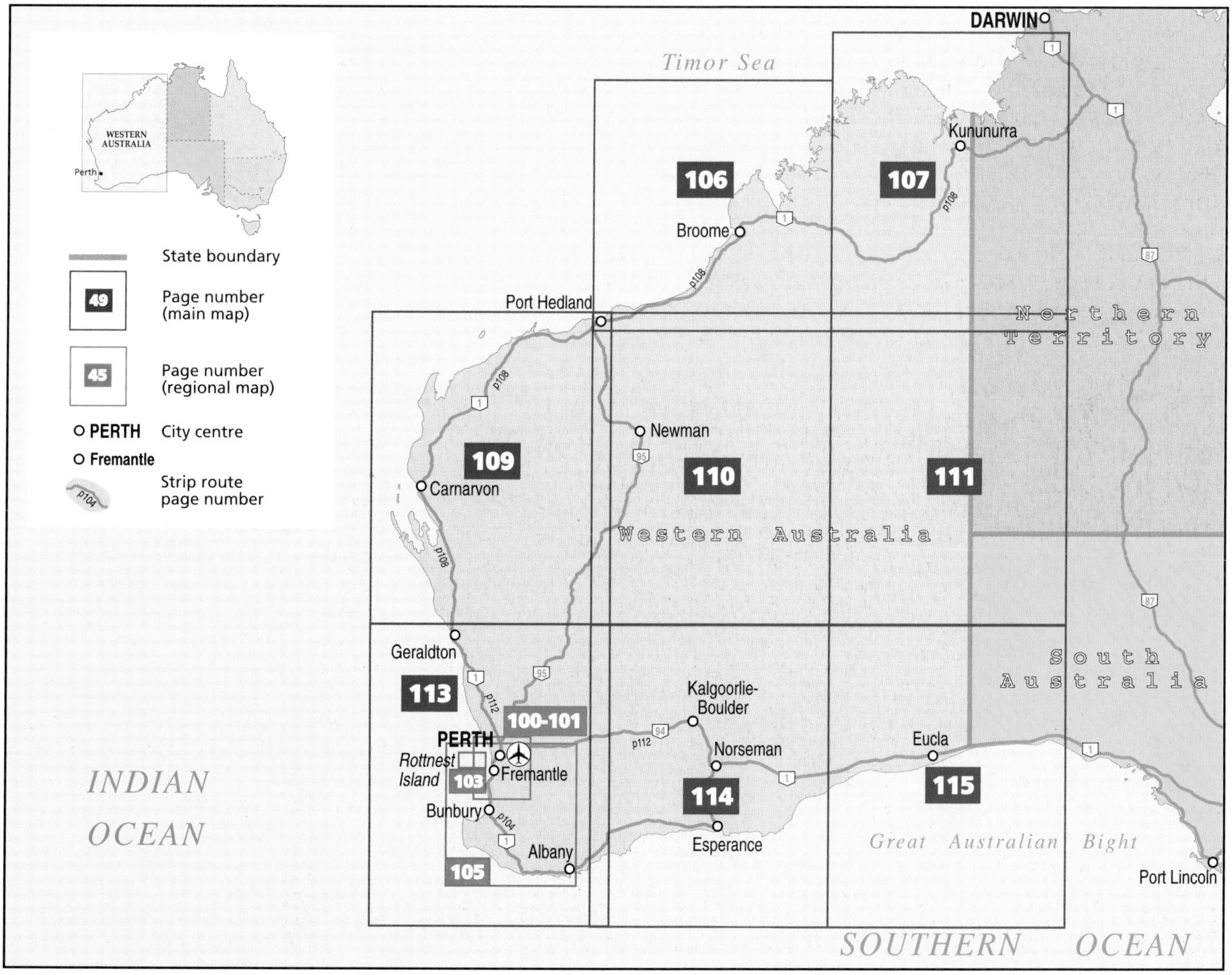

Perth

With its network of freeways Perth is a modern, dynamic city, and one of great charm and beauty. Elegant riverside parks and gardens along the Swan River lend the city grace and distinction. The city centre, particularly the area around St Georges Terrace, is a pleasant mixture of colonial and modern architecture with high-rise buildings standing beside many gracious 19th-century churches and public buildings. To the west are a number of attractive beaches, and to the south lies the port of Fremantle, where the 1987 America's Cup yacht race was held, the first to be held outside the United States.

Top: *Perth, the capital of Western Australia, started out as a fragile settlement on the shores of the Swan River in 1829.*
Above: *Perth's majestic Parliament House, built in 1904, had extensions added in the 1960s.*

CALENDAR OF EVENTS

JANUARY: Hopman Cup, Tasar National Sailing Championships, Vines Golf Classic, Perth Cup (a major racing event), Fremantle Sardine Festival.
FEBRUARY: Festival of Perth with a variety of cultural activities.
MARCH: Asian Baseball Championships.
APRIL: Australian Masters Games, National Boomerang Championships.
MAY: Australian Masters Games.
JUNE: Sunshine Festival held at Geraldton, north of Perth.
JULY: People's Marathon.
AUGUST: Australian Ice Hockey Championships.
SEPTEMBER: Wildflower Festival, AFL Football finals, Perth Royal Show.
OCTOBER: Spring in the Valley.
NOVEMBER: Fremantle Festival.
DECEMBER: Australian Derby, Boxing Day racing carnival, WA Open Tennis Championship.

PERTH	J	F	M	A	M	J	J	A	S	O	N	D
AV. TEMP. °F	77	79	75	70	63	57	55	57	59	64	68	72
AV. TEMP. °C	25	26	24	21	17	14	13	14	15	18	20	22
DAILY SUN hrs	11	10	9	7	6	5	6	6	7	8	10	10
RAINFALL in	0	0.5	1	2	5	8	7	5	3	2	1	0.5
RAINFALL mm	9	12	19	46	123	182	173	135	80	54	22	14
RAINFALL days	3	3	4	8	14	17	18	17	14	11	7	4

TOP ATTRACTIONS

Central Government Offices: the original heart of Perth, close to the site where a tree was felled in 1829 to mark the foundation of the capital.
Kings Park: also known as Mount Eliza, offers superb views of Perth and the graceful Swan River.
London Court: an interesting and colourful shopping alley with mock Tudor frontages.
St George's Cathedral: designed by eminent Australian architect Edmund Blacket, built between 1879 and 1888.
Stirling Gardens: a wonder to behold in springtime when blooms and exquisitely maintained lawns offer a dramatic contrast to the canyons of iron and concrete that surround it.

WHERE TO STAY

Baileys Parkside Hotel, Bennett St, tel: (08) 9325 3788, fax: 9221 1046. Self-contained, centrally located.
Hyatt Regency, 99 Adelaide Terrace, tel: (08) 9225 1234, fax: 9325 8899. One of the city's most prestigious five-star hotels.
Metro Inn Apartments, Nile St, tel: (08) 9325 1866. Self-contained apartments and hotel rooms, close to city centre.
Miss Maud European Hotel, Murray St, tel: (08) 9325 3900. Scandinavian style in city centre.
Perth Parkroyal, 54 Terrace Rd, tel: (08) 9325 3811, fax: 9221 1564. Luxury accommodation, overlooking the Swan River.
Perth Parmelia Hilton, Mill St, tel: (08) 9322 3622, fax: 9481 0857. Old-world elegance, in city centre.
Sheraton Perth, 207 Adelaide Terrace, tel: (08) 9325 0501, fax: 9325 4032. Comfortable and very convenient.
The Mercure Hotel Perth International, 10 Irwin St, tel: (08) 9325 0481, fax: 9221 3344. Quality hotel.
The Sebel Hotel, Pier St, tel: (08) 9325 7655, fax: 9325 7383. Excellent facilities, well located.
Wentworth Plaza, Murray St, tel: (08) 9481 1000, fax: 9321 2443. Comfortable and affordable accommodation.

1. HOSTEL
2. MISS MAUD SWEDISH HOTEL
3. INNTOWN PERTH HOTEL
4. SEBEL
5. HOTEL REGATTA
6. KINGS PERTH HOTEL
7. MERCURE HOTEL

0   500 m
0   500 yd

N

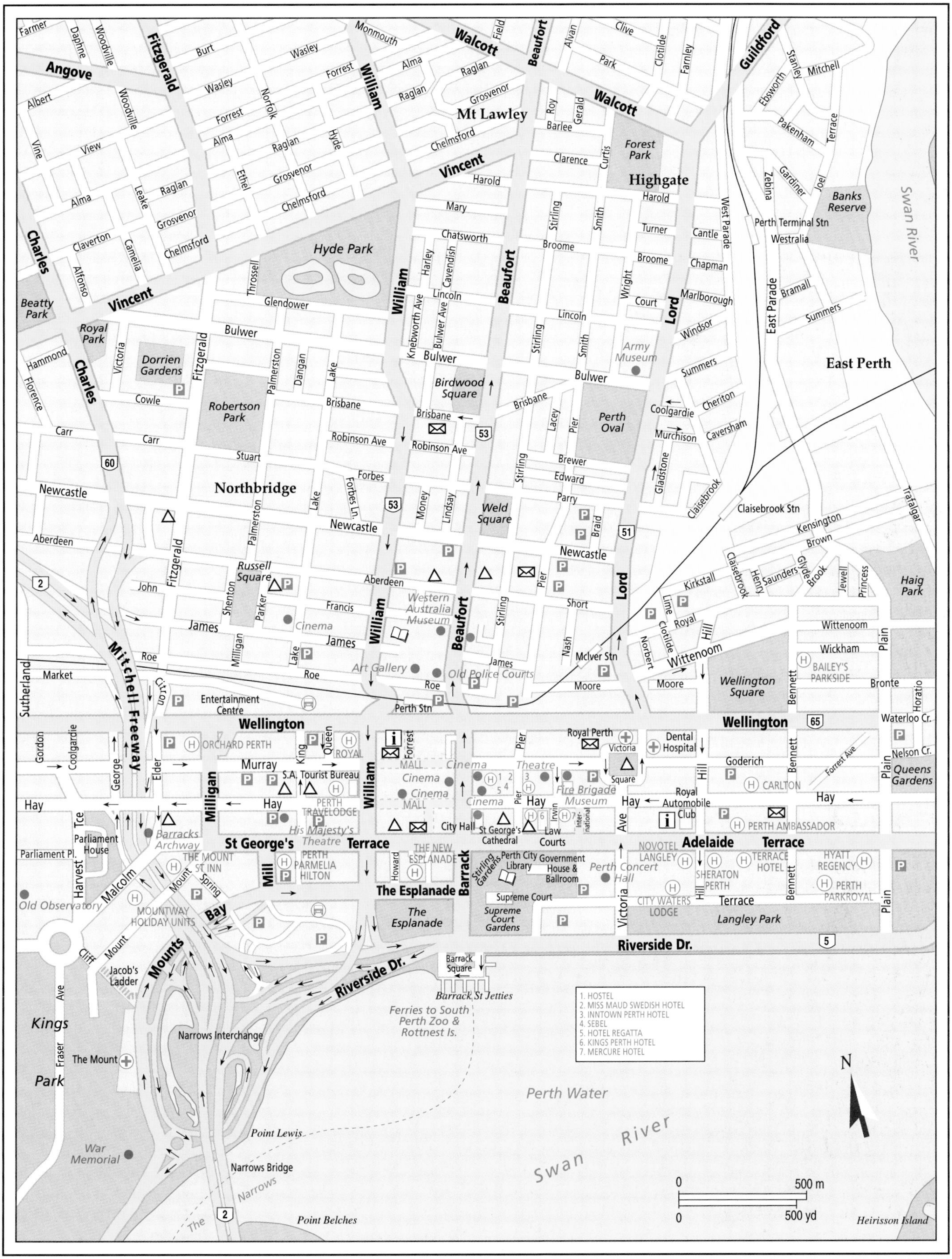

△ St Patrick's	Place of worship	🚍 Bus terminus	✉ Post office
Ⓗ Hotel		● Police station	● *Market* Place of interest
ⓘ Information		Ⓟ Parking	⊕ Hospital

Perth Daytrips

The population of Western Australia is concentrated in the south-east corner of the state and consequently there are many interesting daytrips from Perth. Fremantle, to the south, is a superb mixture of historic buildings and seaside graciousness. Further south, visit the lazy beach townships of Rockingham and Mandurah. To the north Yanchep Beach is a popular day out. East of the city the historic centres of Guildford, York, Northam and Mundaring are all worth visiting, and off the coast Rottnest Island is accessible by both boat and plane.

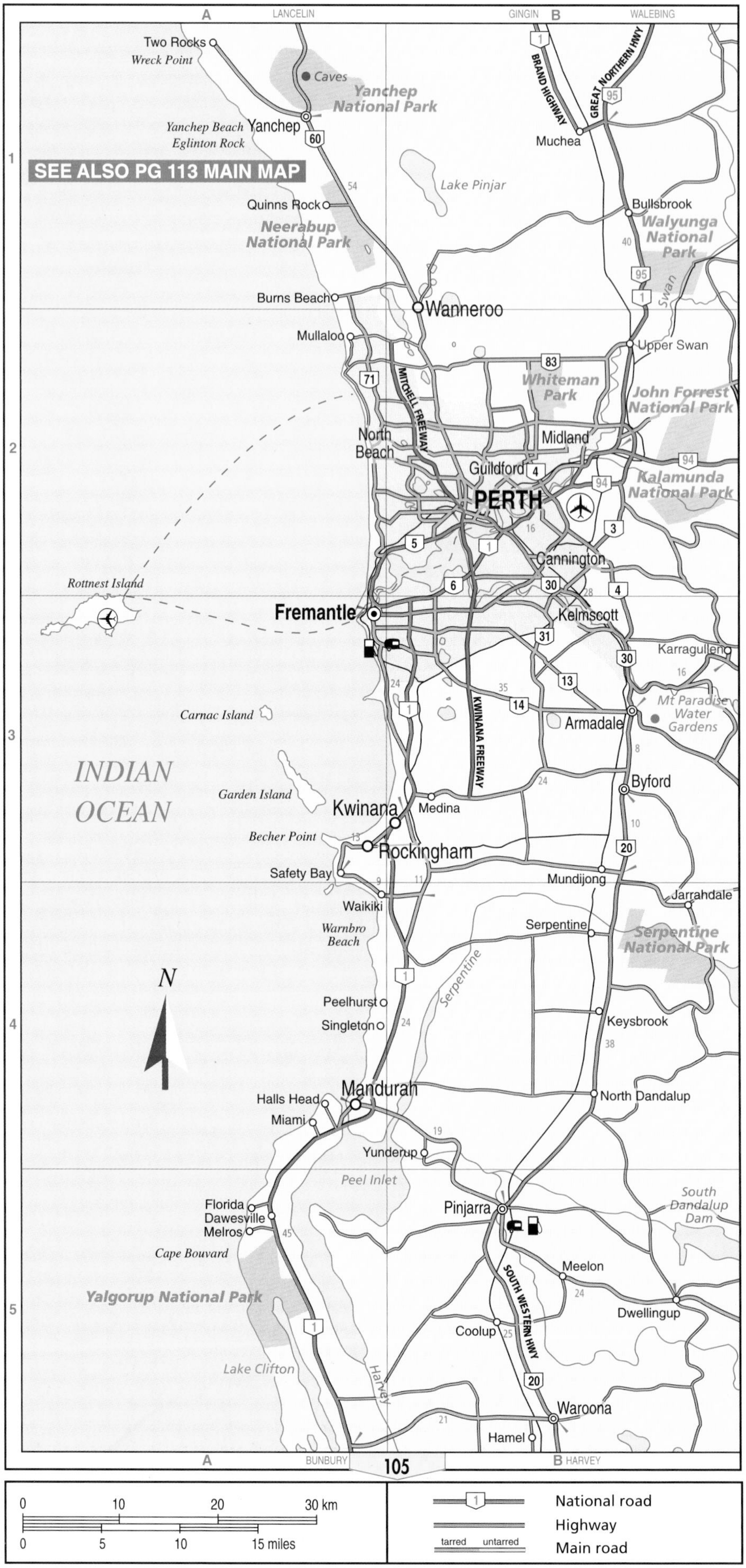

TOP ATTRACTIONS

Fremantle: delightful township with interesting historic buildings, gracious modern hotels, extensive seaside parks.
Northam: picturesque town located on the Avon River.
Rockingham: a pleasant seaside resort, site of the first European settlement in Western Australia.
Rottnest Island: favourite holiday and daytripper destination.
York: first township in the Avon Valley, full of really beautiful old buildings. There is little doubt that it is one of the best preserved and restored 19th-century towns in Australia. A true monument to the architecture of that era.

Above: *The old buildings on Avon Terrace in York are a reminder that the town was established in the 1830s, not long after Perth.*

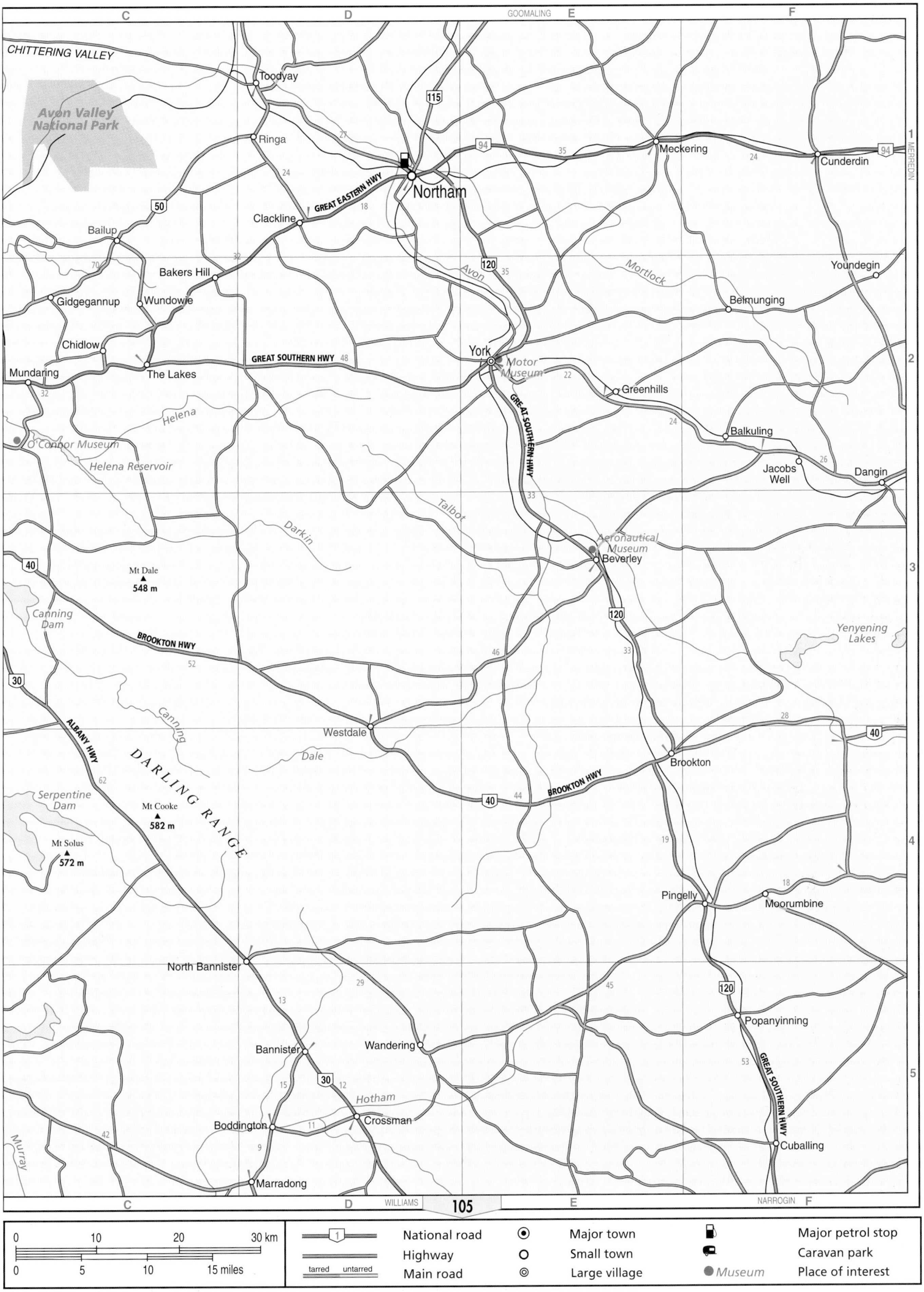
C
D
GOOMALING E
F
CHITTERING VALLEY
Avon Valley National Park
Toodyay
115
Ringa
27
94
35
Meckering
24
Cunderdin
94
MERREDIN
1
24
GREAT EASTERN HWY
Northam
18
50
Clackline
Bailup
70
32
Bakers Hill
Avon
120
35
Mortlock
Youndegin
Gidgegannup
Wundowie
Belmunging
Chidlow
York
Motor Museum
2
GREAT SOUTHERN HWY
48
Mundaring
The Lakes
22
Greenhills
32
Helena
O'Connor Museum
24
Balkuling
Helena Reservoir
GREAT SOUTHERN HWY
Jacobs Well
26
Dangin
33
Talbot
Darkin
Aeronautical Museum
Beverley
40
Mt Dale
548 m
3
120
Canning Dam
Yenyening Lakes
BROOKTON HWY
33
46
52
30
Canning
ALBANY HWY
28
Westdale
40
Brookton
Dale
DARLING RANGE
62
BROOKTON HWY
44
40
Serpentine Dam
Mt Cooke
582 m
Mt Solus
572 m
19
4
18
Pingelly
Moorumbine
North Bannister
29
120
45
13
Popanyinning
Wandering
Bannister
GREAT SOUTHERN HWY
53
30
12
5
15
Hotham
Crossman
Boddington
11
42
Murray
9
Cuballing
Marradong
C
D
WILLIAMS
105
E
NARROGIN F
0 10 20 30 km
0 5 10 15 miles
National road
Highway
Main road
tarred untarred
Major town
Small town
Large village
Major petrol stop
Caravan park
Museum
Place of interest

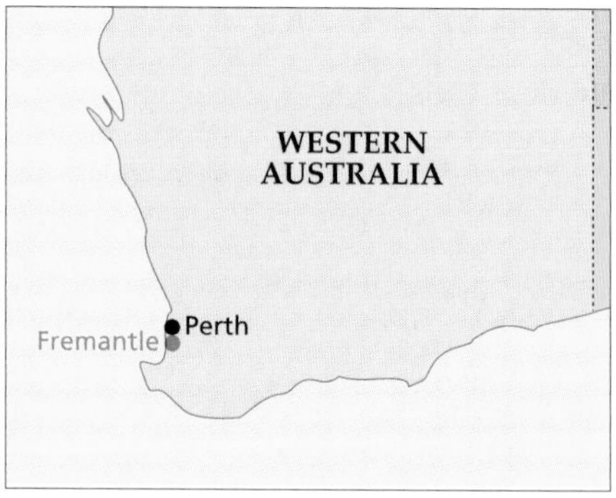

Fremantle

In the past decade Fremantle has become the great tourist destination in the Perth area. There are seemingly row upon row of interesting historic buildings, modern hotels, seaside parks and enough attractions to make it an ideal daytrip. Have a picnic, or a meal in one of the dozens of restaurants in the area, wander along the shoreline, visit the museums or gaze at the conspicuous wealth at the yacht club – in 1987 Fremantle was the site of the America's Cup yacht race. No visit is complete without seeing the Round House, the Fremantle Gaol, the Maritime Museum, the markets and the Art Gallery.

TOP ATTRACTIONS

Freo Markets: over 140 shops open on Fridays, Saturdays and Sundays. The first markets began in 1897.
The Round House: built in 1831, the Swan River colony's first gaol and claimed to be Western Australia's oldest public building.
Western Australia Maritime Museum: marvellous display of artefacts recovered from the depths of the Indian Ocean.

APPROX. DISTANCES IN KM FROM PERTH	
Albany	409
Broome	2229
Bunbury	185
Carnarvon	900
Esperance	721
Geraldton	420
Kalgoorlie/Boulder	584
Manjimup	317
Meekatharra	738
Port Hedland	1762
Wyndham	3231

Right: *The Round House is the state's oldest building.*

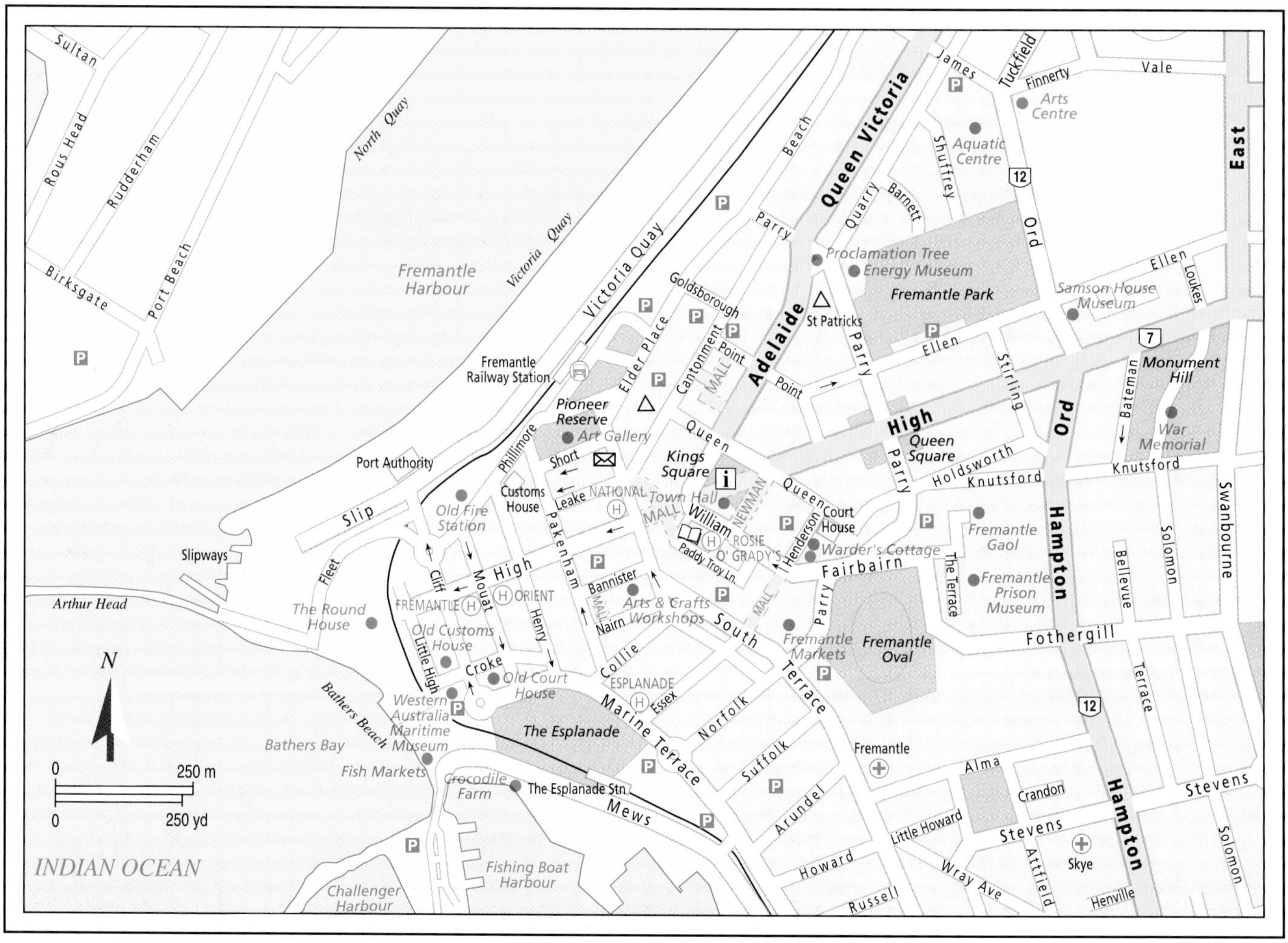

Rottnest Island

Located 19km (12 miles) off the coast of Perth, Rottnest Island is a wonderful holiday and daytripper destination. The island was named by the explorer Willem de Vlamingh who mistook the quokkas (small wallabies that inhabit the island) for rats and named the island 'Rat's Nest Island'. Over the years Rottnest has been a pilot station for Fremantle, an internment camp, and during World War II, a military post. The absence of cars, the historic buildings, the charm of the huge Moreton Bay figs and the quiet waters around the island have all been a magnet for the people of Perth since the 1850s.

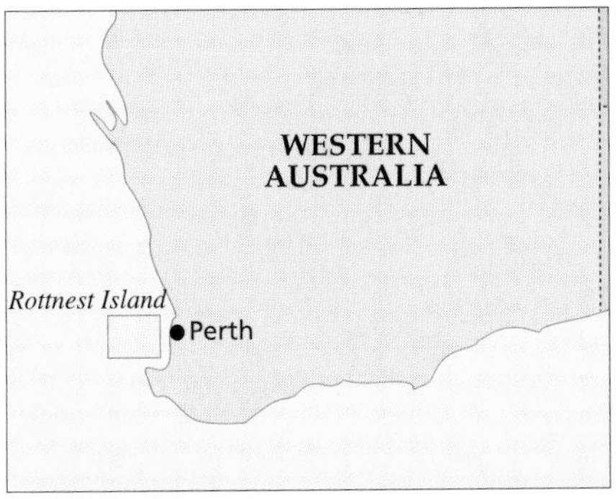

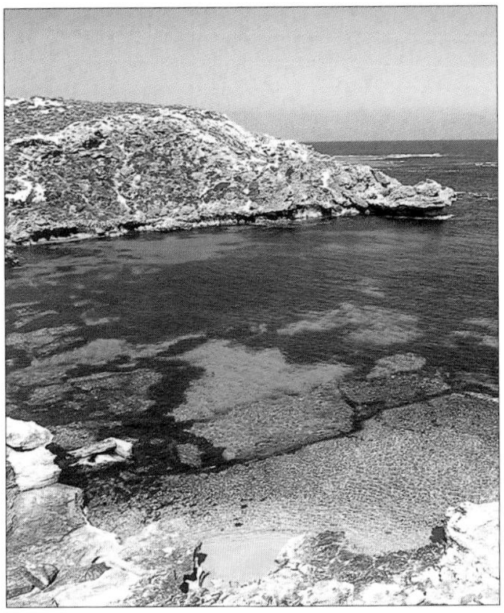

TOP ATTRACTIONS

Cape Vlamingh Heritage Trail: a 30-minute walk, with opportunities to see the *Kirya Maru* shipwreck. The island's fauna includes quokkas, dugites, fairy terns and dolphins. Don't miss Bridge Rock and the blowhole.
Vincent Way Heritage Trail: a 45-minute walk, the most important of the Heritage Trails as it encompasses all Rottnest Island's Old Settlement buildings.

Left: *Rottnest Island is an accessible holiday destination, 12 minutes by air and two hours by boat from Perth.*
Above: *There are no cars on Rottnest Island so everyone rides a bicycle or walks.*

ROTTNEST ISLAND	J	F	M	A	M	J	J	A	S	O	N	D
AV. TEMP. °F	79	79	75	72	66	63	61	61	63	66	70	73
AV. TEMP. °C	25	26	24	22	19	17	16	16	17	19	21	23
DAILY SUN hrs	11	10	9	7	6	5	6	6	7	8	10	10
SEA TEMP. °F	70	72	70	70	70	68	66	63	63	66	66	68
SEA TEMP. °C	21	22	21	21	21	20	19	17	17	19	19	20
RAINFALL in	0	0	0.5	1	4	6	6	4	2.5	1.5	0.5	0
RAINFALL mm	7	11	14	38	107	158	150	105	61	39	17	10
RAINFALL days	2	2	4	8	15	18	20	18	14	11	6	3

SEE ALSO PG 113 MAIN MAP

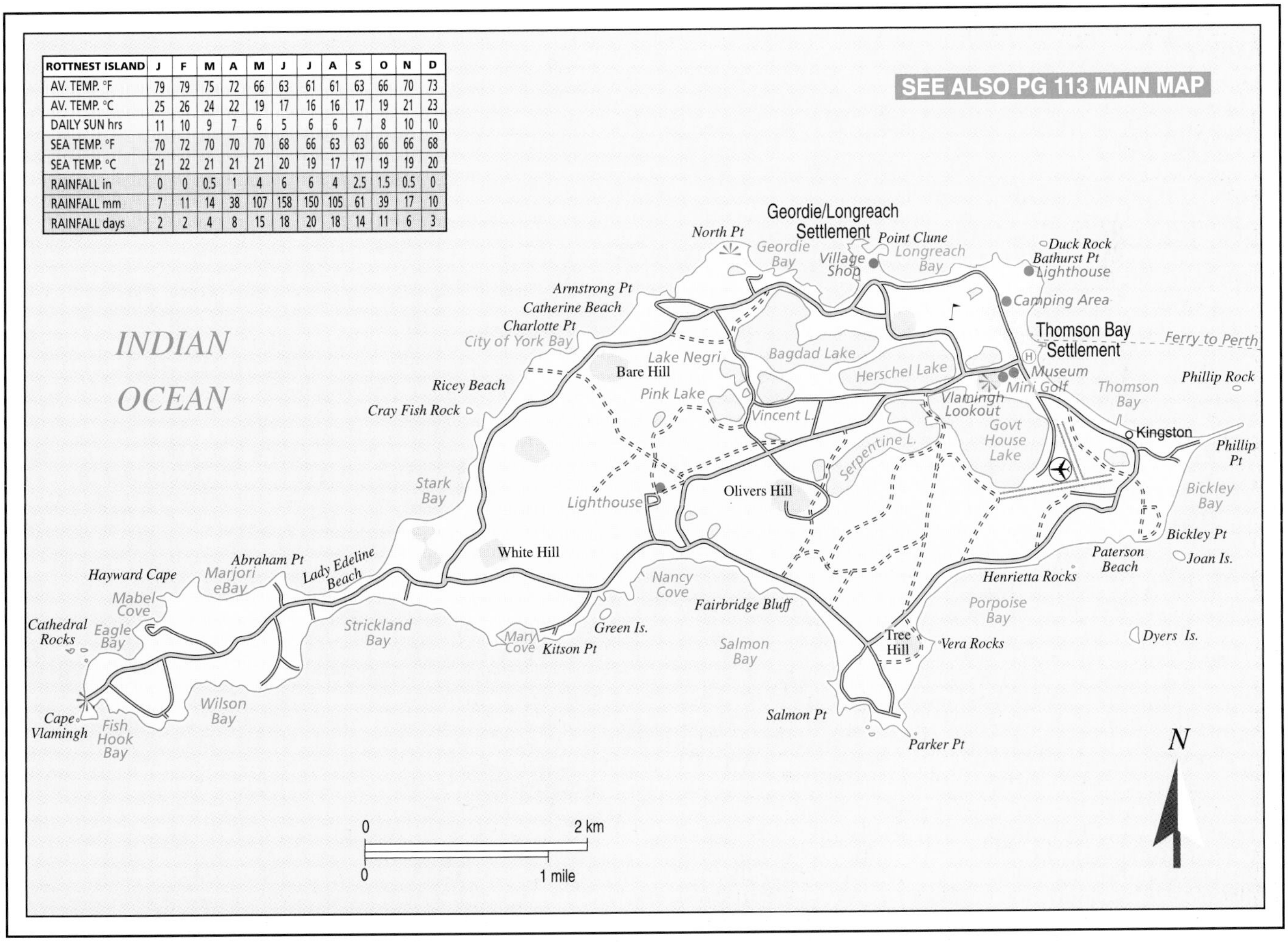

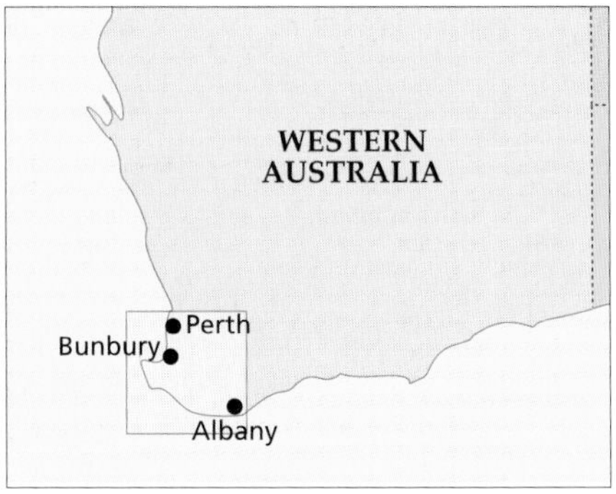

South-west Western Australia

One of the most beautiful areas in Australia, south-west Western Australia is characterised by white beaches, aquamarine seas, impressive rugged cliffs, towering trees, attractive villages and towns, and a charm that seems to have remained untouched for 50 years. The whalers and timber cutters left behind an area of unique attraction. In the south-west there is so much to enjoy that it would be easy to wander through the area for a month and scratch only the surface. The sand dunes of the coastline push up against headlands of wildflowers, and nearby the Stirling Ranges provide fabulous views and the Margaret River very impressive wineries.

TOP ATTRACTIONS

Albany: interesting town with exceptionally beautiful rock formations nearby.
Bunbury: one of the most attractive towns in Australia with abundant parks and gardens, interesting historic buildings and a very handsome beachfront.
Leeuwin-Naturaliste National Park: some of the state's most beautiful coastline combined with dense native forests and beaches that are popular with surfers.
Margaret River: chic township nestled in the hills, this area is famous for its wine.
Stirling Range: exceptionally beautiful but isolated region, well worth visiting.

ON THE ROAD

This is a major tourist area, which means that even the roads through the Leeuwin-Naturaliste National Park and around the major attractions like Mammoth Cave and Cape Leeuwin are sealed and reliable. Smaller centres may not have adequate facilities, but the major townships – Busselton, Margaret River, Augusta, Bunbury – all have petrol stations, accommodation and a range of restaurants and cafés. The roads through the jarrah and karri forests are particularly beautiful, although sometimes they can wind on for many kilometres. The state's motoring organisation, the Royal Automobile Club of Western Australia, has a branch office at Bunbury (check local directory, or for more information contact the head office at Perth).

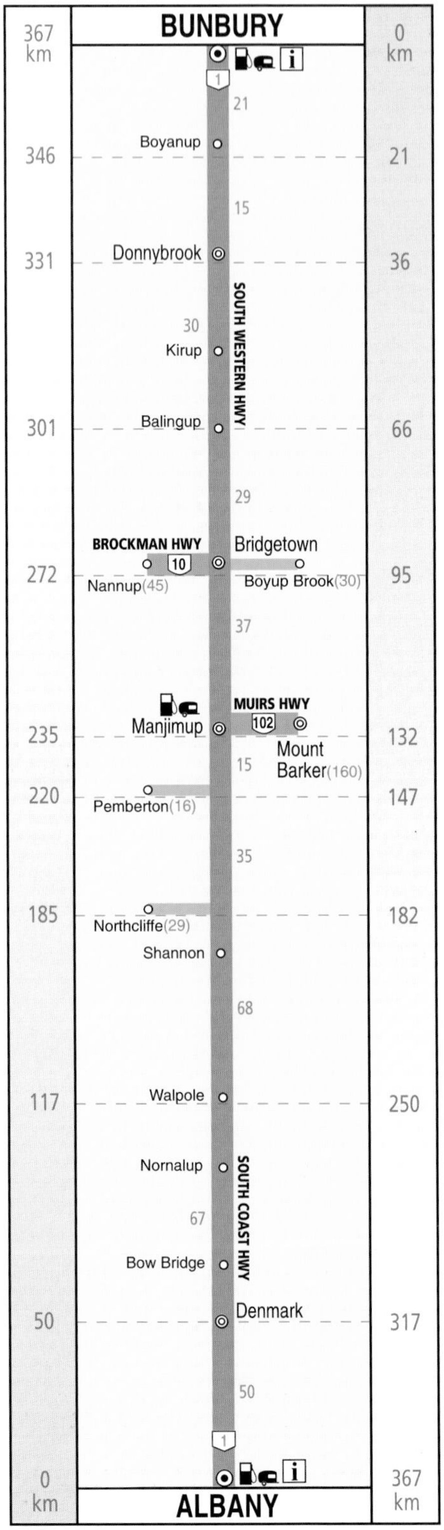

Below: *An unsealed road leads to Toolbrunup Peak of the Stirling Ranges, which is often shrouded in mist.*

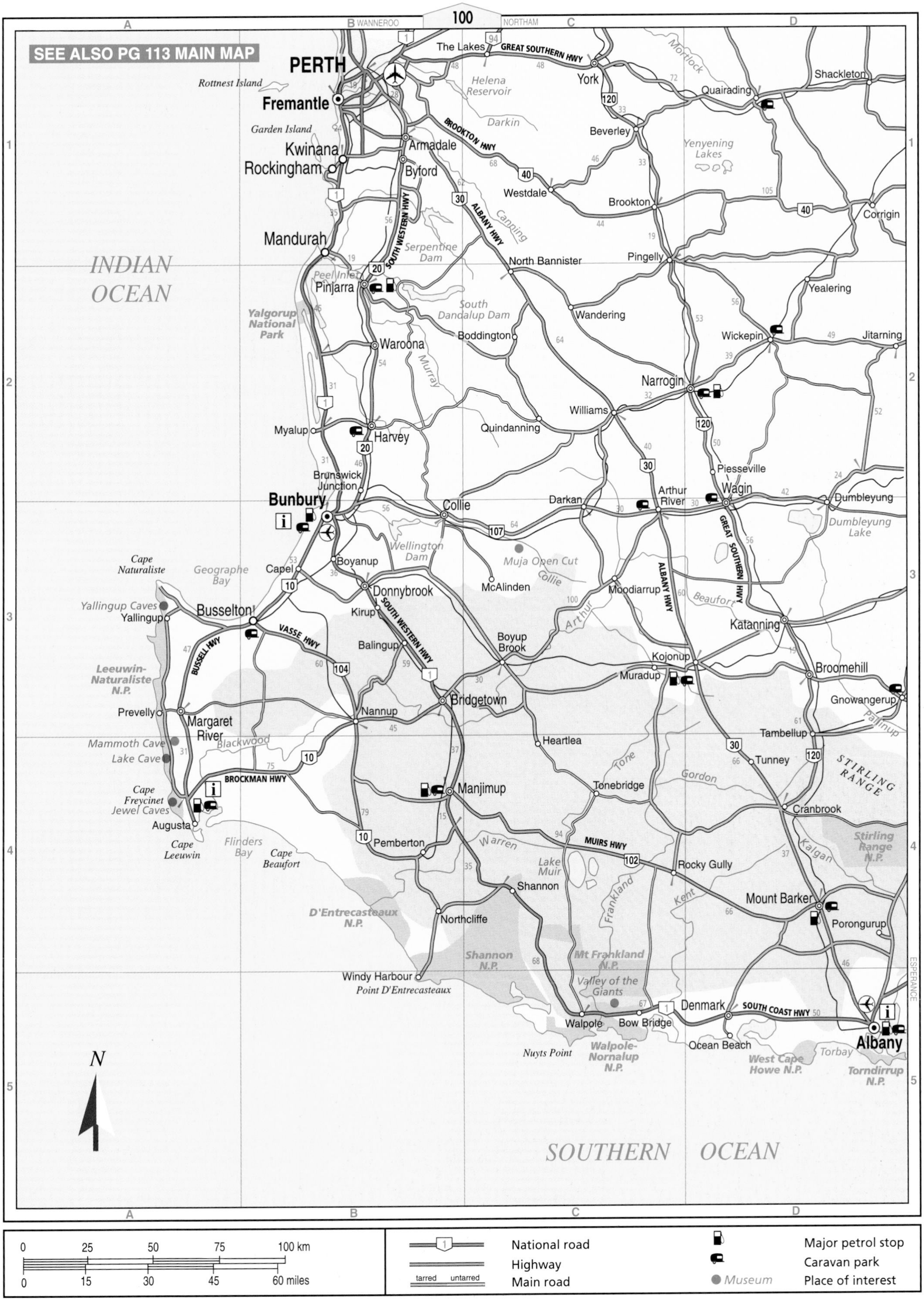
SEE ALSO PG 113 MAIN MAP
100
WANNEROO
NORTHAM
ESPERANCE
PERTH
Fremantle
Rottnest Island
Garden Island
Kwinana
Rockingham
Mandurah
Peel Inlet
Pinjarra
Yalgorup National Park
Waroona
Myalup
Harvey
Brunswick Junction
Bunbury
INDIAN OCEAN
Cape Naturaliste
Geographe Bay
Capel
Boyanup
Yallingup Caves
Yallingup
Busselton
Donnybrook
Kirup
Balingup
Leeuwin-Naturaliste N.P.
Prevelly
Margaret River
Mammoth Cave
Lake Cave
Blackwood
Cape Freycinet
Jewel Caves
Augusta
Cape Leeuwin
Flinders Bay
Cape Beaufort
Nannup
Bridgetown
Manjimup
Pemberton
D'Entrecasteaux N.P.
Northcliffe
Windy Harbour
Point D'Entrecasteaux
Shannon N.P.
Shannon
Lake Muir
Mt Frankland N.P.
Valley of the Giants
Walpole
Bow Bridge
Nuyts Point
Walpole-Nornalup N.P.
Denmark
Ocean Beach
West Cape Howe N.P.
Torbay
Albany
Torndirrup N.P.
SOUTHERN OCEAN
The Lakes
GREAT SOUTHERN HWY
Helena Reservoir
York
Mortlock
Shackleton
Quairading
Darkin
Beverley
Yenyening Lakes
BROOKTON HWY
Armadale
Byford
SOUTH WESTERN HWY
ALBANY HWY
Westdale
Brookton
Corrigin
Canning
Serpentine Dam
North Bannister
Pingelly
Yealering
South Dandalup Dam
Wandering
Boddington
Wickepin
Jitarning
Murray
Narrogin
Williams
Quindanning
Piesseville
Arthur River
Wagin
Darkan
Collie
Dumbleyung
Dumbleyung Lake
Wellington Dam
Muja Open Cut
McAlinden
Moodiarrup
Beaufort
Arthur
Katanning
Boyup Brook
VASSE HWY
BUSSELL HWY
Kojonup
Muradup
Broomehill
Gnowangerup
Pallinup
Heartlea
Tambellup
Tunney
STIRLING RANGE
BROCKMAN HWY
Tone
Gordon
Tonebridge
Cranbrook
Warren
MUIRS HWY
Rocky Gully
Stirling Range N.P.
Kalgan
Frankland
Kent
Mount Barker
Porongurup
SOUTH COAST HWY
0 25 50 75 100 km
0 15 30 45 60 miles
National road
Highway
tarred untarred
Main road
Major petrol stop
Caravan park
Museum
Place of interest

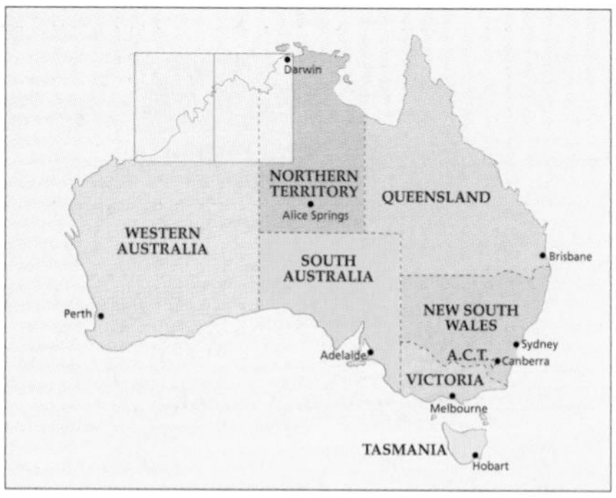

The Kimberley

This vast region is a wonderland of desert scenery, and contains the strikingly unusual Bungle Bungle Ranges. The lookout at Lake Argyle village affords a view of the lake and makes it seem like some strange desert fjord. The Five Rivers Lookout at Wyndham has magnificent views of the Forrest, Pentecost, King, Durack and Ord rivers and the mudflats that have formed at the confluence of these waterways. There are views from vantage points along Geikie Gorge near Fitzroy Crossing and along the coastline near Broome where red soils meet white beach sands and the blue waters of the Indian Ocean.

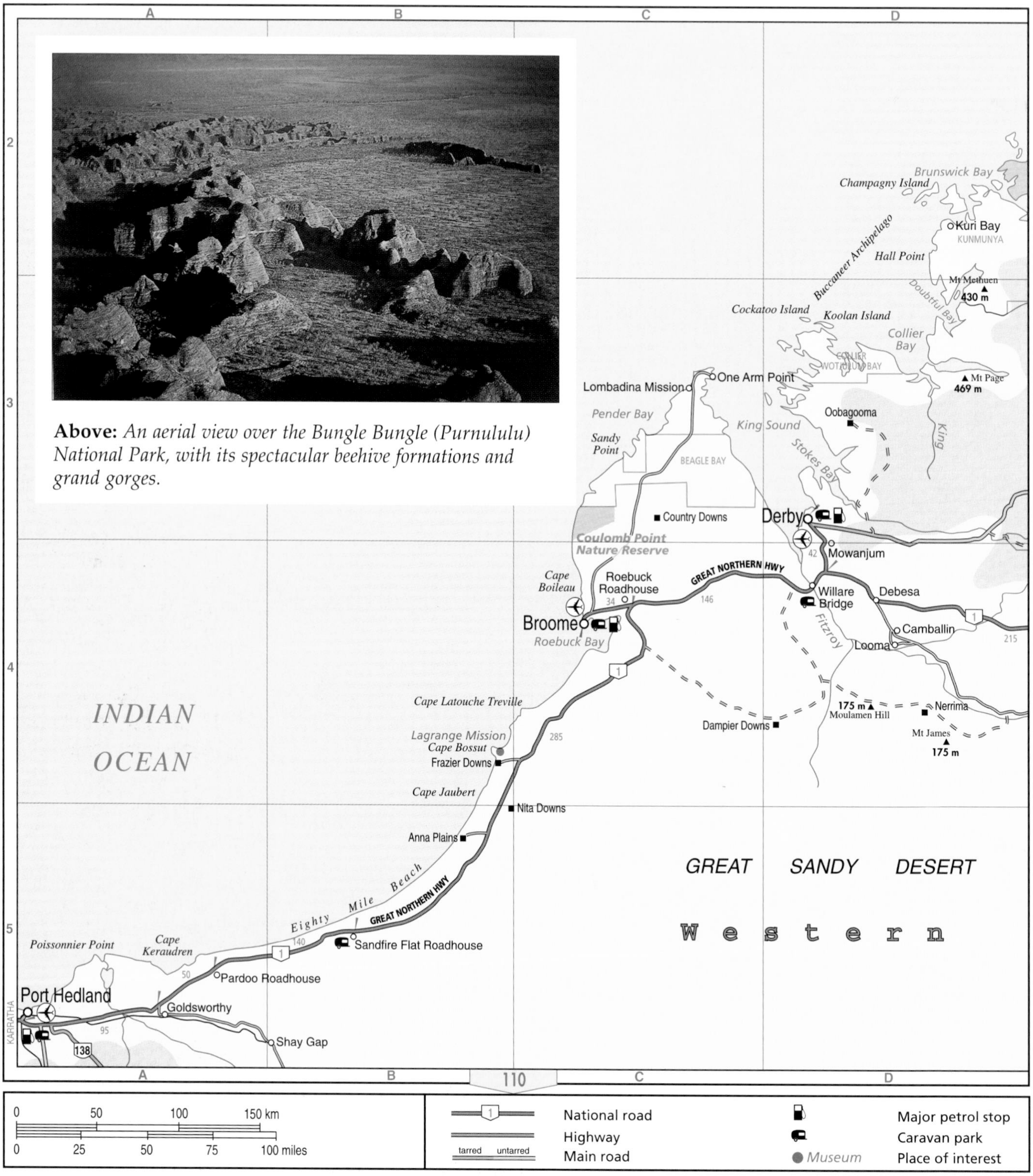

Above: *An aerial view over the Bungle Bungle (Purnululu) National Park, with its spectacular beehive formations and grand gorges.*

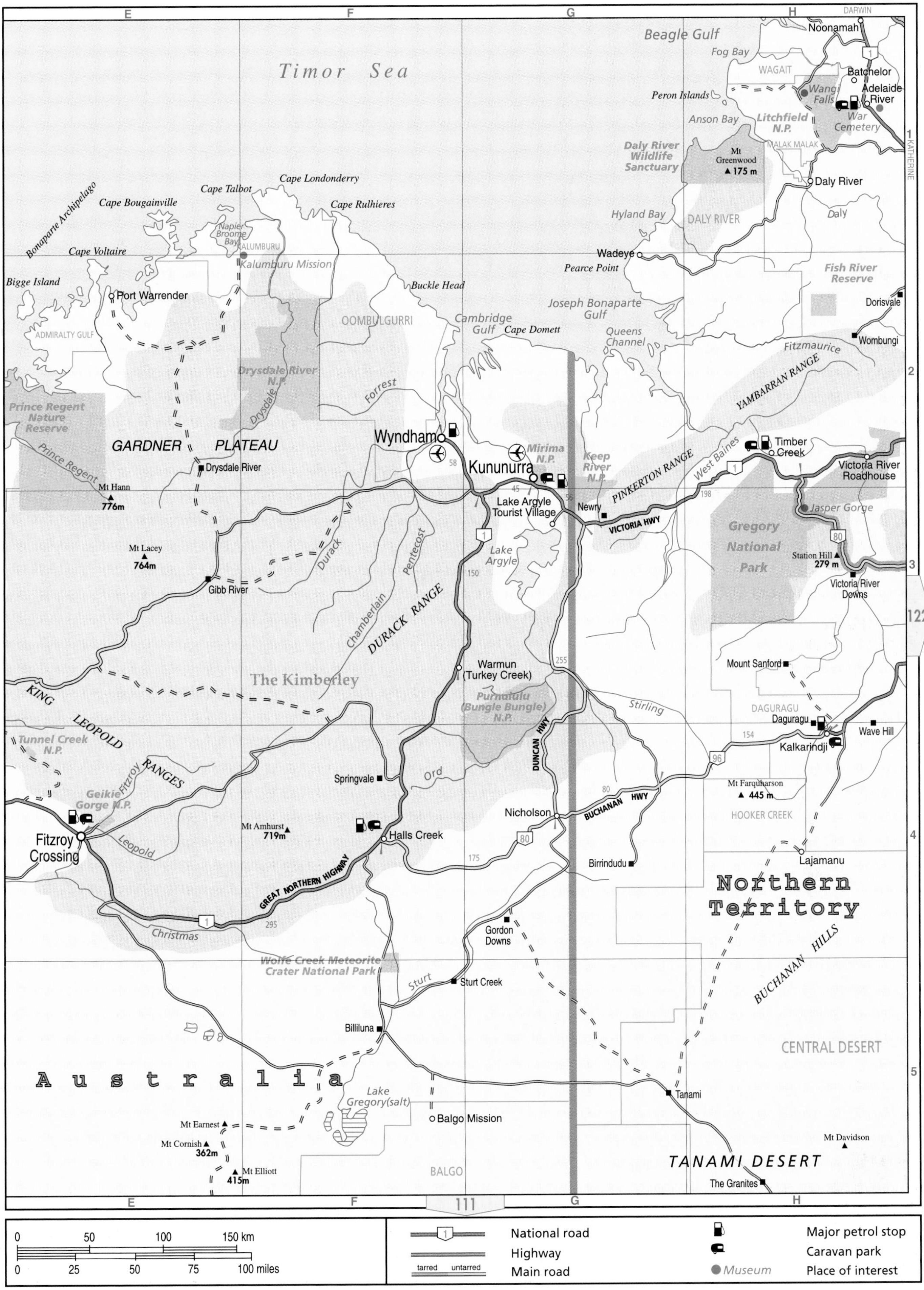

E
F
G
H
DARWIN
Beagle Gulf
Noonamah
Fog Bay
Timor Sea
WAGAIT
Batchelor
Adelaide River
Peron Islands
Wangi Falls
War Cemetery
Anson Bay
Litchfield N.P.
Daly River Wildlife Sanctuary
Mt Greenwood
175 m
MALAK MALAK
KATHERINE
Daly River
Cape Londonderry
Cape Talbot
Cape Bougainville
Cape Rulhieres
Bonaparte Archipelago
Napier Broome Bay
KALUMBURU
Kalumburu Mission
Hyland Bay
DALY RIVER
Daly
Cape Voltaire
Wadeye
Pearce Point
Bigge Island
Buckle Head
Fish River Reserve
Port Warrender
Joseph Bonaparte Gulf
Dorisvale
OOMBULGURRI
Cambridge Gulf
Cape Domett
ADMIRALTY GULF
Queens Channel
Wombungi
Fitzmaurice
Drysdale River N.P.
YAMBARRAN RANGE
Forrest
Prince Regent Nature Reserve
Drysdale
Wyndham
Mirima N.P.
Keep River N.P.
Timber Creek
GARDNER PLATEAU
Prince Regent
Kununurra
West Baines
PINKERTON RANGE
Victoria River Roadhouse
Drysdale River
Mt Hann
776m
Lake Argyle Tourist Village
Newry
VICTORIA HWY
Jasper Gorge
Mt Lacey
764m
Durack
Pentecost
Lake Argyle
Gregory National Park
Station Hill
279 m
Gibb River
Victoria River Downs
Chamberlain
DURACK RANGE
Mount Sanford
Warmun (Turkey Creek)
The Kimberley
Purnululu (Bungle Bungle) N.P.
KING LEOPOLD RANGES
Stirling
DAGURAGU
Daguragu
Wave Hill
Tunnel Creek N.P.
DUNCAN HWY
Kalkarindji
Fitzroy
Ord
Springvale
Geikie Gorge N.P.
Mt Farquharson
445 m
Nicholson
BUCHANAN HWY
HOOKER CREEK
Mt Amhurst
719m
Fitzroy Crossing
Halls Creek
Leopold
Birrindudu
Lajamanu
GREAT NORTHERN HIGHWAY
Northern Territory
Christmas
Gordon Downs
BUCHANAN HILLS
Wolfe Creek Meteorite Crater National Park
Sturt
Sturt Creek
Billiluna
CENTRAL DESERT
Australia
Lake Gregory (salt)
Tanami
Mt Earnest
Balgo Mission
Mt Cornish
362m
Mt Davidson
Mt Elliott
415m
TANAMI DESERT
BALGO
The Granites
122
111
0 50 100 150 km
0 25 50 75 100 miles
National road
Highway
tarred untarred
Main road
Major petrol stop
Caravan park
Museum
Place of interest

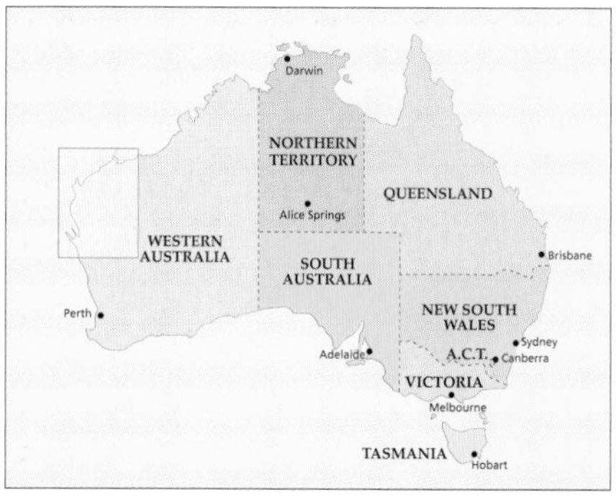

Pilbara and Shark Bay

The Pilbara is a strange mixture of large iron-ore ports, mining towns, and endless kilometres of desert. From Port Hedland to Kalbarri the landscape changes from barren coastal desert to an area of fabulous wildflower displays. The region in the south contains the beautiful Ningaloo Coral Reef, strange domed stromatolites and Shell Beach at Shark Bay. One of the biggest attractions are the dolphins at Monkey Mia. There are also thousands of kilometres of unspoilt, white sand beaches, game fishing off coastal islands, and the near-deserted, old gold-mining towns of Cue and Meekatharra.

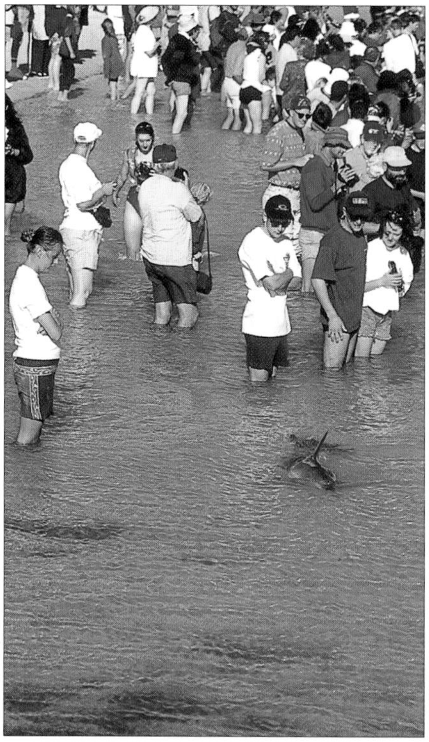

TOP ATTRACTIONS

Cape Inscription: the point where the first Europeans stepped onto Australian soil.
Cue and Meekatharra: fascinating old mining settlements, now nearly ghost towns.
Hamelin: location of ancient, domed stromatolites.
Shark Bay: beautiful, isolated bay offering a range of attractions such as Monkey Mia.
Monkey Mia: dolphins come to shore to be fed and petted.
Pilbara's mining towns: Mount Tom Price, Paraburdoo, Shay Gap, Newman, Pannawonica and Goldsworthy are all interesting.
Roebourne, Onslow and Cossack: fascinating, appealing post-war townships.

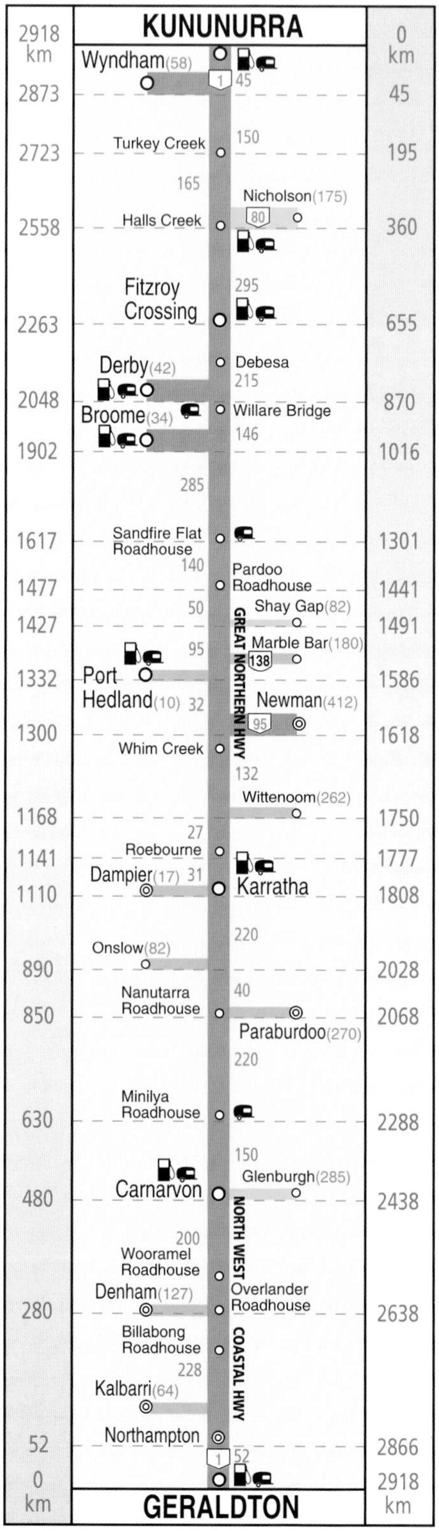

ON THE ROAD

It is vital to stay on the main roads in this area. The rainfall is low and the temperatures in summertime frequently above 40°C (104°F) for days on end. This means that the numerous roads that head off into the desert can be extremely dangerous if you experience vehicle problems. The distances between the main centres are considerable and precautions should be taken so you don't break down or run out of petrol. Main roads are all sealed, but the minor roads are invariably dirt. Usually they are in good condition because there is little traffic and little rainfall to create potholes and corrugations. Stay with your vehicle if it breaks down.

Above, left: *The dolphins of Monkey Mia are world-renowned for their fondness of the people who visit them.*
Left: *Emma Whitnell was the first female settler in the region; crumbling walls are all that remain of her school.*

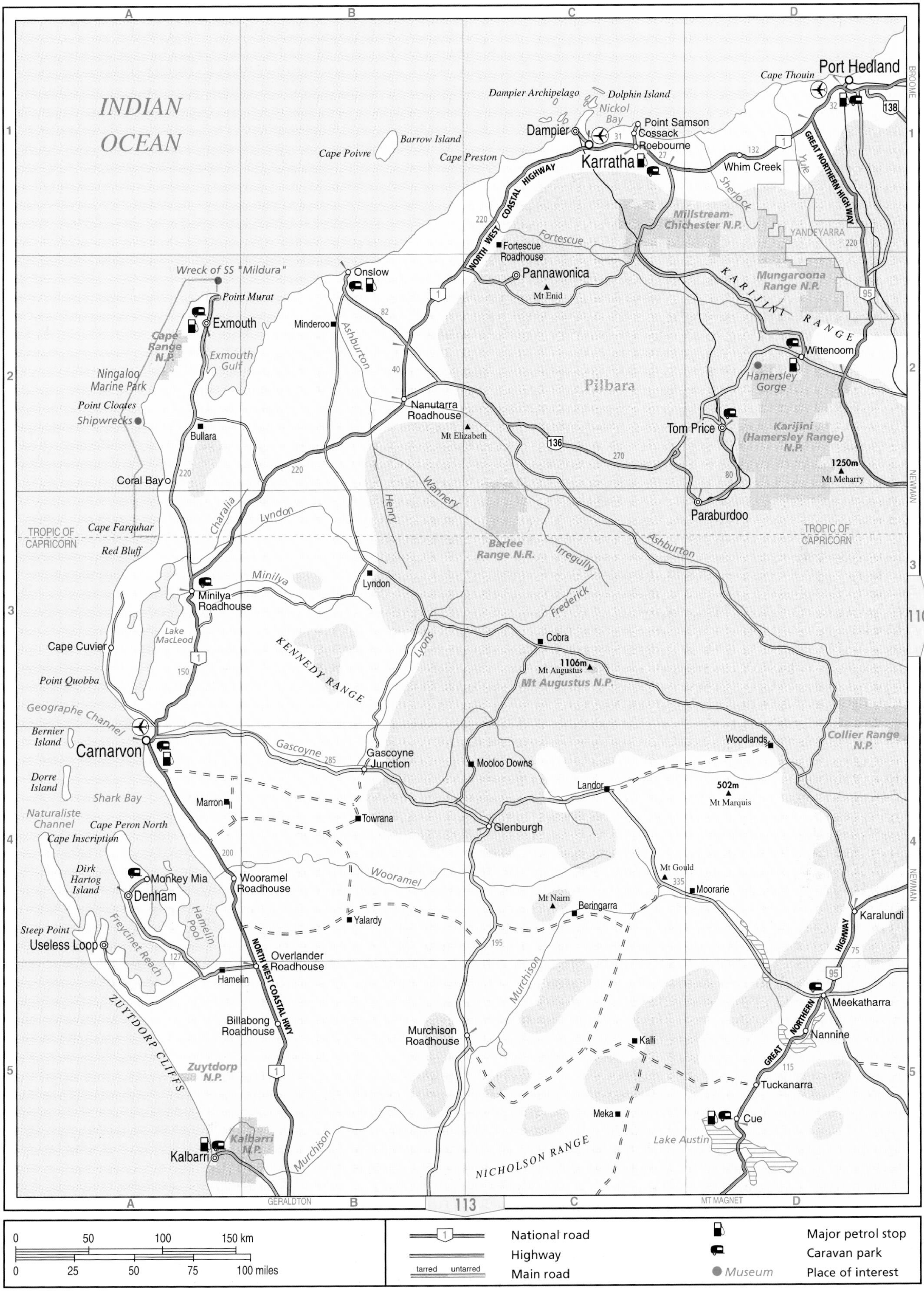
INDIAN OCEAN
Port Hedland
Cape Thouin
Dampier Archipelago
Dolphin Island
Nickol Bay
Dampier
Point Samson
Cossack
Roebourne
Karratha
Barrow Island
Cape Poivre
Cape Preston
Whim Creek
Sherlock
Yule
GREAT NORTHERN HIGHWAY
NORTH WEST COASTAL HIGHWAY
Millstream-Chichester N.P.
YANDEYARRA
Fortescue
Fortescue Roadhouse
Pannawonica
Mt Enid
Onslow
Wreck of SS "Mildura"
Point Murat
Exmouth
Cape Range N.P.
Exmouth Gulf
Ningaloo Marine Park
Point Cloates
Shipwrecks
Minderoo
Ashburton
Mungaroona Range N.P.
KARIJINI RANGE
Wittenoom
Hamersley Gorge
Pilbara
Nanutarra Roadhouse
Mt Elizabeth
Bullara
Tom Price
Karijini (Hamersley Range) N.P.
1250m
Mt Meharry
Coral Bay
Charalia
Lyndon
Henry
Wannery
Paraburdoo
TROPIC OF CAPRICORN
Cape Farquhar
Red Bluff
Barlee Range N.R.
Irregully
Ashburton
Minilya
Minilya Roadhouse
Frederick
Lake MacLeod
Cape Cuvier
KENNEDY RANGE
Lyons
Cobra
1106m
Mt Augustus
Mt Augustus N.P.
Point Quobba
Geographe Channel
Bernier Island
Carnarvon
Gascoyne
Gascoyne Junction
Woodlands
Collier Range N.P.
Mooloo Downs
Dorre Island
Shark Bay
Marron
Landor
502m
Mt Marquis
Naturaliste Channel
Cape Peron North
Towrana
Glenburgh
Cape Inscription
Dirk Hartog Island
Monkey Mia
Denham
Wooramel Roadhouse
Wooramel
Hamelin Pool
Mt Gould
Moorarie
Mt Nairn
Beringarra
Yalardy
Karalundi
Steep Point
Useless Loop
Freycinet Reach
Overlander Roadhouse
Hamelin
NORTH WEST COASTAL HWY
Murchison
HIGHWAY
ZUYTDORP CLIFFS
Meekatharra
GREAT NORTHERN
Nannine
Billabong Roadhouse
Murchison Roadhouse
Kalli
Zuytdorp N.P.
Tuckanarra
Meka
Cue
Kalbarri N.P.
Kalbarri
Lake Austin
NICHOLSON RANGE
BROOME
NEWMAN
GERALDTON
MT MAGNET
110
113
0 50 100 150 km
0 25 50 75 100 miles
National road
Highway
Main road
tarred
untarred
Major petrol stop
Caravan park
Museum
Place of interest

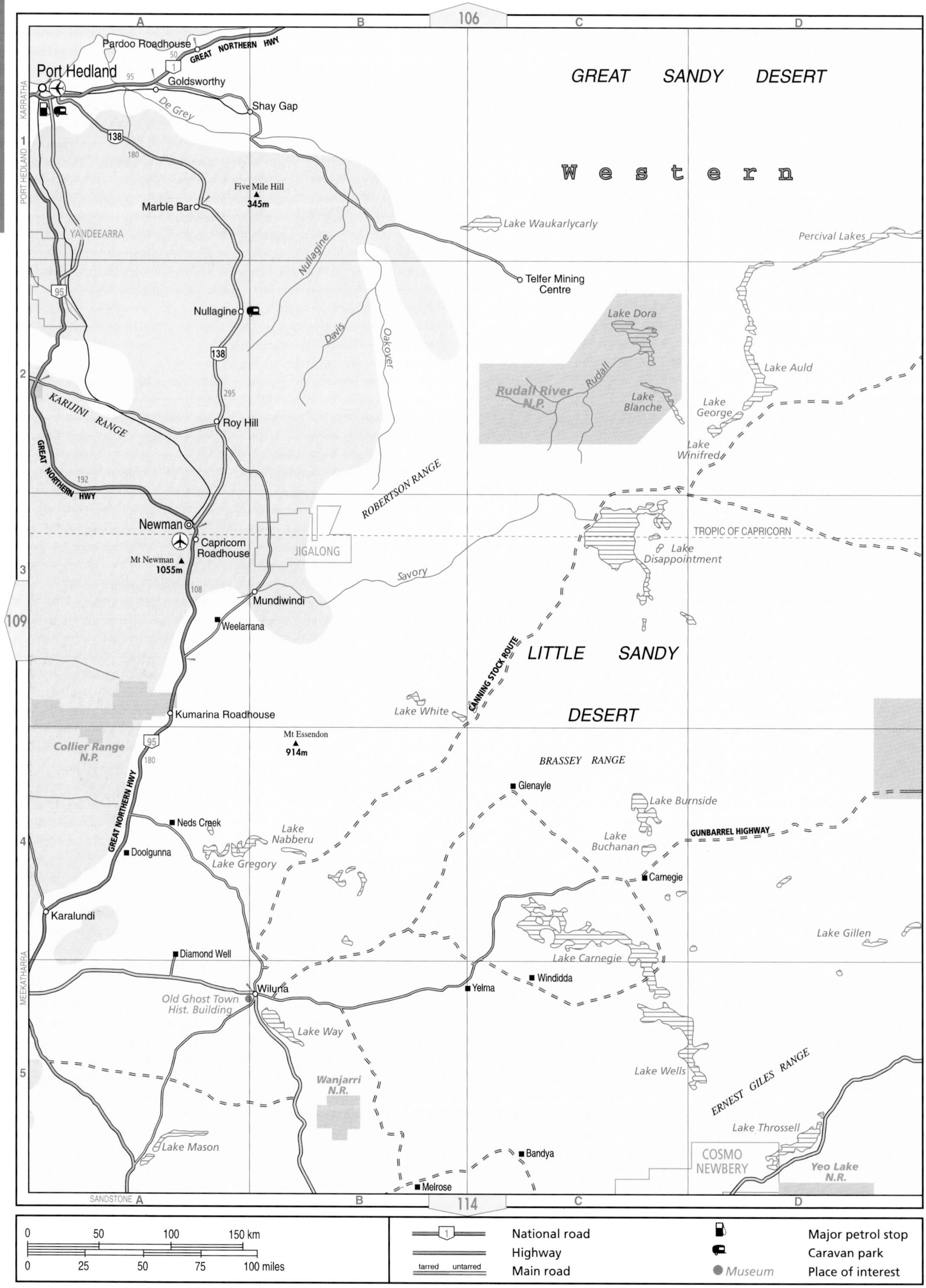
106
109
114
A
B
C
D
1
2
3
4
5
KARRATHA
PORT HEDLAND
MEEKATHARRA
SANDSTONE
GREAT SANDY DESERT
Western
LITTLE SANDY
DESERT
Pardoo Roadhouse
GREAT NORTHERN HWY
Port Hedland
Goldsworthy
Shay Gap
De Grey
Five Mile Hill
345m
Marble Bar
YANDEEARRA
Nullagine
Nullagine
Davis
Oakover
Lake Waukarlycarly
Telfer Mining Centre
Percival Lakes
Lake Dora
Rudall
Rudall River N.P.
Lake Blanche
Lake Auld
Lake George
Lake Winifred
KARIJINI RANGE
Roy Hill
GREAT NORTHERN HWY
ROBERTSON RANGE
Newman
Capricorn Roadhouse
JIGALONG
Mt Newman
1055m
TROPIC OF CAPRICORN
Lake Disappointment
Savory
Mundiwindi
Weelarrana
CANNING STOCK ROUTE
Kumarina Roadhouse
Lake White
Collier Range N.P.
Mt Essendon
914m
BRASSEY RANGE
Glenayle
Lake Burnside
GREAT NORTHERN HWY
Neds Creek
Lake Nabberu
Lake Buchanan
GUNBARREL HIGHWAY
Doolgunna
Lake Gregory
Carnegie
Karalundi
Lake Gillen
Diamond Well
Lake Carnegie
Windidda
Yelma
Wiluna
Old Ghost Town Hist. Building
Lake Way
Wanjarri N.R.
Lake Wells
ERNEST GILES RANGE
Lake Mason
Lake Throssell
Bandya
COSMO NEWBERY
Yeo Lake N.R.
Melrose
0 50 100 150 km
0 25 50 75 100 miles
National road
Highway
tarred untarred
Main road
Major petrol stop
Caravan park
Museum
Place of interest

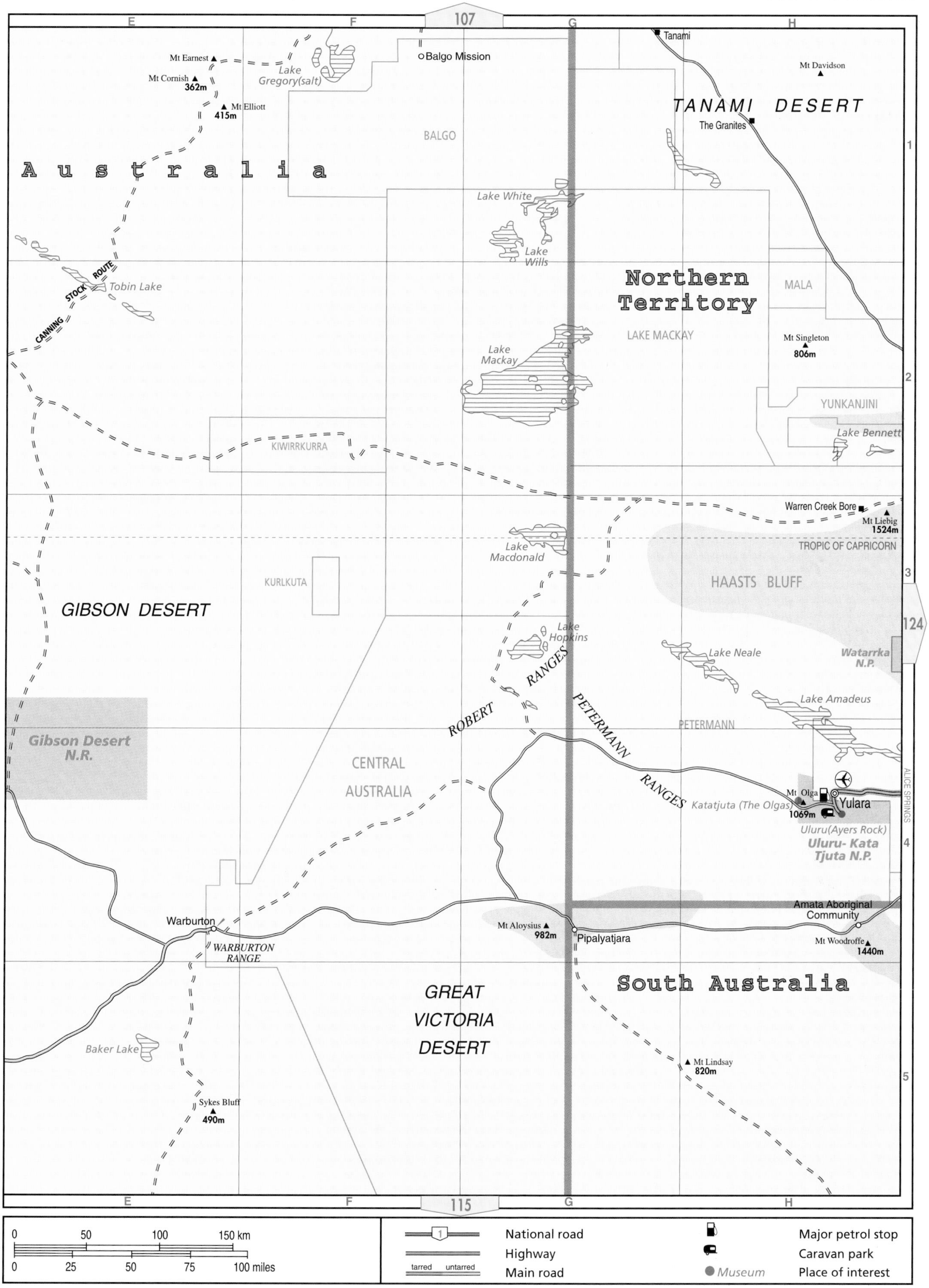
107
E
F
G
H
Tanami
Balgo Mission
Mt Davidson
Mt Earnest
Mt Cornish
362m
Lake Gregory(salt)
Mt Elliott
415m
TANAMI DESERT
The Granites
BALGO
Australia
Lake White
Lake Wills
Tobin Lake
CANNING STOCK ROUTE
Northern Territory
MALA
LAKE MACKAY
Mt Singleton
806m
Lake Mackay
YUNKANJINI
Lake Bennett
KIWIRRKURRA
Warren Creek Bore
Mt Liebig
1524m
TROPIC OF CAPRICORN
Lake Macdonald
HAASTS BLUFF
KURLKUTA
GIBSON DESERT
124
Lake Hopkins
Lake Neale
Watarrka N.P.
ROBERT RANGES
PETERMANN RANGES
Lake Amadeus
PETERMANN
Gibson Desert N.R.
CENTRAL AUSTRALIA
ALICE SPRINGS
Mt Olga
1069m
Yulara
Katatjuta (The Olgas)
Uluru(Ayers Rock)
Uluru- Kata Tjuta N.P.
Amata Aboriginal Community
Warburton
Mt Aloysius
982m
Pipalyatjara
Mt Woodroffe
1440m
WARBURTON RANGE
South Australia
GREAT VICTORIA DESERT
Baker Lake
Mt Lindsay
820m
Sykes Bluff
490m
1
2
3
4
5
115
0 50 100 150 km
0 25 50 75 100 miles
National road
Highway
tarred untarred
Main road
Major petrol stop
Caravan park
Museum
Place of interest

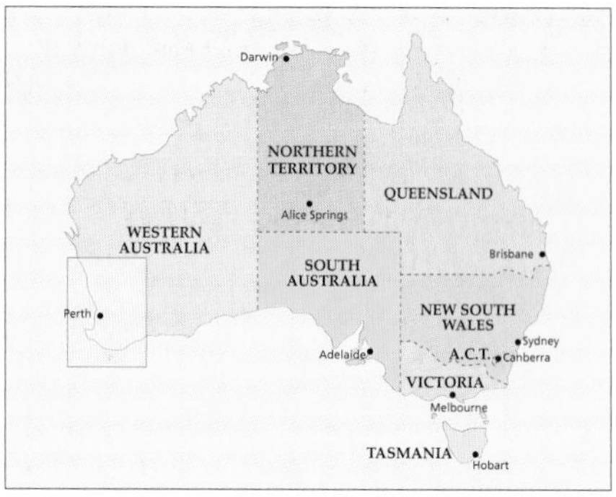

The South-west

Most Western Australians live in the south-western corner of the state. This area includes the substantial and gracious coastal towns of Geraldton, Bunbury, Busselton, Albany and Margaret River and fascinating wheat belt towns such as Merredin, Northam and Hyden. The beaches of the south-west are breathtaking: bone-white sand, slate-grey granite cliffs, and water that changes from aquamarine near the shore to a dark cobalt-blue further out. The Albany Doctor, Esperance Doctor and Bunbury Doctor are strong, cool winds which blow in off the Southern Ocean, whipping up waves and sculpting coastal trees into fantastic shapes.

TOP ATTRACTIONS

Bunbury to Albany: famed for its granite cliffs and its stands of giant karri and jarrah trees.
Kalbarri to Lancelin: characterised by small fishing villages, dramatic cliffs and unusual rock formations like the Pinnacles in the Nambung National Park near Cervantes, as well as beautiful wildflower displays.
The Inland Region: attractions of this area include the famous Wave Rock near Hyden, the water pipeline built to serve the gold-mining towns of Kalgoorlie and Coolgardie, Lake Dumbleyung where Sir Donald Campbell set the world water speed record in 1964 and the charming, historic villages of York and Northam.

Above: *Millions of years of weather erosion has created the awesome Wave Rock formation near the town of Hyden.*

ON THE ROAD

The south-west corner has a relatively high population density and contains most of the state's major tourist attractions. Consequently the region has good sealed roads. The larger towns all have adequate accommodation, petrol and other car services. The smaller wheat belt towns are often little more than a service station, a hotel-motel and a grain loading facility. Minor roads in this area are, as a general rule, reliable, but tend to deteriorate further west and north.

Below: *The Pinnacles at Nambung National Park were thought by 17th-century maritime explorers to be the remnants of a city.*

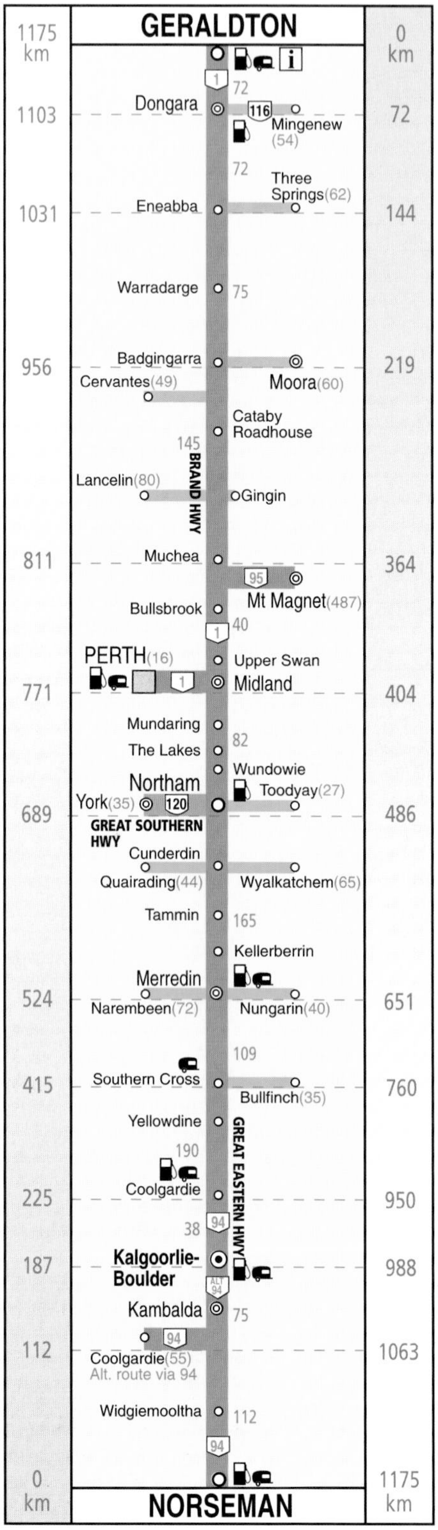

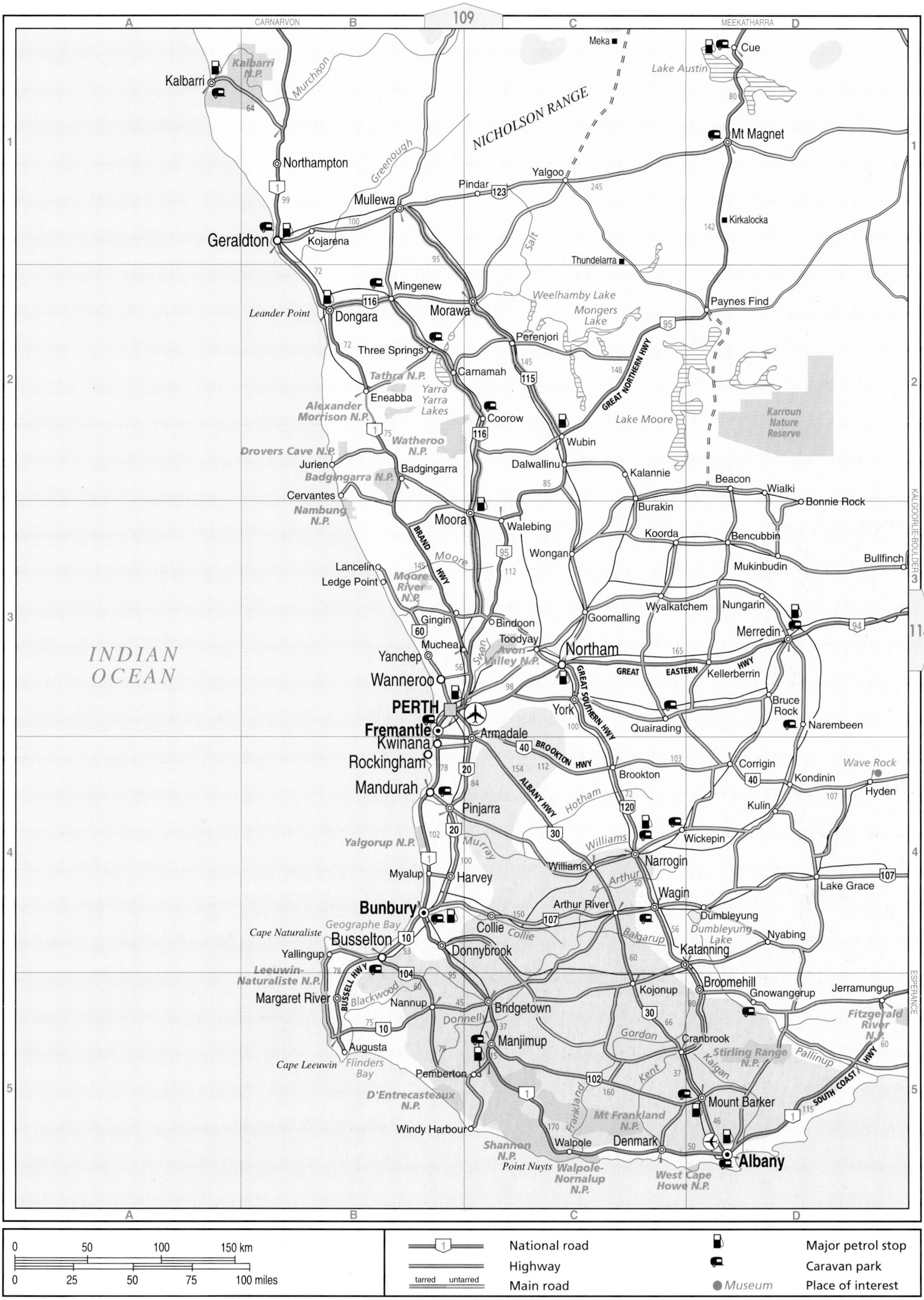

109
CARNARVON
MEEKATHARRA
KALGOORLIE-BOULDER
ESPERANCE
114
INDIAN OCEAN
NICHOLSON RANGE
Kalbarri
Kalbarri N.P.
Murchison
Northampton
Greenough
Mullewa
Pindar
Yalgoo
Meka
Cue
Lake Austin
Mt Magnet
Kirkalocka
Geraldton
Kojarena
Thundelarra
Salt
Mingenew
Dongara
Leander Point
Morawa
Weelhamby Lake
Mongers Lake
Paynes Find
Perenjori
Three Springs
Carnamah
Tathra N.P.
Yarra Yarra Lakes
Eneabba
Alexander Morrison N.P.
Coorow
GREAT NORTHERN HWY
Lake Moore
Karroun Nature Reserve
Watheroo N.P.
Wubin
Drovers Cave N.P.
Jurien
Dalwallinu
Badgingarra N.P.
Badgingarra
Kalannie
Beacon
Wialki
Bonnie Rock
Cervantes
Burakin
Nambung N.P.
Moora
Walebing
BRAND HWY
Koorda
Bencubbin
Wongan
Moore
Lancelin
Ledge Point
Moore River N.P.
Mukinbudin
Bullfinch
Nungarin
Wyalkatchem
Goomalling
Gingin
Bindoon
Merredin
Toodyay
Avon Valley N.P.
Muchea
Swan
Northam
Yanchep
GREAT EASTERN HWY
Kellerberrin
Wanneroo
PERTH
York
GREAT SOUTHERN HWY
Bruce Rock
Fremantle
Quairading
Narembeen
Kwinana
Armadale
BROOKTON HWY
Rockingham
Brookton
Corrigin
Wave Rock
Kondinin
Mandurah
ALBANY HWY
Hotham
Hyden
Pinjarra
Kulin
Yalgorup N.P.
Murray
Williams
Wickepin
Narrogin
Myalup
Harvey
Lake Grace
Arthur
Wagin
Bunbury
Arthur River
Dumbleyung
Dumbleyung Lake
Cape Naturaliste
Geographe Bay
Collie
Nyabing
Busselton
Balgarup
Yallingup
Donnybrook
Katanning
Leeuwin-Naturaliste N.P.
BUSSELL HWY
Blackwood
Broomehill
Kojonup
Jerramungup
Margaret River
Gnowangerup
Nannup
Bridgetown
Fitzgerald River N.P.
Donnelly
Gordon
Augusta
Manjimup
Cranbrook
Stirling Range N.P.
Pallinup
Kalgan
Cape Leeuwin
Flinders Bay
Pemberton
Kent
SOUTH COAST HWY
D'Entrecasteaux N.P.
Frankland
Mount Barker
Mt Frankland N.P.
Windy Harbour
Shannon N.P.
Walpole
Denmark
Albany
Point Nuyts
Walpole-Nornalup N.P.
West Cape Howe N.P.
0 50 100 150 km
0 25 50 75 100 miles
National road
Highway
tarred untarred
Main road
Major petrol stop
Caravan park
Museum
Place of interest

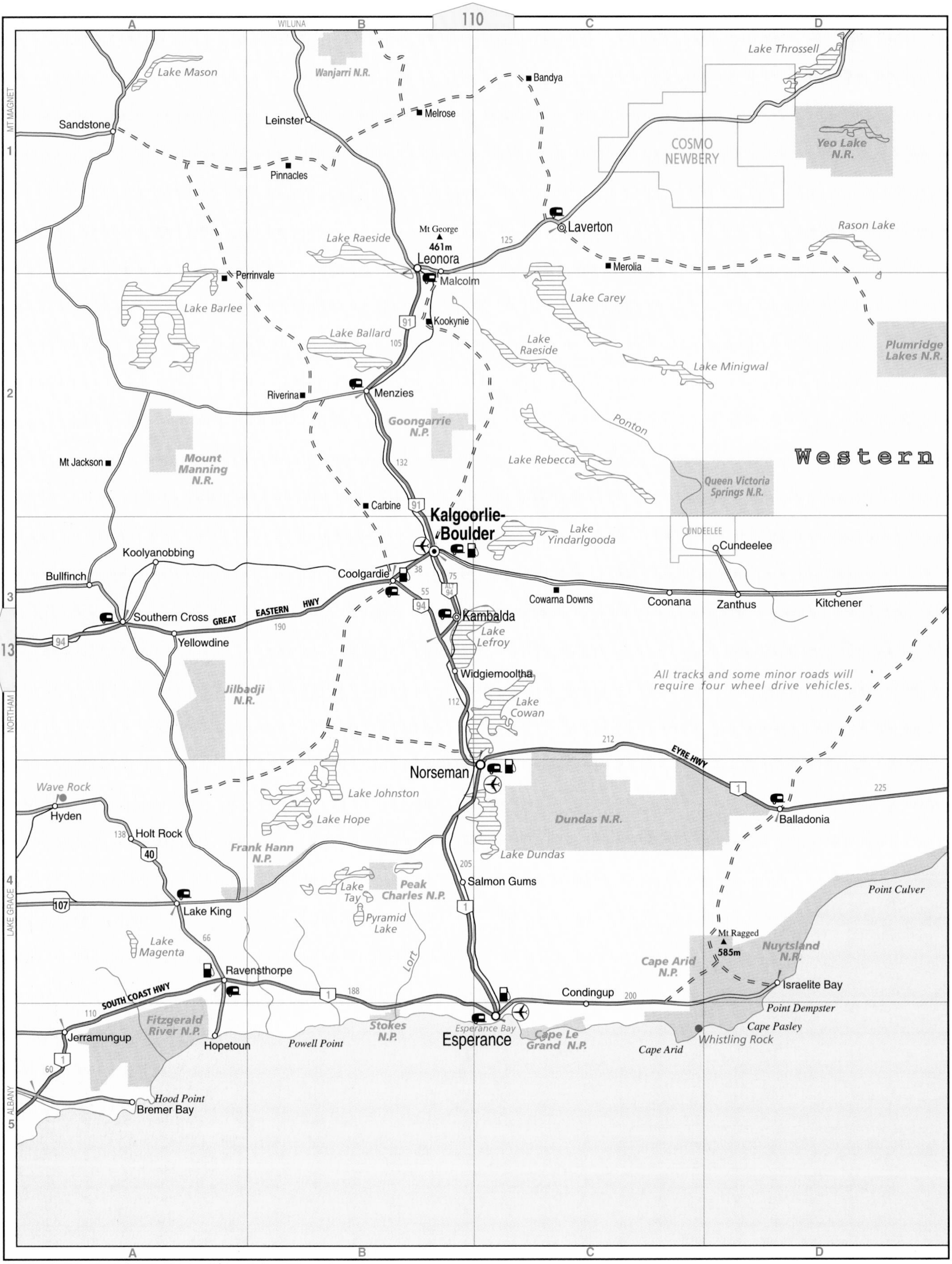
110
113
WILUNA
MT MAGNET
LAKE GRACE
NORTHAM
ALBANY
A
B
C
D
1
2
3
4
5
Western
Lake Mason
Wanjarri N.R.
Bandya
Melrose
Lake Throssell
Sandstone
Leinster
Pinnacles
COSMO NEWBERY
Yeo Lake N.R.
Mt George
461m
Lake Raeside
Leonora
Laverton
Rason Lake
Perrinvale
Malcolm
Merolia
Lake Barlee
Kookynie
Lake Carey
Lake Ballard
Lake Raeside
Plumridge Lakes N.R.
Lake Minigwal
Riverina
Menzies
Goongarrie N.P.
Ponton
Mt Jackson
Mount Manning N.R.
Lake Rebecca
Queen Victoria Springs N.R.
Carbine
Kalgoorlie-Boulder
Lake Yindarlgooda
CUNDEELEE
Cundeelee
Koolyanobbing
Bullfinch
Coolgardie
Cowarna Downs
Coonana
Zanthus
Kitchener
Southern Cross
GREAT EASTERN HWY
Kambalda
Yellowdine
Lake Lefroy
Widgiemooltha
Jilbadji N.R.
All tracks and some minor roads will require four wheel drive vehicles.
Lake Cowan
EYRE HWY
Norseman
Wave Rock
Hyden
Lake Johnston
Balladonia
Lake Hope
Dundas N.R.
Holt Rock
Frank Hann N.P.
Lake Dundas
Salmon Gums
Lake Tay
Peak Charles N.P.
Point Culver
Lake King
Pyramid Lake
Lake Magenta
Mt Ragged
585m
Nuytsland N.R.
Cape Arid N.P.
Lort
Ravensthorpe
Israelite Bay
Condingup
SOUTH COAST HWY
Point Dempster
Fitzgerald River N.P.
Stokes N.P.
Esperance Bay
Cape Pasley
Jerramungup
Hopetoun
Powell Point
Esperance
Cape Le Grand N.P.
Whistling Rock
Cape Arid
Hood Point
Bremer Bay

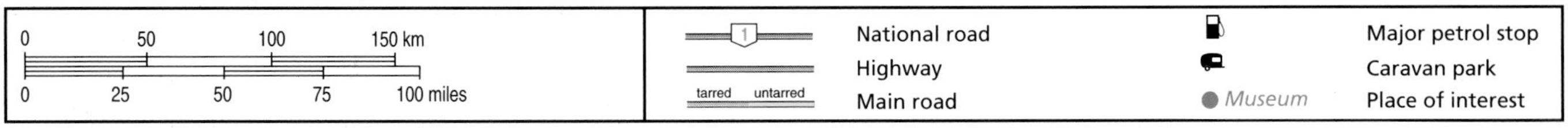
0 50 100 150 km
0 25 50 75 100 miles
National road
Highway
tarred untarred
Main road
Major petrol stop
Caravan park
Museum
Place of interest

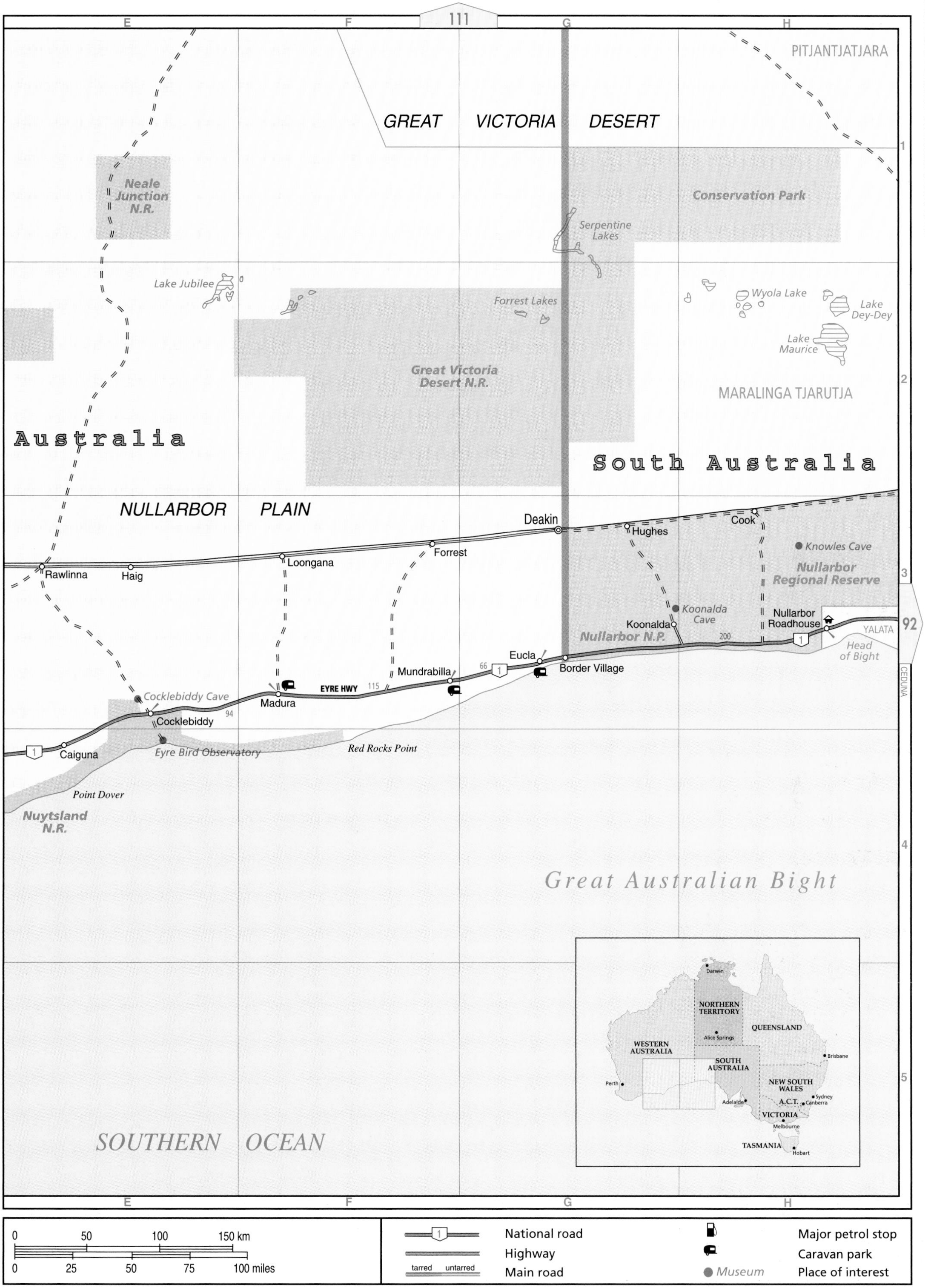
111
PITJANTJATJARA
GREAT VICTORIA DESERT
Neale Junction N.R.
Conservation Park
Serpentine Lakes
Lake Jubilee
Forrest Lakes
Wyola Lake
Lake Dey-Dey
Lake Maurice
Great Victoria Desert N.R.
MARALINGA TJARUTJA
Australia
South Australia
NULLARBOR PLAIN
Deakin
Cook
Hughes
Knowles Cave
Forrest
Loongana
Rawlinna
Haig
Nullarbor Regional Reserve
Koonalda Cave
Koonalda
Nullarbor Roadhouse
YALATA
92
Nullarbor N.P.
Head of Bight
CEDUNA
Eucla
Border Village
Mundrabilla
EYRE HWY
Madura
Cocklebiddy Cave
Cocklebiddy
Caiguna
Eyre Bird Observatory
Red Rocks Point
Point Dover
Nuytsland N.R.
Great Australian Bight
SOUTHERN OCEAN
Darwin
NORTHERN TERRITORY
Alice Springs
QUEENSLAND
WESTERN AUSTRALIA
SOUTH AUSTRALIA
Brisbane
Perth
NEW SOUTH WALES
Sydney
A.C.T.
Canberra
Adelaide
VICTORIA
Melbourne
TASMANIA
Hobart
0 50 100 150 km
0 25 50 75 100 miles
National road
Highway
tarred untarred
Main road
Major petrol stop
Caravan park
Museum
Place of interest

NORTHERN TERRITORY

Travellers will be overwhelmed by the flat terrain and vast isolation of the Northern Territory, where you can drive for 200–300km (125–185 miles) without passing a single service station or seeing another human being. Uniform vegetation and lonely, straight roads that disappear into the horizon are characteristic of central and northern Australia. The population of about 168 600 is spread over a vast 1 346 200km² (519 633 sq miles), yet, for all its remoteness, the Territory contains some significant landmarks. Both Litchfield and Kakadu national parks are notable for their wealth of Aboriginal heritage, cool and beautiful waterfalls and crocodile-infested rivers. Other landmarks include Uluru (Ayers Rock) and Kata Tjuta (the Olgas). This is the Australia of red deserts, impossibly blue skies, people who live hard simple lives, and a landscape that will take your breath away with its raw beauty.

Undoubtedly, the greatest attractions of the Northern Territory lie around Alice Springs. The awesome sight of Uluru and the 36 smaller monoliths known as Kata Tjuta attract tourists from all over the world. Further north are the beautiful MacDonnell Ranges, stretching to the east and west of Alice Springs and cut by a number of gorges offering a cool respite from the desert heat. The most notable gorges include Simpson's Gap, Standley Chasm and Glen Helen.

A journey to Katherine along the Stuart Highway passes through the unusual Mataranka Homestead Tourist Resort, where thermal springs bubble up in a region dominated by scrub and ant hills. Further south is the superb Nitmiluk (Katherine Gorge) National Park located 32km (20 miles) north-east of Katherine. You can hire canoes and make your own way up the gorge, however, the most popular and convenient way of exploring the area is on one of the organised cruises. Kakadu National Park is noted for its wildlife, Aboriginal rock art, waterfalls and vast wetlands that spring to life in the wet season.

Opposite: *Darwin, Australia's 'Gateway to the North', has survived cyclones and a World War II bombing attack.*

DARWIN	J	F	M	A	M	J	J	A	S	O	N	D
AV. TEMP. °F	82	82	82	84	80	78	78	80	82	84	84	84
AV. TEMP. °C	28	28	28	29	27	26	26	27	28	29	29	29
DAILY SUN hrs	6	6	7	9	9	10	10	10	10	10	8	7
RAINFALL in	16	13.5	12	4	1	0	0	0	1	3	5	9
RAINFALL mm	414	345	315	100	21	1	1	7	18	72	141	233
RAINFALL days	21	20	19	9	2	1	0	1	2	6	12	16

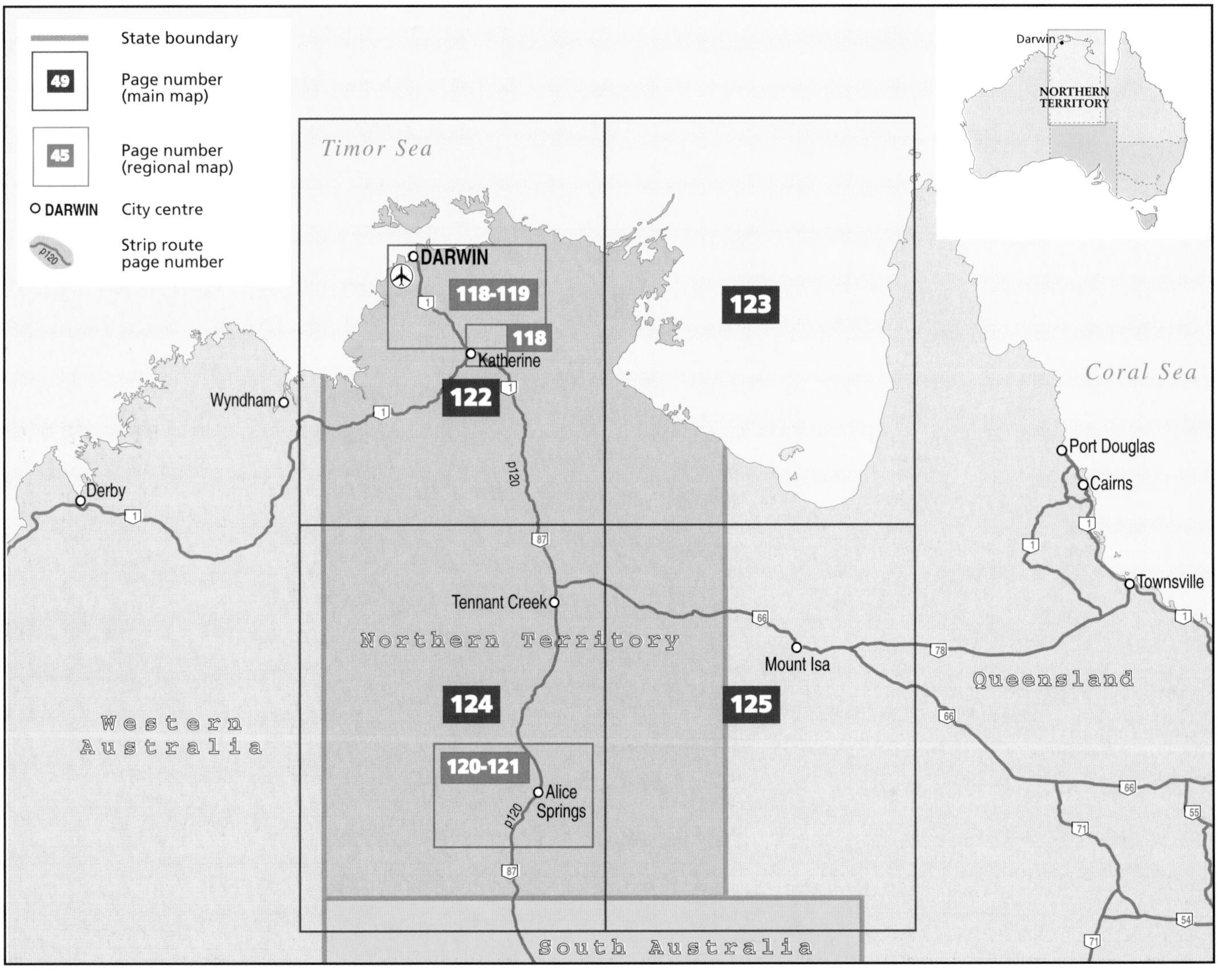

Darwin

Darwin is the capital city of the Northern Territory. Located between Beagle Gulf and Port Darwin and situated on Fannie Bay, Darwin is a thriving centre of nearly 75 000 people. It is both geographically and temperamentally a 'city in the tropics'. This is an ideal starting point for visits to Kakadu National Park, the various crocodile farms in the area and Litchfield National Park, one of the secrets of the far north. Darwin has survived two major disasters this century – it was entirely flattened by Cyclone Tracy on Christmas Day 1974 and it is the only city in Australia to have been bombed in World War II.

TOP ATTRACTIONS

Botanical Gardens: over 400 species of tropical plants.
Chinese Temple: still used by Buddhists, Taoists and Confucians.
Esplanade Gallery: built out of cypress pine in 1937.
Government House: beautiful old seven-gabled house which overlooks Darwin Harbour.

WHERE TO STAY

Novotel, cnr Peel & Esplanade, tel: (08) 8941 0755, fax: 8981 9025.
Asti Motel, cnr Smith & Packard, tel: (08) 8981 8200, fax: 8981 8038.
Beaufort, Esplanade, tel: (08) 8980 0800, fax: 8980 0888.
Darwin Travelodge, Esplanade, tel: (08) 8981 5388, fax: 8981 5701.
MGM Grand, Mindil Beach, tel: (08) 8943 8888, fax: 8943 8999.

CALENDAR OF EVENTS

JANUARY: Territory Sevens Rugby Union Tournament, Australia Day Celebration.
MAY: On the Beach.
JUNE: Bougainvillea Festival, Casino Golf Classic, Expo.
JULY: Kakadu Safari Ride, Royal Darwin Show, Cup Carnival, Darwin Turf Club Gala Ball.
AUGUST: Barefoot Mudcrab Tying Championships, Rodeo, Beer Can Regatta, Australian Safari.
SEPTEMBER: National Aboriginal Art Award.

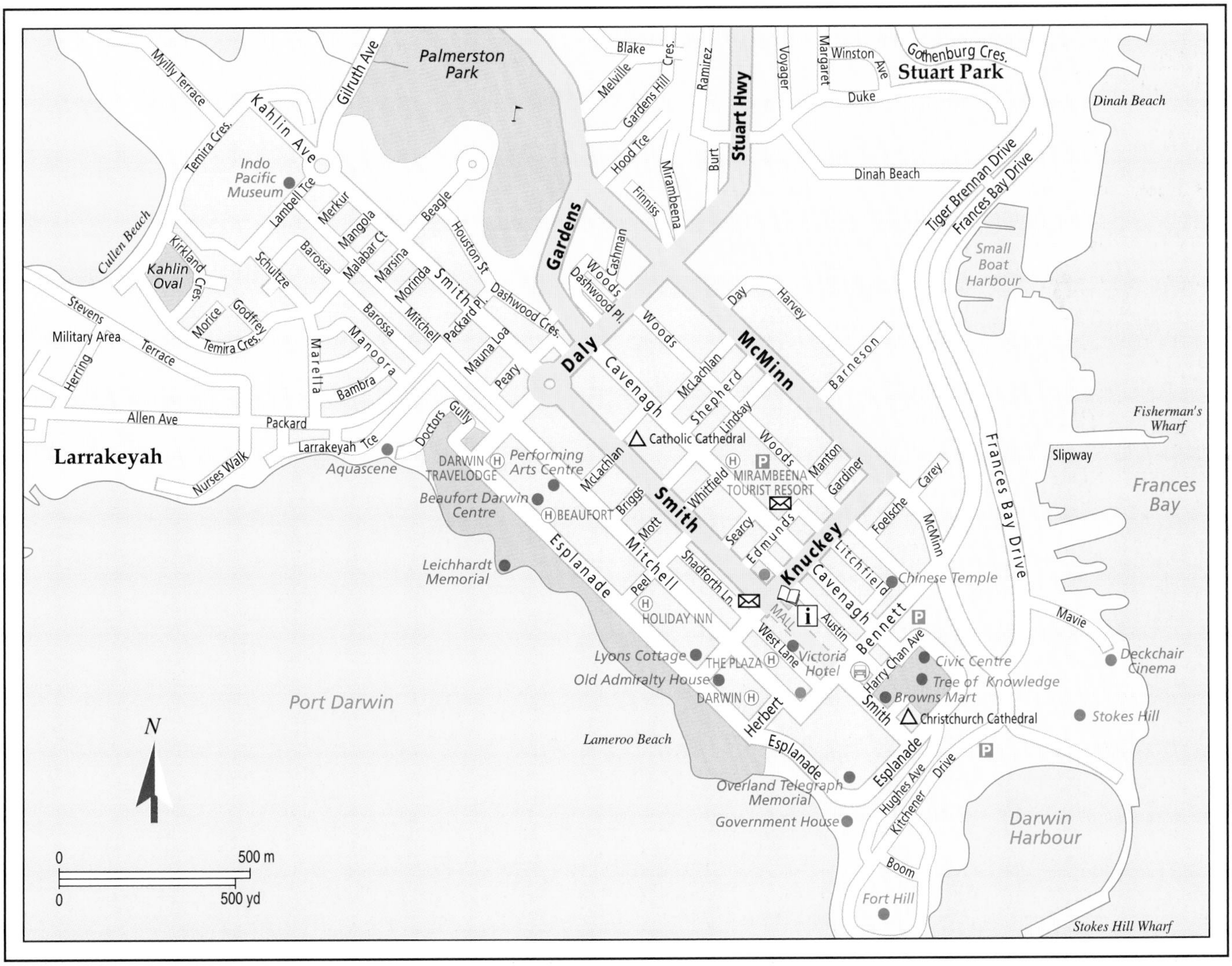

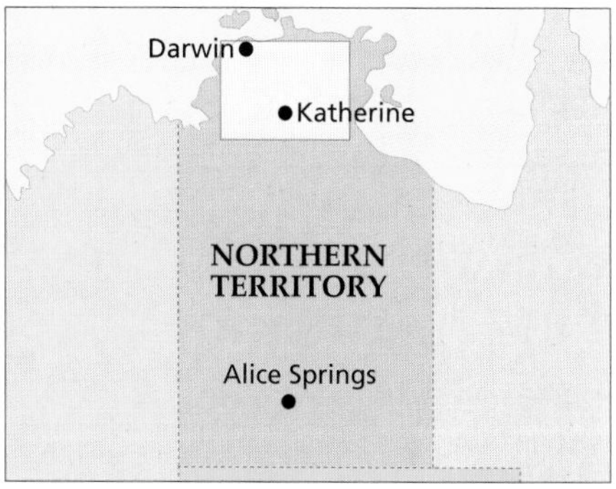

Kakadu and Nitmiluk National Parks

Two of the premier tourist attractions in northern Australia are the Kakadu and Nitmiluk (Katherine Gorge) national parks. Kakadu covers 1 307 300ha (3 230 338 acres), and is an important World Heritage region with superb Aboriginal rock paintings, teeming wildlife (particularly crocodiles and birds in the wetlands) and waterfalls that turn into raging torrents in the wet season. Nitmiluk contains the Katherine River which has carved 13 separate ravines, including the impressive 180 352-ha (445 650-acre) Katherine Gorge.

APPROX. DISTANCES KM FROM DARWIN	
Adelaide River	112
Alice Springs	1492
Borroloola	974
Daly Waters	586
Finke	1911
Katherine	314
Mataranka	417
Pine Creek	224
Tennant Creek	985
Uluru	1937
Wauchope	1100

Left: *The Yellow River cruises at Kakadu National Park set off at sunrise so that guests can see nature awaken. During the wet season (November to March) the water rises, flooding the tidal flats of the Alligator rivers and creating one huge wetland.*

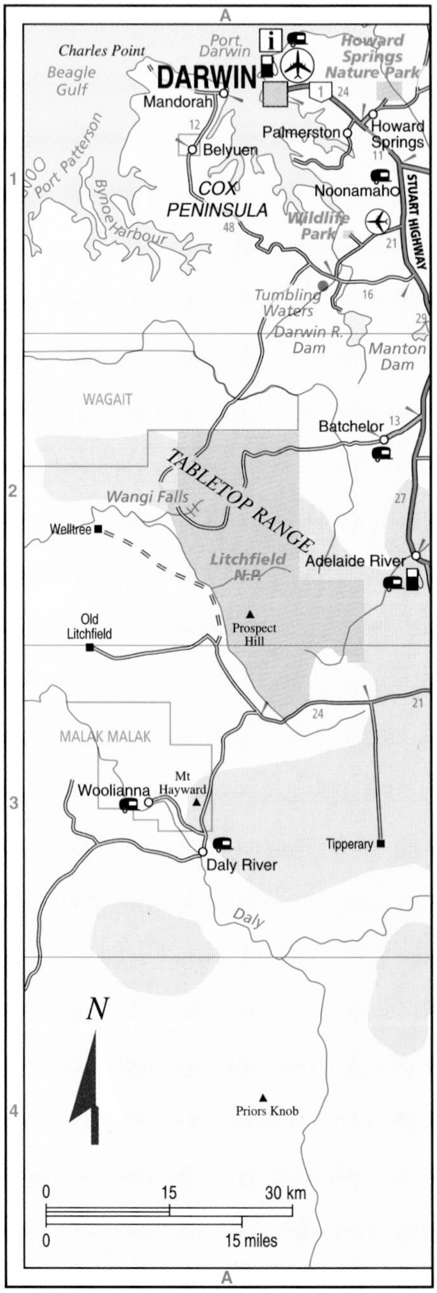

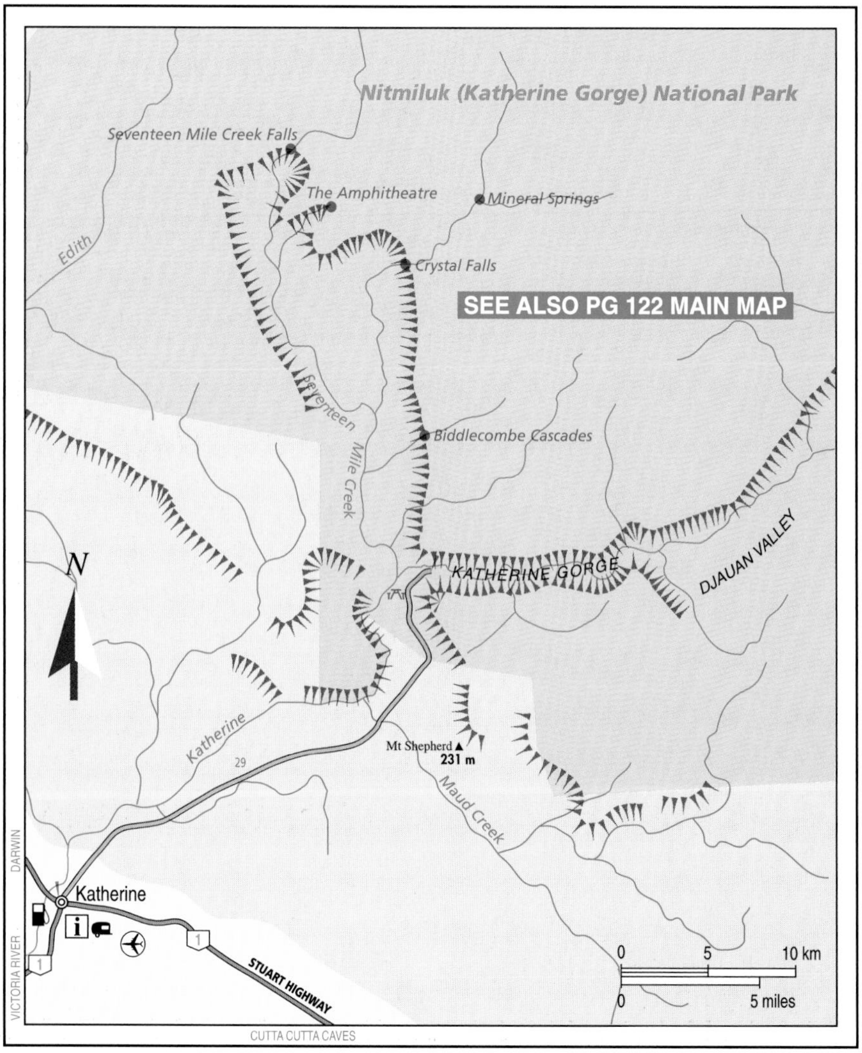

TOP ATTRACTIONS

Arnhem Land Escarpment: formidable barrier with seasonal creeks tumbling over rock face.
Edith Falls: clear pools fringed with greenery and red cliffs.
Jabiru: uranium mine and crocodile-shaped motel.
Katherine Gorge: deep sandstone gorge carved through the rugged escarpment.
Nourlangie Rock: over 100 Aboriginal sacred sites.
Ubirr Rock: impressive Aboriginal rock art site.

WHERE TO STAY

Gagadju Lodge Cooinda, Kakadu Hwy, tel: (08) 8979 0145, fax: 8979 0148.
Dunmarra Wayside Inn, Stuart Hwy, Katherine, tel: (08) 8975 9922.
Kakadu Holiday Village, Arnhem Land, tel: (08) 8979 0166.
Camping sites: there are a large number of camping sites within the boundaries of both Kakadu and Nitmiluk, including Malabanbandju, Mardukal and the Jim Jim Billabong camping areas. It is sensible to call in at the Ranger Headquarters near Jabiru to get details, brochures and maps. Contact Bowali Visitors Centre, Kakadu Highway on (08) 8938 1100. The parks' relative proximity to Darwin means that many visitors stay in Darwin and make daytrips to these wilderness areas. While this is quite feasible, it means that some of the early morning appeal – the mists rising from rivers and wetlands – is missed unless you leave Darwin very early.
The distance from Darwin to Jabiru is 247km (154 miles). It takes about two and a half hours to complete the one-way journey.

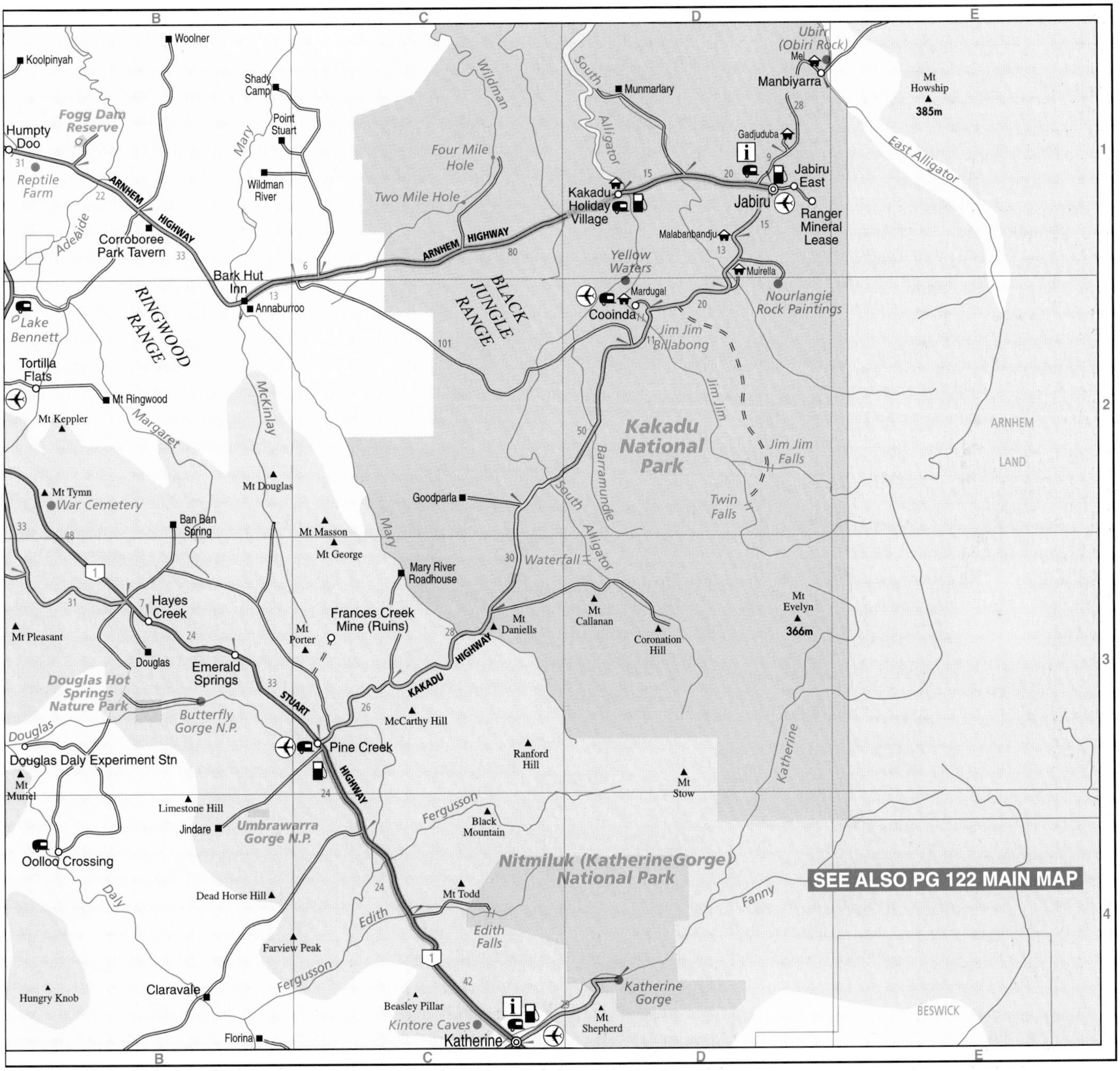

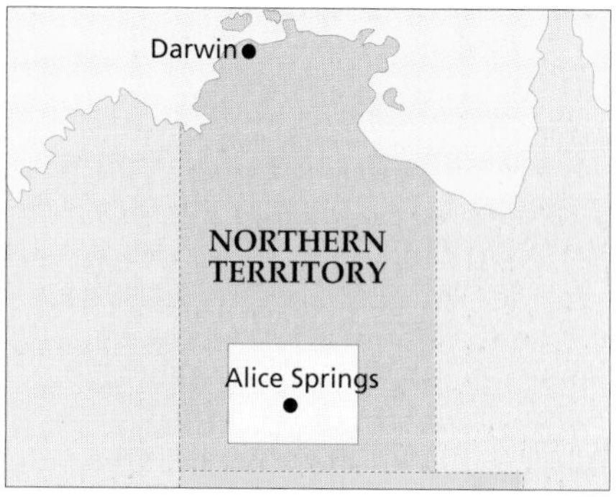

Alice Springs

It's easy to spend two or three weeks in Alice Springs and do something interesting and different every day. The greatest magnets are Uluru and Kata Tjuta, which rise out of the flat desert wasteland and mesmerise travellers with their changing colours and strangely haunting spirituality. Uluru rises 348m (1141ft) above the surrounding countryside and has a circumference of 9.4km (5.8 miles). To its north lie the 36 smaller monoliths known as Kata Tjuta, as well as Kings Canyon. Alice Springs is framed by the MacDonnell Ranges with their dramatic gorges, and nearby is the Lutheran mission at Hermannsburg.

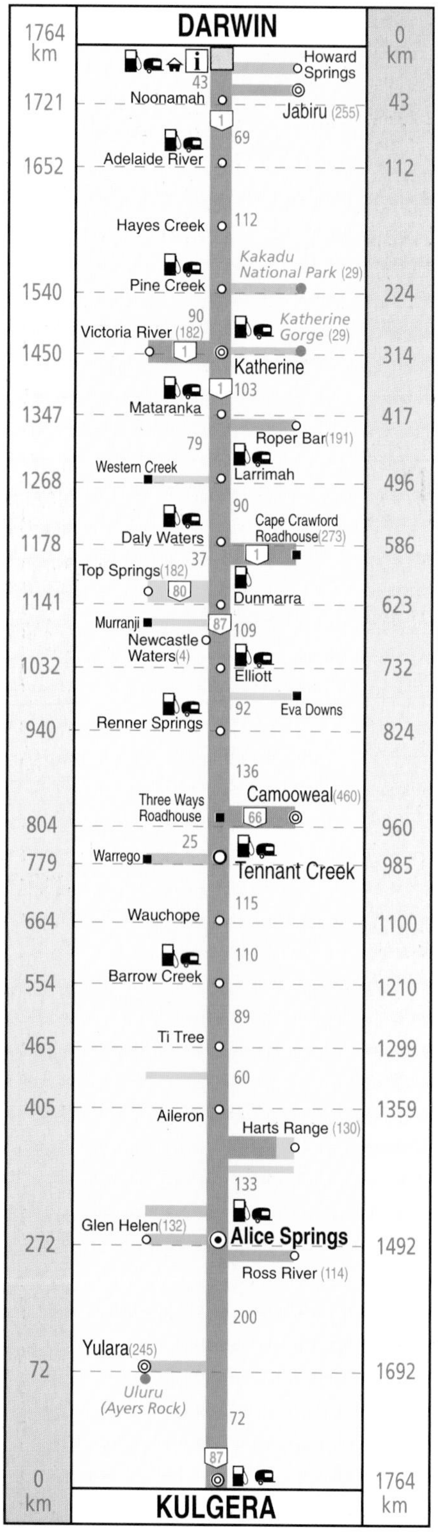

Above: *Alice Springs, once a telegraph repeater station, was made famous by Nevil Shute's 1950s novel A Town Like Alice.*
Opposite: *It is possible to drive around the circumference of Uluru, revered by the Aborigines as a sacred site.*

TOP ATTRACTIONS

Alice Springs Overland Telegraph Repeater Station: restored buildings allow insight into life in the early days of settlement in the region.
Arltunga: fascinating old gold-mining town.
Bushwalking: at Ormiston Gorge and Pound, Kings Canyon and N'Dhala Gorge.
Henbury Meteorite Craters: 200-m (656-ft) meteor craters created thousands of years ago.
Hermannsburg's Lutheran mission: captures the spirit of central Australia.
MacDonnell Ranges: dramatic gorges with hidden valleys.
Uluru–Kata Tjuta National Park: best at sunrise and sunset when the rocks change colour as the sun rises or falls below the horizon.

ON THE ROAD

Keep to the main roads and you'll have no trouble. Dirt tracks lie beyond, and given the area's climatic extremes, can be very dangerous. Stay with your car if it breaks down. Beware of dehydration, and speeding road trains 50m (165ft) long; if you see one coming, head for the bush!

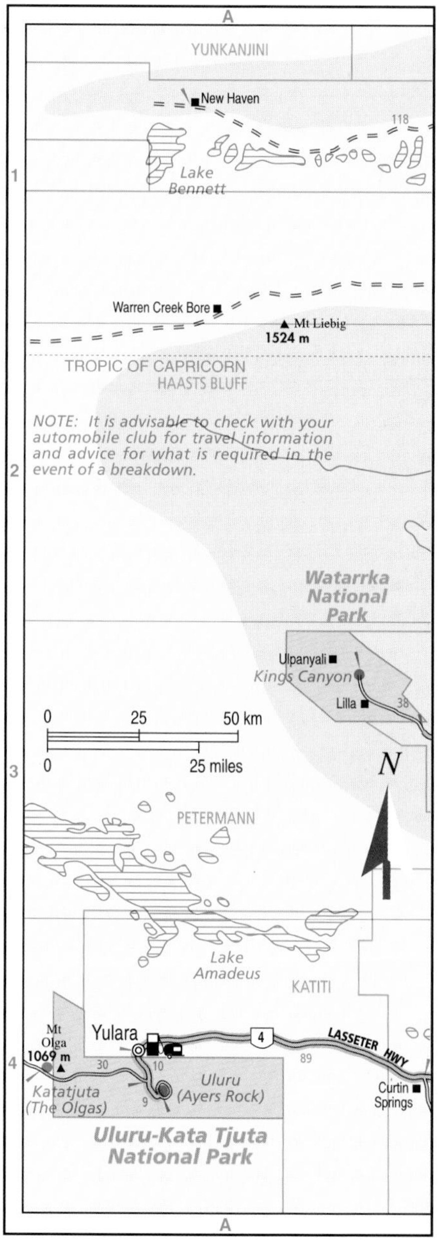

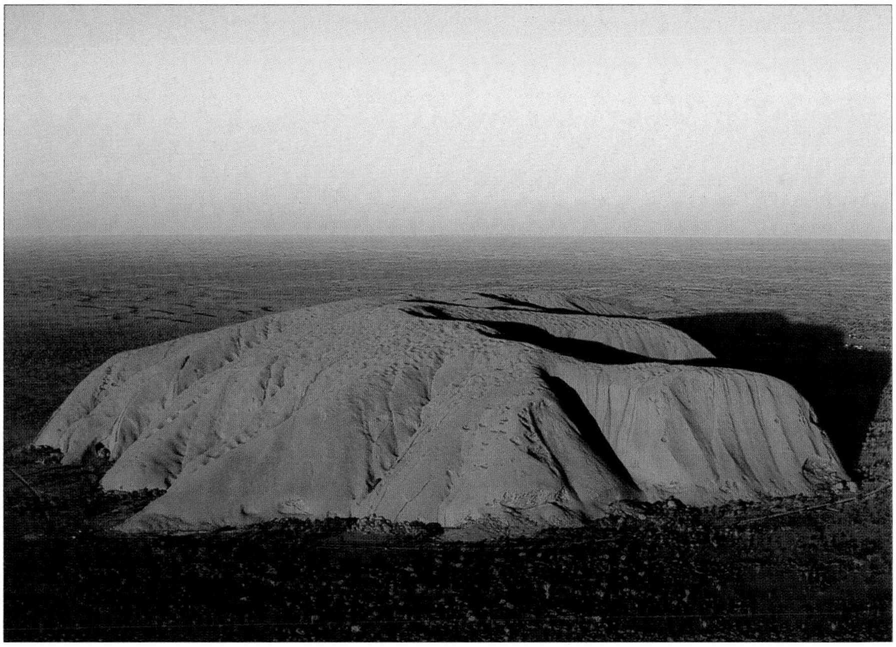

WHERE TO STAY

Alice Springs Pacific Resort, Stott Tce, tel: (08) 8952 6699, 1 800 805 055, fax: 8953 0995.
Diplomat Hotel, Cnr Gregory Tce & Hartley St, tel: (08) 8952 8977, 1 800 804 885, fax: 8953 0225. Centrally located.
Frontier Oasis, Gap Rd, tel: (08) 8952 1444, 1 800 891 101, fax: 8952 3776. Reasonably priced.
Lasseters Hotel Casino, Barrett Dve, tel: (08) 8950 7777, 1 800 808 975, fax: 8953 1680. Luxury hotel attached to Alice Springs casino.
Plaza Hotel Alice Springs, Barrett Dve, tel: (08) 8952 8000, fax: 8952 3822. Luxury resort at base of MacDonnell Ranges.

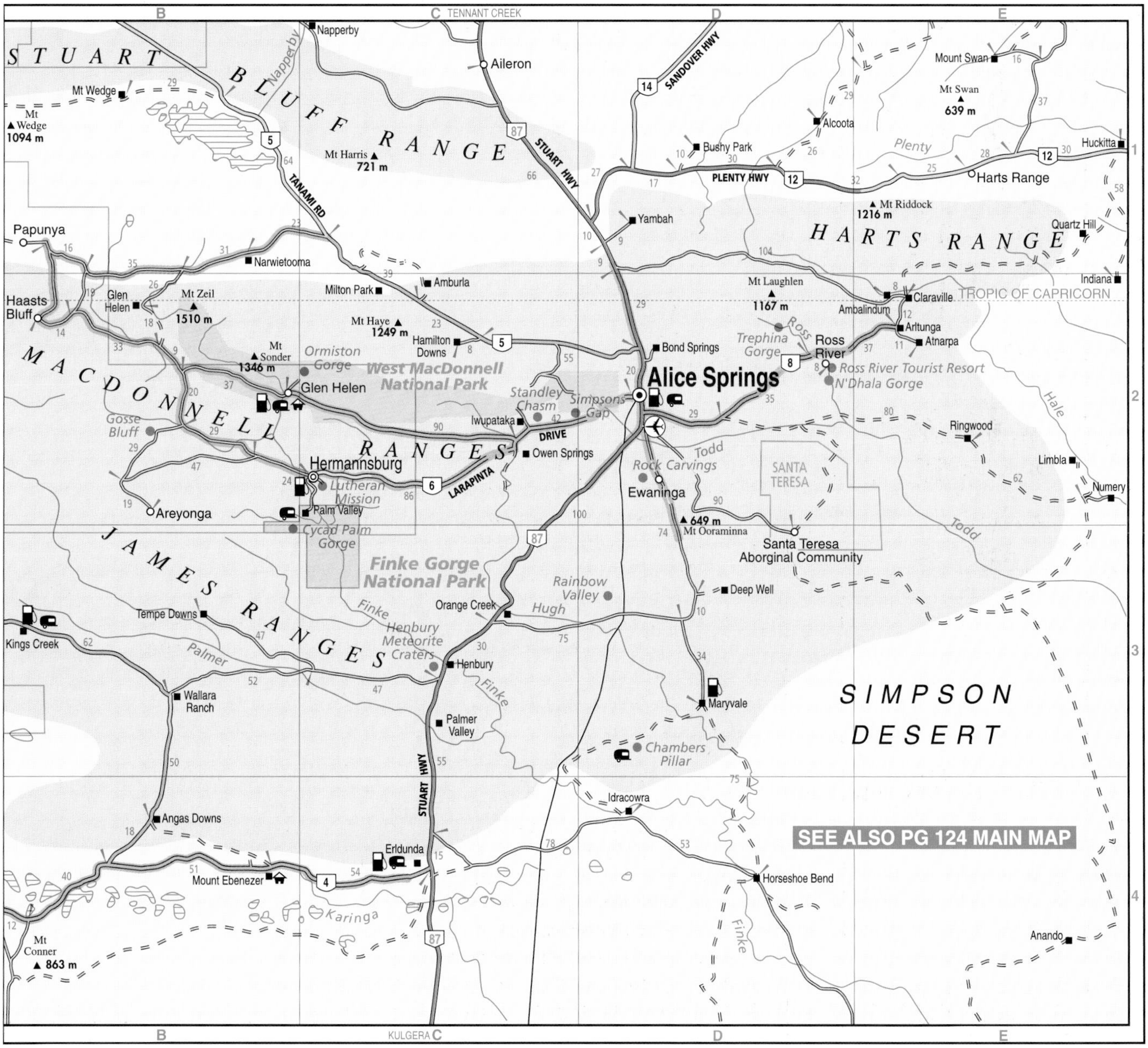

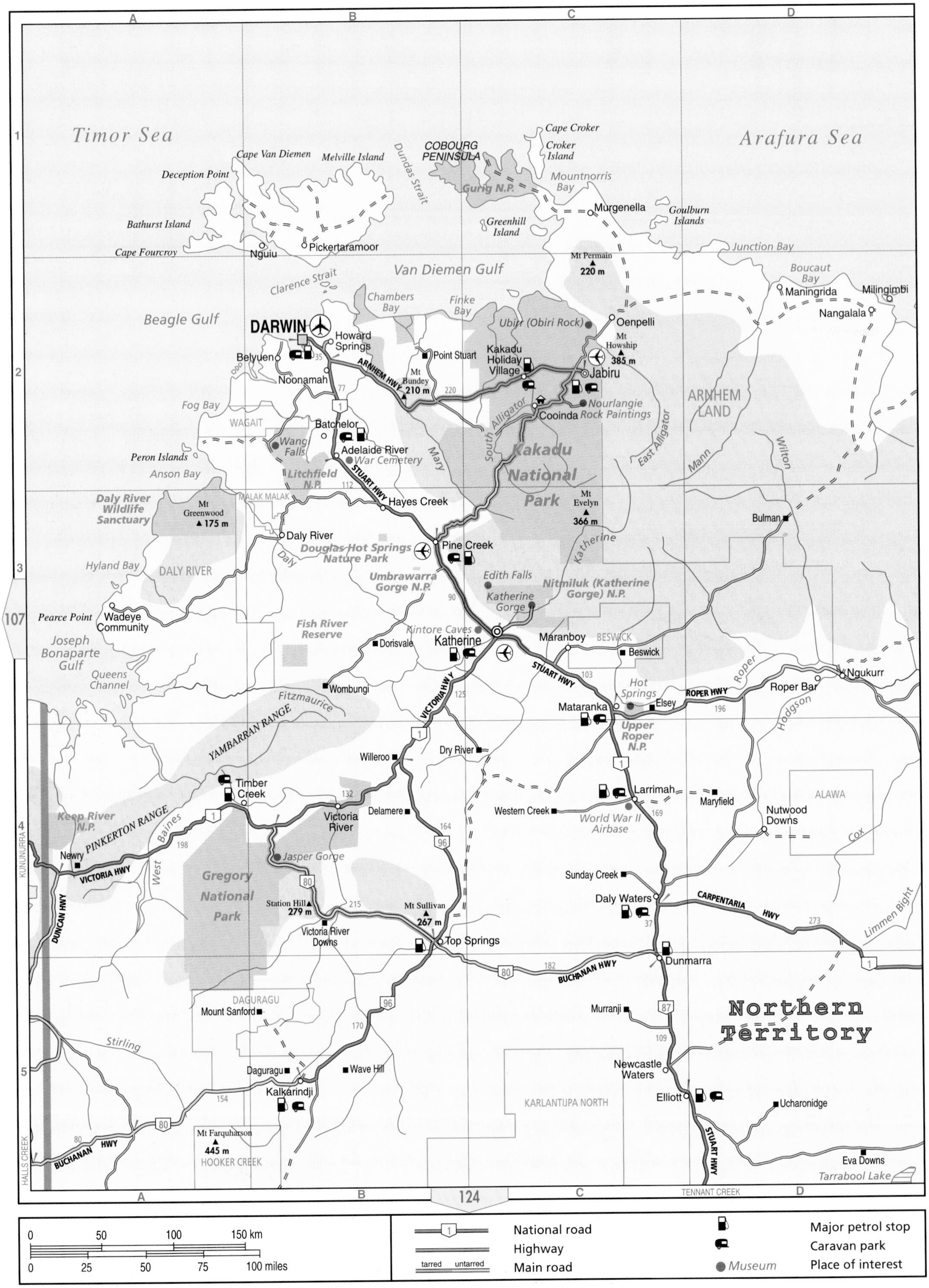

Timor Sea
Arafura Sea
Cape Van Diemen
Melville Island
Deception Point
Bathurst Island
Cape Fourcroy
Nguiu
Pickertaramoor
Dundas Strait
COBOURG PENINSULA
Gurig N.P.
Cape Croker
Croker Island
Mountnorris Bay
Murgenella
Goulburn Islands
Greenhill Island
Junction Bay
Boucaut Bay
Maningrida
Milingimbi
Nangalala
Mt Permain 220 m
Van Diemen Gulf
Clarence Strait
Chambers Bay
Finke Bay
Beagle Gulf
DARWIN
Howard Springs
Belyuen
Noonamah
Point Stuart
Mt Bundey 210 m
Ubirr (Obiri Rock)
Oenpelli
Mt Howship 385 m
Kakadu Holiday Village
Jabiru
Cooinda
Nourlangie Rock Paintings
ARNHEM HWY
ARNHEM LAND
Fog Bay
WAGAIT
Batchelor
Wangi Falls
Adelaide River
War Cemetery
Litchfield N.P.
Peron Islands
Anson Bay
South Alligator
East Alligator
Mary
Mann
Wilton
Kakadu National Park
STUART HWY
Hayes Creek
MALAK MALAK
Daly River Wildlife Sanctuary
Mt Greenwood 175 m
Daly River
Mt Evelyn 366 m
Bulman
Douglas Hot Springs Nature Park
Pine Creek
Hyland Bay
DALY RIVER
Daly
Umbrawarra Gorge N.P.
Edith Falls
Katherine
Nitmiluk (Katherine Gorge) N.P.
Katherine Gorge
Pearce Point
Wadeye Community
Joseph Bonaparte Gulf
Fish River Reserve
Kintore Caves
Dorisvale
Maranboy
BESWICK
Beswick
Queens Channel
Wombungi
Fitzmaurice
VICTORIA HWY
Hot Springs
ROPER HWY
Roper
Roper Bar
Ngukurr
Mataranka
Elsey
Upper Roper N.P.
Hodgson
YAMBARRAN RANGE
Willeroo
Dry River
Timber Creek
Larrimah
Maryfield
ALAWA
Keep River N.P.
PINKERTON RANGE
Baines
Victoria River
Delamere
Western Creek
World War II Airbase
Nutwood Downs
Cox
Newry
VICTORIA HWY
West
Jasper Gorge
Gregory National Park
Sunday Creek
Daly Waters
CARPENTARIA HWY
Limmen Bight
DUNCAN HWY
KUNUNURRA
Station Hill 279 m
Mt Sullivan 267 m
Victoria River Downs
Top Springs
Dunmarra
BUCHANAN HWY
DAGURAGU
Mount Sanford
Murranji
Northern Territory
Stirling
Daguragu
Wave Hill
Newcastle Waters
Kalkarindji
KARLANTIJPA NORTH
Elliott
Ucharonidge
Mt Farquharson 445 m
HOOKER CREEK
BUCHANAN HWY
HALLS CREEK
Eva Downs
Tarrabool Lake
TENNANT CREEK
107
124
0 50 100 150 km
0 25 50 75 100 miles
National road
Highway
Main road
tarred untarred
Major petrol stop
Caravan park
Place of interest
Museum

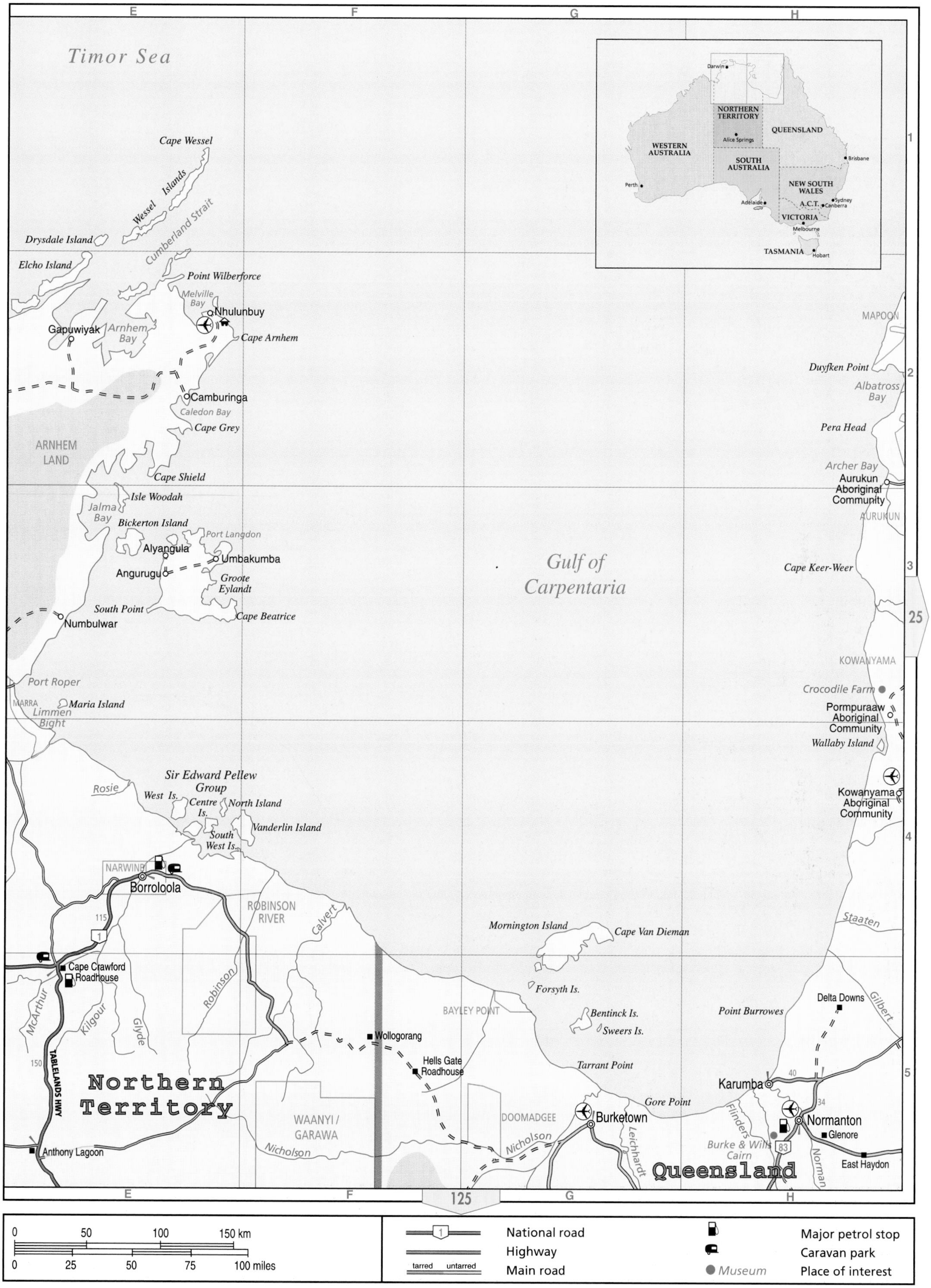

E
F
G
H
Timor Sea
Cape Wessel
Wessel Islands
Cumberland Strait
Drysdale Island
Elcho Island
Point Wilberforce
Melville Bay
Nhulunbuy
Gapuwiyak
Arnhem Bay
Cape Arnhem
Camburinga
Caledon Bay
Cape Grey
ARNHEM LAND
Cape Shield
Isle Woodah
Jalma Bay
Bickerton Island
Port Langdon
Alyangula
Umbakumba
Angurugu
Groote Eylandt
South Point
Cape Beatrice
Numbulwar
Port Roper
MARRA
Maria Island
Limmen Bight
Rosie
Sir Edward Pellew Group
West Is.
Centre Is.
North Island
Vanderlin Island
South West Is.
NARWINBI
Borroloola
ROBINSON RIVER
Calvert
115
1
Robinson
Cape Crawford Roadhouse
McArthur
Kilgour
Glyde
150
TABLELANDS HWY
Northern Territory
Anthony Lagoon
Wollogorang
Hells Gate Roadhouse
WAANYI / GARAWA
Nicholson
BAYLEY POINT
DOOMADGEE
Gulf of Carpentaria
Mornington Island
Cape Van Dieman
Forsyth Is.
Bentinck Is.
Sweers Is.
Tarrant Point
Gore Point
Burketown
Leichhardt
Queensland
Flinders
Burke & Wills Cairn
83
Karumba
40
34
Normanton
Glenore
Norman
East Haydon
Point Burrowes
Delta Downs
Gilbert
Staaten
Kowanyama Aboriginal Community
Wallaby Island
Pormpuraaw Aboriginal Community
Crocodile Farm
KOWANYAMA
25
Cape Keer-Weer
AURUKUN
Aurukun Aboriginal Community
Archer Bay
Pera Head
Albatross Bay
Duyfken Point
MAPOON
1
2
3
4
5
125
Darwin
NORTHERN TERRITORY
Alice Springs
QUEENSLAND
WESTERN AUSTRALIA
SOUTH AUSTRALIA
Brisbane
Perth
NEW SOUTH WALES
Adelaide
A.C.T.
Sydney
Canberra
VICTORIA
Melbourne
TASMANIA
Hobart
0 50 100 150 km
0 25 50 75 100 miles
National road
Highway
tarred untarred
Main road
Major petrol stop
Caravan park
Museum
Place of interest

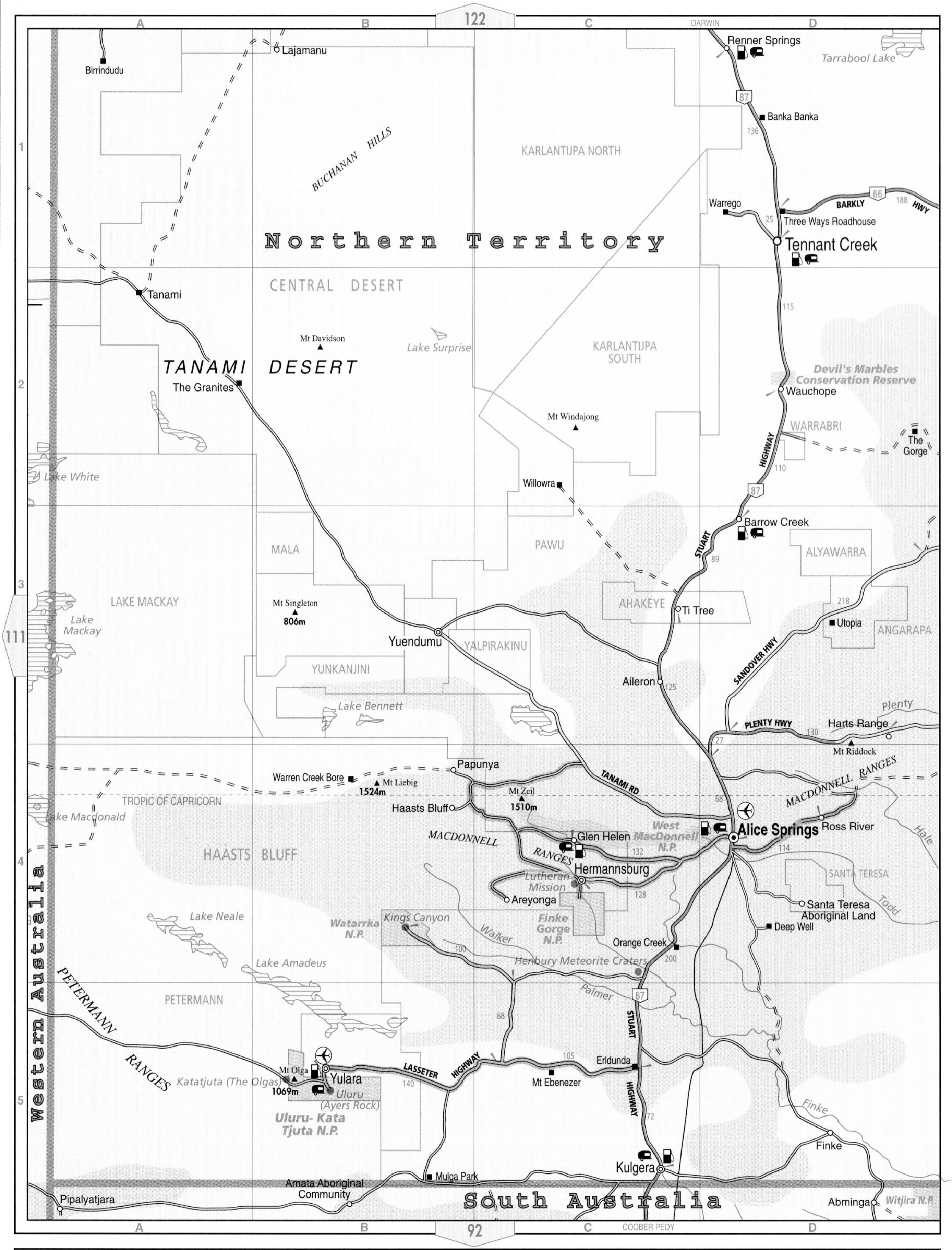

Scale		Legend			
0 50 100 150 km		1	National road	(petrol pump)	Major petrol stop
0 25 50 75 100 miles			Highway	(caravan)	Caravan park
		tarred untarred	Main road	● *Museum*	Place of interest

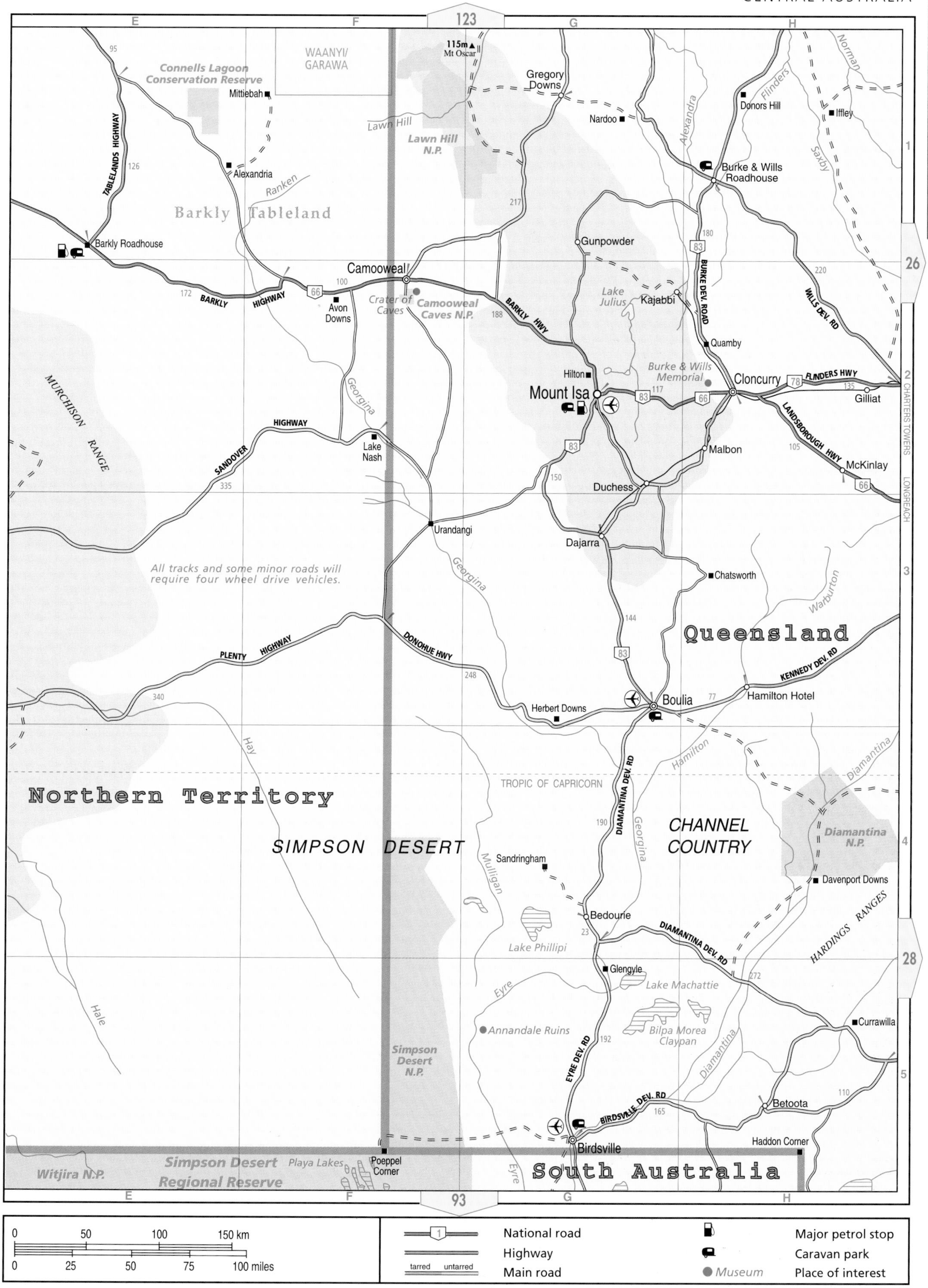

Northern Territory
Queensland
South Australia
Barkly Tableland
SIMPSON DESERT
CHANNEL COUNTRY
All tracks and some minor roads will require four wheel drive vehicles.
Connells Lagoon Conservation Reserve
WAANYI/ GARAWA
Lawn Hill N.P.
Camooweal Caves N.P.
Diamantina N.P.
Simpson Desert N.P.
Simpson Desert Regional Reserve
Witjira N.P.
TROPIC OF CAPRICORN
Camooweal
Mount Isa
Cloncurry
Boulia
Birdsville
Bedourie
Gregory Downs
Burke & Wills Roadhouse
Barkly Roadhouse
Alexandria
Mittiebah
Avon Downs
Lake Nash
Urandangi
Dajarra
Duchess
Malbon
Hilton
Gunpowder
Kajabbi
Quamby
Nardoo
Donors Hill
Iffley
Gilliat
McKinlay
Chatsworth
Hamilton Hotel
Herbert Downs
Sandringham
Glengyle
Davenport Downs
Currawilla
Betoota
Haddon Corner
Poeppel Corner
Annandale Ruins
Burke & Wills Memorial
Crater of Caves
115m Mt Oscar
Lake Julius
Lake Phillipi
Lake Machattie
Bilpa Morea Claypan
Playa Lakes
MURCHISON RANGE
HARDINGS RANGES
TABLELANDS HIGHWAY
BARKLY HIGHWAY
BARKLY HWY
SANDOVER HIGHWAY
PLENTY HIGHWAY
DONOHUE HWY
BURKE DEV. ROAD
WILLS DEV. RD
FLINDERS HWY
LANDSBOROUGH HWY
KENNEDY DEV. RD
DIAMANTINA DEV. RD
EYRE DEV. RD
BIRDSVILLE DEV. RD
Georgina
Mulligan
Hay
Hale
Eyre
Diamantina
Hamilton
Warburton
Flinders
Norman
Saxby
Alexandra
Ranken
Lawn Hill
CHARTERS TOWERS
LONGREACH
123
26
28
93
E F G H
1 2 3 4 5
National road
Highway
Main road
tarred
untarred
Major petrol stop
Caravan park
Museum
Place of interest
0 50 100 150 km
0 25 50 75 100 miles

Text Index

Names in bold indicate top attractions
Names with • indicate photographs

Names in italics indicate useful categories such as the following:

accommodation
aquariums
beaches
botanic gardens
islands
lakes
mining towns
mountains
museums
national parks
rock art
shopping
ski resorts
state parks
theme parks
zoos

Map Index

PLACE NAME INDEX
[EXCLUDING VILLAGES]
[SEE VILLAGES ON PG 133]

M

N

O

P

Q

R

S

T

U

V

W

PLACE NAME INDEX
[VILLAGES ONLY]

C

G

H

M

Ravine	C2	47
Rawlina	E3	115
Raymond Terrace	C3	51
Red Hills	A5	77
Red Range	B3	43
Red Rock	D3	43
Redesdale	A1	61
Redesdale	B1	63
Redhill	C3	89
Redland Bay	C5	13
Redlynch	C4	23
Reedy Creek	B4	15
Reedy Marsh	A4	77
Regents Park	C3	37
Regentville	B3	37
Relbia	C4	77
Remine	B3	79
Renison Bell	C2	79
Renner Springs	D1	124
Repton	C4	43
Retreat	A4	43
Rheban	C4	81
Rhyll	C5	61
Rhyndaston	B1	75
Riana	C2	79
Richmond	B2	75
Richmond	B4	81
Richmond	D3	26
Ridgley	C2	79
Ringa	D1	101
Ringarooma	C2	81
River Heads	B3	19
Rob Roy	A3	43
Robe	D4	95
Roberts Point	B4	75
Robertson	D1	45
Robertstown	C2	95
Robertstown	D3	89
Robertstown	E5	93
Robina	B3	15
Rochford	A2	61
Rochford	B2	63
Rock Flat	B4	45
Rock Flat	D3	47
Rockbank	A3	61
Rockbank	B3	63
Rockton	B5	45
Rockton	D1	65
Rockvale	B4	43
Rocky Gully	C4	105
Rocky Plains	C3	47
Rocky River	A2	90
Rocky River	A4	43
Rodney	B4	45
Rodney	C1	65
Rodney	D5	47
Roebourne	C1	109
Roebuck Roadhouse	C4	106
Roger River	B1	79
Rokewood	C1	62
Rolleston	G2	29
Rolleston	A2	31
Romsey	B2	61
Romsey	C2	63
Roper Bar	D3	122
Rosebud	B4	61
Rosevale	B4	77
Rosewood	A2	47
Rosewood	A5	13
Roseworthy	D3	87
Roslyn	B1	45
Ross	B3	81
Ross River	D2	121
Ross River	D4	124
Rossendale	A5	19
Roto	C3	49
Rowella	B2	77
Rowella	B2	81
Rowes	D5	47
Roy Hill	A2	110
Royal George	C3	81
Royalla	B2	45
Royalla	C3	55
Royalla	D1	47
Rubyvale	G2	29
Rubyvale	G5	27
Rudall	B3	89
Ruffy	D1	63
Rugby	B1	45
Rules Point	C2	47
Rumula	B3	23
Runaway Bay	C1	15
Runnymede	B4	81
Runnymede	C2	75
Rye Park	A1	45

S

Saddleworth	C2	95
Saddleworth	D1	87
Saddleworth	D3	89
Saddleworth	E5	93
Safety Bay	A3	100
Salmon Gums	B4	114
Saltwater River	C3	75
Saltwater River	C4	81
Samford	B3	13
San Remo	C5	61
Sandfire Flat Roadhouse	B5	106
Sandford	C3	75
Sandilands	A3	87
Sandon	A2	63
Sandon	D3	43
Sandstone	A1	114
Sandy Hill	B2	43
Sandy Point	A3	64
Sans Souci	D4	37
Santa Teresa Aboringinal Land	D4	124
Sapphire	A3	43
Sapphire	G5	27
Sapphiretown	C1	90
Sawpit Creek	C3	47
Sawtell	D4	43
Scamander	C2	81
Scarborough	C5	37
Scarness	B3	19
Scenes Creek	C3	62
Scotts Head	C4	43
Sea Lake	B2	67
Sea Lake	B5	49
Seaspray	B2	64
Seaspray	B3	69
Seaton	A2	64
Second Valley	C5	89
Selbourne	B2	81
Selbourne	B4	77
Serpentine	B4	100
Seven Mile Beach	C2	75
Seymour	C1	61
Seymour	C1	63
Seymour	D3	67
Shackleton	D1	105
Shannon	A3	81
Shannon	C4	105
Shannon	D3	79
Shannons Flat	D2	47
Shay Gap	B1	110
Shay Gap	B5	106
Sheffield	A2	81
Sheffield	D2	79
Shelford	C1	62
Shelley	A3	47
Sheringa	A3	89
Sherlock	D3	95
Shoalhaven Heads	D1	45
Shute Harbour	B3	21
Sidmouth	B2	77
Silverton	A3	49
Simpson	B2	62
Simpsons Bay	B4	75
Simpsons Bay	B5	81
Singleton	A4	100
Sisters Beach	C1	79
Slowport	C2	79
Smiggin Holes	C3	47
Smithfield Heights	C4	23
Smithtown	C5	43
Smoky Bay	C5	93
Snowtown	B1	87
Snowtown	C2	95
Snowtown	C3	89
Snowtown	E5	93
Snug	B3	75
Somers	C5	61
Somersby	B3	39
Somersby	D1	37
Sorell	B4	81
Sorell	C2	75
Sorent	D2	79
Soreyton	D2	79
Sorrento	B4	61
Sotala	B3	51
South Arm	B3	75
South Arm	B4	81
South Forest	B1	79
South Kilkerran	A2	87
South Riana	C2	79
South Springfield	B2	81
South Springfield	D2	77
South West Rocks	C5	43
South West Rocks	D2	51
Southern Cross	A3	114
Southport	A5	75
Southport	B5	81
Spalding	D3	89
Spargo Ck	A3	63
Sprent	A2	81
Spreyton	A2	81
Springbeach	D1	75
Springsure	A2	31
Springsure	G2	29
St Lawrence	B1	31
St Lawrence	H1	29
St Lawrence	H4	27
St Leonards	B4	61
St Marys	C2	81
St Patricks River	D3	77
Stafford	B4	13
Stamford	D4	26
Stanborough	A3	43
Stanley	B1	79
Stannifer	A3	43
Stannum	B2	43
Stanthorpe	B1	43
Stanthorpe	C1	51
Stanthorpe	C5	31
Stephens	B4	15
Steppes	B3	81
Stirling	D4	87
Stirling North	A3	91
Stirling North	C2	89
Stokes Bay	B1	90
Stokes Bay	C5	89
Stonehenge	B3	43
Stonehenge	C1	75
Stonehenge	C3	81
Stonehenge	D2	28
Stoneyford	B2	62
Stonor	B1	75
Stonor	B3	81
Stony Pt	C5	61
Storeys Creek	C2	81
Stormlea	C4	75
Stormlea	C5	81
Stradbroke	B2	64
Strahan	B3	79
Stratford	B2	64
Stratford	C4	23
Strath Ck	C1	61
Strath Ck	C2	63
Strathblane	A4	75
Strathbogie	D1	63
Strathbogie	A2	43
Strathgordon	C4	79
Strathpine	B3	13
Streaky Bay	C5	93
Stuarts Point	C5	43
Suggan Buggan	A5	45
Suggan Buggan	B5	47
Suggan Buggan	C1	65
Sunnybank	C4	13
Surat	A4	31
Surat	H4	29

T

U

V

W

Y

Z